REASON NOT

REASON NOT

EMOTIONAL APPEAL
IN SHAKESPEARE'S DRAMA

Omry Smith

PETER LANG

Oxford • Bern • Berlin • Bruxelles • Frankfurt am Main • New York • Wien

Bibliographic information published by Die Deutsche Nationalbibliothek
Die Deutsche Nationalbibliothek lists this publication in the Deutsche
Nationalbibliografie; detailed bibliographic data is available on the Internet at
<http://dnb.d-nb.de>

A catalogue record for this book is available from The British Library.

Library of Congress Cataloging-in-Publication Data:

Smith, Omry, 1968–
    Reason not : emotional appeal in Shakespeare's drama / Omry Smith.
        p. cm.
    Includes bibliographical references and index.
    ISBN 978-3-03911-400-9 (alk. paper)
    1. Shakespeare, William, 1564-1616--Criticism and interpretation. 2.
Shakespeare, William, 1564-1616--Knowledge--Psychology. 3. Emotions in
literature. 4. Persuasion (Psychology) in literature. 5. Rhetoric and
psychology. I. Title.
    PR3065.S58 2009
    822.3'3--dc22
                                2009017968

ISBN 978-3-03911-400-9

Cover design: Kara Trapani, Peter Lang Ltd

© Peter Lang AG, International Academic Publishers, Bern 2009
Hochfeldstrasse 32, CH-3012 Bern, Switzerland
info@peterlang.com, www.peterlang.com, www.peterlang.net

All rights reserved.
All parts of this publication are protected by copyright.
Any utilisation outside the strict limits of the copyright law, without the
permission of the publisher, is forbidden and liable to prosecution.
This applies in particular to reproductions, translations, microfilming,
and storage and processing in electronic retrieval systems.

Printed in Germany

To my parents

Contents

Acknowledgements

This book is based on my PhD dissertation, 'Emotional Appeal in Shakespeare's Drama', written under the supervision of Prof. Harai Golomb. I am grateful to this unique man and scholar for his good advice; for sharing his knowledge, his diverse talents and his saucy sense of humour; and for being my ever-fixed mark, unaltered in the face of some unacademic impediments. This study owes him much; it is the fruit of our shared Will.

I wish to thank Susan Rosenfeld for her major role in the translation of this book into English, and for her editing of the entire manuscript. During this challenging process I have enjoyed her creative solutions, critically helpful criticism, patience, and dedication. I would also like to thank each of the following for their contribution to the process of translation: Prof. Eddie Levenston; Anat Schultz; Glendyr Sacks; and Dr Uri Golomb.

Significantly significant thanks are extended to Prof. Ahuva Belkin, without whom this study would never have been completed. I am grateful to Prof. Aaron Ben-Ze'ev and Prof. Avraham Oz, for their kind help on a range of issues and their learned professional advice.

I wish to thank my teachers, colleagues and friends, each of whom has been an inspiration and contributed to this study in ways that, unfortunately, cannot be elaborated here: Aaron Mondry; Israel Sherez; Eric Storm; Prof. Tom Levi; Prof. Freddie Rokem; Dr Jennie Ebeling and Menachem Rogel, 'The Noble Two Whatevers'; Dr Vered Lev Kenaan; Dr Ronnie Mirkin; Prof. Adolfo Sacchetta; Dr Cristina Marras; Prof. Martin Orkin; Dr Atay Citron; Dr Dorit Yerushalmi; Dr Shai Frogel; Dr Tzachi Zamir; Prof. Nurit Yaari; Dr Liora Malka-Yelin; Arik Yelin; Prof. Eyal Berkowitz-Zidane-Balachsan; Tomer Reuveni; Rakefet Levy and the Rakefet Levy Design School for the Performing Arts; Lika Marutian; Paz Ordan; Inna Elkonin; Orli Popper; and Adi Fridberg.

Introduction

If a Tree Falls in a Forest

In *King John* IV, i, an event occurs that is exceptional in Shakespeare's early drama. The king, seeking to eliminate the constant threat to his crown, instructs Hubert to murder Arthur, the child-prince and rightful heir to the English throne. When Hubert, accompanied by 'executioners', arrives at the room in which Arthur is imprisoned and informs him of his intention to put out his eyes with hot irons, the prince pleads with his captor for mercy. This exceptionally long speech – spanning eighty lines – employs a variety of rhetorical devices and passion-inducing techniques that have led a number of critics to consider it 'unnatural' and unsuited to the characterisation of a child, particularly that of a terrified child.[1] Whether natural, unnatural, or simply in keeping with the theatrical conventions to which Shakespeare's rhetoric-loving audience was accustomed, this elaborate speech proves highly effective in the fictional world of the play: Hubert is overwhelmed with pity and completely abandons his intention of killing Arthur, preferring instead to endanger himself by reporting falsely to the king that he has carried out his order.

I refer to this event as 'exceptional' because Shakespeare, in his early plays, tends to deafen the ears of his characters to attempts by other characters to influence their opinions, will or actions by arousing their passions. As demonstrated at length in Appendix A, such attempts to exert an influence usually fail from the very outset in Shakespeare's drama written before 1599; here I shall make do with one of the more clear-cut examples of this trend, namely, the failure of Lord Say's plea for his life to influence Jack Cade and his fellow-

---

1 See, e.g.: E. A. J. Honigmann, 'Introduction to *King John*', *King John*, ed. E. A. J. Honigmann (London and New York: Methuen, 1983), pp. lxvi–lxvii.

rebels in *2 Henry VI* (IV, vii, 48–101). What Say says on his own behalf is impressive in matter and 'art' alike, considering the difficult position in which he finds himself as he appeals to the pity of those present; the playwright, however, provides Cade with an original escape from the emotional trap laid by the speech:

CADE:　　[*Aside*] I feel remorse in myself with his words; but I'll bridle it: he shall die, an it be but for pleading so well for his life. (Ibid., 90–91)

Although there is considerable cruelty in this moment, the arbitrary reasoning Cade uses to justify the murder is not without a humorous touch. Furthermore, when examined within the context of all other failed attempts by Shakespeare's characters to sway one another's emotions, Cade's admirable evasion seems an amused allusion by the playwright to his own tendency to doom to failure all such appeals to emotion. Against this background, Prince Arthur's success in causing Hubert to betray his oath to the king, and thereby endanger his own life, certainly deserves to be classified as an exceptional event.

　　Yet even this exceptional speech of Arthur's cannot be considered an exception in Shakespeare's early drama, if we take into account the negligible effect it has on the plot as a whole – as opposed to its effect at a given moment on a specific character. *In the plays written before 1599, Shakespeare does not use emotional influence by characters on one another as a structural device to advance the plot.* Limitations of space prevent an exhaustive survey here of Shakespeare's drama written before 1599, discussing the many attempts therein by characters to move other characters emotionally, and illustrating the negligible effect these attempts have on the plot: Appendix A demonstrates the validity of this generalisation in seven of Shakespeare's early plays, which, due to their political, military or 'Roman' character, involve a particularly intensive use of formal classical rhetorical devices, including passion-arousing speeches. The very numerousness of these speeches emphasises their lack of functionality in the plot development of these early plays.

　　The instance from *King John* discussed above seems at first particularly exceptional in the context of this trend: the audience witnesses a character exerting a strong emotional influence on another character, who changes his course of action in a manner that appears highly significant to the development of the plot. In other words, the playwright seems to channel the plot by means of emotional influence on one of the central characters. In the broad scheme of the play, however, Shakespeare in effect bypasses this seemingly decisive event: the rumour that the king has ordered Hubert to murder the prince reaches the ears of Pembroke and Salisbury; the two earls have strong moral objections to such an act, and, witnessing Hubert's report to the king on Arthur's alleged death, they decide to rebel and join forces with the French in their invasion of England; Arthur, meanwhile, attempting to escape from his prison, leaps from the wall to his death; when Pembroke and Salisbury, on their way to join the French, find his body, they consider this to be concrete proof that he was murdered by Hubert; the latter, arriving on the scene, denies all responsibility for the death of the prince, but encounters the complete disbelief of the two noblemen, who carry out their intention to desert to the French side.

Thus Arthur's effective speech does not ultimately affect the development of the plot. The room in which Hubert intended to put out the prince's eyes and in which he was persuaded not to do so, constitutes a kind of isolated space, and the other characters are not aware of what took place there; these characters act on rumours and on the misleading evidence they see with their own eyes. The room of Arthur's imprisonment and Hubert's yielding to the prince's passion-arousing speech, are thus comparable to the remote forest and to the tree that falls there when no one is present to record the event with his senses: at least for the characters that were not present in this room, the events that took place in it – as presented to the audience – never happened. Pembroke and Salisbury would have lost faith in their king and deserted him if Hubert had not been influenced by Arthur's speech, and acted in an identical manner even though he *was* influenced by it. Even the reversal in the plot, in which they return toward the end of the play to the English camp, arises not from any change in their perception of the death of Arthur, but rather from their own pragmatic considerations: from the words of the dying Melun they

learn that the French king intends to make use of them during his war
with the English, but to behead them once it has ended.

Shakespeare's Early and Later
Use of Passion-Inducing Speeches

Such stirring speeches as Arthur's plea to Hubert's mercy are usually
referred to in the terminology of rhetoric as *emotional appeals*. This
term will be further clarified below. Shakespeare, whose work
abounds in forms and devices drawn from the repositories of classical
rhetorical tradition, makes substantial use of formulae for presenting
emotional appeals, as conceived by Cicero, Quintilian and their latter-
day English successors. In his early plays, as indicated above, these
frequent and extensive emotional appeals exert only a limited influence on the progression of the plot. Later in his creative life, Shakespeare's use of emotional appeal evolved in conjunction with other
developments in his writing technique, gradually growing in complexity and sophistication and assuming a more influential role. In a
number of plays from 1599 onwards, they become powerful 'plot
engines', in ways not found in plays written previously. In other
words, in plays written before 1599, most of the factors that motivate
the characters' actions (emotions, ambitions, external forces and other
dictates) have already been established *before* the starting point of the
play's plot. The characters act under their influence from beginning to
end, or change their course of action due to the manner in which they
comprehend substantive, imagined or falsely-reported events. These
events might alter the balance of powers within the fictional world
they inhabit, leading characters to change their attitude, or to recon-
sider which actions serve their best interest.

Beginning in 1599, this trend changes. In three plays in particular
– *Julius Caesar* (1599), *Othello* (1601–1604) and *Coriolanus* (1607–
1608) – emotional appeals clearly function as plot engines, in addition
to their role in enriching the plays' thematic content. This doubly

crucial role of emotional appeal has motivated me to devote an entire chapter to each of these plays. *Henry V* (1599), which has also received its own chapter, abounds in emotional appeals, although it is not possible to determine unambiguously whether they actually affect the concatenation of the play's events. The questionable effect of emotional appeals in *Henry V* is demonstrated at length in Appendix B, which examines some of the play's most salient speeches of persuasion. The decision to include this history play in my study arose primarily from the unprecedented scope of the play's emotional appeals, as well as their central thematic role within it.

The only criterion in choosing the four plays upon which this study focuses was the centrality of emotional appeal to both the thematic and the structural dimensions. Thus, with no consideration of genre, no comedy was included in the final list. In the course of my research for *Reason Not*, I tried to reason regarding the absence from the Shakespearean corpus of a comedy whose plot is motivated by emotional appeals.[2] The various hypotheses I considered are all related to two major traditional characteristics of the comic genre: comedy does not tend to represent complex emotional processes; and comedy tends to allot chance and arbitrary devices a dominant role in shaping the course of events (as opposed to plays driven by emotional appeals, which convert emotions to dramatic action in a direct connection of cause and effect).

At the time of this writing, however, I see the following as a more plausible explanation for the phenomenon in question: the emotions that traditionally dominate the world of comedy are inherently

---

2   In *The Merchant of Venice*, for example, despite the prominence, from our point of view, of the speeches of the Duke of Venice and Portia, which are directed to Shylock and the 'dram of mercy' they hope to find in him (VI, i, 17–34; 180–201), and which can be classified as emotional appeals, Shylock is completely insensitive to these appeals. Shakespeare prefers to resolve the entanglement of the plot with what appears to be a completely arbitrary device, one characteristic of the comic tradition: a young maid with no prior practical experience in the legal profession, is able to brilliantly control the legal proceedings and force Shylock to retreat from his demand to have his bond. In other words, although emotional appeals do exist in this comedy, they do not have a role in propelling the plot.

different from those Shakespeare generates through his plot-motivating emotional appeals. As I shall demonstrate, choler plays a central role in all four plays studied: readers will have frequent encounters with this emotion, which might be termed the 'main protagonist' of this study. Choler was considered in early modern Europe to be the most vehement and powerful among the human passions, unique in that it has the power to set in motion far-reaching actions not only by individuals, but even by entire kingdoms.[3] In light of Shakespeare's choices of emotions in the four plays addressed in this study, it would appear that he considered anger best suited for representing effective processes of emotional appeal leading to drastic actions. It seems that choler, which colours the worlds of the plays in question and determines their character to a great extent, was not considered appropriate as a dominant emotional backdrop in the comedies. Although anger and rage do make occasional 'guest appearances', most of the dominant emotions portrayed in the comedies are of an entirely different nature. Nevertheless, because we are concerned with art, it cannot be stated that a comedy in which anger rules is not within the realm of the possible, and the same is true of a play driven by emotional appeals in which the driving emotion is not anger; the fact that there is no Shakespearean comedy shaped by emotional appeals may, therefore, be quite fortuitous.

What is *Emotional Appeal*?

This study focuses on the use of emotional appeal by Shakespearean characters, and on the ways in which the playwright employs this device in his texts, both structurally and thematically. The term *emotional appeal* appears in research literature and in translations of classical sources also as *appeal to emotion*, *appeal to passion*, or *use of pathos*. Emotion (*pathos*) is one of the three means of persuasion defined by Aristotle in his *Rhetoric*; in a given rhetorical situation, it

3   See Chapter Two, p. 69.

influences the addressee in conjunction with the *logos* (logical argumentation) and *ethos* (the speaker's character as perceived by the audience in light of their knowledge of his or her past actions, and their impression of it during the speech).[4] Ancient and Renaissance rhetoricians – as well as modern scholars – view the emotion stirred by the orator and his image in the eyes of his audience as having greater influence than his logical argumentation; the specific characteristics of a given situation determine which of the first two is the dominant persuasive force; yet, while both *ethos* and *pathos* may strongly influence the addressee's mind and divert his judgement, only the power of *pathos* can stir him to action. This observation is of considerable relevance to the matter at hand – Shakespeare's drama – since characters who act constitute the core of every dramatic work.

Throughout this study, the term *emotional appeal* will usually denote an appeal by one character to another, to a group of other characters, or even to himself, employing devices designed to arouse an emotion in order to influence the addressees' judgements or motivate their actions. An emotional appeal might consist of a well-made speech, meticulously constructed according to Roman models. Such a speech would draw on the lists of topics formulated by such theoreticians as Cicero and Quintilian, and would be moulded using emotionally effective formal models. Sometimes, however, a single word, uttered at the right time and place, is sufficient to arouse an intense emotional response in the object of manipulation. For example, Coriolanus' loss of self-control (and consequently of his life) is the result of having the words 'traitor' and 'boy of tears' hurled at him.

In the context of Shakespeare's plays, I also use the term *emotional appeal* to refer to a character's words or actions that in effect arouse an emotional response, even if this was not the character's explicit aim. A case in point is my discussion of Brutus' instruction to his fellow-rebels in *Julius Caesar* to smear blood on their hands and swords, and wave their swords while marching in the streets of Rome. Brutus views this as a ceremonial act; I will argue that it constitutes an emotional appeal. As demonstrated in the relevant chapter, this act would have been recognised as an emotional appeal by the play-

4   For further clarification of this definition of *ethos*, see Appendix C.

wright's contemporaries: the sight of red – and of blood in particular – was perceived in Shakespeare's time as arousing anger, inciting people to shed more blood. The justification for classifying Brutus' act as an (unintentional) emotional appeal can be found in its context – namely, its appearance in a play that consists largely of a series of emotional appeals. As shown in Chapters Two and Five, Shakespeare characterises Brutus and Antony, among other things, through the use of contrastive comparison. Antony's conscious emotional appeals are shown as highly effective in promoting his plans. By contrast, Brutus' unconscious emotional appeals are shown as counterproductive, achieving the opposite effects from those sought by Brutus himself.

The specific context will occasionally prompt me to classify words or actions of a given character as an 'emotional appeal to the self'. A typical example of such an appeal occurs in *Coriolanus* III, ii, 111–124: the protagonist begins this short monologue by expressing his decision to accede to the exhortations of his mother and to stand before the tribunes and the people; a mere ten lines later, however, he resolutely expresses a diametrically opposed decision. The change that takes place in Coriolanus within these few lines is emotional, and arises from his having enumerated the expected implications of facing the people. This brief monologue is in effect a typical *amplification* figure,[5] arousing his anger, influencing his judgement and causing him to view the same circumstances in a completely different light. The broad context of this monologue leads me to classify it as an 'emotional appeal to the self': the three main sharp reversals in the plot of *Coriolanus* result directly from the effects that emotional appeals have on the protagonist, and in two of these instances his enemies succeed in overcoming him by inflaming his rage; Coriolanus' vulnerability to such appeals, and the degree of his own active contribution to the arousal of his rage, are thus embodied in the monologue.

5   On the figure of amplification, see pp. 142–144.

Isolating the Component of *Pathos*

To the best of my knowledge, there has been no systematic inquiry into emotional appeals in Shakespearean drama. I am not aware of any study (either of Shakespeare's plays generally, or of any of his plays in particular) that isolates the emotional component and examines its role in processes of persuasion. At most, some of the speeches and processes of persuasion in these plays have been examined under the general designation of 'persuasion' or 'rhetoric'. The decision to isolate the emotional component of these processes in my study was partly motivated by the growing scholarly interest in emotion – both generally, and specifically in Shakespeare studies. My primary motivation, however, was the undeniable centrality of emotion within the processes of persuasion in the plays under discussion. Even a cursory glance at the literal surface of *Henry V*, *Julius Caesar*, *Othello* and *Coriolanus* reveals Shakespeare's considerable interest in the emotions: he focuses upon them in his descriptions of the mental processes that his characters experience, and he emphasises the influential power of emotions over events in the worlds that he constructs in these plays. As the quotes woven into this study repeatedly demonstrate, these plays are saturated with words emanating from the semantic field of emotions. The characters resort to these words frequently to describe their own or others' emotional states, and their psychic and physiological manifestations.

Of course, the examination of emotional appeals is not an end in itself, but an additional tool in the continuing effort to decode and understand Shakespeare's dramatic creation and artistic system. Given the prominent role of emotional appeals at both the thematic and plot levels of these plays, an examination of them in isolation is likely to shed more light on central issues that existing research has frequently addressed from other angles.

Stirring the Characters and Stirring the Audience

Readers of this study will find themselves 'imprisoned' for the most part within the confines of the fictional worlds of the plays: the focus will be on the effect of emotional appeals on the various characters, rather than on their potential effect on the audience. It must be borne in mind, however, that the rhetorical devices of which the various characters make use in order to influence the emotions of their fellow characters, are simultaneously being employed by the playwright himself to influence the emotions of his audience. The opening soliloquy of *Richard III* is a clear example of Shakespeare's use of emotional appeal to manipulate the emotions of his spectators. This soliloquy is in effect a typical figure of amplification, detailing the circumstances of the protagonist's alleged misfortune. According to Richard, this misfortune is the result of his deformed appearance, which is particularly conspicuous against the background of the courtly 'fair, well-spoken days' following the civil war. This speech appears to be a typical appeal to the pity of the audience: it presents Richard as the innocent victim of 'dissembling nature', and contrasts his private misery with the overall well-being of society as a whole. It is clear, however, that the nature and intensity of emotion aroused in the audience in response to this appeal depend on a multiplicity of elements, such as the acting choices made by the actor. The actor playing Richard may deliver these lines at face value, that is, as an appeal to the pity of the audience; on the other hand, these very same lines easily submit themselves to deliveries of quite another nature, deliveries which may arouse emotions very different or even opposed to pity.

It should be pointed out that not only is the soliloquy open to a variety of interpretations, it actually invites the audience to take an ambivalent emotional approach to Richard: as a passive victim who arouses pity, on the one hand; and as an active agent responsible for choosing the path of villainy – and who therefore arouses emotions such as anger, hatred or disgust – on the other. This ambivalence is embodied in the word 'determined', which appears in the crucial lines in which Richard explains the reason for his wickedness (ll. 28–31).

The two accepted meanings of this word – in Shakespeare's time as well as in ours – enable two completely different readings of Gloucester's declaration:

And therefore, since I cannot prove a lover ...
I am *resolved* to prove a villain ...

And therefore, since I cannot prove a lover ...
I am *destined* to prove a villain ...

The actor may thus portray Richard in the opening soliloquy as either a passive victim or a villain by choice, alternately as villain and victim, or even as victim and villain simultaneously – each of these options has limitless performance possibilities. Such acting choices will carry far-reaching implications for the audience's emotional stance regarding the protagonist, and hence for the manner in which they will later 'judge' him for his deeds – and perceive the events in the play as a whole.

At a number of points throughout the study I shall demonstrate my awareness that various appeals to emotion directed by characters towards other characters, contain the potential for considerable emotional influence on the audience as well (it can, of course, be said that almost any word or event in a play has the potential for exerting an emotional influence on the spectator; my reference is to those appeals whose effect would seem to be particularly powerful). The most significant example of such an appeal is perhaps Antony's stirring speech before the people in *Julius Caesar* (III, ii, 65–242). This long, meticulously constructed speech, which ingeniously combines verbal rhetorical devices with visual ones – such as the public display of Caesar's corpse, his blood, his wounds and his 'will' – cannot but have some emotional effect on the spectators, who sit or stand facing the actor and experience the event directly through their own senses. Because of its specific focus, this study will not examine such interesting implications, but will occasionally refer to the potential effect of certain emotional appeals beyond the borders of Shakespeare's fictional worlds.

Modern and Early Modern Theories of the Emotions

This study is based upon a process of continuous comparison between Shakespeare's dramatic text and relevant Roman, Elizabethan and Jacobean sources. These sources focus on, or at least refer to, classical rhetorical techniques of emotional appeal, or to the emotions in general. The assumption is that the content of these sources represents, to some extent, information available to Shakespeare and his audience, and expresses at least some of the 'facts' and 'truths' generally accepted by the contemporaneous society.

Classical rhetorical education is not common in modern western culture, and the perception and conceptualisation of emotions – as stressed in valuable recent studies by Gail Kern Paster and others – has changed markedly in the last four centuries.[6] Many contemporary readers, playgoers and even scholars are therefore 'blind', to some extent, to the various rhetorical devices employed by Shakespeare and his characters, and to descriptions, hints, *double entendres* and processes, related to emotions and emotional rhetoric, that are embedded in his plays. Reading Shakespeare's text through the prism of Roman and English rhetorical treatises, and of the various relevant treatises that discuss emotions, exposes these devices, processes and events. For example, familiarity with the physiological characteristics of the emotions, as presented in early modern sources and in the play itself, allows us to discern the sophisticated system of allusions built into

---

6   See, e.g.: Robert L. Reid, 'Humoral Psychology in Shakespeare's *Henriad*', *Comparative Drama* 30 (4), (1996), pp. 471–502; Maurice Charney, *Shakespeare on Love and Lust* (New York: Columbia University Press, 2000); Lynn Enterline, *The Rhetoric of the Body from Ovid to Shakespeare* (Cambridge: Cambridge University Press, 2000); Peter Rollins and Allan Smith (eds), *Shakespeare's Theories of Blood, Character, and Class* (New York, Bern, Berlin, Bruxelles, Frankfurt/M., Oxford, Wien: Peter Lang, 2001); Gail Kern Paster, Katherine Rowe and Mary Floyd-Wilson (eds), *Reading the Early Modern Passions: Essays in the Cultural History of Emotion* (Philadelphia: University of Pennsylvania Press, 2004); Gail Kern Paster, *Humoring the Body: Emotions and the Shakespearean Stage* (Chicago and London: The University of Chicago Press, 2004).

Julius Caesar, which points to the specific passion that rules Brutus. This intense passion, as suggested by several ingenious textual hints, distorts Brutus' ability to reason and motivates him to murder Caesar. Similarly, identifying the primary rhetorical figure employed by Iago, and the specific term ('Reasoning') applied to it in Richard Sherry's treatise,[7] has provided valuable insights into the emotional process that Othello experiences. Examining Shakespeare's use of this figure has proved helpful in distinguishing a significant trait in Othello's mental characterisation, which enables Iago to undermine his general's high immunity to powerful emotional stimuli.

By exposing and examining such processes and events in my four case-studies, it is possible to trace the unique way in which Shakespeare uses emotional appeals in each of them. As noted above, emotional appeal has been assigned a very significant place in the thematic and structural levels of these plays. For this reason, and because the interactions between compositional planes in Shakespeare's works are extraordinarily manifold, the findings that emerge from an analysis of emotional appeals in each play provide new data that can contribute to our general understanding of it. Such new data also offer the basis for a fresh examination of major research questions associated with that play.

The first four chapters of this study contain occasional references to modern theories of emotion. These are employed to examine, demonstrate or enrich various arguments from a purely complementary perspective. In the final chapter, however, these theories will take centre stage, and will be compared systematically with the various findings presented in the preceding chapters. Through this comparison, I shall attempt to characterise the unique nature of Shakespeare's emotional dynamics[8] and examine the extent to which it corresponds to its 'real-world' equivalents – not as described in writings preserved

---

7   Richard Sherry, *A Treatise on Schemes and Tropes* (1550), ed. Herbert W. Hildebrandt (Gainesville, Florida: Scholars' Facsimiles & Reprints, 1961), p. 76.

8   In other words, to examine the place and function of emotion as an influential factor in the characters' psyches and in the fictional world in general (that is, in microcosmic and macrocosmic processes), and to characterise the interplay between emotion and other factors – such as sensual perception, imagination, thought, will and the rational faculty.

from the playwright's lifetime, but as perceived in modern studies of the emotions. The premise of this final chapter is that several modern theories, far removed from Shakespeare's own world, can provide valuable and relevant insights into his work, notwithstanding the newer formulations and latter-day ways of thinking that have brought them into existence. Such modern theories were written and formulated on the basis of universal and 'timeless' emotional processes and behavioural principles. Shakespeare's works, while not entirely free of the constraints of their time and place, also display a profound observation of human nature. They often feature insights whose relevance transcends the customs, conventions, assumptions and beliefs of Elizabethan and Jacobean England. Shakespeare's plays, besides being works of art that construct their own unique and self-oriented worlds, and beyond their mimetic relation to the society in which they were created, also 'hold as 'twere a mirror up to nature'. Shakespeare might not be 'our contemporary', but his legacy still has substantial relevance.

Chapter One
Henry V

'Sweet smoke of rhetoric!'
(*Love's Labour's Lost*, III, i, 35)

Studies of *Henry V* frequently refer to its close connection with *The Prince*, Niccolo Machiavelli's influential treatise, and with Chapter 17 in particular. This chapter discusses whether a ruler should inspire fear (*timore*) or love (*amore*) in his subjects. Machiavelli, who usually gives his readers clear and explicit answers, writes that the Prince – a generalised term for any ruler – would be wise to engender fear, first-and-foremost, in his subjects. He argues that the Prince should not be concerned about gaining a reputation as a cruel man (*el nome di crudele*), and should not avoid any deterring actions which would ensure the continuing presence of fear in his subjects' hearts. *The Prince* teaches, through historical examples, that political and military leaders who have adopted this strategy of inducing fear in their subordinates have succeeded in maintaining long-term obedience and loyalty; this enabled them to lead their armies on difficult campaigns of conquest, or to stabilise their civil rule and remain securely in power for long periods.

To date, scholars attempting to enhance the understanding of *Henry V* by comparing it with *The Prince*, have focused on Shakespeare's characterisation of the young king's 'moral qualities'. Interpreting a variety of textual evidence relating to Henry and his actions, they have placed him along a spectrum that stretches between two extremes: the cruel Machiavellian – dissembling, brutal, opportunist, homage-seeking, rational and heartless – and the very image of the merciful Christian ruler, who might occasionally use 'Machiavellian' means, but only to further his pursuit of moral aims.[1] This chapter, too, compares events and characters in *Henry V* with descriptions and insights from *The Prince*, and examines the affinity between the Shakespearean king and the various rulers whose successes or failures are outlined in Machiavelli's book. However, in contradistinction to prevailing scholarly trends, I have chosen to look at this affinity from a worldly, practical perspective, without passing moral judgement on Henry's character. It is doubtful whether such judgements could be substantiated, in any case: as is often true of Shakespeare's plays, *Henry V* offers many contradictory bits of evidence and makes others deliberately ambiguous, thus limiting our ability to peer into the character's very 'soul'. Like so many Shakespearean characters, Henry is an enigma, and the playwright thwarts all efforts to determine his true motives and their 'morality'.

Thus, instead of focusing on the king's morality, as it were, I have examined, in light of Machiavelli's book, the rhetorical-emotional strategies, tactics and techniques he employs and through which he seeks to establish his rule and lead his army on French soil. The examination of Henry's tactics and techniques as a rhetorician is not merely an end in itself; it also serves to promote our understanding of the play as a whole. The king is a shrewd and skilled rhetorician, whose speeches and declarations are designed, first-and-foremost, to influence the actions of others. A major shortcoming in those studies that seek to pass conclusive moral judgement on Henry's character is their ignoring of this crucial aspect. They tend to take Henry's statements at face value, as if they were spoken on the psychiatrist's couch and express his innermost thoughts and feelings. These words, however, are in fact spoken publicly and aim above all to manipulate the

---

1   For a representative sample of the range of judgemental opinions on Henry's 'moral character', see: Harold C. Goddard, *The Meaning of Shakespeare*, vol. I (Chicago and London: The University of Chicago Press, [1951] 2003), pp. 215–268; Vickie Sullivan, 'Princes to Act: Henry V as the Machiavellian Prince of Appearance', *Shakespeare's Political Pageant: Essays in Literature and Politics*, ed. Joseph Aulis and Vickie Sullivan (Lanham, MD: Rowman & Littlefield, 1996), pp. 125–152; Stephen Hollingshead, *Shakespeare's Answer to Machiavelli* (North Carolina: Carolina Academic Press, 2005); John Roe, *Shakespeare and Machiavelli* (Cambridge: Brewer, 2002).

actions of other characters, hence their relevance to Henry's moral and mental profile is tenuous.

Emotions in general, and fear in particular, occupy a central thematic role in *Henry V*. As will be shown in this chapter, the play's main protagonist displays an ambivalent attitude towards the fear that arises, in different circumstances, in his subjects' hearts. As *The Prince* recommends, Henry finds it necessary to inspire fear in his subjects in order to establish his authority and retain the unity of his army: after all, this army is fighting in harsh conditions, and its heterogeneous ethnic and human make-up makes it prone to internal conflicts. On the other hand, when leading his soldiers into battle, Henry must aspire to remove all fear from their hearts. In Shakespeare's time, anger was considered the ultimate motivating emotion for a fighter: this emotion was believed to enhance courage and physical strength by *warming* the blood and *raising* the spirits[2] upwards within the body, channelling them towards the extremities. Fear, on the other hand, was deemed to have the opposite physiological characteristics: it *cools* the blood and the spirits, causes them to abandon the face, and channels them *downwards* towards the heart, thereby weakening the body. In light of these widely-held beliefs, which are expressed explicitly and extensively in the play, anger and fear are obviously deemed 'contradictory' emotions and cannot exist simultaneously within the same body. If Henry, who requires the bravest and strongest soldiers, does not drive all traces of fear from their bodies, then the battle-rage indispensable for their proper performance on the battlefield will never emerge. Thus, when the battle of Agincourt is looming and conditions in his army are deteriorating, the king radically alters his emotional-rhetorical policy, adopting a new tactic that will rid his soldiers' bodies entirely of the 'cold fear' (IV, chorus, l. 45). On the

---

2   In the emotional language of medieval and renaissance medicine, the *spirits* are tiny particles or fluids that reside in the blood, moving among the organs and providing them with the necessary force to function (*OED*, 'spirit', n., 16a). There are three types of *spirits* – animal, natural and vital – which are differentiated by their degree of refinement, the manner in which they move in the body, and the bodily functions for which they are responsible. See also: Thomas Elyot, *The Castel of Helthe* (1539), (New York: Scholars' Facsimiles & Reprints, 1979), p. 11.

altar of this critical goal, he temporarily abandons the Machiavellian strategy of intimidating his subjects and of enforcing military and social hierarchies, and, through his speeches and conduct alike, inspires a sense of equality and brotherhood in his camp. When the battle reaches its successful conclusion, Henry once more needs united and obedient subjects, rather than brave and raging soldiers; the 'prince' therefore returns to his principal strategy of enforcing his authority through intimidation and renewed emphasis on hierarchical distinctions.

1.1 *The Prince*, *Henry V* and the Rhetoric of Intimidation

1.1.1 *Henry V and Chapter 17 of The Prince*

Moments before the departure of the English fleet from the port of Southampton, the conspirators Cambridge and Grey flatter Henry with exaggerated praise of the ideal relations that exist between him and his subjects. Cambridge's flattery outdoes that of his comrade, and from the point of view of the modern spectator or reader, may be seen as not only exaggerated, but paradoxical:

> Never was monarch better *feared* and *loved*
> Than is your majesty ... (II, ii, 25–26; my italics)

In order to capture the full significance and force of this flattery, consideration should be given to the direct connection between Cambridge's words and one of the central questions posed in Machiavelli's *The Prince*, a work whose influence on Elizabethan and Shakespearean drama, and on *Henry V* in particular, has been widely studied. This seemingly paradoxical compliment, which to my knowledge has not been addressed by scholars, seems to be derived directly from Chapter 17 of *The Prince*; this chapter focuses on the measure of mercy and cruelty a prince should show his subjects. Machiavelli opens the chapter with a title that presents an explicit question: should

28

the prince arouse fear or love in his subjects? He immediately answers that it is, of course, preferable to nurture both simultaneously, but that this ideal is very difficult to achieve, as love and fear cannot easily be combined into a single dough; hence, writes Machiavelli, the ruler in most instances must decide between love and fear.[3] This is why Cambridge's flattery appears so far-fetched: he credits his king with achieving this Machiavellian ideal, so difficult to attain.

Machiavelli, in his practical and matter-of-fact writing, does not waste words on ideals that are difficult to attain, but moves on to provide an immediate answer to the question he has posed:

> ... if you have to make a choice, to be feared is much safer than to be loved. For it is a good general rule about men, that they are ungrateful, fickle, liars and deceivers, fearful of danger and greedy for gain. While you serve their welfare, they are all yours, offering their blood, their belongings, their lives, and their children's lives, as we noted above – so long as the danger is remote. But when the danger is close at hand, they turn against you ... [And] People are less concerned with offending a man who makes himself loved than one who makes himself feared: the reason is that love is a link of obligation which men, because they are rotten, will break any time they think doing so serves their advantage; but fear involves dread of punishment, from which they can never escape.[4]

Echoes of these remarks can be found in the two history plays that preceded *Henry V*. In *1 Henry IV*, for example, the king learns in retrospect and the hard way that if he wants to prevent internal strife, he must inspire fear in his subjects (I, iii, 1–9). His son, as the play focused upon by this chapter shows, rules better than he, and is endowed with the genius to calculate the appropriate means and timing to arouse, alternately, the fear and love of his subjects. This virtuosity of Shakespeare's Henry is so great that Cambridge's exaggerated compliment does not fall far from the reality presented in the play.[5]

---

3   Machiavelli, *The Prince*, translated by Robert M. Adams (New York: W. W. Norton and Company, 1977), p. 47.

4   Ibid., pp. 47–48.

5   Throughout the play a number of characters express their affection, love, or appreciation of Henry, when he is not present and in circumstances which do not cast doubt upon their sincerity. Among these characters we find even Pistol

Cambridge's obsequious words constitute a sort of prologue to the scene's preoccupation with the Machiavellian question presented above. Immediately following these words, Henry orders an action by which he shows himself to be a merciful ruler; showing mercy (*pietà*), according to Machiavelli, is one of the means by which a ruler can awaken the love of his subjects:

> KING: ... Uncle of Exeter,
> Enlarge the man committed yesterday
> That railed against our person. We consider
> It was excess of wine that set him on,
> And on his more advice we pardon him. (II, ii, 39–43)

The conspirators, knowledgeable in matters of sovereignty, continue pretending to be exemplary subjects, and warn Henry that such a display of mercy also indicates an excess of confidence, which may, in time, cause him harm; but since their king seems determined to show mercy, they advice him to punish the offender before his release, and thus preserve his power of deterrence:

> SCROOP: That's mercy, but too much security.
>   Let him be punished, sovereign, lest example
>   Breed, by his sufferance, more of such a kind.
> KING: O let us yet be merciful.
> CAMBRIDGE: So may your highness, and yet punish too.
> GREY: Sir,
>   You show great mercy, if you give him life,
>   After the taste of much correction. (II, ii, 44–51)

The lords' advice, in light of Machiavelli's book, is of course sound, practical and realistic; but, ironically, the three are unaware of the bit of information that would provide them with a broader perspective and a fuller understanding of their king's display of mercy. This bit of information exposes their advice as superfluous: in a few moments Henry will order their execution; thus he will raise the level of fear in

---

(see IV, i, 44–48), who has good reason to bear a grudge against the king – who has confirmed the execution of his friend and turned his back on his patron.

his camp immediately before the departure for the difficult mission in France, and will put into correct proportion the release of the insubordinate man from detention.

The events and substance of this scene invite the audience to examine Henry's actions henceforth as a sequence of acts intended to preserve the ideal balance between love and fear in the hearts of his subordinates. These actions, despite the considerable emotional charge they arouse, are the result of a strictly rational calculation by one of the most calculated characters in Shakespeare's drama. After announcing the sentence of the three traitorous lords, Henry declares that from his point of view their execution is not personal vengeance, but a means of safeguarding the kingdom (II, ii, 175–178). Considering his actions throughout the play, some of which I shall discuss at length, there seems no reason to doubt the sincerity of this statement. The fact that Henry is the new ruler of England (and intends to become the new ruler of France), explains why he is at pains to establish his threatening image:

> A new prince, above all others, cannot possibly avoid a name for cruelty, since new states are always in danger.[6]

Henry's awareness of the intimidating aura surrounding the sovereign is expressed explicitly in his Night Scene soliloquy. In this soliloquy Henry makes an enquiry concerning the essence of 'ceremony', during which he is revealed as an 'enhanced', more humane version of the cold Machiavellian prince:

> Art thou aught else but place, degree and form,
> Creating awe and fear in other men,
> Wherein thou art less happy, being feared,
> Than they in fearing? (IV, i, 243–246)

6 Machiavelli, *The Prince*, p. 47.

1.1.2 *Fear as a Means of Unifying Subjects*

One of the primary tasks of the prince, according to Machiavelli, and one that can be realised by 'creating awe and fear in other men,' is to preserve the internal unity of the hierarchy which he heads. Subjects who fear the might of their ruler will refrain from forming 'sects and sections', and will themselves act to resolve personal and group disputes. As a sterling example of this general principle Machiavelli points to Hannibal, who stood at the head of a large army made up of members of different nations. Machiavelli stresses that this army was free of internal strife, and claims that this achievement is entirely attributable to the inhuman cruelty of its much-vilified leader. Machiavelli distinguishes himself from earlier writers who, having considered the matter superficially, praise the unity of Hannibal's army but criticise his cruelty, not realising that the two are inseparably joined as cause and effect.[7]

In *Henry V*, Shakespeare uses a variety of means to demonstrate the special nature of the English army, which comprises a hodgepodge of nationalities. He even points out the real potential for the outbreak of strife among the various ethnic groups. Differences among the nationalities that make up Henry's army are tangibly expressed on stage by means of the conspicuous accents the playwright assigns to the characters. This phenomenon reaches a theatrical climax in scene ii, III, when four officers of Henry's army are on stage simultaneously, each speaking in a different accent: Fluellen the Welshman ('athversary, by Cheshu'), Jamy the Scot ('it sall be vary gud'), Macmorris the Irishman ('the work ish ill done tish ill done...'), and Gower the Englishman. The potential for internal strife within the military framework, against this background of national differences, is clearly illustrated when the tension between Fluellen and Macmorris mounts to the point of an explicit threat of murder (1. 136). This scene may be comic in nature, by virtue of the different accents and the amusing character of Fluellen, yet it clearly reveals the dangerous potential built into Henry's multi-national army.

---

7   Ibid., p. 48.

The theme of the ruler's task of uniting many human elements in order to achieve a shared objective is introduced as early as I, ii, in the Archbishop of Canterbury's parable of the bees. Observing these creatures, Canterbury says, teaches man how discipline and 'obedience' (l. 187) to one authority helps preserve order in the human kingdom. One desired goal, so preaches the Archbishop after having surveyed the different kinds of bees and their varied roles, can be achieved when all the different strata of society are harnessed together and work jointly:

> ... many things having full reference
> To one consent may work contrariously,
> As many arrows loosed several ways
> Come to one mark,
> As many ways meet in one town,
> As many fresh streams meet in one salt sea,
> As many lines close in the dial's centre.
> So may a thousand actions once afoot
> End in one purpose and be all well borne
> Without defeat. (I, ii, 205–214)

Henry's primary mission, as well as the secondary missions leading to its realisation, can in effect be defined in terms of unifying different and at times hostile human groups. His main goal is the conquest of France and the unification, under one crown, of two traditionally hostile kingdoms 'whose very shores look pale / With envy of each other's happiness' (V, ii, 344–345). In order to realise this objective, he must unite soldiers of different nationalities under his rule; yet this union of nations is not in itself sufficient when each nation, far from being a homogeneous social unit, is itself divided into different social strata.[8] Even Henry's principal objective, the conquest of France, is presented as an act of unification intended to advance yet another goal – the long-sought subjugation of the Turks:

---

8   Shakespeare uses a variety of means to draw the attention of his audience to the different social classes to which the soldiers of the English army belong. A prominent example of this differentiation is Henry's separate appeals to nobles and yeomen in his speech during the assault on Harfleur (see p. 62).

KING: [*To Katherine*] Shall not thou and I, between Saint Denis and
               Saint George, compound a boy, half French, half English, that
               shall go to Constantinople and take the Turk by the beard?
               (V, ii, 204–207)

1.1.3 Bardolph as the 'Awesome Prince'

As early as scene II, i, Shakespeare introduces a theatrical caricature
of a Machiavellian 'prince' who acts to unite his divided people by
means of intimidation. This caricature presents the audience with a
concise and exaggerated version of processes and actions that will
later be enacted onstage in a more refined, implied fashion. In order to
demonstrate Henry's rhetorical stratagem towards his subjects and
soldiers, the playwright focuses on a small social-military framework:
the band of clowns consisting of Bardolph, Nym and Pistol. The
threesome plans to join Henry's army on its mission to France in order
to improve their financial circumstances. The unity of this group is
undermined by the animosity that exists between Nym and Pistol for
financial and romantic reasons: Pistol has married Nell Quickly, who
was engaged to Nym, and to make matters worse, refuses to return the
eight shillings he borrowed from him in the past.

In the opening lines of II, i, in which Nym and Bardolph meet
and exchange greetings, Shakespeare formulates a brief, concentrated
exposition in which he reveals to the audience the hierarchy that exists
in the group: 'Corporal' Nym is lowest in rank, above him is 'Ancient' Pistol, and the highest – or for our purposes 'the Prince' – is
Bardolph, whose rank at this point is 'Lieutenant'. The latter, as the
highest ranking individual, is aware of the split between his two
'subjects', and realises that he must act to unite them if they are to
achieve their joint objective in going to France:

> BARDOLPH: Come, shall I make you two friends? We must to France
>   together. Why the devil should we keep knives to cut one
>   another's throats? (II, i, 90–92)

At the beginning of the scene, Bardolph expresses his readiness to
forego his breakfast for the sake of restoring good relations between

34

Nym and Pistol (ll. 11–13); but this gesture of benevolence makes no impression whatsoever on Nym. The moment Pistol, accompanied by his new wife, enters and joins the other two, passions flare and swords are drawn. Bardolph, in the face of this emergency, abandons his soft policy of benevolence and turns to the more effective Machiavellian method, intimidation:

> BARDOLPH: Hear me, hear me what I say. He that strikes the first stroke, I'll run him up to the hilts, as I am a soldier. (Ibid., ll. 64–66)

Pistol, characterised in the play as the very embodiment of cowardice, is affected by these resolute words; the speech arouses his fear and thus quells his anger (ll. 67–68). Nym, by contrast, has a much hotter temperament,[9] and his rage does not abate. He threatens the life of his rival, who responds with a show of contempt. Bardolph tries once again to extinguish the fire by means of intimidation, but this time amplifies it by swearing upon his sword:

> By this sword, he that makes the first thrust, I'll kill him. By this sword, I will ... Corporal Nym, an thou wilt be friends, be friends. An thou wilt not, why, then, be enemies with me too. (Ibid., ll. 99–104)

These threats, combined of course with his natural cowardice, cause Pistol to promise that he will repay his debt soon and in full; Nym is satisfied, and Prince Bardolph has succeeded in uniting his forces.

1.1.4 The Narrow Boundary between Fear and Hatred

To his advice that the ruler should intimidate his subjects, Machiavelli attaches a condition. The prince must prevent the fear that he inspires from being accompanied by hatred:

> Still, a prince should make himself feared in such a way that, even if he gets no love, he gets no hate either; because it is perfectly possible to be feared and not hated ...[10]

---

9   His spirits are concentrated in the upper part of his body (l. 69).
10   Machiavelli, *The Prince*, p. 48.

As I shall demonstrate, the spirit of this instruction is apparent in the way Henry comports himself in the presence of his soldiers. Interestingly, it also dictates his treatment of the French: Henry is well aware that they are his enemies only temporarily; and because his ultimate goal is the French throne, he must view them both as present enemies and future subjects. This understanding would appear to be behind the briefing he gives Exeter when he names him temporary governor of Harfleur, shortly after its surrender:

> Open your gates.
> > Come, uncle Exeter,
> Go you and enter Harfleur; there remain,
> And fortify it strongly 'gainst the French.
> *Use mercy* to them all. (III, iii, 51–54; my italics)

From the moment its gates are opened to the English army, the people of Harfleur become Henry's subjects, and he must prevent the accumulation of animosity towards him. The above instructions to Exeter should be examined in the light of the exceptionally blunt intimidation speech he delivered but a few seconds earlier (III, iii, 1–43), during which he vividly described what his wild soldiers would do to the infants, maids and elderly of the city, should its governor not surrender. From the broader viewpoint of the rhetorical strategy and the Machiavellian policy of intimidation employed by Henry throughout the play, it is clear that the harsh words are intended to achieve a specific goal: the speediest possible surrender of the city. Henry can make use of the most ruthless imagery, because words are destined to be forgotten; deeds, on the other hand, are not forgotten, and he must be very cautious when establishing his rule in the city. In this context it should be mentioned that in Holinshed's *Chronicles*, Henry's army plundered Harfleur after its conquest,[11] and in Hall's version the English sacked the surrounding villages during the siege.[12] Shakespeare chose not to follow his two main sources in this instance. The calculated, 'Machia-

---

11   Raphael Holinshed, 'Henrie the Fift, Prince of Wales', *Chronicles* (1587), vol. 3 (New York: AMS Press, 1965), p. 73.
12   Edward Hall, *The Union of the Two Noble and Illustre Families of Lancaster and York*, ed. H. Ellis (New York: AMS Press, 1965), p. 61.

vellian', Henry he has created cannot afford for such acts to be committed, being aware of the actual forces that shape reality:

> ... but above all, he [the Prince] should not confiscate people's property, because men are quicker to forget the death of a father than the loss of a patrimony.[13]

Taken at face value, Henry's response to the announcement of Bardolph's execution can be seen as an expression of the king's moral inclinations. However, a more mundane interpretation would link it to utilitarianism and Machiavellian foresight: both the execution and the king's public response can be regarded as mere rhetorical means aimed at achieving a specific objective. Henry seeks thereby to deter his soldiers from performing acts likely to precipitate hatred among the local population towards the English, particularly their ruler:

> We would have all such offenders so cut off; and we give express charge that in our marches through the country there be nothing *compelled* from the villages, nothing taken but paid for, none of the French upbraided or abused in disdainful language ... (III, vi, 106–110; my italics)

This injunction of Henry's, much like his instructions to Exeter upon entering Harfleur, seems to contradict previous declarations of his. Shakespeare's use of the verb 'compel' (l. 108) in this speech of Henry's echoes its earlier use in the ultimatum delivered by Exeter at the French court:

> Therefore in fierce tempest is he coming,
> In thunder and in earthquake, like a Jove,
> That if requiring fail, he will *compel* ... (II, iv, 99–101; my italics)

The use of this same verb in two seemingly contradictory declarations accentuates the significant difference between the intimidating rhetoric Henry addresses to his enemies, and his actual deeds.

Bardolph's execution should be examined within the context of the larger Machiavellian picture. The hanging itself, which is carried out on Exeter's orders, and the king's approval of it, are not merely means of deterring the English soldiers from mistreating the local

---

13   Machiavelli, *The Prince*, p. 48.

population (that is, from committing acts likely to arouse the French people's hatred towards their future ruler); through them Henry also readjusts the level of fear in which his soldiers hold him, and which he must preserve and nurture. The execution and Henry's speech referring to it occur at a critical point in time: winter has begun, and the English army is dwindling in numbers as hunger and disease spread through the ranks. The harsh conditions have created a breeding ground for problems within the army, and as the potential for internal conflict increases, Henry must intensify the awe and fear in which his soldiers hold him. Much can be learned about the Shakespearean king and his methods by studying the source from which the playwright took the general design of his plot: the soldier put to death in Holinshed's *Chronicles* is nameless, whereas in Shakespeare's version he is familiar to the audience as an amusing character from the subplot. Some of the spectators must even have remembered Bardolph as one of Henry's companions in his wilder days, as presented in the two parts of *Henry IV*. The outcome of this modification by Shakespeare is an increased dimension of 'coldness' or 'cruelty' in the characterisation of the king: from Fluellen's report it would seem that the execution has not yet taken place, and Henry, who explicitly hears from Fluellen the name of the condemned man, does not act to cancel the sentence, nor does he utter any word that might indicate sorrow (Of course, the actor playing Henry could choose to express a sense of scruple and internal conflict while delivering the king's resolute and 'cruel' words; however, the text itself carries not the slightest clue to support such an interpretation).

Machiavelli argues that, in particular, the prince who leads his army in war with many soldiers under his command should not be troubled if he earns a reputation for cruelty.[14] Such a prince will even be forced from time to time to execute one of his men in order to preserve the level of fear. Nevertheless, as mentioned above, Machiavelli is aware that overly extreme acts on the part of a ruler are liable to arouse the hatred of his subjects; for this reason he explains the circumstances in which a subject can be executed without the risk of arousing this undesirable emotion:

14   Ibid.

When he does have to shed blood, he should be sure to have a strong justification and just cause ...[15]

Thus, as I shall show, Henry takes the life of a subject or threatens to do so only when he is armed with a pretext that will be seen by his men as *clear and justified*; for this purpose he makes use of the unchallenged and broadest consensus, religion. The church-icon that Bardolph has stolen, from the point of view of Henry the ruler and rhetorician, is no mere 'pax of little price' (III, vi, 44), as it is presented by Pistol, whose point of view and emotional involvement in the situation differ from those shared by most English soldiers. A church-icon stolen from a French church, from both the English and the French viewpoints, is not an object of small monetary value, but rather a sacred object of spiritual and emotional value that transcends national boundaries. For this reason no one will consider – or at least will not let on that he considers – the execution of a desecrating thief to be a disproportionate and unjust act. Henry, who approves the hanging and dictates the general policy which has probably caused Exeter to order it, guarantees himself an image as an awesome and perhaps cruel ruler, but one who is also just. An understanding of the rhetorical thinking behind this event illustrates the method behind Henry's intimidating acts in general: it is no accident that the next time he threatens to impose the death penalty, he will harness religion to his cause once again.[16]

---

15   Ibid.
16   IV, viii, 114–117.

1.2 Control of Anger as a Key to Victory

1.2.1 Anger as a Weapon

Anger was regarded in early modern Europe as the soldier's most basic and effective weapon in battle. Although sources of the time do not agree on the exact nature of its influence on the mind of the warrior, they all explicitly indicate that this emotion can motivate a person to perform acts that he would not dare to carry out in normal circumstances. A number of sources indicate that anger is only capable of intensifying the courage of an already courageous person, or of spurring him to act in a way that *appears* to be courageous.[17] By contrast, other sources consider anger to be the central, even essential, condition for human courage. According to Coeffeteau, 'choler makes men hardy',[18] and Montaigne accepts as an established fact that anger is a necessary condition for courage:

> It is said that valour cannot be achieved without the help of anger ... that we do not attack the wicked or our foes vigorously enough, unless we are angry.[19]

This concept is employed by Montaigne in his broader argument that Man's noblest achievements are made possible by the driving force of the passions. In order to give this argument a convincing basis, he makes use of a fact about which he considers there to exist a consensus.

This widely-accepted concept is evinced in Shakespeare's plays, in which there are a number of heroic figures characterised in accordance with the conventional tradition of the 'raging warrior'. Most of

---

17 See, e.g.: Aristotle, *Nicomachean Ethics*, III, viii; Cicero, *Tusculan Disputations*, 4, 23. Compare: 'To be furious, / Is to be frighted out of fear' (*Antony and Cleopatra*, III, xiii, 199–200).

18 F. N. Coeffeteau, *A Table of Humane Passions with their Causes and Effects*, translated by E. Grimeston (1621), (Ann Arbor, MI: University Microfilms, 1981), p. 422.

19 Montaigne (1533–1592), *The Complete Essays*, translated by M. A. Screech (Harmondsworth: Penguin, 1993), pp. 638–639.

Shakespeare's great warriors – including Talbot, Hotspur, Hector, and Coriolanus – are characterised above all by their angry natures, or by the fact that their outstanding deeds of courage are achieved with the help of their rage.[20] In *Henry V* this convention is represented by the character of Fluellen, who is endowed with 'manly rage' (III, ii, 22–25), and by the ludicrous figure of Pistol the coward, who, in his pretentious declarations, portrays himself as the embodiment of the raging warrior.[21] The favourable influence of anger on the warrior is not limited to the courage it inspires in him; this emotion was also thought at the time to increase a man's physical prowess and implant in him the desire to kill. Coeffeteau writes explicitly that because heat is the source of strength, and the blood of an angry man is hot, people become stronger when they are angry.[22] Wright claims that from choler arise fighting, blood and wounds, and a man whose blood rises up through his body (which is the physiological effect accompanying anger), wants to shed the blood of others.[23] The paramount soldier, one who shows courage, physical strength, endurance, and blood-thirstiness towards his enemies, should therefore have a fierce temper or the ability to develop anger upon entering battle.

20 See for example: *1 King Henry VI*, IV, vi, 6–15; *1 King Henry IV*, III, i, 174–183; *Troilus and Cressida*, I, ii, 2–11; IV, v, 105–108; *Coriolanus*, I, iv, 27–28; I, ix, 84–85.

21 See, e.g.: II, i, 53–54; II, iii, 53–54; IV, iv, 64.

22 F. N. Coeffeteau, *A Table of Humane Passions with their Causes and Effects* (1621), p. 466. Thomas Elyot's *Castel of Helthe* also refers to anger as warming the extremities: 'Ire is kendlyd in the harte ... and then is sent forthe in to the members, and doth superfluously heate them ... Where naturall heate is feeble, the heate may nat be dispersed unto the extreme partes, and then dothe the extreme members, that is to say, which are farre from the harte, remayne colde, and tremblynge'. Thomas Elyot, *The Castel of Helthe* (1539), (New York: Scholars' Facsimiles & Reprints, 1979), p. 62.

23 Thomas Wright, *The Passions of the Minde in Generall* (1604), pp. 65, 166–167. Compare: 'My burning breast that rowles in wrath, and doth in rancour boyle, / Sore thrysteth after blood, and wounds with slaughter, death and spi-yle'. John Studley, 'translation to *Medea*', *Seneca: His Tenne Tragedies*, ed. Thomas Newton (1581), (Bloomington and London: Indiana University Press, 1964), Act I, p. 57.

In Henry's army there are no mythological fighters such as Hector, Coriolanus, Talbot or Hotspur. From the words of the Chorus we learn of the amateur standard of the English soldiers, who are no more than simple citizens carried away on the wave of enthusiasm that sweeps the kingdom following the declaration of war; many of them are mere boys 'whose chin is but enriched / With one appearing hair', or men who 'sell the pasture now to buy the horse' (II, Chorus, 1, 5; III, Chorus, 22–24). In the first half of the play Shakespeare acquaints his audience intimately with three cowardly and opportunistic soldiers, whose declared intentions in going to war are financial.[24] Bardolph, Nym and Pistol are, as the latter testifies when they stay behind and do not join the attack on Harfleur, 'man of mould' (III, ii, 22). The significance of this expression is twofold: Pistol apparently means that he and his comrades are 'only human beings' – offspring of the first man, created from clay – simple people who experience the human emotion most natural at such a moment, fear; but the expression also echoes the medical language of the time, instructing the audience to see the three soldiers as human beings whose bodily complexion is dominated by the coldest of the four elements, earth;[25]

---

24   Shakespeare chooses not to present any soldiers except Bardolph, Nym and Pistol on stage, until the eve of the Battle of Agincourt. In this way he manipulates the audience into projecting what they know of these three onto the English army in general (on the eve of the battle three other, quite different, soldiers are presented intimately to the audience, for a different manipulative purpose). The worldly, opportunistic nature of Bardolph, Nym and Pistol contradicts the patriotic and heroic descriptions given by the Chorus at the beginning of Acts II and III: in scene III, ii, the boy reports that Bardolph has stolen a lute-case (the sale of which earns him three-and-a-half pence) and cooperated with Nym in stealing a fire-shovel (42–45). Even before the campaign begins, Pistol declares his true motives for going to France: '... For I shall sutler be / Unto the camp, and profits will accrue' (II, i, 111–112); 'For Falstaff he is dead, And we must earn therefore' (II, iii, 6).

25   Fluellen, who orders Bardolph, Nym and Pistol to join the assault on the walls of Harfleur, reviles them as 'cullions' (i.e., 'rascals' [III, ii, 21]). As the editors of the Arden and Cambridge editions note, the original meaning of this word was 'testicles'. The cold nature of these reproductive organs was emphasised two scenes earlier in a comic pun (testicles were referred to at the time as 'stones of generation', and in usage termed 'vulgar' by the *Oxford English Dictionary*, simply 'stones' [*OED*, n., 11a]): 'I put my hand into the bed and

Bardolph, Nym and Pistol are unsuited to the battlefield, in which 'the humour of it is too hot' (ibid., 4–6). By comparison, the horse of the French Dauphin – whose body, according to its owner, is lacking the cold elements of earth and water – is 'pure air and fire', as though created for warfare (III, vii, 20–23).

1.2.2 'Imitate the Action of the Tiger'

Thomas Wright describes the way in which it was customary in his day to arouse anger in soldiers before entering battle:

> Let a souldiour heare a trumpet or a drum, and his bloud will boile and bend to battell ... In europe we neuer see soldiors almost fight, but first prououked to warres, with trumpets and drummes ... musicke and instruments in one kind causeth souldiers blood to rise, and thirst after the shedding of the blood of their enemies.[26]

However, in a most interesting passage, Wright explains that the sounding of a trumpet or other musical effect does not necessarily arouse the same passion in the minds of different people; the arousal of any passion depends upon a variety of factors such as natural bodily disposition, physical condition, moral character,[27] and an additional factor that in modern usage might be called 'conditioning':

> ... I cannot imagine, that if a man neuer had heard a trumpet or a drum in his life, that he would at the first hearing be mooued to warres.[28]

This quotation clearly illustrates the impediment facing Henry in scene III, i, as he stands before his newly-recruited troops in the first battle on French soil. At the beginning of the scene, the king and his soldiers are seen retreating from an attempted attack on the walls of

---

felt them, and they were as cold as any stone. Then I felt to his knees, and so up'ard and up'ard, and all was as cold as any stone' (II, iii, 22–25).

26   Thomas Wright, *The Passions of the Minde in Generall.* (1604), pp. 166–171.
27   Ibid., p. 171.
28   Ibid.

Harfleur; Henry delivers a speech meant to urge his men on into a renewed attack on a breach that has apparently been opened in the wall. The purpose of Henry's speech is to bring about what would have happened of its own accord if his soldiers were more seasoned and of a higher quality, transforming themselves in the blinking of an eye when they hear the tumult of battle:

> In peace there's nothing so becomes a man
> As modest stillness and humility;
> But when the blast of war blows in our ears,
> Then imitate the action of the tiger ... (III, i, 3–6)

The editor of the Arden edition glosses the expression 'the blast of war' as 'the warlike trumpet sound', whereas the editor of the Cambridge edition leaves it to the reader to choose between this interpretation and 'cannon shot'. A study of the entry 'blast' in the *Oxford English Dictionary* seems to show that 'trumpet blast' alone is the more logical choice,[29] because the use of the word 'blast' to indicate 'an explosion' or 'blowing up by gunpowder' apparently came to be accepted only later (the earliest appearance of this definition in the *OED* is from 1635, some 35 years after the first performance of the play[30]). For this reason and in light of the above references to Wright's book, the phrase 'when the blast of war' is not a metaphor indicating the moment the battle begins, but rather a specific reference to the moment when the trumpeter plays the sounds intended to move the blood of the soldiers, make it boil, and raise it up through the body.[31] Henry's instruction is very specific, and he explains to his untried soldiers how they are to respond, physiologically and mentally, to the sound of the trumpet blast. Because the soldiers' response is not the desired 'conditioned' one –

---

29 *OED*, 'blast', n., 3a.

30 Ibid., 8a.

31 Compare: 'Now, when the angry trumpet sounds alarum / ... Clifford, I say, come forth and fight with me ...' (*2 Henry VI*, V, ii, 3–5); 'And when he saw my best alarumed spirits / Bold in the quarrel's right, roused to the encounter, / ... Full suddenly he fled' (*King Lear*, II, i, 52–55).

they do not imitate the action of the raging tiger[32] – Henry himself turns to arousing their anger, replacing the effect of the trumpet with the power of his own speech.

As a military leader and orator, Henry faces a number of obstacles on the occasion in question. The first is lack of time: because the battle is already in progress, he does not have the same advantage of time and relative quiet that he will have, for example, on the morning of the battle of Agincourt. The effectiveness of the long, carefully structured St Crispin's Day speech will greatly depend upon his soldiers' attentiveness and understanding, which will not be attainable once the fighting has begun. The second obstacle, relevant not only to the occasion in question but to the entire duration of Henry's stay in France, is related to the problematic cause of the war. The play, from the opening scene, does not provide the audience with a clear and unequivocal reason for Henry's decision to invade France, and along with numerous declarations by characters justifying it, we encounter comments and evidence that indicate the opposite. The belief of soldiers that they are fighting for a good cause is, according to Coeffeteau, an important prerequisite if they are to fight with courage and determination.[33] In Holinshed's and Hall's versions of the life story of Henry V, the king emphasises before his soldiers, in his speech at Agincourt (neither writer mentions a speech at Harfleur), the 'just cause' for which they are about to go into battle;[34] in these two sources Henry explicitly instructs his soldiers to see the justice of their

32 On the angry temperament of the tiger, see, for example: 'Exile all foolish Feamale feare, and pity from my mynde, / And as th'untamed Tygers use to rage and rave unkynde, / ... permit to lodge and rest, / Such salvage brutish tyranny within thy brazen brest' (John Studley, 'translation to *Medea*' [1581], Act I, p. 57); 'One word more, one word! / This tiger-footed rage, when it shall find / The harm of unscanned swiftness, will, too late, / Tie leaden pounds to's heels' (*Coriolanus*, III, i, 316–318); 'Pluck the keen teeth from the fierce tiger's jaws ...' (Sonnet 19, l. 3).

33 F. N. Coeffeteau, *A Table of Humane Passions with their Causes and Effects* (1621), p. 421.

34 '... the just cause for which they fought ...', '... if God of his clemencie doo favour us, and our just cause (as I trust he will) we shall speed well inough ... God and our just quarrel shall defend us ...'. Raphael Holinshed, 'Henrie the Fift, Prince of Wales', pp. 79–80.

cause as evidence that god desires their victory over the French.[35] In Shakespeare's play, by contrast, the king makes use of no such argumentation in his speeches at Harfleur and at Agincourt; the only reference he makes during his stay in France to the purportedly just cause of the war is in his nocturnal conversation with the soldiers Williams, Bates and Court. This exceptional moment only serves to prove the rule, since Henry is not speaking publicly, in his own name, but is impersonating an anonymous 'gentleman of a company'. Furthermore, when his declaration regarding the king's just cause encounters Williams' doubting response (IV, i, 126–129), Henry does not try to defend his claim, but rather ignores the comment.

We return to Henry as he faces his soldiers and tries to motivate them to renew their attack on the walls of Harfleur. The solution he finds to the two rhetorical impediments mentioned above is to avoid a 'standard' emotional appeal, that is, one that enters the mind of the addressee through the cognitive system; instead, he improvises an appeal that bypasses this system, and directly affects the soldiers' emotional physiology. Henry fights their fear by instructing them to imitate the outward characteristics of the emotion of anger:

> Stiffen the sinews, conjure up the blood,
> Disguise fair nature with hard-favoured rage.
> Then lend the eye a terrible aspect;
> Let pry through the portage of the head
> Like the brass cannon; let the brow o'erwhelm it
> As fearfully as doth a galled rock
> O'erhang and jutty his confounded base,
> Swilled with the wild and wasteful ocean.
> Now set the teeth and stretch the nostril wide,
> Hold hard the breath and bend up every spirit
> To his full height. (III, i, 7–17)

35 Ibid.; Edward Hall, *The Union of the Two Noble and Illustre Families of Lancaster and York*, p. 67. This instruction is in accordance with what is written in *The French Academie* regarding fear: this emotion is so powerful and influential that only God is capable of uprooting it from the heart of man. The only cure for fear, then, is belief – the belief in God and doing his will – or 'the true feare of GOD.' See: Pierre de La Primaudaye, *The French Academie* (London, 1618), (Ann Arbor, MI: University Microfilms), pp. 472–473.

The gestures and facial expressions Henry dictates to his soldiers are none other than the physical manifestations of anger in its most 'pure' or 'basic' form, that is, anger 'unstained' by other emotions or blurred by behavioural conventions common to a specific time and place.[36] Any angry man, if not hiding or suppressing his anger, will display some or all of the following characteristics: heightened muscular tension, a piercing glance, scowling, baring his teeth,[37] flaring nostrils, shallow breathing, and curving of the spine.[38]

With regard to the expression 'conjure up the blood' (l. 7), disagreement has arisen due to problems of transcription, and it is difficult to determine whether Shakespeare originally wrote 'conjure up' or 'summon up'. The expression 'conjure up', if that is indeed what appeared in the original, does not in my opinion indicate the meaning suggested by the editor of the Cambridge edition, 'to perform some kind of a "bawdy magic" upon the blood'. Even if this suggestion applies to a number of instances in which the play draws an analogy between war and sexual activity and rape, it does not fit Henry's *specific* rhetoric in the speech in question. This interpretation contradicts the spirit of Henry's focused and purposeful instructions, and the specific physical effects he is attempting to bring about. Bewitching the blood to awaken love or desire in his soldiers would severely hinder their performance in combat, and contradict Henry's attempts to cause them to imitate 'hard-favoured' raging tigers. It seems to me that the meaning of this phrase when spoken by Henry is 'To call upon, constrain ... to appear to do one's bidding, by the ... use

---

36   Anger is classified in current studies as one of the 'six basic emotions', along with fear, disgust, sadness, joy, and surprise. Each of these emotions is characterised by a distinctive facial expression, universally recognisable. See: P. Ekman, 'Basic Emotions', *Handbook of Cognition and Emotions*, ed. T. Dalgleish and M. Power (Chichester: John Wiley and Sons, 1999), pp. 45–60.

37   Baring the teeth as an expression of the rage of 'the soldier' on his mission appears in Valeria's worshipful description of young Martius hunting a butterfly: '... whether his fall enraged him, or how 'twas, he did so set his teeth and tear it. O, I warrant how he mammocked it!' (*Coriolanus*, I, iii, 55–58).

38   P. Ekman and Richard J. Davidson (eds), *The nature of emotion: fundamental questions* (1994); P. Ekman, 'Basic Emotions', *Handbook of Cognition and Emotions* (1999).

of some spell', 'to raise ... as by magic, occult influence, the art or tricks of the conjuror'.[39] At the time, the expression was commonly used in references to devils and spirits, and usually meant to raise them aboveground, so that they would be visible to those present. In the same way, when in times of anger the blood rises up through the body, it colours the face red and thus becomes visible.

These remarks are also relevant with regard to the suggestion put forward by Rowe, who reads the expression in question 'summon up'. It seems to me that the appropriate interpretation of this reading is not the more general 'call up', but rather 'call upwards'. In other words, for our purposes the significance of this disputed phrase is to be found in the second word, which is not disputed, 'up'. Raising the blood up to the top part of the body is, as explained, a specific act, most suitable for arousing anger, and it suits and completes the parallel command that Henry gives later in reference to the spirits, which he calls to his soldiers 'to bend up' to their 'full height' (ll. 16–17): in times of anger, as mentioned, these distilled particles or fluids also rise up through the body.

The rhetorical-emotional tactic Henry chooses is not as groundless as it might seem, and is not effective only in the realms of literary and theatrical fiction. Contemporary research recognises that, just as emotions shape facial expressions and alter the tonicity of various muscular systems in the body, they are also aroused or altered as the result of such physical changes.[40] Achieving a desired emotional effect by means of a physical action, such as a gesture or facial expression, is a well known method in theatrical practice: actors and acting students who have difficulty in reproducing a specific emotional state through the power of imagination, are often instructed by the director or teacher to begin the process from its 'end', that is, to produce the physical effect that will bring about the desired emotional

---

39   *OED*, 'Conjure', v., III, 5a, 9c.
40   R. B. Zajonc, S. T. Murphy, and M. Inglehart, 'Feeling and Facial Efference: Implications of the Vascular Theory of Emotion', *Psychological Review* 96 (1989), pp. 395–416; R. J. Larsen, M. Kasimatis, and K. Frey, 'Facilitating the Furrowed Brow: an Unobtrusive Test of the Facial Hypothesis Applied to Unpleasant Affect', *Cognition and Emotion* 6, (1992), pp. 321–338.

change. In this connection the editor of the Cambridge edition points out that in the monologue in question Henry uses words that belong to the semantic field of theatrical acting ('imitate', 'action'). In *Coriolanus* III, ii, which is replete with expressions from this field, we find an explicit awareness of the power of gestures to bring about in the gesturer the emotional effect which they usually denote. Volumnia, instructing her angry, stubborn son before he faces the people and tribunes, teaches him how to neutralise his warrior's heart (the heart, it will be recalled, was considered the seat of the emotions) and impose mildness upon it:

> ... waving thy head,
> Which often, thus, correcting thy stout heart,
> Now humble as the ripest mulberry
> That will not hold the handling ... (III, ii, 78–81)

Coriolanus, convinced at first by his mother's arguments, expressing his readiness to face the people and tribunes, quickly changes his mind again. From the reason he gives for his refusal, it is evident that a theatrical gesture – or 'action'[41] – can influence the mind:

> I will not do't,
> Lest I surcease to honour mine own truth
> And by my body's action teach my mind
> A most inherent baseness. (Ibid., 121–124)

Henry does not repeat this unique emotional tactic of arousing anger by imitating its physiological effects. In his next combat speech, instead of arousing the anger of his soldiers, he stimulates their desire for honour. The play does not refer to the fact that Henry desists from devoting time and resources to arousing anger in his soldiers; however, in light of the above comments by Thomas Wright regarding the role of emotional 'conditioning' on the battlefield, it is possible to reconstruct the reason for the change in the king's war rhetoric: after he explains to his soldiers how they are expected to respond to 'the blast of war', and after he has performed with them in a 'guided' manner the entire emotional-physical process, they cease to be 'virgins' in this

41   For a clarification of this term, see pp. 194–195.

area. In subsequent battles, accordingly, there is no longer any need for such a speech, and the soldiers' anger will awaken with the trumpet blast, which is sounded at the beginning of every battle. Scene III, i, then, presents the emotional learning process undergone by Henry's soldiers: at its very beginning, while the stage is empty, an alarum is heard, the purpose of which is apparently to arouse the anger of the soldiers and motivate them to a renewed attack on the city wall;[42] this blast does not achieve the desired physical and mental effects, and natural fear drives the soldiers to retreat; Henry arrives in their wake and delivers the speech, the purpose of which is explained above; at its completion, the trumpet blast is once again sounded, (1. 34 SD), this time accomplishing its purpose, and helping to create the desired emotional conditioning.

In his Harfleur speech Henry does not make do with motivating his soldiers to attack by means of anger, but also plays on their sense of shame (as he will do in his St Crispin speech, to be discussed in the closing chapter). At the beginning of the play Canterbury, Ely, Exeter, and Westmoreland try to exert emotional pressure on their king, with the intention of inducing him to declare war on France. The rhetorical technique chosen by the four is based on evoking the valorous feats of his great predecessors Edward III and Edward 'the black prince of Wales' (I, ii, 100–135) in the fields of France; this evocation suggests, of course, a comparison of the deeds of past heroes with the idleness of their descendent in the present. It cannot be determined, from the text, to what degree, if at all, this emotional appeal influences Henry, but as he faces the walls of Harfleur he adopts precisely the same technique and practices it on his soldiers; the king calls up from the past the subjects of his heroic ancestors, who are the ancestors of his present-day subjects, and challenges his soldiers not to shame the precedent of their predecessors:

---

42   The editors of the Arden and Cambridge editions were evidently unaware of the role of the trumpet in the battlefield in arousing anger in the soldiers; for this reason they gloss the word 'alarm / alarum' in the stage directions, III, i, 0 and III, Chorus, 33, as a 'military signal', and define the purpose of the trumpet as 'to transmit battlefield messages'.

> On, on, you noblest English,
> Whose blood is fet from fathers of war-proof,
> Fathers that like so many Alexanders
> Have in these parts from morn till even fought,
> And sheathed their swords for lack of argument.
> Dishonour not your mothers; now attest
> That those whom you called fathers did beget you. (III, i, 17–23)

Diluted with a bit of flattery, he presents a similar challenge immediately afterwards to his lower-class soldiers (ibid., ll. 25–30). It should be explained that the emotion of shame is certainly likely to be awakened when the subject grasps in his imagination a future occurrence that is liable to stain his reputation, and not only in light of present circumstances or events.[43] In his discussion of the emotion of shame, Coeffeteau notes its power to inspire even in cowards the courage to follow their commanders into battle.[44] The potency of this emotion as a motivating force in war is stressed in the play,[45] and from a physiological viewpoint it is most suited for the advancement of Henry's goals, as he tries to eradicate the fear of his soldiers. Although shame is defined by some as 'a kind of fear',[46] it is significantly different from that fear which weakens and paralyses, and with which Henry has to deal at Harfleur. When such weakening fear arises in a man whose life is in danger, the blood leaves the face and descends to the heart.[47] When a man feels shame, on the other hand, an excess of blood rises to his face and colours it red.[48] This physical reaction is identical to the change brought about by the emotion of anger; Henry, then, tries in various ways during his speech to counter the negative physical effects that fear has caused in his soldiers, and to raise the blood back to the upper part of their bodies.

43   See Chapter Four, p. 189.
44   F. N. Coeffeteau, *A Table of Humane Passions with their Causes and Effects* (1621), pp. 503–504.
45   See, for example, III, ii, 110–112; III, v, 36–39, 46–47; IV, v, 3–10, 23.
46   'Shame, say the philosophers, is a kind of feare, which ariseth, for that man doubts some blame and some censure of his actions'. F. N. Coeffeteau, *A Table of Humane Passions with their Causes and Effects* (1621), p. 496.
47   Ibid., p. 497.
48   See Appendix B, p. 298.

1.2.3 The Absence of Anger Among the French

Parallel to his close surveillance of the balance of emotions in the English camp, Shakespeare allows a similar glimpse into the opposing camp. This glimpse tempts the audience to draw a straight line linking the emotional state of the French with their performance on the battle-field. Just as the absence of anger from the minds and bodies of the English soldiers at Harfleur interfered with their fighting, so too can the failure of the French be explained in emotional terms, namely, the complete lack of anger within their army at critical moments.

At the beginning of the second act, the Chorus reports that the French 'shake in their fear' when they hear the intelligence regarding England's 'most dreadful preparation' (ll. 12–15). This report receives no textual confirmation in scene II, iv, in which the French court is first presented to the audience. The French king and his constable at this point express what is termed in Coeffeteau's work 'moderate fear'; despite the word 'fear', this emotion is significantly different from 'normal' fear, which paralyses: it does not impair the warrior's physical and mental functioning, but rather guides him in thinking out his actions wisely and protecting himself.[49] In sharp contrast to the king and the constable, the Dauphin's emotional state in this scene can be described as the complete opposite of moderate fear (II, iv, 23–29). It is precisely this emotional state that will dominate the entire French camp prior to the battle of Agincourt, as will be discussed later.

The beginning of scene III, v presents the French after the 'mod-erate fear' that has governed them gives way to anger and the desire for revenge. Their anger arises from the severe blow to their honour brought about by the march of the English – whom the French consider their inferior offspring, the product of their ancestors' vented lust (ll. 5–9) – undisturbed across their country. This anger is intensi-

---

49 '... disordered Feare ... doth wholly trouble the imagination of man ... there is a kinde of moderate Feare, which striking reason but genteley, makes us advised (to the which the stoickes give the name circumspection) to provide with iudgement for that which concernes us: for that it makes us carefull and atten-tive to looke to our affaires, and to give order for that which is necessary to shelter us from storms'. F. N. Coeffeteau, *A Table of Humane Passions with their Causes and Effects* (1621), p. 472.

fied by the mockery they endure from their wives, as the Dauphin reports (ll. 27–35). In the thinking of the time, contempt was thought to arouse particularly intense anger,[50] and the display of contempt by those whom the subject considers inferior to himself (the marching English, the mocking Madams), lead to the most intense anger of all.[51] This anger erupts towards the end of the scene, when the king orders his men to put an end to this intolerable situation, to mobilise the army and defeat the English. But precisely at this moment, when their anger and desire for revenge are at their peak, they quickly begin to fade, quenched by overconfidence certainty of knowing the outcome of the battle before it even begins. Even the constable, who, it will be remembered, demonstrated circumspection during scene II, iv, undergoes a sharp emotional transition from anger to complacency, seconds after his king announces the general mobilisation:

> This becomes the great.
> Sorry am I his numbers are so few,
> His soldiers sick and famished in their march,
> For I am sure, when he shall see our army
> He'll drop his heart into the sink of fear
> And for achievement offer us his ransom. (III, v, 55–60)

These lines clearly indicate the emotional problem from which the French are suffering: from the anger and frustration he showed a mere 40 lines earlier, the constable moves to a demonstration – albeit ironic – of *sorrow* (l. 56); in the Night Scene Shakespeare will put into his mouth words indicating that he continues to distance himself from the emotional state befitting a warrior, when he expresses *pity* for his enemies ('Alas, poor Harry of England' [III, vii, 130]).

The distancing of the French from anger, and their entrenchment in the realms of overconfidence and pride, is expressed above all in their visions as the battle nears:

---

50   See Chapter Three, p. 145.
51   F. N. Coeffeteau, *A Table of Humane Passions with their Causes and Effects* (1621), pp. 567–570.

DAUPHIN: ... Will it never be day? I will trot to-morrow a mile, and my way
shall be paved with English faces. (III, vii, 80–81)

ORLEANS: It is now two o'clock; but, let me see, by ten
We shall have each a hundred Englishmen. (Ibid., 155–156)

In one of his observations on the emotion of anger, Aristotle describes the transition of the angry man's consciousness back and forth from the wrong that has been done him, to the revenge he will wreak upon the wrongdoer. This observation also appears in writings of the time relevant to our subject. It refers to the uniqueness of anger, which involves sensations of both pain and pleasure (unlike most emotions, which are associated with either pain or pleasure): we feel pain when we recreate in our imaginations a wrong that has been done us; the pain of these memories directs us to thoughts of retribution, and when the later is realised in our imaginations, we feel pleasure.[52] Considering this unique characteristic of anger, it is clear that the French are so far removed from it that their consciousness has entirely abandoned the injuries to their country and their honour, perpetrated by the English army. They feel no pain, only pleasure, as they repeatedly realise revenge in their imaginations.

The description by the Chorus of the French as 'over-lusty' (IV, Chorus, 18) is accurate; their desire to realise their pleasure-giving imaginings grows stronger in the final hours before the battle, and reaches a peak at its beginning: at midnight the Dauphin already takes leave of his fellow noblemen and sets to work arming himself; a few moments before the beginning of the battle the French are still growing in complacence, as Grandpre and the constable elaborate with exaggerated detail upon the miserable English camp and its famished, weak and bloodless soldiers (IV, ii, 15–33, 38–53). These two amplifications – which can be classified as 'emotional appeals to the self'[53] – overcome the French constable's temperance, and he begins his assault even before he is joined by his guidon (IV, ii, 59–61).

---

52   F. N. Coeffeteau, *A Table of Humane Passions with their Causes and Effects* (1621), pp. 557–558.

53   For a clarification of the term 'emotional appeal to the self', see Introduction, p. 18.

Holinshed describes a similar incident, but the assault is attributed to the Duke of Brabant;[54] Shakespeare, then, has chosen to demonstrate the intensity of the French over-lustiness through its embodiment in the man who heads the army and who should, therefore, be working to eradicate it. In Holinshed's version this incident is no more than an anecdote; in the Shakespearean play it marks the peak of an entire emotional process, presented on stage in detail.

The most ironic and felicitous expression of the inadequate physical-emotional state of the French prior to the battle, is uttered by the Dauphin. He is troubled, just before the assault, over the low level of competitiveness he will be encountering in combat against so weak an enemy. In compensation, he suggests a creative solution:

> CONSTABLE: Hark, how our steeds for present service neigh!
> DAUPHIN: Mount them, and make incision in their hides,
>   That their *hot blood* may spin in English eyes
>   And dout them with superfluous courage, ha!
>   (IV, ii, 7–10; my italics)

In the closing chapter I shall show how *Henry V* focuses on the role of the faculties of appraisal and reckoning in processes of emotional arousal, and how the significant numerical imbalance between the English and French armies – after it is grasped and processed in the intellect[55] – is liable to arouse different emotions in different characters. It is this perception of the imbalance that leads the French to give free rein to their harmful pride; the French steeds, by contrast, precisely because of their lack of intellect, face the battle in the most appropriate emotional and physical state possible.

54   Raphael Holinshed, 'Henrie the Fift, Prince of Wales', p. 80.
55   See Chapter Five, pp. 228–232.

1.3 Henry's Rhetoric for the Management of Fear

1.3.1 The Physiological Incompatibility of Anger and Fear

Our discussion so far can be summarised in one sentence: advancing towards his goal of conquering France, Henry must control his men, maintain their unity, and infuse them with courage and physical strength; in order to control his men and maintain their unity, he must arouse their *fear*; in order to infuse them with courage and physical strength, he must arouse their *anger*. This twofold emotional task of Henry's is not without difficulty. According to the perception common in Shakespeare's day, the two passions that he must arouse in his army while in France are incompatible: they affect the human body in opposite ways and thus cannot exist therein simultaneously.

That fear and anger are mutually exclusive, one giving way to the other, is demonstrated in the words of Pistol, on whom Bardolph's death threats make a deep impression and allow his natural cowardice to resume control of him:

> An oath of mickle might; and fury shall abate. (II, i, 67)

The contradiction between fear and anger arises from the difference in the temperature each induces in the blood, and from the different location of blood and the spirits in the body, depending upon which emotion is dominant. As explained in the discussion of Henry's speech at Harfleur, the blood and the spirits become hot when one is angry; they rise up through the body to the face and are channelled to the extremities. In times of fear, on the other hand, they move in the opposite direction: when one discerns a life-threatening situation, the heart contracts and becomes weak, and 'provident nature' sends the blood from the face to the heart, in an attempt to keep it secure.[56] When fear is strong and there is insufficient blood in the face to protect the heart, the blood elsewhere in the body descends to reinforce it;

---

56 Thomas Wright, *The Passions of the Minde in Generall* (1604), pp. 26–36; Pierre de La Primaudaye, *The French Academie*, p. 471.

in the event of extreme fear, the blood descends even lower than the heart (the sources do not indicate what purpose this serves).[57] People blessed with excess blood are hardy: even when they are in danger and their blood descends to their hearts, sufficient amounts remain in their faces and hands; for this reason their strength does not desert them and their limbs do not tremble.[58] Most human beings are not blessed with excess blood, so that at any given moment it is likely to be located either in their faces and limbs, or close to their hearts – thus ordinary people grow pale in a fear-inspiring situation. The hands of the fearful shake and become weak because they are cold: the blood and the spirits are the source of bodily heat, and when they desert the hands, this heat leaves with them (spirits grow cold in times of fear, thus becoming thicker and heavier, and, like the blood, descend through the body).[59]

The above are not merely learned theories gathered from writings by Shakespeare's contemporaries, of interest only to men of letters. *Henry V* itself displays a keen awareness of the physiological mechanisms of the passions of anger and fear, as described, and deals with them frequently and explicitly: the hot temperature that accompanies anger (and hence situations of military conflict) is referred to on several occasions, as well as the elevated place of the blood and spirits in the bodies of angry or hardy men.[60] Correspondingly, the text demonstrates awareness of the opposite symptoms – that is, of coldness, of the draining of blood from the face to the interior of the body and of the low location of the spirits – as characterising fear.[61] The manner in

---

57   F. N. Coeffeteau, *A Table of Humane Passions with their Causes and Effects* (1621), pp. 461–462, 464.

58   Ibid., pp. 422–423.

59   Ibid., pp. 462–463; Pierre de La Primaudaye, *The French Academie*, p. 471. It seems, according to the sources, that although the spirits reside in the blood and move about the body through the blood vessels, they are 'autonomous', and their location does not necessarily coincide with that of the blood. This is evident in the 'physical guidance' Henry imparts to his soldiers in his speech at Harfleur, during which he refers to raising the blood and raising the spirits as two separate undertakings (III, i, 7, 16–17).

60   I, ii, 151; II, i, 68–69; II, iv, 68; II, iv, 123; III, i, 7, 17; III, ii, 2–6, 106–108; III, iii, 21; IV, ii, 9; IV, vii, 175–177; III, v, 18–20.

61   I, Chorus, 8–11; II, ii, 71–76; III, v, 16–25; IV, Chorus, 43–45.

which Shakespeare refers in *Henry V* to the body and its passions indicates that he assumed his audience to be knowledgeable about the physical mechanism of emotions; this is clearly demonstrated in the soliloquy delivered by the boy who stays behind during the assault on Harfleur. He expresses his opinion on the excessive cowardice of his patrons, Nym, Pistol and Bardolph, treating the latter as an exceptional phenomenon in the area of emotional physiology:

> For Bardolph, he is *white-livered* and *red-faced*, by the means whereof 'a faces it out but fights not. (III, ii, 32–33; my italics)

The meaning of the term 'white-livered' at the time was 'coward': the liver is the source of blood, and a low reserve of blood, as has been explained, does not allow the body to deal well with the changes brought about by fear.[62] The 'flaming-red' colour of Bardolph's face[63] is misleading: it would seem to indicate an abundance of blood, or that most of his blood is concentrated in his upper body, and therefore that he is either naturally courageous, or courageous by virtue of being choleric.[64]

As has been shown, the opposing characteristics of fear and anger create a considerable problem for Henry: on the one hand, he must avoid a situation in which there is even a trace of fear in his attacking soldiers, as this emotion will prevent their anger from awakening when they hear the trumpet blast of war, and their performance as warriors will be severely impaired; on the other hand, as a sovereign and a general, he must strike fear into the hearts of his subjects in order to maintain his authority and the unity of his army. Henry must, therefore, find an intermediate solution, to orchestrate between the two opposing emotions and to regulate them in keeping with his perception of time and circumstances.

---

62   Compare: *Twelfth Night*, III, ii, 48–49.
63   'Good Bardolph, put thy face between his sheets and do the office of a warming-pan' (II, i, 84–85); '... 'a saw a flea stick upon Bardolph's nose and 'a said it was a black soul burning in hell-fire?' (II, iii, 38–40).
64   'Cholerik ... is discerned by these sygnes folowinge ... Visage and skyn red as fyre ... Hardy and fyghtynge'. Thomas Elyot, *The Castel of Helthe* (1539), p. 2.

1.3.2 Henry Lowers the Level of Fear in his Camp

The physiological incompatibility between fear and anger did not pose a great difficulty for Henry during the early stages of the fighting in France, when his soldiers were fresh and healthy and were not yet opposed by a large and well organised army. Leading up to the decisive encounter with the French at Agincourt there is a change in circumstances, and with it, a change in the emotional balance: the state of the English army has deteriorated due to loss of life, disease, fatigue, and the harsh conditions of winter. To these new impediments must of course be added the ever-present doubts about the justness of the cause of the war, mentioned above. This doubt is expressed explicitly on stage by one of the soldiers on the eve of battle (IV, i, 126–129). Furthermore, the French army, with its impressive numbers, has been mobilised in its entirety for the encounter with the English, who have so far fought against civilian targets and have met with only limited local resistance. In other words, leading up to the last and decisive battle, there is increased potential for an awakening of fear among Henry's soldiers.[65] Henry – aware of the new circumstances, of the danger posed by this growing fear (VI, i, 286–289), and of the probability that he is facing a battle that will determine the outcome of the entire campaign – adjusts the emotional policies he has been employing, and undertakes a broad rhetorical effort to eliminate fear among his men altogether. In keeping with this temporary policy, he suspends for the moment the Machiavellian intimidation he has taken care to nurture since the beginning of the play.

Students of the play point out that as the battle of Agincourt approaches, Henry tends to 'suppress', 'hide' or 'blur' the military and class hierarchies that differentiate among his men. Andrew Gurr devotes a substantial part of his introduction to the play to this phenomenon, emphasising that in his declarations at Agincourt, Henry is attempting to conceal the very social distinctions that he reaffirms at

---

65   The word 'fear' occurs in the play 27 times. It appears with ever-increasing frequency as the battle of Agincourt approaches, but from the moment the battle begins until the end of the play it does not appear even once.

other times and in other places.[66] Scholars have referred to this phenomenon primarily from a social perspective, and aside from observing that Henry tries to raise morale in his camp and encourage his soldiers 'to fight lustily for him', they have not examined its emotional implications. It seems to me useful to point out the direct connection between the king's suppression of hierarchies and his rhetoric of emotion: as suggested below, this suppression is one of the means he uses to banish fear from the hearts of his subjects. The hierarchical structure and its frequent reaffirmation lead the individuals who make it up to be in constant fear of those who rank above them in the social order; the cancellation of this order, or at least its temporary camouflage, reduces their fear or causes it to disappear entirely.

Henry's efforts to temporarily suspend the social order and the fear in which his subjects hold him, are evident in the opening speech of Act IV. In this speech, the Chorus describes an idyllic picture of the king walking through the English camp the night before the battle, a man among his people:

> O now, who will behold
> The royal captain of this ruined band
> Walking from watch to watch, from tent to tent,
> Let him cry 'Praise and glory on his head!'
> For forth he goes and visits all his host,
> Bids them good morrow with a modest smile,
> And calls them *brothers*, *friends* and *countrymen*.
> ...
> That every wretch, pining and *pale* before,
> Beholding him plucks comfort from his looks.
> A largess universal, like the sun,
> His liberal eye doth give to every one,
> *Thawing cold fear* ... (IV, Chorus, 28–45; my italics)

Indeed, as mentioned above in another context, there are occasional glaring contradictions between the words of the Chorus and the 'reality' seen on stage, and this passage is a case in point: the audience does not witness, following the above lines, their theatrical realisation,

---

66   Andrew Gurr, 'Introduction to *King Henry V*', *King Henry V*, ed. Andrew Gurr (Cambridge: Cambridge University Press, 1992), pp. 32–37.

and does not see Henry giving his subjects (certainly not 'all' his subjects, as the Chorus states in line 32) 'A little touch of Harry in the night' (l. 47). Instead they see him, wrapped in the robe of Erpingham to disguise his identity, in confrontational and argumentative encounters with Pistol, Williams, Bates, and Court. Nevertheless, the words of the Chorus manipulate the way the spectator perceives the reality shown subsequently, particularly as they fit in well with the atmosphere Henry creates during the night, in the company of characters he meets when he is not hiding behind a false identity (and with the warm words with which Henry describes, in a theatrical aside, Captain Fluellen [IV, i, 84–85]). The words of the Chorus, furthermore, are entirely compatible with the messages of fellowship that Henry articulates to his soldiers in his St Crispin's Day speech, moments before the battle begins:

> Then shall our names,
> Familiar in his mouth as household words,
> Harry the king, Bedford and Exeter,
> Warwick and Talbot, Salisbury and Gloucester,
> Be in their flowing cups freshly remembered. (IV, iii, 51–55)

In the course of this speech the king goes so far as to make a declaration of brotherhood, and a promise that those who fight by his side will in the future all belong to a single, high, social class:

> We few, we happy few, we band of brothers.
> For he to-day that sheds his blood with me
> Shall be my brother; be he ne'er so vile,
> This day shall gentle his condition. (IV, iii, 60–63)

In the chronicles of Holinshed and Hall there is no hint of any such rhetorical tactic or declaration of brotherhood; the only rhetorical expression indicating an attempt by the king to create a sense of affinity between himself and his soldiers is found in the opening lines of the speech in Hall's version: 'Welbeloved frendes and contrymen'.[67]

---

67   Edward Hall, *The Union of the Two Noble and Illustre Families of Lancaster and York*, p. 66.

The extraordinary change in Henry's emotional policy can be illustrated by comparing the statements cited above from the St Crispin's Day speech, with the concealed social messages in his speech at Harfleur at the beginning of the war. His separate appeals to nobles and commoners emphasise and perpetuate the social disparity in the English army:

> On, on, *you noblest English,*
> Whose blood is fet from fathers of war-proof ...
> ... *And you, good yeoman,*
> Whose limbs were made in England, show us here
> The mettle of your pasture; let us swear
> That you are worth your breeding – which I doubt not,
> For there is none of you so *mean and base*
> That hath not noble lustre in your eyes. (III, i, 17–30; my italics)

Henry continues to use the rhetoric of suppressing class differences employed in the St Crispin speech after the speech has ended. When the French herald Montjoy arrives in the English camp and delivers a demoralising speech, the king takes advantage of the public nature of the occasion: in his answer to the French he conceals messages aimed primarily at his own soldiers, who are present. Apparel is perhaps the social symbol that perpetuates social class more than any other, and differentiates individuals from those above and beneath them in rank; Henry, rhetorically exploiting the physical deterioration wreaked upon his army by time, hardship and the ravages of winter, describes in his speech a sort of uniform that would unite him and all his soldiers into a single class. This external unity is supported, according to him, by internal unity:

> Let me speak proudly. Tell the constable
> We are but warriors for the working-day;
> Our gayness and our gilt are all besmirched
> With rainy marching in the painful field.
> There's not a piece of feather in our host
> (Good argument, I hope, we will not fly),
> And time hath worn us into slovenry.
> But by the mass, our hearts are in the trim ... (IV, iii, 108–115)

An additional means Shakespeare uses to imply Henry's temporary policy of blurring hierarchies, is the contrasting characterisations of the English and French camps. In opposition to the suppression of social disparities on the English side, the separatism of the French is strikingly emphasised when they request Henry's permission to allow their men to re-enter the battlefield to separate the bodies of nobles from those of commons (IV, vii, 73); in the eyes of the French, this separation will put an end to the woeful situation in which 'many of our princes ... / Lie drowned and soaked in mercenary blood, / So do our vulgar drench their peasant limbs / In blood of princess' (ibid., ll. 74–77).

The Chorus, describing Henry 'Walking from watch to watch, from tent to tent', devotes six lines to the king's outward appearance, which radiates cheerfulness and freshness:

> Upon his royal face there is no note
> How dread an army hath enrounded him,
> Nor doth he dedicate one jot of colour
> Unto the weary and all-watched night,
> But freshly looks and overbears attaint
> With cheerful semblance and sweet majesty ... (IV, Chorus, 35–40)

Literally, these lines and those that follow indicate that Henry wishes to thaw the 'cold fear' gripping his soldiers: this he attempts to do by publicly displaying his confidence and using what is termed in modern research 'emotional contagion',[68] that is, by directly inducing in his soldiers the emotions he is displaying. The secondary meaning of the lines also testifies to Henry's efforts to suppress fear, but in the Machiavellian sense, subtly suggested by the playwright's choice of words: the play's various editions provide a number of possible interpretations of the expression 'overbears attaint' (l. 39); in addition to the accepted literal meanings ('subdues weariness', 'puts down the pressures on his mind'), Andrew Gurr suggests the associated meaning 'ignores criminal charges'; if we translate his suggestion into the terminology of this chapter, Henry desists from his Machiavellian policy of intimidation, in keeping with which he severely punishes his

---

68   See Chapter Three, p. 125.

soldiers for certain offences (as in the case of Bardolph's hanging). The considerable likelihood that the words 'colour' and 'choler' were pronounced in Shakespeare's time similarly or identically,[69] reinforces Gurr's reading and applies the double meaning he suggests for the entire sequence of lines 37–40.

In light of this interpretation it is possible to move back through the play's events and re-examine Henry's declaration regarding Bardolph's execution. Such a re-examination reveals a linguistic nuance that indicates the degree of the king's rationality, foresight and Machiavellian calculation. In reference to future crimes his soldiers might commit, Henry promises every similar offender a fate identical to Bardolph's:

> We *would* have all such offenders so cut off ... (III, vi, 106–112; my italics)

In contrast to his practice elsewhere in the play, by which he seeks to be perceived by his subjects as resolute and decisive, Henry does not in this instance make use of the word 'shall'. This auxiliary verb is frequently employed by the king for asserting his determination or certainty of future events.[70] His unusual choice of the word 'would' may therefore hint at the possibility that Henry, even at this early stage, is already aware that there may be times when he will have to set aside his policy of intimidating punishment.

The moment Henry has accomplished his critical mission and has won the battle of Agincourt, the circumstances that influence his rhetorical-emotional policy change: since his soldiers will not be expected to function as warriors in the foreseeable future, there is no longer any need to take action to banish their fear. Furthermore, in the absence of any external military threat, the only potential for development of problems and dangers lies within the English army itself.

---

69   See Chapter Two, p. 84.
70   Henry clearly demonstrates his awareness of the significant difference between 'will' and 'shall' in his meeting with Katharine (V, ii, 243–246). Throughout the play it is clear that the English king knows how to choose the word that will best convey a sense of confidence, determination and decisiveness, usually as part of his rhetoric of intimidation. See, for example: I, ii, 264, 284–289; III, iii, 10–12; III, iv, 160; IV, iii, 36–67, 97–125.

Thus as soon as Henry has ascertained beyond all reasonable doubt that the French have been defeated, he immediately reinstates his intimidating aura by threatening capital punishment:

> Come, go we in procession to the village,
> And be it death proclaimed through our host
> To boast of this, or take the praise from God
> Which is his only. (IV, viii, 114–117)

As in the case of Bardolph's execution, here too the 'prince' makes a calculated use of religion to serve his Machiavellian rhetoric. In the lines above, Henry guarantees that his men will be aware that his 'cruelty' is not arbitrary, and that he does not intend to take the life of any man without a *clear and justified* cause.

I agree with Goddard's claim regarding the impression created by Henry's reading of the list of the English dead at the end of the battle. There is a clear sense of the significant difference between the king's separatist approach on this occasion and the substantially different social messages he has communicated, as demonstrated above, earlier that very same day:[71]

> Edward the Duke of York; the Earl of Suffolk;
> Sir Richard Ketly; Davy Gam, esquire;
> None else of name, and of all other men
> But five and twenty. (IV, viii, 104–107)

Shakespeare's audience, of course, did not live in our 'politically correct' world, and I do not wish to examine Henry's behaviour in terms of the conventions of our day: the Elizabethan audience would have found nothing amiss in the reading of the names of the fallen in descending social-hierarchical order. But the words in which the king refers to the slain commoners seem discordant, particularly when compared with those he let fly in the hyperbolic declarations of brotherhood of the St Crispin speech. The expression 'of name' (l. 106), in this context, means 'of a notable family'; the unpleasant ring of the words 'none else of name' to the modern ear, is apparently what caused Olivier to remove them from his film version of the play;

---

71   Harold C. Goddard, *The Meaning of Shakespeare*, vol. I, p. 255.

but it seems to me that these words carried a disharmonious effect even in the original performances of the play, or at least in the mind of the playwright: in one of the stage directions found in the Night Scene – one exceptionally detailed in comparison with his stage directions in general – Shakespeare reveals his awareness that simple soldiers also have names:

> *Enter three Soldiers*, JOHN BATES, ALEXANDER COURT *and* MICHAEL WILLIAMS. (IV, i, 85 SD)

1.3.3 Ending the Intimidation of the French

Simultaneously with the elimination of his subjects' fear, Henry employs additional means to improve his chances of victory at Agincourt; these include modifying the rhetorical-emotional manipulations he aims at the French. In the first half of the play – as was customary in the martial traditions of both the fictional and the real worlds – he attempts to arouse fear in his enemies by means of intimidating speeches;[72] in the second half of the play, however, Henry acts to eliminate this emotion, not only from his own camp – as discussed above – but from the enemy's as well. The English king no longer aims threatening speeches at the French; instead, when replying to their messages through Montjoy the herald, he acknowledges their supposed superior strength, emphasising the poor condition of his own army, the decreasing numbers of his soldiers, and the disease that has exhausted the survivors (III, vi, 141–146). Even as Henry is describing to the French herald the fame that awaits his soldiers at the end of the battle, he chooses to focus on that of the fallen, whose bodies, left lying on French soil, will cause plagues, which will decimate her people (IV, iii, 98–107).

Henry faces Montjoy, not in an intimate space, but in the presence of his peers, captains and soldiers. Consequently he must balance his words meticulously and choose the rhetorical tactic that will work best on all of his diverse addressees. In his words to the French herald

---

72   I, ii, 260–298; II, iv, 76–112; III, iii, 1–43.

he thus takes care not to completely denigrate his army and its chances of success. He creates instead a rhetorical medley in which he expresses, on the one hand, awareness of the apparent inferiority of his men in quantity and strength, and on the other hand, his belief in their determination to fight without compromise:

> Go therefore, tell thy master here I am.
> My ransom is this frail and worthless trunk,
> My army but a weak and sickly guard.
> Yet, God before, tell him we will come on,
> Though France himself and such another neighbour
> Stand in our way. (III, vi, 152–157)

> The sum of all our answer is but this:
> We would not seek a battle, as we are,
> Nor as we are, we say, we will not shun it:
> So tell your master. (Ibid., 162–165)

> Good God, why should they mock poor fellows thus?
> The man that once did sell the lion's skin
> While the beast lived, was killed with hunting him. (IV, iii, 92–94)

>   Tell the constable
> We are but warriors for the working-day;
> Our gayness and our gilt are all besmirched
> With rainy marching in the painful field;
> There's not a piece of feather in our host
> (Good argument, I hope, we will not fly),
> And time hath worn us into slovenry.
> But by the mass, our hearts are in the trim,
> And *my poor soldiers* tell me yet ere night
> They'll be in fresher robes, or they will pluck
> The gay new coats o'er the French soldiers' heads
> And turn them out of service. (Ibid., 108–119; my italics)

As shown, the French do not in fact feel the slightest fear in the face of the critical military encounter, and as it draws closer, their pride, lust for victory, and even joy in their yet-to-be-achieved triumph grows stronger.

Despite the considerable rhetorical effort that Henry and Shakespeare invest in the speeches quoted above, my general claim regarding the questionable effect of emotional appeals on the plot applies to them as well.[73] As demonstrated in Chapter Five, the main cause of the French complacence is their perception of the great disparity between their army and that of the English in terms of numbers and freshness of troops. We have no way of determining the effect of other factors on the emotions of the French, including these emotional appeals by Henry: the play supplies no information whatsoever regarding the way these fear-reducing messages were received in the French camp, nor does it give any indication as to what degree, if any, they affect the growing complacency there. Each and every spectator is invited to complete the picture himself, and to attach whatever weight he deems appropriate to Henry's fear-reducing rhetoric and to his emotional rhetoric in the play in general. On the one hand, the king's success in conquering France can be attributed to his strength as an orator who brilliantly controls the balance between the fear and anger both of his soldiers and of his foes. The temptation is great to see Henry as the hero who conquers France through the power of the word alone, particularly in light of the fact that during the war he is revealed to the audience only when acting verbally: the king does not fight on stage, and the play is completely lacking in battle scenes like those found in *Henry VI*, *Richard III*, *Macbeth*, and *Coriolanus*. On the other hand, the play allows spectators to assess the abundance of words Henry utters in the fields of France as if they were mere 'airy nothings', scattered alongside the mighty forces activated by God or Fortune,[74] who have chosen for a brief period to subordinate France to English mastery. Between these two reductive possibilities there exists a range of countless others, and each spectator or reader is free to realise them in his mind's eye.

73   See Appendix B, pp. 295–308.
74   The allusions that might lead spectators to see God as being solely responsible for events are discussed at length in Appendix B. Fortune is also mentioned during the play (eight times), and the epilogue credits her with the conquest of France while at the same time adopting ambiguous wording, leaving the audience to subjectively interpret Henry's part in the victory: '*Fortune* made his sword / By which the world's best garden *he* achieved ...' (ll. 6–7; my italics).

Chapter Two
Julius Caesar

'I did not think you could have been so angry.'
(Cassius to Brutus, *Julius Caesar*, IV, iii, 143)

Julius Caesar is the first of Shakespeare's plays to employ emotional appeal as a primary plot mechanism. The playwright dramatised a famous literary-historical episode, in which a stirring speech changes the course of history, and shaped his play to make emotional rhetoric a dominant factor at the levels of theme and plot, both implicitly and explicitly. The dominant emotion in the play, generated by its emotional appeals and motivating its plot, is *anger*. This passion was considered in early modern Europe to be the most powerful and dangerous of the emotions, distinguished not only by its sheer force, but also by its operation at a level beyond interpersonal relationships:

> Of all the passions of the soul, there is not any one that takes such deep root, or extends her branches farther than *Choler* ... Yea, she enflames whole kingdoms and empires; whereas the other passions doe only trouble and agitate private persons.[1]

Employing sophisticated arrays of words and images, the play allows us to trace the progress of this passion: it hints at how anger, initially burning hidden within a single character, later intensifies and spreads inexorably until its flame consumes the whole of Italy.

To date, scholarly references to the rhetoric of emotional appeal in this play have focused on its two central speeches – those delivered by Brutus and Antony after Caesar's murder. Scholars have linked the

---

1   F. N. Coeffeteau, *A Table of Humane Passions with their Causes and Effects*, (1621), pp. 547–548.

characterisation of the heroes to their qualities as orators: Brutus, in keeping with his ostensibly 'stoical' conduct, focuses on the logical aspects of the speech, whereas the hedonistic Antony, who knows the nature of emotional thrills and stimulations, is appropriately capable of exciting the populace through his speech. Thus, some scholars tend to 'criticise' Brutus' rhetorical abilities, as they compare his ostensibly logical, symmetry-based prose speech to Antony's passionate, eloquent and moving words, which motivate the Roman citizens to a wave of violence. This criticism ignores the clear-cut reality that every spectator or reader can note: Brutus's speech is actually an overwhelming success; when it begins, the outraged citizens demand explanations for the murder, but by the end they support Brutus enthusiastically.

This chapter presents a systematic analysis of emotional appeals throughout the play, examining the nature and operation of its mechanisms of emotional arousal, as well as the emotional profiles of the chief characters. In light of the reading I propose, it would clearly be simplistic to view Brutus as 'cold-blooded', incapable of arousing excitement or agitation in others. Such a simplistic view of his characterisation ignores the complex reality woven beneath the surface: in contrast to the general opinion that dominates *Julius Caesar*'s fictional Rome, as well as modern Shakespearean criticism, Brutus' body and mind are ruled by the intense passions generally referred to as 'anger', characterised in Shakespeare's time as 'boiling', 'burning', or 'blood-inflaming'; these same passions are the actual force that motivates him to murder Caesar. They distort his rational thinking and allow him to justify the deed by means of ostensibly logical reasoning. Brutus is totally unaware of these facts, and – ironically – throughout the play unwittingly produces emotional appeals, which spread the 'fire' burning within him into his surroundings, and finally into the entire domain of the body politic. Far from portraying Brutus as 'a man of Reason' or as a melancholic hero tormented by moral doubts and scruples, Shakespeare presents him as one who is unaware of his own emotions, who misunderstands human emotional mechanisms in general, and is not aware of their decisive power in human life.

2.1 The Anger Hidden Within Brutus' Heart

2.1.1 Brutus' Emotional Image

Critics of *Julius Caesar* have yet to examine, to the best of my knowledge, the relationship between the tragedy's protagonist and the emotion of anger. On the face of it, the passions classified as 'irascible' – those that inflame the blood and involve aggressive behaviour – are incompatible with the main traits of Brutus' character. This general impression seems to stem from two main factors: the direct linkage drawn in the play between Brutus and Stoic philosophy; and some textual references that tempt spectators and readers to ascribe to him melancholic emotions.

Brutus is characterised as perceiving himself – and being perceived by others – as one whose life is guided by Stoic philosophy. On various occasions he gives voice to conceptions that are typically Stoic,[2] and from his very first words is portrayed as one who appears to seek fulfilment of this pragmatic philosophy: the avoidance of immoderate emotional agitation.[3] He strives constantly to externalise calmness, moderation, discretion, self-control and restraint,[4] and at the same time tries to placate the immoderate emotions that possess other characters, by instructing them to exhibit calmness and emotional self-control.[5] Brutus' self-image and public reputation as the very embodiment of emotional balance is commemorated at the end of the play in the eulogy which Mark Antony utters over his corpse. Antony, attempting to illustrate the hero's exceptional emotional stability, uses

---

2   See, e.g.: IV, iii, 190–192; V, i, 103–107, 124–125.

3   'A soothsayer bids you beware the ides of March' (I, ii. 19). Granville-Barker points out the 'measured' and 'dispassionate' quality of this line, and its significance for the exposition of Brutus' character. Harley Granville-Barker, *Preface to Julius Caesar* (London: Heinemann, 1995), p. 33.

4   His efforts to display these qualities can be seen in the literal and structural levels of his reaction to Cassius' emotional manipulations: '... What you have said / I will *consider*; what you have to say / I will with *patience* hear and find a time / Both meet to hear and answer such high things' (I, ii, 167–170; my italics).

5   III, i, 22; III, i, 82–83, 180; III, ii, 12; IV, ii, 42–45.

the conventional language of Shakespeare's time for describing the passions: there are Four Elements that compose the human body, and any imbalance in the proportions among them leads to an imbalance in the Four Humours – but in Brutus, according to Antony, these elements existed in the proper proportions.[6]

Brutus' presumed stoic calmness, which had been his normal everyday state of mind, leaves him some short time before the beginning of the plot. Ostensibly, he is suffering from some internal emotional storm, of the kind involving misery and self-destruction, rather than aggressive behaviour. For example, he describes himself as 'poor Brutus with himself in war' (I, ii, 46), and is seen late at night in his orchard, suffering from insomnia and internal conflict (II, i, 4, 61–62). As he perceives it, ever since Cassius began to 'whet' him against Caesar, his days and nights have become one continuous hideous dream (ibid., 65). Some critics, naturally assuming that emotion is the force that skews Brutus' power of reason – and produces his false interpretation of reality, whereby he sees Caesar's murder as a just and necessary act – have diagnosed him as melancholic.[7] It seems that these scholars have fallen into some of the traps scattered by Shakespeare throughout the play. *Julius Caesar* certainly tempts the spectator and reader to classify Brutus as a melancholic, or one who is suffering temporarily from a melancholic seizure – especially if we consider his statements regarding his 'sadness' ('my sad brows ...

---

6   'His life was gentle, and the elements / So mixed in him that Nature might stand up / And say to all the world, "This was a man!"' (V, v, 73–75). Compare: 'In the composition of the bodie politique (as of the naturall) there is required a concurrence or euen mixture of the foure Elements ... in our bodies by the unequall temper of the elements the humors get masterie each ouer other (of which humors the diuersities of complexions do arise) ...'. Edward Forset, *A comparative discourse of the bodies natural and politique* (1606), (Farnborough, Hants: Gregg International Pub., 1969), p. 38. See also: Thomas Elyot, *The Castel of Helthe* (1539), pp. 2–3.

7   'Brutus is melancholic ... Brutus' black depression darkens his reason ...'. Thomas McAlindon, *Shakespeare's Tragic Cosmos* (Cambridge: Cambridge University Press, 1996), p. 79. See also: D. J. Palmer, 'Tragic Error in *Julius Caesar*', *Shakespeare Quarterly* 21 (4), (1970), p. 403; Ernest Schanzer, 'The Tragedy of Brutus', *Shakespeare Julius Caesar: A Casebook*, ed. Peter Ure (London: Macmillan, 1969), p. 186.

my sad heart' [II, i, 290, 308]). Another misleading clue, tempting scholars to classify Brutus as a melancholic, is planted shortly after Cassius' suicide. The latter was deceived by Pindarus' false report of Titinius' 'captivity', and gave way to despair. When Messala discovers his lifeless body, he utters a line that seems at first to be one of those key Shakespearean phrases that provide tiny yet crucial clues for the understanding of the entire play:

> Mistrust of good success hath done this deed.
> O hateful error, *melancholy's child*,
> Why dost thou show to the apt thoughts of men
> The things that are not? (V, iii, 66–69; my italics)

As some scholars have justly observed, the play is certainly concerned with some of its characters' fatal mistakes and wrong evaluations, brought about by the effect of emotion upon their rational thinking,[8] and Messala's words are indeed relevant to this broad theme. Yet we must not be tempted to regard them as a specific clue referring to Brutus and his emotional characteristics throughout the entire play. As demonstrated here and in the following chapters, Shakespeare's drama abounds in such 'invitations', scattered in each and every play, encouraging the spectator to adopt hasty interpretations, whilst at the same time providing him with subtle hints that guide him to doubt and re-evaluate his overhasty conclusions. As I shall show below, this is exactly the case with Brutus' emotions: a cursory acquaintance with *Julius Caesar* encourages the spectator or reader to classify them as 'melancholic'; yet a pattern of sophisticated clues reveals a totally different emotional reality.

Other scholars who have attempted to explain Brutus' hidden motives and distorted justification for the murder (without resorting to vague emotional terms[9]), have assumed that Brutus is envious of Caesar, and that his envy stems from a hidden ambition. Such an assump-

---

8   See, e.g.: D. J. Palmer, 'Tragic Error in *Julius Caesar*', pp. 399–409.
9   Such as the terms used by the influential Knights, when referring to Brutus' emotional state: 'obscure personal emotion', 'personal feelings'. See: L. C. Knights, 'Personality and Politics in *Julius Caesar*', *Shakespeare Julius Caesar: A Casebook*, ed. Peter Ure (London: Macmillan, 1969), pp. 129, 131.

tion cannot be substantiated, as the play does not offer any data to sustain it. It is far from coincidental, therefore, that these scholars do not offer any citation to support this interpretation. They seem to be influenced by a general impression of Brutus' alleged 'pride', which causes him to compare his worthiness and status to those of Caesar, a comparison that gives rise to the typical emotion predominant in such situations.[10] Another piece of evidence that leads scholars to ascribe envy to Brutus is the intense manifestation of this passion by Cassius: the latter, according to this interpretation, 'contaminates' Brutus with his own emotions, or functions in the play as a personification of the evil elements in Brutus' soul, one of which is Envy.[11] It is far from my intent to argue that this intuitive interpretation is completely groundless, and that Brutus' character cannot be portrayed onstage as having a touch of envy: the arousal of this passion is indeed plausible in situations such as the one he is placed in at the beginning of the play. In fact, there is no fundamental contradiction between this interpretation and the reading suggested below, since envy and anger are by no means strangers to one another, but rather relatives of the first degree: long-term envy that fails to find relief is often expressed in a fit of rage.[12] However, considering the ramified pattern of literal hints and

10 Thus, for example, states Barton: 'Cassius plays upon this feeling. His persuasion is as deadly as it is because it recognises and takes advantage of a deeply buried jealousy of Caesar, lurking behind all of Brutus' republican principles'. Anne Barton, 'Julius Caesar and Coriolanus: Shakespeare's Roman World of Words', Shakespeare's Craft: Eight Lectures, ed. Philip H. Highfill Jr (Carbondale: Southern Illinois University Press, 1982), pp. 45–47.

11 The interpretation offered by Harold Goddard pictures Brutus as the hero of a 'tragic' Moral Play, given to the influence of several opposing mental forces; these forces are externalised through the 'evil angels' Cassius and Caesar, and the 'good' – Portia (Brutus' wisdom) and the boy Lucius (his innocence). See: Harold C. Goddard, The Meaning of Shakespeare, vol. 1, pp. 307–330. Virgil Whitaker is the first to point to the relation between Julius Caesar and the genre of Morality plays, particularly in the design of the hero's internal conflict (such as the psychomachia of Mankind or The Castle of Perseverance). See: Virgil K. Whitaker, 'Brutus and the Tragedy of Moral Choice', Shakespeare Julius Caesar: A Casebook, ed. Peter Ure (London: Macmillan, 1969), pp. 172–182.

12 This emotional dynamics is clearly expressed throughout the sedition speech addressed by Cassius to Brutus at the beginning of the play. Cassius' bitterness at

stage effects surveyed below, it seems far more relevant to pinpoint anger as the emotion that dominates Brutus. This specific emotional observation also contributes to our general understanding of the play: anger assumes a major role in *Julius Caesar*, both at the thematic level and in motivating the plot; the hints and effects that indicate Brutus' anger also link him to the anger aroused in other characters and to the emotional transformation undergone by the entire body politic.

2.1.2 Textual Clues Indicating Brutus' Anger

One of the ways in which Shakespeare hints at the hidden anger within Brutus, is the subtle indication of the affinity between him and the storm that rages on the night preceding the murder of Caesar. This storm is portrayed as an entity that powerfully externalises its anger. The analogical linking of the storm with Brutus is a cunning device, enabling the playwright to present his audience with an introverted protagonist who does not tend to externalise raging emotions, but contains them within his own heart, hidden from view. The storm is 'personified' and portrayed in the same language often used to describe the human passions,[13] and various descriptions characterise it above all as an angry being: Casca uses the word 'rage' when expressing to Cicero the profound impressions it has stamped on his mind (I, iii, 7),[14] and considers the possibility that it is none other than the gods' revenge upon 'the world', whose sauciness '*incenses* them to send destruction' (I, iii, 13; my italics). Calpurnia describes to Caesar the extraordinary sights reported by Romans, among them 'Fierce fiery warriors' (II, ii, 19), fighting upon the clouds.

---

the unbearable reality, in which he must publicly express subordination and submissiveness to a man he believes to be his inferior, occasionally bursts out as fits of rage (I, ii, 128–131, 135–138, 150–151).

13   Thus, for example, Cicero describes the sky as 'disturbed' (I, iii, 39), and Cassius refers to the heavens' 'impatience' (ibid., 61).

14   Casca employs this word in describing some *other* storms he has experienced, yet he refers to them solely for the purpose of illustrating the fact that he has yet to witness such a mighty storm as the one raging in the present.

The placing of the words 'fierce' and 'fiery' in such close proximity is significant to our discussion, since it directly links the storm's fire to the emotion of anger; words denoting fire, inflammation, burning and boiling, are frequently employed in references from Shakespeare's day to choler, its arousal and its physical effects on men:

> Yea, she [Choler] inflames ... whereas the other passions do only trouble and agitate ... *Choler* is accompanied with heat ... for this passion enflames the blood ... the heat of choler is boiling ... it is kindled suddenly ... so it is quenched with little pain ... his eyes are full of fire and flame which this passion doth kindle ... his face is wonderfully inflamed as by a certain reflux of blood which ascends from the heart.[15]

Calpurnia's depiction of the 'Fierce fiery warriors' is but a single item in a pattern of descriptions based on words such as 'flame', 'torches', 'burn', 'fiery' and 'fire', with which Shakespeare verbally paints the storm and its effects in fiery colours. Such evocative activation of the mind's eye of his spectators, supported by stage effects that act strongly upon their senses[16] – in addition to the characters' explicit references to the storm's dominating emotion – result in the characterisation of the storm as an extreme frenzy of choler/rage/anger.[17]

The traditional view of Man as a microcosm of the world, prevalent since antiquity, features extensively in Renaissance essays and drama. Shakespeare analogises between Man and the State, the world or the cosmos in some of his plays; the most outstanding instance is of course the storm that blows within Lear's mind, and its

15 See: F. N. Coeffeteau, *A Table of Humane Passions with their Causes and Effects* (1621), pp. 547–602. For further illustration: '... for they but *kindle* and *inflame* his choler more and more ... this *stirred coales* among the people ... turmoyled with sundry thoughts and kynde of thoughts, suche as *the fyre of his choller* dyd sturre up ...'. Thomas North, 'The Life of Caius Martius Coriolanus', from Plutarch's *Lives of The Noble Greacians and Romans* (1579), *Shakespeare's Coriolanus*, ed. Philip Brockbank (London and New York: Methuen, 1980), pp. 333–343. See also: Pierre de La Primaudaye, *The French Academie*, pp. 497–498.

16 The play's original stage directions indicate some effects resembling 'Thunder and lightning' in the beginning of scenes I, iii and II, ii, as well as a 'Thunder' towards the end of II, i, and the continuation of the thundering ('Thunder still') around I, iii, 100.

17 See: I, iii, 10, 16, 17, 18, 25, 63, 130.

relation to the actual storm raging over Albion. Spectators of *Julius Caesar* are also invited to find such analogies between aspects of certain characters and Italy, the powers of Nature, celestial bodies, and the storm with all its accompanying effects.[18] Thus, with regard to the affinity between Caesar and the storm's 'eruptions', this invitation is delivered both implicitly – through the use of similar words in their descriptions[19] – and explicitly:

> CASSIUS: Now could I, Casca, name to thee a man
> Most like this dreadful night,
> That thunders, lightens, opens graves, and roars
> As doth the lion in the Capitol –
> A man no mightier than thyself, or me,
> In personal action, yet prodigious grown
> And fearful, as these strange eruptions are.
> CASCA: 'Tis Caesar that you mean, is it not, Cassius? (I, iii, 72–79)

The descriptions of the storm, however, do not refer solely to Caesar – the character linked with it most extensively is in fact Brutus: the protagonist, the storm and its effects are all referred to by the words 'strange',[20] 'impatience',[21] 'fire',[22] 'firm/unfirm'[23] and 'stare'.[24] Cassius' description of the 'man most like this dreadful night', quoted above, constitutes a far more faithful reflection of Brutus – the hidden Brutus – than of Caesar, who is seen on-stage as an unthreatening character, abounding in human weaknesses overstated to the verge of

---

18   I, iii, 72–78; I, iii, 128–130; II, i, 63–69.
19   Caesar and the effects accompanying the storm are both referred to by certain characters using the words 'foam' (I, ii, 246; I, iii, 7) and 'ambitious' (I, iii, 7; III, ii, 22, 70).
20   I, ii, 35; I, iii, 33, 61, 78, 138.
21   I, iii, 61; II, i, 248. This word was synonymous in the relevant period with 'anger/rage/choler' (*OED*, 'impatience', n., 1), and frequently appears in this sense in Shakespeare's drama. Ironically, Brutus reveals throughout the play his strong affection for the word 'patience', by which he expresses his striving for emotional self-control, and his expectations that the characters surrounding him will moderate their emotions (I, ii, 169; III, i, 179; III, ii, 13; IV, iii, 192; V, i, 105).
22   I, ii, 177; II, i, 110.
23   I, ii, 301; I, iii, 4.
24   I, iii, 2; II, i, 242.

a caricature. Indeed, through Cassius' enigmatic reply, Shakespeare instructs his audience to view Casca's naive assumption with some scepticism:

Let it be who it is ... (Ibid., 80)

As interpreters of *Julius Caesar* have shown, Shakespeare guides his spectators to observe the difference between the private and public behaviours of some of his characters. According to these interpreters, the characters 'put on' a certain 'mask' when appearing in the public arena:[25] this mask is designed according to the prevailing ideals of Shakespeare's Roman society, and its purpose is to promote the masked characters' image in the eyes of the public (as well as in their own eyes). In their private lives, shielded from the scrutiny of the populace, the characters sometimes allow themselves to relinquish this heavy histrionic burden, remove the mask, and expose human qualities perceived by society as weaknesses.

As mentioned briefly at the beginning of this chapter, Brutus sees himself and is seen by the Romans as a 'Stoic', namely, a man whose life is not ruled by his passions, and who is not prone to immoderate emotional agitation. It is his behaviour and utterances in the public arena that have created this image. I have referred to some of them earlier, but in order to illustrate them in their most palpable fashion, let us examine a moment in which Brutus' conscious self-image as a passion-proof Stoic is evident. This instance is sometimes referred to as 'The double report of Portia's death'. Brutus, who has been aware of Portia's death for some time, reacts to Messala's report of her demise as if he were hearing it for the first time, uttering a Stoic moral sentiment which draws a worshipful response from Messala:

MESSALA: ... like a Roman bear the truth I tell,
For certain she is dead, and by strange manner.
BRUTUS: Why, farewell, Portia. We must die, Messala.
With meditating that she must die once,
I have the patience to endure it now.
MESSALA: Even so, great men great losses should endure. (IV, iii, 188–193)

25   L. C. Knights, 'Personality and Politics in *Julius Caesar*', pp. 121–139.

Harold Goddard rejects any suggestion that we interpret the 'double report' as the outcome of some text-copying/editing error – due to the negligence of either the playwright or his publisher – and quotes this instance as evidence supporting his interpretation, according to which Brutus is 'acting a part' in public.[26] Likewise, Alexander Leggatt – focusing on Brutus' inflated self-image and his constant efforts to nourish his public image – refers to these lines as a 'public display of stoic calm'. Leggatt does not seem obliged to prove that the 'double report' is not the outcome of a possible editing or copying error: as he justly argues, Brutus is already taking advantage of Portia's death in order to manifest his virtues after the first report of her death (IV, iii, 146); if indeed the text of this scene is not corrupted, Shakespeare is further inflating Brutus' demonstration of self-control after the second report, taking it to a level of caricature.[27]

In contrast to his public proceedings and utterances, Brutus' behaviour in the private arena is completely different; hidden from the public gaze, he shows no tendency to curb his passions and their external manifestations. In the Orchard Scene (II, i), Portia describes her husband's behaviour during the past evening as a succession of signs of anger. The staring, the foot stamping and the angry hand gesture she refers to, are by no means characteristic of a melancholic man, and the words with which she describes Brutus' behaviour belong to the semantic field of anger: 'impatiently', 'angry', 'impatient', 'enkindled', 'grief'[28] (ll. 237–256). Portia further sharpens her emotional diagnosis by excluding the possibility that Brutus suffers from what was known in Elizabethan times as a slight and temporary imbalance of the Four Humours ('an effect of humour', l. 250). Anyone may suffer from time to time from such an anomaly, due to the interaction among diverse, ever-changing factors such as nutrition, air quality,

26   Harold C. Goddard, *The Meaning of Shakespeare*, vol. 1, p. 326.
27   Alexander Leggatt, *Shakespeare's Political Drama: the History Plays and the Roman Plays* (London and New York: Routledge, 1988), p. 148.
28   The meaning of the word 'grief' in Shakespeare's time was not restricted, as in our days, to 'sorrow' or 'sadness'; this noun is often used in Elizabethan and Jacobean texts to denote 'anger' (*OED*, n., 4a). In *Julius Caesar* it appears with a range of senses: sorrow (IV, iii, 153); sorrow or anger (I, iii, 111); anger (IV, iii, 115); a cause of anger and revenge-seeking (I, iii, 118; III, ii, 203).

physical exercise, and rest.[29] Portia claims that at first she had hoped her husbands' behaviour was the result of such 'effect of humour', but in the light of the symptoms she has listed – as well as their strength and duration – she negates this possibility and assumes that within Brutus' mind broods 'some sick offence' (l. 268). The word 'offence' is often used in Elizabethan and Jacobean sources to denote one of the most common causes of the arousal of anger.[30]

Having surveyed some of the allusions to Brutus' hidden anger, it is now possible to examine the protagonist's first reference in the play to his irregular emotional state:

> *Vexed* I am
> Of late with passions of some *difference* ... (I, ii, 39–40; my italics)

The literal meaning of the above, as the various editors of *Julius Caesar* have noted, is that Brutus is troubled lately by some internal mental conflict; but the specific words that Shakespeare has chosen to put in his hero's mouth are equivocal, and belong to the semantic field of anger. Thus, Brutus' utterance may indicate that he finds himself of late *in a state of anger* ('vexed'), dominated by emotions typical to *disputes* and *quarrels* ('difference').[31]

Shakespeare provides two additional, significant clues that hint at the storm of anger hidden under Brutus' tormented exterior; these will be revealed in detail in the next section.

---

29   Thomas Wright, *The Passions of the Minde in Generall* (1604), p. 65.
30   Thus, for example, it appears in the pithy definition to the headword 'Ira' (anger, rage, wrath), in Thomas Elyot's Latin–English dictionary (1538): 'Ira, wrathe, an appetite to punish him of whom we be offended' (Thomas Elyot, 'Ira', *Dictionary*, 1538 [Menston: Scolar Press, 1970]). Compare: 'Offended or wounded feeling ... displeasure, annoyance, or resentment caused ... to a person' (*OED*, 'offence', n., 5a). As a verb, this word denotes the act of stirring anger or hostility ('offence' is an obsolete form of the verb 'offend'): 'To hurt or wound the feelings ... to vex, annoy, displease, anger ... To excite a feeling of personal annoyance, resentment ...' (*OED*, 'offence/offend', v., 7).
31   '... a dispute or quarrel caused by ... disagreement: used in various shades of intensity from simple estrangement or dispute to open hostility ... [*obs.*]' (*OED*, 'difference', n., 3a).

2.2 Anger and the Hero's Self-Persuasion

2.2.1 Reason and Passion in the Orchard Soliloquy

The widely accepted view of our age – that the so-called 'negative' emotions are more dangerous when suppressed – should not be regarded as one of the novelties of modern psychology: its manifestations can be found in ancient and renaissance European writings. Thus, for example, Montaigne describes the danger involved in the concealment of anger:

> By hiding our choler we drive it into our bodies ... I would advise you to give your valet a rather unseasonable slap on the cheek rather than to torture your mind so as to put on an appearance of wisdom; I would rather make an exhibition of my passions than brood over them to my cost: express them, vent them, and they grow weaker; it is better to let them jab outside than be turned against us ...[32]

Regarding this matter, he cites a pithy saying of somewhat more general relevance, ascribed to Seneca:

> All defects are lighter in the open ... they are most pernicious when concealed beneath a pretence of soundness.[33]

Hidden anger, therefore, is particularly dangerous because it grows and intensifies.[34] In the specific case under discussion the danger is even greater, since Brutus is striving to be a man of reason; he makes decisions and acts on the basis of what he erroneously considers to be a dictate of reason, unaware that his thinking is governed by a force considered in Shakespeare's time to be Reason's arch enemy:

---

32 Montaigne, 'On Anger', *The Complete Essays*, pp. 814–815.
33 Ibid. (Seneca, *Epist. Moral*. LVI, 10).
34 Compare: '... when offence is as it were shut up, that it cannot range at will, then it turneth into rage, and offereth violence to it selfe, extending it selfe euen vnto those that have not offended it at all. For it is stirred vp, and waxeth sharpe in it selfe, and by this meane it increaseth more and more continually'. Pierre de La Primaudaye, *The French Academie*, p. 495.

> For that the other passions ... even at the very instant when they are as it were in
> the height of their transport, give way some-what to reason, and yeeld in some
> sort unto her commandments, when as she presents herself to pacifie them.
> Whereas *Choler* doth like unto mariners which are amazed or corrupted, and
> will give no ear to the voice of their pilot ... who doth not then see that this *Passion*, (more then any other) quencheth the light of reason?[35]

Brutus is convinced that his decision to assassinate Caesar is the outcome of a purely rational thinking process, and is totally unaware of the double influence of his hidden anger over his mind: this emotion is the very force that motivates him to perform such a radical action, distorts his rational thinking and causes him to justify the murder by faulty logical argumentation. Shakespeare supplies two critical clues that reveal this dynamics: these clues are planted in the Orchard Soliloquy, that is, during the key moments when Brutus seeks justification for the murder, 'finds' it, and expresses his final determination to act. The characteristic features and specific placement of these clues suggest a direct linkage between Brutus' anger, his process of self-persuasion, and the distorted logic by which he justifies the murder. But before disclosing these clues, we must first demonstrate the severe degree of distortion present in the protagonist's rational thinking, as manifested in the Orchard Soliloquy (II, i, 10–34).

This soliloquy is an excellent example of circular argumentation, beginning with the conclusion it is forced to reach at its end ('It must be by his death', l. 10); the space between the argument's beginning and its final conclusion can be defined as an extreme effort to eliminate the immense gap separating the *possible* from the *certain*. While at the beginning of this speech Brutus refers to Caesar as one who might pose some danger, by its end he becomes an unquestionable danger, and must be eliminated. Brutus' own words reveal how great is the gap between the 'possible' and the 'certain' in this case, and how distorted the logic that would bridge it. At the time he is pondering the murder there is no certainty that Caesar will be crowned

---

35 F. N. Coeffeteau, *A Table of Humane Passions with their Causes and Effects*
(1621), pp. 607–609. On anger as the disruptor of reason, see also: Thomas Elyot,
The Castel of Helthe (1539), p. 62.

and, of course, no certainty that – if crowned – he will become dangerous:

> He *would* be crowned:
> How that *might* change his nature, there's the question. (II, i, 12–13; my italics)

The lines following are also heavily weighted with words denoting uncertainty (in order of appearance: may, may, may, would, think, would); the frequency with which these words occur in the soliloquy keenly illustrates the failure of Brutus' logic. In Rome's circumstances at this juncture, it would be reasonable to wait and observe if indeed Caesar is crowned; even if this possibility becomes reality, it is only logical to wait and monitor any signs that might indicate an alarming transformation in his character or way of governing. A personage such as Brutus – familiar to Caesar – could certainly have closely followed any developments and reacted, if necessary, in the proper manner and at the appropriate time.

Let us now examine the quality and influence of the emotion in Brutus' flawed process of argumentation.[36] An instant after noting that to the best of his knowledge Caesar's passions never 'swayed more than his reason' (II, i, 19–21), he continues to vacillate between the possible and the certain:

> And since the quarrel
> Will bear no colour for the thing he is,
> Fashion it thus: that what he is, augmented,
> Would run to these and these extremities. (II, i, 28–31)

The *Arden* and *Cambridge* editors gloss lines 28–30 and explain that Brutus is employing legal terminology; from the point of view of our discussion, the meaning they suggest is similar: 'since the cause of

---

36 Once it is clear that Brutus' mind is not functioning rationally and that Caesar's murder is not dictated by reason, there remains no alternative but to conclude that the factor influencing Brutus is emotion: 'These passions have a free commanding might, / And divers actions in our life do breed; / For all acts done without true Reason's light / Do from the passion of the Sense proceed'. John Davies, *Nosce Teipsum (The Soul of Man)* (1599), *Silver poets of the sixteenth century* (London: J. M. Dent, 1947), p. 378.

complaint is not plausible, considering what he [Caesar] is now, modify it/make it appear thus ...'. However, both editors refer only to the literal meaning of these lines, whereas Brutus' words are crucially ambiguous. From the various spelling forms customary for the words 'colour' and 'choler', it appears that in Shakespeare's time they were pronounced similarly or even identically.[37] The word 'choler' was used to denote the 'orange-red humour',[38] secreted in the body during the arousal of anger, or to denote this emotion *per se*. Thus, its double meaning refers to the word 'quarrel' (l. 28) in its 'natural' and commonly accepted meaning (as opposed to the legal meaning), namely a 'dispute' or a 'conflict' (note again the double meaning embodied in Brutus' first reference in the play to his emotional state, 'vexed I am with passions of some *difference*'). The secondary meaning of Brutus' utterance is therefore 'since the cause of complaint will not arouse anger, considering what he [Caesar] is now, modify it thus ...', or 'since the dispute/conflict will not arouse anger, considering what he [Caesar] is now, modify it thus ...'. In other words, Caesar and his actions, as they are in reality, fail to constitute a cause substantial enough to arouse anger in Brutus; but Brutus needs this emotion: it will supply him with a motive and distort his logic to the point where he can 'discover' an appropriate justification for murder; he is thus guiding himself to modify reality, in order to stimulate the desired emotion.

37 Among the various spellings of the nouns 'choler' and 'colour' cited by the *Oxford English Dictionary*, four are completely identical: coloure, colour, color, collor (*OED*, 'choler', n.; 'colour', n.). Helge Kokeritz explicitly refers to the trio 'choler-collar-colour' as one of the main homonymic word-groups often employed in Shakespeare's puns. Kokeritz demonstrates the poet's use of this trio by quoting puns which rely upon the duos 'collar-colour' and 'collar-choler'; he does not, however, refer to or quote any instances in which Shakespeare exploits the duo discussed here, namely 'choler-colour'. See: Helge Kokeritz, *Shakespeare's Pronunciation* (New Haven: Yale University Press, 1953), pp. 98–99, 241.

38 'Natural coler is the fome of blood, the color whereof is redde and clere, or more lyke to an orange colour, and is hot and drye, wherein the fire hath dominion ...'. (Thomas Elyot, *The Castel of Helthe*, 1539), p. 9.

This secondary meaning is further reinforced by Shakespeare's use of the word 'fashion' (l. 30); the meanings of this verb in 16th and early 17th Century English sources – including Shakespeare's drama, and *Julius Caesar* in particular – are varied. Thus, in the lines discussed, it might mean 'beautify'[39] or even 'distort an argument'.[40] This verb accumulates further meanings and implications throughout *Julius Caesar*'s unique world, and these meanings shed further light on the dynamics hidden below the surface of the Orchard Soliloquy. Thus, on its next occurrence in the same scene, its signification moves between 'excite/stir emotion', 'influence, motivate or persuade through emotion', and even 'set the heart on fire':

> BRUTUS: Send him [*LIGARIUS*] but hither and I'll *fashion* him. (II, i, 220; my italics)
>
> ...
>
> LIGARIUS: Thou, like an exorcist, hast conjured up
>   My mortified spirit. Now bid me run
>
>   ...
>
>   And with a heart *new-fired* I follow you
>   To do I know not what ... (323–333; my italics)

The word 'fashion', both as a verb and a noun, belongs to *Julius Caesar*'s semantic field of emotions, and occurs in several contexts in which Shakespeare is dealing with emotional phenomena. It is used as a synonym for 'humour', in the sense of 'the fundamental emotional disposition of a specific man or woman',[41] as well as 'a character's present emotional state'.[42] Thus, the sophisticated pattern of meanings and reciprocal references of the words 'fashion' and 'humour' sheds

---

39   *OED*, 'fashion', n., 1c.
40   Compare, e.g.: 'And God forbid, my dear and faithful lord, / That you should *fashion*, wrest or bow your reading / Or nicely charge your understanding soul / With opening titles miscreate, whose right / Suits not in native colours with the truth' (*Henry V*, I, ii, 13–17; my italics).
41   'CASSIUS: Bear with him, Brutus, 'tis his *fashion*. / BRUTUS: I'll know his *humour* when he knows his time ...' (IV, iii, 135–136; my italics); 'CASSIUS: As they pass by, pluck Casca by the sleeve / And he will (after his sour *fashion*) tell you / What hath proceeded worthy note today' (I, ii, 179–181; my italics).
42   'CAESAR: Mark Antony shall say I am not well, / And for thy *humour* I will stay at home' (II, ii, 55–56; my italics).

some light on Cicero's utterances from the Storm Scene, which are – in their literal sense as well – a kind of early interpretive comment on the dynamics of Brutus' thinking during the Orchard Soliloquy and the play as a whole:

> ... men may construe things after their *fashion*
> Clean from the purpose of the things themselves. (I, iii, 32–35; my italics)

Another hint in the Orchard Scene referring to the intense anger that dominates Brutus' mind, is placed immediately after the soliloquy. Just as Brutus seals his argument and pronounces Caesar's final 'sentence', the boy Lucius enters and reports to his master the fulfilment of his task:

> BRUTUS: ...
> And kill him in the shell.
> *Enter LUCIUS*
> LUCIUS: The taper burneth in your closet, sir. (Ibid., 35)

By using the word 'closet', Lucius refers to Brutus' private chamber. This word was often employed in Shakespeare's time to denote a place where a man may seek seclusion and avoid the scrutiny and influence of other people. This denotation yields its figurative use, referring to the interior and hidden spaces of the body, such as the womb and the chest, as well as to such hidden faculties of the mind as consciousness, understanding, intention, and the heart (in the sense of 'emotion', since the heart was considered to be the seat of the passions).[43] Shakespeare himself uses this word elsewhere as an explicit metaphor for the heart:

> My heart doth plead that thou in him dost lie,
> A closet never pierced with crystal eyes ... (*Sonnet 46*, ll. 5–6)

The apparently innocent report that Shakespeare puts in Lucius' mouth is therefore a reference to the fire burning at this critical moment inside the protagonist's heart, the hidden anger raging within him. That Shakespeare's use of this double meaning is deliberate is

43   *OED*, 'closet', n., 6a, 6b.

86

confirmed later in the play when he draws another analogy between Brutus' emotional state and the burning of a candle:

> BRUTUS: How ill this *taper burns*! Ha, who comes here?
>
> ...
>
> Art thou some god, some angel, or some devil,
> That makest my *blood cold* and my hair to stare?
> (IV, iii, 275–280; my italics)

While in the Orchard Scene the burning of the candle functions as a metaphor for the burning state of Brutus' heart and blood, on the night before the final battle of Philippi – an instant before Caesar's ghost appears to him – its disordered burning functions as a metaphor for his blood's lowering temperature, a result of the fear which gradually takes hold of him.[44]

2.2.2 Reason and Passion in Brutus' Speech to the People

Through the Orchard Soliloquy, Shakespeare provides a glimpse into a mental process to which I shall henceforth refer as 'rationalising of emotion': Brutus' will to murder Caesar derives, as shown, from his anger; yet, for the sake of feeding his self-image as a man of Reason, he 'fashions' reality, persuades himself that he is acting out of rational imperatives, and wraps the emotional kernel in a pseudo-logical construction of a passion-free legal discussion. Throughout the tragedy, the protagonist is persistent in his tendency to rationalise emotion, a tendency which culminates in his speech before the Roman people.

However, before I examine the rationalisation of emotion found in Brutus' public speech, a few words should be devoted to the widespread tendency to perceive it as a rhetorical 'flop'. Some scholars, focusing their analysis on Brutus' rhetorical devices, trace numerous

---

44   In the beginning of the scene, when Brutus instructs Lucius to light the candle, he refers to his private room as 'study' (l. 7). Lucius' reference to the same room, after fulfilling his task, using a different word ('closet'), provides an additional hint of Shakespeare's consciousness of the double meaning embedded in the boy's plain report.

'flaws' in his speech and then refer to it using pejorative expressions such as 'ineffective' or 'Brutus' failure'.[45] These scholars seem to ignore the fact that Brutus did not address his speech to them, but rather to the Roman people, who did not notice its alleged flaws and deficiencies. In fact, Brutus' speech must be described as a sweeping rhetorical triumph. When the orator first ascends the pulpit, the attending citizens loudly demand an explanation as to the cause of the murder. When he descends, they support him enthusiastically, convinced that 'This Caesar was a tyrant', and feel 'blest that Rome is rid of him' (III, ii, 40–62).[46] For the rhetorician, who evaluates a speech primarily for its effect on the audience, there is no significance to the fact that Brutus' speech is 'cold', based on circular argumentation, contrived, and drenched in rhetorical self-awareness. Nor is there any significance to the fact that the citizens have failed to delve deeply into the speech and its faulty logic, or that they wish at its end to 'Let him [Brutus] be Caesar'. The major influential factor throughout this speech is Brutus' *ethos*,[47] which causes the common people – thought by ancient and early-modern rhetoricians to be incapable of grasping logical argumentation[48] – to perceive his arguments as logical and valid. Brutus' speech must not, therefore, be catalogued along with the

45 See: Brian Vickers, *The Artistry of Shakespeare's Prose* (London: Methuen, 1968), pp. 240–245. For a totally different interpretation, stressing the great power and effectiveness of Brutus' speech over its specific audience, see: Ernest Schanzer, 'The Tragedy of Brutus', pp. 183–194.

46 In these lines Shakespeare significantly strays from North's translation to Plutarch, which stresses that the citizens gave Brutus and his confederates '... such audience that it seemed they neither greatly reproved nor allowed the fact'. Thomas North, 'The Life of Julius Caesar', from Plutarch's *Lives of The Noble Greacians and Romans* (1579), *Julius Caesar*, ed. Marvin Spevack (Cambridge and New York: Cambridge University Press, 2000), p. 161.

47 Brutus is known to his audience as an honourable man of Reason prior to this speech, and this public image is further amplified during his oration. The two components constituting his *ethos* (namely, the speaker's image in the eyes of his addressees, based on their knowledge of his past activities, and his image as grasped during his speech) support and amplify one another in this scene through recurrent feedback. For further clarification of the term *ethos*, as used in this study, see Appendix C.

48 See Chapter Three, notes 17, 18; and Chapter Four, pp. 194–195.

errors he commits throughout the play, such as the decisions to murder Caesar, to spare Antony, and to grant him permission to speak before his friends, Romans and countrymen.

Although it can not be regarded in itself as a 'tragic error', Brutus' speech reveals the essential symptoms of the 'disease' which has led him to commit his fatal mistakes: the problematic relation within his mind between Reason and Passion, or in less flattering words, his emotional blindness. As I shall show below and in the fifth chapter, the errors mentioned above derive primarily from Brutus' inability to identify his own and other people's emotions, as well as his lack of understanding of the crucial part played by emotion in the pageant of life.

The common view referred to above, regarding the 'coldness' of the speech under discussion, is in itself valid and one can certainly sense the strong scent of 'logic' it conveys.[49] Throughout the play, Brutus reveals his tendency to relate to emotional situations by using the language of reason[50] – never more so than during this scene, in which his entire speech is constructed in a rhetorical style appropriate to logical argumentation, providing a *rational justification* for an action motivated by intense passions:

> Those that will hear me speak, let 'em stay here;
> Those that will follow Cassius, go with him;
> And public *reasons* shall be rendered
> Of Caesar's death. (III, ii, 5–8; my italics)

> Romans, countrymen, and lovers, hear me for my *cause* ...
> (Ibid., 13; my italics)

The rigid structure of Brutus' oration strives to conceal the clearly irrational reality, and confine it within the bounds of logic. The speech is written in prose, which is often interpreted as Brutus' attempt to

---

49 Even the rhetorical questions addressed by Brutus to the people in lines 25–29, must not necessarily be held as a means of inducing guilt or shame, but rather a part of an 'if ... than ...' argument, through which the speaker attempts to prove that the content of his speech is inoffensive to his audience: '*If* any, speak ... *If* any, speak ... *If* any, speak ... *Then* none have I offended' (my italics).

50 For example: 'Now, good Metellus, go along by him. / He *loves* me well, and I have given him *reasons*' (II, i, 218–219; my italics).

'descend' toward the simple citizens; however, Brutus' prose, far from being 'common', is elaborate and crammed with rhetorical schemes. Formal prose is a typical instrument employed by Shakespearean characters when constructing logical arguments:[51] the characters who speak this prose are 'freed' from the constraints of fixed rhyme and rhythm, and can therefore employ a variety of rhythmic effects and sentence-lengths to support a logical argument. Symmetry, for example, can serve a speaker to enforce a given comparison, or to refute it. This is precisely what Brutus does, assisted by a prose that rationalises reality through the use of conditional clauses and reasoning (ll. 25–31). This rationalising prose is constructed of rhetorical schemes that feature both symmetry and inverted symmetry, presenting an ostensibly organised and lucid world in which, behind every act or reaction, lies a reasonable cause (the following lines have been re-arranged, in order to clearly demonstrate the structure of the speech):

> ... not that I loved *Caesar less*,
> but that I loved *Rome more*.
>
> Had you rather Caesar were *living*, and *die* all slaves,
> than that Caesar were *dead*, to *live* all free men?
>
> *As* Caesar loved me, *I weep for him*;
> *as* he was fortunate, *I rejoice at it*;
> *as* he was valiant, *I honour him*;
> but,
> *as* he was ambitious, *I slew him*.
>
> There is *tears* for his love,
> *joy* for his fortune,
> *honour* for his valour,
> and *death* for his ambition. (Ibid., 19–25; my italics)

Brutus' habit of wrapping the irrational in a formal structure that suggests rationality is not exclusive to the Orchard Soliloquy and the speech to the people, but occurs throughout the play. Cassius exposes this habit of Brutus' during their tumultuous dialogue in scene IV, ii,

---

51   See, e.g.: *Hamlet* V, i, 9–20, 201–205.

immediately after the latter has formulated an argument that uses inverted symmetry to disguise itself as logical:

BRUTUS: Judge me, you gods! Wrong I mine enemies?
           And, if not so, how should I wrong a brother?
CASSIUS: Brutus, this *sober form* of yours hides wrongs ...
           (IV, ii, 38–40; my italics)

The above line uttered by Cassius may be the fittest means to define Brutus' rhetoric in general. This definition can be further sharpened by an examination of Shakespeare's specific choice of words: the meaning of the word 'sober' was not confined in Shakespeare's time – as it is in ours – to 'moderate', 'temperate', 'clear-headed', etc., but could also be used to denote 'guided by sound reason ... rational'; the word 'form' was used also as a rhetorical term denoting 'method of arranging the ideas in logical reasoning'.[52]

Brutus, in his speech to the Romans, does not *deliberately* 'hide(s) wrongs' (to use Cassius' words). He cannot be regarded as a 'sophist', at least not in the conventional meaning of this word; perceiving him as such strips the play of its complexity and tragic sense. The text does not supply any evidence of deliberate manipulation by which he seeks to influence the people, or any degree of self-awareness as to the failure of his logical argumentation. As can be seen in the Orchard Soliloquy, which offers a glimpse into his mind (since there are no other characters present, it is obvious that he is not trying to deceive anyone but himself), Brutus is simply unaware of the emotion that motivates him, and is convinced of his righteousness. His public speech should be seen in this respect as a direct continuation of the Orchard Soliloquy, precisely because of the deterioration in logic that it reveals. In contrast to the Orchard Soliloquy, none of Brutus' words in this speech to the citizens denotes uncertainty; he does not refer to Caesar as someone who might one day have grown ambitious; rather, he refers to him as someone who actually *was* ambitious. The increase of distortion in Brutus' references to Caesar may be linked to the parallel increase in his emotional agitation during the period of time separating the night of the storm and the public speech.

52   *OED*, 'sober', a., 11; 'form', n., 9.

2.2.3 'The Cause is in the Will'

The hints concerning the *modus operandi* of Brutus' mind, on which our discussion has focused thus far, are subtle and elusive, hidden for the most part under the play's surface. In contrast with this elusiveness in the characterisation of Brutus, Shakespeare places beside him certain characters whose mental characteristics are similar, but in a much 'cruder' and more obvious way. The actions and emotional reactions of these characters can be seen as an exaggerated manifestation of those displayed by the hero, guiding the spectators to grasp the subtler version. This technique is similar to the one Shakespeare employed in *Henry V*, portraying Bardolph as a caricature-like reflection of the 'intimidating prince', as argued here in the first chapter. Just as the ridiculous means that Bardolph employs in order to unite Pistol and Nim may direct the spectator's attention to the sophisticated, covert methods of control used by the king, so Shakespeare uses the characters of Caesar and the citizens in *Julius Caesar* to expose the basic quality of Brutus' mental mechanism.

The conduct of the citizens toward Cinna the poet (III, iii) is a clear demonstration of this mechanism, which renders the characters possessed by it unable to distinguish between an *emotional motive* and a *just and rational cause*. The citizens have become exceptionally angry during Antony's stirring speech, and this same passion – infusing them with a strong will to kill – seeks immediate relief:

> Revenge! About! Seek! Burn! Fire! Kill! Slay! Let not a traitor live! ... Pluck down benches ... Pluck down forms, windows, any thing ... (III, ii, 195–249)

Because the conspirators have already left Rome, having heard of these events, the citizens' rage must find an alternative outlet. When they accidentally run into Cinna, they begin an investigation aimed at finding a cause that will justify his murder. When such cause is not found, the 'rationalising of emotion' mechanism is recruited, and anger forces Reason to produce it:

3 PLEBEIAN:	Your name, sir, truly.
CINNA THE POET:	Truly, my name is Cinna.
1 PLEBEIAN:	Tear him to pieces, he's a conspirator.

CINNA THE POET:	I am Cinna the poet, I am Cinna the poet.
4 PLEBEIAN:	Tear him for his bad verses, tear him for his bad verses.
	(III, iii, 24–28)

Shakespeare provides a somewhat subtler version of such mental dynamics in the characterisation of Caesar, who – as opposed to his false self-image of a passion-proof man – is shown by the play to be essentially an emotional rationaliser. This tendency of Caesar's is dramatised in II, ii, first when he produces a ridiculous rationalisation of the ominous sign of the heartless sacrificial beast (ll. 41–44), and later when he enthusiastically adopts Decius' flattering rationalisation of Calpurnia's dream (l. 91). In these two instances Caesar is motivated by emotion (pride, which overcomes fear), but at the same time, aided by his impressive capacity for self-delusion, he strives to present himself to himself and to his surroundings as one who makes decisions and acts purely through Reason. His true irrational nature emerges in his tyrannical and/or childish reply to Decius, who wishes to 'know some cause' why Caesar 'will not come today' to the senate-house:

The cause is in my will. (II, ii, 71)

According to Thomas Wright's *The Passions of the Mind in General*, the *will* – 'which of it selfe, being blinde, and without knowledge' – is subject to the influence of two external factors, Passion and Reason; it is the relative strength of one as well as the weakness of the other that causes us to act rationally or irrationally.[53] It follows that the 'cause' of any human decision or act – including, of course, Caesar's temporary decision not to come out of doors – does not stem from the will, but from either Reason or Passion. Thus, by placing Caesar's reply, quoted above, within a sequence of rationalisations and Stoic clichés

---

53 When one's mind is sound, Will obeys the instruction of its guide, Reason (also 'wit', 'judgement'); however, Passion may disrupt this desirable condition by influencing Will through two possible channels: directly, or by applying its distorting force upon Reason (and thus Reason provides Will with wrong guidance). See: Thomas Wright, *The Passions of the Minde in Generall* (1604), pp. 57–59.

(ll. 34–37, 26–27), Shakespeare exposes his character's pathological inability to distinguish between the separate and fundamentally different influences of Reason and Passion upon his will.

Shakespeare makes similar use of the word 'will' in characterising the hero of the tragedy and his parallel patterns of thought. In scene IV, iii, a controversy arises between Brutus and Cassius, as to the best tactics to use in the inevitable encounter between their army and the forces led by Antony and Lepidus. Cassius argues that they must remain in their present location until the expected arrival of the enemy, whose journey from Philippi to Sardis is expected to exhaust its men. Brutus, characteristically, errs in rejecting his friend's opinions and suggestions, and provides some arguments of his own, ostensibly proving that the optimal tactical move would be to march towards the enemy. Brutus' arguments are far from well-grounded, and just as in the Orchard Scene, he relies on generalisations and forces them on the particular matter under discussion: he produces maxims about the circular nature of the 'tide', the 'flood' and the 'current' (ll. 218–224), yet presents no specific datum derived from present reality to demonstrate the validity of the analogy he is using. Brutus' conviction that he and his army are at the 'tide' (that is, an instant before the beginning of low-tide), is not supported by facts, and therefore cannot be regarded as the outcome of a rational thinking process. Nevertheless, from the outset of his 'refutation' of Cassius' arguments, his words reveal his personal conviction that he is guided by his Reason, which is superior to his friend's:

> Good *reasons* must of force give place to better ... (IV, iii, 203; my italics)

Cassius, consistently tending to self-effacement in the presence of Brutus, yields again:

> Then with your *will* go on ... (IV, iii, 224; my italics)

Nevertheless, it is possible that the inclusion of the word 'will' in Cassius' reply implies his awareness of the fact that his friend's 'reasons' – which are, as always, presented in the form of a well-constructed logical argument – are not necessarily the fruit of Reason.

Yet even if this specific word does not express the conscious awareness of the speaker himself, it may certainly be regarded as one of those subtle Shakespearean hints that encourage spectators to broaden their perspective and consider the range of circumstances and the complexity of a given situation.

The quality and extent of Brutus' tragic awareness is a subject of dispute among scholars. Some, stressing its total absence – or at least its relative deficiency[54] – rely upon two major facts: firstly, the absence of any statement by Brutus that might indicate his perception of Caesar's murder as an erroneous or unjust act; and secondly, Brutus' reference to Antony's and Lepidus' expected victory, some short time before his death, as a 'vile conquest' (V, v, 38). In contrast to these scholars, others credit Brutus with some awareness of his errors, and argue that throughout the second half of the play he acknowledges the loss of everything he held dear: his wife, his friends, and the goal for which he joined the conspiracy and murdered his 'best lover'. I believe that these scholars substitute their own awareness, shaped by extensive reading and analysis of the play, for that of the hero, and it is no coincidence that they do not support their observations with any kind of textual evidence.[55] It seems to me inadvisable, if not impossible, to give preference to either of these two attitudes: the fact that Brutus does not express remorse for the murder does not necessarily indicate its absence. Moreover, even if his reference to his enemy's victory as 'vile' expresses his conviction of the righteousness of the murder, considerable time separates this utterance from the moment of his death; this time space abounds in crucial occurrences, which may produce changes in his consciousness. It should be noted, above all, that the specific choices of behaviour adopted by the actor who portrays Brutus may be the most crucial factor influencing any given

54 See, e.g.: J. I. M. Stewart, 'Character and Motive in *Julius Caesar*', *Shakespeare Julius Caesar: A Casebook*, ed. Peter Ure (London: Macmillan, 1969), p. 116. Virgil K. Whitaker, 'Brutus and the Tragedy of Moral Choice', pp. 179, 181.

55 See: Harold C. Goddard, *The Meaning of Shakespeare*, vol. 1, p. 329; L. C. Knights, 'Personality and Politics in *Julius Caesar*', p. 137; Ernest Schanzer, 'The Tragedy of Brutus', p. 193; T. S. Dorsch, 'Introduction to *Julius Caesar*', *Julius Caesar*, ed. T. S. Dorsch (London and New York: Methuen, The Arden Shakespeare, 1985), pp. vii–lxxii.

spectator in this matter. In any case, it seems that Shakespeare – as he does in his other tragedies – leaves this key problem deliberately vague and open to subjective interpretation.

Harold Goddard and L. C. Knights, crediting Brutus with a complete tragic awareness, quote his final lines as its expression:

> Caesar, now be still,
> I killed not thee with half so good a will. (V, v, 51)

Goddard and Knights do not clearly explain how this quotation attests to Brutus' alleged awareness,[56] nor do they refer to its most significant word, which is also the last uttered by the hero in his life. This is the first instance in which Brutus refers to Caesar's murder as a fulfilment of the *will*, as opposed to the fulfilment of a dictate of Justice or Reason, which is what he has consistently suggested throughout the play. In fact, this is the very first time he utters this word, which receives significant emphasis due to its position at the end of a couplet. Thus, this 'Man of Reason' ends his life as he utters the word that denotes the entirely neutral mental faculty: as explained above, the will is at times guided by the light of Reason, and at other times subject to the power of Passion. Brutus, then, at the moment of his death, comes close to a more accurate description of the mental mechanism that led him to the assassination, and dominated him in general. Yet here, just as in scene IV, iii, quoted above, it is not possible to determine to what extent, if any, this key word is consciously chosen by the speaker himself, and if so, expresses any form of tragic awareness.

---

56   Harold C. Goddard, *The Meaning of Shakespeare*, p. 329; L. C. Knights, 'Personality and Politics in *Julius Caesar*', p. 137.

2.3 Brutus Inflames Italy

Thus far, the focus of my reading has been Brutus' blindness to the quality of his emotions and their distorting influence upon his Reason. As I shall now show, the scope of his emotional disability is much wider: the play reveals his failure to perceive the crucial place of emotion in the sphere of rhetoric, as well as the 'contagious' quality of the passions, spreading among humans through direct communication. In fact, Brutus is characterised as being completely blind to emotion, totally unaware that passions are the main force that moves his world. His severe emotional disability causes him – without his being even remotely aware of the fact – to spread his inner 'fire' throughout the whole of Italy.

2.3.1 The Denial of Emotion in Rhetorical Situations

Brutus' denial of emotion, particularly of its profound effect in any given rhetorical situation, is evident in his dialogue with Portia on the night before Caesar's murder. Portia enters the orchard, seeking her withdrawn husband in the hope of discovering the cause of his strange behaviour. Answering her searching questions, Brutus argues evasively that he is 'not well in health, and that is all'; the wife, intensifying her efforts, kneels and performs an emotional appeal:[57]

> And upon my knees
> I charm you, by my once-commended beauty,
> By all your vows of love, and that great vow
> Which did incorporate and make us one,
> That you unfold to me, yourself, your half,
> Why you are heavy ... (II, i, 270–275)

---

57 Kneeling is one of emotional appeal's most characteristic gestures (see pp. 179, 192, 282). Compare: 'I must prevent thee, Cimber. / These couchings and these lowly courtesies / Might fire the blood of ordinary men / ... Be not fond / To think that Caesar bears such rebel blood / That will be thawed from the true quality / With that which melteth fools ...' (III, i, 35–42).

Her efforts, however, fail to produce the desired effect. Brutus does not reveal his secret, and puts an end to the emotional appeal:

> Kneel not, gentle Portia. (II, i, 278)

This reaction does not indicate that the appeal has had any effect on Brutus, and Portia thus alters her rhetorical tactics: henceforth she relies upon her *ethos*.[58] With regard to this factor, Portia, as a woman, is at a considerable disadvantage: women, as opposed to men, were not thought to excel in emotional stability ('constancy'),[59] and were therefore considered incapable of safeguarding a secret.[60] But Portia finds a way to bypass this obstacle; she chooses not to ignore or deny the undisputable facts (her being a woman, the nature of women in general), but rather to prove herself different, an exception among womankind:

> I grant I am a woman, but withal
> A woman that Lord Brutus took to wife.
> I grant I am a woman, but withal
> A woman well-reputed, Cato's daughter.
> Think you I am no stronger than my sex,
> Being so fathered and so husbanded?
> Tell me your counsels, I will not disclose 'em. (II, i, 292–298)

Portia's arguments do not prove that she is 'stronger than my [her] sex', but only suggest that this is highly probable; she saves the un-equivocal, persuasive, logical proof of her claim for the end of her

---

58   For a clarification of the term of *ethos*, see Appendix C.

59   The *Oxford English Dictionary* defines 'constancy' as 'The state or quality of being unmoved in mind' (*OED*, n., 1a). Yet in the light of Thomas Wright's comments on this word, as well as *Julius Caesar* III, i, 58–70, it is evident that it refers to the firmness of emotion (since emotion is the sole factor that directly generates the motions of the mind). Wright stresses that the flawed constancy of women (and young men) stems from lack of prudence and judgement, and that a constant woman is an exceptional phenomenon that must be commended and prized. Thomas Wright, *The Passions of the Minde in Generall* (1604), pp. 40–42.

60   See, e.g.: 'O constancy, be strong upon my side, / Set a huge mountain 'tween my heart and tongue! / I have a man's mind, but a woman's might. / How hard it is for women to keep counsel!' (II, iv, 6–9).

speech, when she presents conclusive evidence of her ability to master the passions:

> I have made strong proof of my *constancy*,
> Giving myself a voluntary wound
> Here, in the thigh. Can I bear that with patience
> And not my husband's secrets? (II, i, 299–302; my italics)

This final proof tips the scales: Brutus promises to reveal his secret, and indeed fulfils his promise later (II, iv, 6–7; 40–43). Portia's success in establishing a solid *ethos*, and the strong impression this means of persuasion makes upon her husband, are reflected in his astounded reaction, as well as in the adjective he grants her:[61]

> O ye gods,
> Render me worthy of this noble wife! (II, i, 302–303)

In North's translation of Plutarch's *Lives*, Portia does not kneel before her husband, but strives to establish her *ethos* from her very first words.[62] It seems that Shakespeare – who closely followed the *ethos* establishing process described in his source but added to his scene the kneeling, the emotional appeal, and Brutus' dismissive reaction to it[63] – intended for his spectators to compare the protag-

---

61 The adjective 'noble' acquires in the course of *Julius Caesar* a variety of meanings, one of which is 'a rational man who is not ruled by his passions and is not prone to be emotionally manipulated' (see I, ii, 297–299). A similar sense is found in Hamlet's reference to Man's commendable attributes: 'What a piece of work is a man: how *noble in reason*, how infinite in faculty ...' (II, ii, 303–304; my italics).

62 Thomas North, 'The Life of Marcus Brutus', from Plutarch's *Lives of The Noble Greacians and Romans* (1579), *Shakespeare's Julius Caesar*, ed. Marvin Spevack (Cambridge and New York: Cambridge University Press, 2000), pp. 165–166.

63 Brutus' pretence of being immune to emotional appeals and to emotion in general, is evident also in the stormy debate he holds with Cassius in IV, iii. Throughout this dispute, Brutus expresses his contempt for his friend's externalised displays of rage and claims that they have no effect upon him (ll. 38–46). Since he himself in this scene is given to extreme anger (l. 143), his statement resembles Caesar's baseless pretension to being resistant to emotional influence (I, ii, 198–201, 211–212; II, ii, 34–37; III, i, 35–43, 58–73).

onist's different reactions to each of the three means of persuasion (Brutus is also influenced here by *logos*, since Portia has combined and shaped her evidence into a logical argument. Obviously, her demonstration of *logos* has contributed to the establishment of her *ethos*, since one who excels in rationality is less prone, in the traditional view, to be ruled by the passions).

The conspirators, during their gathering in Brutus' orchard, are preoccupied with the practical implications of their actions. Cassius expresses his fear of obstacles that might be placed in their way by Antony: he holds him to be 'a shrewd contriver' (II, i, 158), and proposes that they murder him along with Caesar. Brutus expresses his objection in principle to such an act, and even adds moral and general reasons to support his objection; however, when he refers specifically to Antony, he does not disqualify Cassius' advice on *moral* grounds, but rather disregards Antony's hazardous potential. Brutus does not sense any danger in Antony, due to his overestimation of *ethos*, both in rhetoric and in life. Antony is reputed among the Romans to be a gamesome and quick-spirited young man, 'a masker and a reveller' who 'revels long a-nights', 'given / To sports, to wildness and much company', that is, a slave to his passions.[64] He therefore has, from Brutus' point of view, a very poor *ethos*,[65] and his political power and influence after Caesar's death are thus likely to be negligible. Brutus does not perceive that Antony's emotional nature may present a serious danger in the near future. The only influential force he ascribes to Antony's emotions is self-destructive: his love for Caesar can but turn into excessive sorrow, which may even prove fatal (ll. 185–189). The irony implicit in Brutus' disdainful outlook is twofold: firstly, Antony's emotional nature is not a weakness but a strength, upon which his great passionate speech will be founded; secondly, his excessive demonstration of *pathos* in this speech will in fact serve to amplify and establish his *ethos*. The reactions of the citizens to his display of passion clearly indicate this amplification of *ethos* by means of *pathos*:

---

64   I, ii, 28–29; II, i, 185–187; II, ii, 116–117; V, i, 62.
65   See Chapter Four, p. 156.

2 PLEBEIAN: Poor soul! His eyes are red as fire with weeping.
3 PLEBEIAN: There's not a nobler[66] man in Rome than Antony.
(Ibid., 107–108)

It is no coincidence that the conspirators have chosen an emo-tionally-blind leader who overemphasises the power of *ethos*: they themselves exhibit a similar inclination, ignoring the existence of *pathos* and acting solely on the basis of *ethos* (Cassius, of course, is an exception here, yet – as pointed out above – he consistently allows Brutus to overrule his instinctive insights). When Cassius, Casca and Cinna consider the possibility of recruiting Cicero, the supporting argument is based on the senator's *ethos*: 'his silver hair', 'judgement' and 'gravity', claims Metellus Cimber, 'Will purchase us a good opinion / And buy men's voices to commend our deeds'. According to Cimber, Cicero's impeccable public image is the proper answer to the problematic image of the conspirators, whose 'youth and wildness shall no whit appear, / But all be buried in his [Cicero's] gravity' (II, i, 144–149). These calculations and their logic are shadowed by two factors: Cicero's historical image, familiar to some of Shakespeare's spectators; and the manner in which he is presented to the audience at the beginning of the play. Cicero achieved his reputation as Rome's greatest orator mainly due to his skills in the use of *pathos*; a consid-erable portion of his writings on rhetoric, which were studied in Elizabethan and Jacobean schools, is devoted to the emotional aspect of oratory, and stresses its decisive influence in rhetorical situations. Moreover, in scene I, ii Cicero is described while onstage as one whose 'ferret and ... fiery eyes' indicate his stormy emotional state, 'As we have seen him in the Capitol, / Being crossed in conference by some senators' (ll. 185–188). This description – uttered by none other than Brutus – ironically foreshadows the description of Antony's eyes as being 'red as fire', and their emotional influence during his great speech; of course, it differs fundamentally and significantly from

66   These lines provide some indication of the process of transformation undergone by the word 'noble', its denotations and connotations, during the course of the play. In this specific context, it ceases to function as an adjective fitting a rational man resistant to emotion (see note 61), and becomes a proper title for a man who externalises immoderate passion.

Metellus Cimber's account, quoted above, which emphasises Cicero's 'gravity' and 'judgement'.

The tendency of the conspirators to overestimate *ethos* is also evident in Cassius' decision to recruit Brutus to the conspiracy:

> CASCA: O, he [*Brutus*] sits high in all the people's hearts,
>   And that which would appear offence in us,
>   His *countenance*, like richest alchemy,
>   Will change to virtue and to worthiness.
> CASSIUS: Him and his *worth* and our great need of him
>   You have right well conceited. (I, iii, 157–162; my italics)

The words by which Cassius and Casca refer to Brutus in these lines are synonymous with *ethos*, as used in rhetorical contexts: the *Oxford English Dictionary* glosses the word 'countenance' as 'Demeanour or manner towards others as expressing good or ill will; show of feeling or manifestation of regard towards another' and 'Estimation; credit or repute in the world';[67] the word 'worth' is used in this sense by Antony, when he describes himself to the people as lacking the essential properties and skills that make an effective orator.[68]

Brutus' perception of *ethos* and *logos* as being superior to *pathos* is clearly demonstrated moments after the assassination. The protagonist grants Antony's request to speak over Caesar's body in the Forum; Cassius, the only conspirator who knows the true value of *pathos*, explicitly alerts his friend to the possibility that Antony may sabotage their enterprise by stirring up the people's emotions. Brutus immediately rebuts this warning,[69] and the dispute is shaped by the

---

67   *OED*, 'countenance', n., I, 1; II, 7; III, 9.

68   'I am no orator, as Brutus is ... / For I have neither wit, nor words, nor *worth*, / Action, nor utterance, nor the power of speech, / To stir men's blood. I only speak right on' (III, ii, 207–213; my italics).

69   Cassius subordinates himself in this moment, as in others, to Brutus' will. As the play draws to an end, he becomes more submissive to the powerful influence of his friend, who 'fashions' him according to his will. Thus, he gradually loses his individuality, which includes his abilities as 'a great observer' who 'looks / Quite through the deeds of men' (I, ii, 202–203). See: Marvin L. Vawter, 'After Their Fashion: Cicero and Brutus in *Julius Caesar*', *Shakespeare Studies* 9 (1976), pp. 211–214.

dramatist like a mathematical equation which proves – according to Brutus – that *logos* combined with *ethos* will outweigh *pathos* (*Logos + Ethos > Pathos*):

CASSIUS:	Brutus, a word with you.	
	[Aside to BRUTUS]	
	You know not what you do. Do not consent	
	That Antony speak in his funeral.	
	Know you how much the people may be *moved*	(*Pathos*)
	By that which he will utter?	
BRUTUS:	By your pardon,	^
	I will myself into the pulpit first	
	And show the *reason* of our Caesar's death.	(*Logos*)
	What Antony shall speak, I will protest	
	He speaks by leave and by permission,	
	And that we are contented Caesar shall	+
	Have all true rites and lawful ceremonies.	
	It shall advantage more than do us wrong.	(*Ethos*)
	(III, i, 231–242; my italics)	

Alexander Leggatt refers to this moment as an expression of Brutus' 'self esteem', which 'blinds' him and causes him to commit the fatal error of allowing Antony's public speech to take place. In order to establish his argument, Leggatt quotes line 236 alone, cut off from its full context.[70] But what this context reveals is that Brutus, rather than comparing the abilities of two orators – his own and Antony's – is comparing the three means of persuasion and their potency in general. He takes lightly the prospect of Antony's speech and the passions it might stir (l. 235), because he is blind to the force of emotion, over-rates *logos* and *ethos*, and has no doubts as to their ability to exert a strong and lasting influence over the people. Another critical reference to this instant is provided by Ernest Schanzer, who finds in lines 238–242 evidence of Brutus' 'shrewd, practical politics'. Schanzer disagrees with scholars who perceive Brutus as a naïve and impractical 'philosopher' undertaking a mission for which he is unfit.[71] However, what emerges from my above interpretation of lines 231–242 suggests

---

70   Alexander Leggatt, *Shakespeare's Political Drama*, p. 145.
71   Ernest Schanzer, 'The Tragedy of Brutus', pp. 183–184.

that Brutus' arguments here show absolutely no indication of 'shrewd, practical politics'. On the contrary, he is oblivious to two central facts of life, of which every politician should remind himself day and night: reason is the force that least influences people, and it is passion that moves the world.

2.3.2 Caesar's Murder as an Act of Rage

On the early morning of the Ides of March, in accord with his general tendency to perceive and display Caesar's murder in a positive light, Brutus tells his confederates of his desire to perform the assassination as a sacrificial act, unmotivated by anger (II, i, 166, 172). It does not require deep analysis in order to perceive the amount of self-delusion inherent in this aspiration, since the play explicitly shows that at least some of the conspirators join the plot because of negative emotions they hold against Caesar. Brutus' anger may be portrayed in a subtle and elusive fashion, but Cassius, the instigator, is clearly shown to be dominated by envy, and Caius Ligarius' belief that Caesar has done him wrong is stressed by Shakespeare twice (II, i, 15–17; II, iii, 4).

Even if these facts are overlooked, the manner in which the conspirators 'stage' the 'scene' of the murder cannot but lead us to define it as *an act of rage*. They assemble around Caesar, entreating him to mitigate Publius Cimber's sentence of banishment. Caesar not only proudly declines their plea (comparing his resolution and emotional stability to the constancy of the northern star), but reinforces his arrogance with a considerable measure of overt contempt, comparing Metellus Cimber's kneeling to canine grovelling, and threatening to 'spurn' him 'like a cur' (ll. 42–46). In their discussions of the human passions, early modern English sources repeatedly emphasise the great power of displays of contempt in igniting anger and the thirst for revenge.[72] The assassination, which follows immediately after the conspirators kneel and Caesar contemptuously repudiates them, therefore becomes a furious act of vengeance; Cassius' early prediction in

---

72   See Chapter Three, p. 145.

the Storm Scene, comparing the emotional quality of the cosmic signs with the nature of the upcoming murder, is thus fulfilled:

> And the complexion of the element
> In favour's like the work we have in hand,
> Most bloody, *fiery*, and most terrible. (I, iii, 128–130; my italics)

2.3.3 Brutus' Unintentional Emotional Appeals

Brutus' unawareness of the anger-laden quality of the murder incurs fatal consequences: the play, as will be demonstrated below, is deeply concerned with the 'contagious' nature of emotion and its strong tendency to spread; the rage embodied in the act of murder will enflame Rome and set the whole of Italy on fire. Brutus, who is ignorant of the mysteries of emotion in general, is unaware of the tendency of the passions to spread; he fails to perceive the 'route' of the distribution of anger, which is clearly depicted to the spectators by means of imagery, and does not sense how he himself has spread this passion into his near surroundings and further afield. Ironically, it is his emotional ignorance that leads him, unwittingly, to produce several emotional appeals that spread anger and cause a general inflammation.

This phenomenon is first seen in II, i, when Brutus recruits Caius Ligarius to the conspiracy. Several moments prior to this encounter, Casca refers to Brutus as 'the sun', which presents 'his fire' (ll. 106–110); within a few minutes, this same fire begins to spread:

> LIGARIUS: [*To BRUTUS*] ...
>   Thou, like an exorcist, hast conjured up
>   My mortified spirit. Now bid me run
>   And I will strive with things impossible ...
>   Set on your foot,
>   And with a heart *new-fired* I follow you
>   To do I know not what ...
>   *Thunder*
>   (II, i, 323–333, 334 SD; my italics)

This enthusiastic proclamation by Ligarius implies that the passion that fires his heart has neutralised his rational capacity ('To do I know not what'). Yet Brutus, the would-be 'man of Reason' who justifies the murder as an essential act dictated by reason, shows no awareness of this implication.

One of the play's theatrical climaxes is no doubt the moment when Brutus, some few seconds after the assassination, attempts to 'fashion' reality and turn the 'savage spectacle' into a 'lofty scene' embodying a ceremonial act:

> Stoop, Romans, stoop,
> And let us bathe our hands in Caesar's blood
> Up to the elbows and besmear our swords. (III, i, 105–107)

This event is not depicted in North's version of Plutarch, and may well be Shakespeare's own invention. Scholars have of course discussed extensively the significance of this theatrical flaunting of Caesar's blood; yet, to the best of my knowledge, the emotional implications of this 'bloody sight' have hitherto been overlooked. Thus, for example, certain scholars have grasped the tragic duality embodied in the smearing of the blood over the conspirators' hands and swords: seen from Brutus' point of view, this blood is a symbol of Rome's enfranchisement and liberation from tyranny, whereas from the opposite viewpoint it can signify nothing but a barbaric and unjust act.[73] But the blood also plays a major role in the play because of the emotional effect it generates: Thomas Wright explicitly reports that the sight of blood – and the colour red in general – inflames the beholder's blood and induces his anger.[74] Wright refers to this matter as a widely accepted truth, based on a variety of sources (such as the books of the Maccabees and 'Galen & other Physitians'). Brutus' emotional ignorance is therefore manifested in his unawareness – or denial – of the most immediate and primal effect that the 'ritualistic' actions he initiates will generate: waving of the blood-smeared hands

---

73   See, e.g.: Maurice Charney, *Shakespeare's Roman Plays: The Function of Imagery in the Drama* (Cambridge: Harvard University Press, 1963), pp. 42, 48–51.

74   Thomas Wright, *The Passions of the Minde in Generall* (1604), pp. 64–65. Compare: 'Then, when the sky shall wax as red as blood, / It shall be said I made it red myself, / To make me think of naught but blood and war' (*The First Part of Tamburlaine the Great*, IV, ii, 53–55).

and swords throughout the city will inevitably stir the citizens to anger, which is, as mentioned in the first chapter, the passion that infuses men with a thirst for blood.[75] Brutus' blindness to the emotional factors inherent in the situation is ironically embodied in the 'text' he instructs his friends to declaim while waving their bloody swords; the essence of this 'text' is in stark contradiction to the emotional effects and messages that will actually accompany its 'performance':

> Then walk we forth, even to the market-place,
> And waving our red weapons o'er our heads
> Let's all cry, '*Peace*, freedom and liberty!' (III, i, 108–110; my italics)

Brutus' complete denial of reality is further stressed by the dramatist when Antony arrives at the murder scene in order to investigate the latest developments. Brutus, standing near Caesar's body with blood-smeared hands, exhibits in his short speech a naïve expectation that Antony will be able to ignore his eyesight (the most potent of the five senses in rousing emotions[76]), focus on the words (*logos*) addressed to him, and believe in the existence of the invisible emotional reality they describe:

> Though now we must *appear* bloody and cruel,
> As by our hands and this our present act
> You *see* we do, yet *see* you but our hands
> And this the bleeding business they have done.
> Our hearts you *see* not, they are pitiful ... (III, i, 165–169; my italics)

Only a short period of time separates Brutus' stage exit, toward the end of III, i, from his entrance at the beginning of the next scene. This fact, as well as dramatic and theatrical common-sense, reinforces the probability that in the play's original performances, the protagonist ascended the pulpit with his hands still smeared in Caesar's blood. This assumption, together with the probability that the actor who portrayed Brutus accompanied his oratory with physical gestures in

75   See Chapter One, p. 41.
76   Thomas Wright, *The Passions of the Minde in Generall* (1604), pp. 57, 149–158.

keeping with its substance and style,[77] leads me to argue that this much discussed speech is the most concentrated theatrical demonstration found in the play of its hero's emotional blindness. As shown earlier, this speech's verbal and syntactic strata – as well as its structure and diverse rhetorical schemes – are typical of the 'Language of Reason', and are employed in order to establish, as it were, the argument according to which Caesar's murder stemmed from a just cause. It therefore follows that the orator's hands should support his speech with fitting movements chosen from the endless inventory of gesture appropriate to illustrating structures of balance, comparison, symmetry, asymmetry, and so on. However, the blood that covers them completely changes the balance between the three means of persuasion in the given rhetorical situation; this blood gives rise to a dynamics in which the speaker is not addressing the rational faculty of his addressees, but mainly their emotions. Thus, the sight of blood on his hands inevitably influences the citizens in a completely opposite way to that of the words he utters, and the hands themselves, red and moving like a Matador's *muleta*, actually act against the purpose of their gestures. Brutus, who opens the speech by asking his hearers to moderate their emotions ('... be *patient* till the last'), using a word that frequently denotes in Shakespeare's writings the opposite state to anger,[78] is actually performing, unconsciously, an appeal to this very

77   The Elizabethan actor in this scene must have made intensive as well as meaning-
     ful use of his hands. This use is not only the outcome of the acting techniques
     dictated by the structure of the Elizabethan theatre (which demands that the actor
     use his body intensively in almost every role and scene), but, above all, of the fact
     that *the actor was enacting a Roman orator*. The Roman treatises of rhetoric
     known to the Elizabethans refer in detail to the orator's use of his hands, and
     stress its significance. The use of the hands constitutes a crucial part of the totality
     of means referred to in early-modern works by the term 'action' (for further
     clarification of this term, see Chapter Four, p. 194); the rhetoric treatises describe
     the diverse 'actions' fitting the diverse rhetorical situations and modes of speech,
     and specify their appropriate hand gestures, their character, range and velocity.
     See: Cicero, *Oratore*, xviii, 59, pp. 349–350; *Rhetorica ad Herennium*, III, xv,
     26–27, pp. 201–205; Quintilian, *Institutio Oratoria*, XI, iii, pp. 85–183.
78   Anger, of course, has no 'opposite' emotion, but the words 'patient' and 'pa-
     tience' are often used by Shakespeare's characters in opposition to words that
     denote anger. See, e.g.: *Antony and Cleopatra*, II, v, 63, 108; *Romeo and Juliet*, I,

same passion. Moreover, this opening line, by which he seeks the appeasement of the commons, calls for a gesture appropriate to hushing or restraining; thus it is actually at the very beginning of the speech that the speaker's emotional ignorance is expressed in the most concentrated fashion: he raises his hand/s to appease the citizens, but in so doing reveals Caesar's blood to their eyes, thus turning their emotions in the opposite direction to that intended.

The speech under discussion not only exhibits Brutus' emotional disability, but also has significant dramatic implications; in the light of the argument presented here, Brutus' speech to the populace can be seen as a sort of early preparation, or – to use show-biz jargon – a 'warm up show' for the speech following. After erring in allowing Antony to speak, Brutus unknowingly continues to play into the hands of his opponent, and furthers the attainment of Antony's goal, namely, to boil the citizens' blood. He assists Antony by delivering the Romans into his hands in a warmer state than they were prior to his own speech. Had Brutus delivered his oration clean handed (physically clean, as opposed to metaphorically), Antony would have had to begin his speech in front of a relatively cold-blooded multitude, thus facing a challenge much tougher than the one he actually faces.

Brutus' agreement to let Antony deliver his speech in the presence of Caesar's corpse must also be added to the list of his unintentional emotional appeals. As the leader who permits the speech, he is directly responsible for whatever it may contain; moreover, as stressed above, Brutus not only *agrees* to Antony giving the speech, but is also *strongly interested* in it being delivered. The public display of a corpse clad in blood-soaked garments constitutes a potent emotional appeal that influences its addressees' minds directly, without any need for their cognitive faculties to mediate. Antony bases his stirring oratory pre-eminently on what they can see; the words he utters merely support, channel and amplify the initial rousing of emotion. Brutus' error is therefore double, since he underestimates not only Antony's skill in

---

v, 88–89; *Titus Andronicus*, I, i, 205–206; *King Lear*, IV, iii, 13–14; *Coriolanus*, II, i, 24–26; III, i, 192; *The Taming of the Shrew*, I, ii, 42; IV, i, 126–127; *Othello*, IV, i, 85–89; II, i, 97–98; *Twelfth Night*, II, v, 60–62.

oratory, but also the quality and potency of the emotion stirred when a bloody corpse is publicly exhibited. Just as he fails to feel the anger beating in his own heart, he does not perceive the potential danger that lies in the eruption of this passion and its tendency to spread; this we witness during the very first moments following the murder. Brutus, on two separate occasions, expresses his concern over the *fear* that may spread from the scene of the crime to the streets of Rome (III, i, 82–83, 180).

At this point I would like the reader momentarily to step out of *Julius Caesar*'s fictional world and observe the theatrical event as a whole: the frequent preoccupation with blood, as well as its extensive presentation onstage, is also likely – from an early modern point of view – to have stirred the Elizabethan spectators to anger, and thus to have influenced their rational judgement and their grasp of the events and of the characters who generated them. These implications must, of course, be investigated separately, and for the time being I wish only to express awareness of their existence, and of the inherent potential for future investigation.

2.3.4 *The Flames of Rage Return to Plague the Fire-Raiser*

The play draws a clear and continuous path by which anger – the same passion that was initially hidden in the protagonist's heart – spreads, and finally 'cumber[s] all the parts of Italy'. Just as this passion is represented throughout the opening scenes by metaphors of fire and burning, so, after its outbreak, Brutus' 'fire of anger' spreads via several way stations (to be described below), sets the entire country on fire, and ultimately, one moment before being extinguished, returns to consume the unwitting fire-raiser himself.

As shown in the discussion of the dialogue between Brutus and Ligarius, the 'fire' spreads from the hero to the other conspirators through 'emotional contagion', and spurs them to action. From the conspirators, through the act of the murder, which was depicted as 'fiery' (I, iii, 128–130) and was in fact carried out assisted by the motivating forces of rage,[79] the fire of anger is embodied in Caesar's corpse. It then erupts and spreads from the corpse via several channels:

1. From Caesar's blood, smeared on the assassins' hands and swords, to their surroundings and to the people present at Brutus' and Cassius' speeches.[80]
2. Through the rhetorical use that Antony makes of his bloody hands.[81]
3. Through the corpse, its open wounds and the blood which pours out of them.

Antony's use of the blood, the literal evocations by which he colours his addressees' imagination red,[82] as well as the reading of the document he presents as 'the will of Caesar' – all these combine to 'inflame' (III, ii, 136) the Romans' blood. In addition, Antony ignites the 'fire' and fans it with his eyes, which are 'red as fire' (ibid., 107).

After kindling the citizens, the fire of rage spreads through the entire city as a real fire –

ALL: Revenge! About! Seek! Burn! Fire! Kill! Slay! (Ibid., 195)

– igniting among others the house of Brutus (ibid., 221), who for the time being escapes its flames by his urgent flight. Shakespeare guides his audience to perceive distinctly the exact path of the spreading passion, when the citizens express their intention to burn Caesar's body: as explained above, the anger that has driven the assassination was embedded in the corpse; following Antony's speech, the citizens declare their intention to kindle the conspirators' houses using the same fire that burns the corpse. Thus, the passion embedded in Caesar's body erupts and spreads through Rome:

79   See above, 2.3.2.
80   The play informs us that Cassius is meant to utter a speech of his own – simultaneous with Brutus, but in a different location (III, ii, 3–6) – but completely neglects this datum, for no apparent reason.
81   Several minutes prior to his speech, Antony shook the bloody hands of the conspirators (III, i, 184–189).
82   See, e.g.: III, ii, 124–125, 184–185.

1 PLEBEIAN: ... We'll burn his body in the holy place
            And with the brands fire the traitors' houses.
            Take up the body.
2 PLEBEIAN: Go fetch fire! (Ibid., 244–247)

            ...

3 PLEBEIAN: ... Come, brands ho, firebrands! To Brutus', to Cassius'; burn
            all! Some to Decius' house, and some to Casca's, some to
            Ligarius'! Away, go! (III, iii, 32–34)

The rage spreads and reaches 'all the parts of Italy' in the form of
'Domestic *fury* and *fierce* civil strife' predicted in Antony's intimate
soliloquy over Caesar's body (III, i, 263–264). Just before the battle of
Philippi ends, the fire begins to return to its source: first, it touches
Brutus' closest surroundings when Portia, in killing herself, 'swal-
lowed fire' (IV, iii, 156). North, in his version of Plutarch's description of the same incident, does not make use of the word 'fire':[83]
Shakespeare's choice of words is evidence of his deliberate placement
of Portia's death directly in the path of anger he traces in the play's
fictional space. This linkage is further reinforced by the choice of the
word 'strange' in Messala's description of the suicide (IV, iii, 189):
as demonstrated in the beginning of this chapter, this same word is
used in the play's opening scenes to describe both the storm and
Brutus' emotional state, and to suggest their affinity. Towards the end
of the play, the fire turns back and reaches the character who
contributed crucially to its ignition: Cassius, still fighting on the
battlefield, sees from a distance how it consumes his tents (V, iii, 12–
14). Ultimately, when the fighting has ended and the fire is almost
totally quenched, it catches up with the fire-raiser himself:

MESSALA: Strato, where is thy master?
STRATO: Free from the bondage you are in, Messala.
           The conquerors can but make a fire of him ... (V, v, 53–55)

It should be noted that the cosmic storm that dominates scene I,
iii, and the fire that accompanies it, are, in themselves, completely

---

83   '... she, determining to kill herself ... took hot burning coals and cast them into her
      mouth, and kept her mouth so closed that she choked herself'. Thomas North,
      'The Life of Marcus Brutus', p. 183.

harmless. When describing to Cicero the lion he has seen in the street, Casca emphasises that the beast only 'glared upon me, and went surly by / Without annoying me' (I, iii, 20–22). In the light of Casca's description of how 'Men all in fire walk up and down the streets' (I, iii, 25), it is evident that the fire does not consume the Men's bodies, since the description denotes an ongoing action, lacking any dimension of urgency. Finally, the fire's harmless nature is clearly evident from Casca's reference to the 'common slave', who 'Held up his left hand, which did flame and burn / Like twenty torches joined, and yet his hand, / Not sensible of fire, remained unscorched' (I, iii, 15–18).

The play reveals how the storm's fire becomes harmful only after passing via Brutus and spreading further along the route described above. As explained, Brutus is totally unaware of the explosion of anger he is likely to generate by murdering Caesar, and prefers to perceive it as an essential and beneficial act:

> We shall be called purgers, not murderers. (II, i, 180)

Brutus uses the word 'purgers' here in its common meaning, and thus ascribes to himself and his confederates the purification of Rome from Caesar's 'ambition'. But the word has an additional sense, one of greater specificity and relevance in this context. In the medical terminology of Shakespeare's time, it is often used to denote purification of the body of excessive humours, by means of various foods and remedies.[84] The use of purgation as a means of curing an excess of the orange-red humour is evident in the dialogue held between Hamlet and Guildenstern, shortly after the premature ending of *The Mouse Trap*:

GUILD.:   The king, sir – …
              Is in his retirement marvellous distempered.
HAMLET: With drink, sir?
GUILD.:   No, my lord, rather with *choler*.

---

84   On purgation as a means of treating an imbalance of the humours, and the recommended treatments in case of excess in each of the four humours, see: Thomas Elyot, *The Castel of Helthe* (1539), pp. 55–59.

HAMLET: Your wisdom should show itself more richer to signify this to his doctor, for for me to put him to his *purgation* would perhaps plunge him into Far more *choler*. (III, ii, 291–299; my italics)

Ironically, the test of time shows how Caesar's murder proves to be the very opposite of an act of purgation. Brutus, through a succession of blind but consistent actions, has violated the balance of humours in the Roman body politic, thus flooding it with the excessive humour that ruled over his own body.

Chapter Three
Othello

'Facts, Hercule, facts! Behind them lies the whole fabric
of deductive truth.'
(Inspector Jacques Clouseau, *A Shot in the Dark*)

Shakespearean scholarship from its inception has focused extensively
on the relationship between Othello and Iago, and on the changes that
the former undergoes under the latter's influence. Yet no satisfactory
explanation has been offered for the links between the ancient's
persuasive techniques and the general's character traits. Some scholars
describe Othello as a faulty human being, focusing on textual expressions that attest as it were to his self-love, pride, and even 'flawed
intellect'; these scholars show how Iago exploits these 'flaws' in his
favour. Others adopt a more positive, forgiving stance towards Othello, stressing Iago's superb rhetorical skills, his 'diabolic intellect' and
even his alleged sexual complexes (latent homosexuality, an aversion
to sex, misogyny), which provide fertile ground for his negative moti-
vations.

Despite these observations and the intense scholarly interest in
the play's chief persuader and persuaded, a study has yet to appear
that points clearly to the supposed 'breach' in Othello's mind, through
which Iago is able to enter surreptitiously and ignite jealousy and
anger in the very man whom 'passion could not shake' (IV, i, 256–
257).[1] This 'breach' – and the process by which Iago identifies,
'zooms in', penetrates, and widens it – have been described in generalised, sometimes inadequate terms. I believe this to be the result of
two main factors. Firstly, no systematic analysis of all the emotional
appeals in this play has yet been carried out, to the best of my know-

---

1   See also: III, iv, 25–27, 128–131.

ledge, despite the centrality of *pathos* to the persuasive processes in this tragedy. To the extent that Iago's rhetorical manipulation of his commander receives scholarly attention, it is usually discussed under the general rubric of 'persuasion'. Secondly, Othello's character is usually discussed with reference to his uniqueness or foreignness in Venetian society, rather than considering his position as an integral part of that society. It is true that Othello is a black man living in a white society, an African among Europeans. However, in stressing his uniqueness and treating him as 'other', or an 'outsider', scholars have ignored a crucial fact: Othello is a classic example of an individual who has climbed to a high status from lowly origins. Such individuals must possess skills or innate qualities highly esteemed by their host society – otherwise, they would never reach such an exalted position.

Scholars have noted that Othello can be viewed as a generic figure, an Everyman operating within a tragic world. But the scholarly literature on this play has hardly made note of the close affinity between certain of Othello's mental traits and similar traits possessed by the characters surrounding him. Particularly neglected is the tendency that Othello shares with other prominent representatives of Venetian society to worship Reason, to view and construct themselves as rational beings, and to establish their reputations as men of reason. As I shall show, this observation is of particular importance in understanding Othello's agitation. Several characters in this play, not least Othello himself, are far removed from rationality, but they perceive themselves as acting and thinking rationally. They tend to deny their own authentic emotions, and remain unaware of the emotional manipulations to which they are subjected. Iago discerns this 'desire for reason' in his commander, as well as in other Venetians, and seeks to take maximal advantage of their fixation when constructing his emotional appeals.

As I shall demonstrate, it is Othello's desire to satisfy his Reason that dictates Iago's rhetorical strategy as he seeks to agitate his commander. The ancient's appeals are all variations on the figure known in Shakespeare's era as 'reasoning'. This figure belongs to the larger group of amplification figures, but it differs from other amplifications in two significant ways: first, it cunningly disguises itself beneath a seemingly rational veneer, so that its object will remain unaware that he is the target of an emotional appeal; second, amplification figures generally consist of long, continuous and eloquent speeches, divided into topics and delivered by an emotionally stirring orator; in 'reasoning', by contrast, the manipulator needs fewer words and the amplification occurs mainly within the target's own mind. This figure flatters the target of persuasion, who considers himself a man of reason, by satisfying his desire for rationality; it encourages his rational faculties to nurture and cultivate the seeds that the manipulator has sown in his mind.

This rhetorical observation clarifies how the walls of reason crumble around the very character who supposedly fortified his soul to an extraordinary degree against the dangerous assaults of passion. Instead of attacking these walls through a direct and conventional emotional appeal, Iago locates what might be termed the 'self-destructive gene' within Othello's mind, and causes it to undermine its own fortifications.

3.1 The Ideal of Reason in *Othello*'s Venice

3.1.1 Impeccable Reason in the Venetian Government

The name of the city of Venice had become legendary throughout early modern Europe. Despite its decline in Shakespeare's time, the city retained its status in European eyes as the quintessence of beauty, virtue, prosperity, civic concord, and – above all – sound government. It was in this city that Giraldi Cinthio chose to locate the opening and closing episodes of the novella that would serve as Shakespeare's primary source for the plot of *Othello*. Yet Cinthio dedicates little of his text to describing Venice and its populace, nor does his novella resonate with the mythical aura surrounding the city's name. By contrast, Shakespeare accords ample space to the characterisation of the city in his dramatic adaptation of the same story, emphasising the enlightened, ideal nature of its ruling body. He structures *Othello* in the mould of a mediaeval morality play, with the characters and the fictional space organised in polarised, antithetical configurations (such as black and white, good and evil, or love and hatred). In this polarised arrangement, enlightened Venice stands in opposition to Turkey and other barbaric lands: the Turks are heathen and savage, whereas the Venetians are Christian and civilised, blessed with divine protection.

Scene I, iii allocates significant stage time to an exposition of the orderly workings of the Venetian government, focusing the audience's attention on this wholesome apparatus. The central trait of this government, and the principal manifestation of its enlightened nature, is its sound and proper use of Reason. In this scene, the duke and the senators are confronted with information, arriving from afar, regarding the deceptive manoeuvres of the Turkish fleet, as well as with Brabantio's accusations that Othello has drugged Desdemona. The way in which the Venetian authorities handle these issues is sober and prudent: they examine the data and the accusations according to the 'assay of reason' (I, iii, 17–19), ignore 'thin habits and poor likelihoods' and attempt to hold a discussion based on clear-cut proof (ll. 106–109). It should be kept in mind that in *The Merchant of Venice*, Shakespeare also characterises Venice as exhibiting an effective government and the rule of law: only in such a law-abiding city can Shylock demand the redemption of his bond – which prior to Portia's learned intervention seemed a legitimate and valid act – and only there can he oblige the duke to honour his demand. Conversely, it is only in such a law-abiding city that the schooled Portia can produce, in an elegant and surprising twist, a long-forgotten law on the basis of which the threat to citizen Antonio is thoroughly annulled. However, the emphasis placed on reason as a central factor in an enlightened government is unique to *Othello* – a play intensely and singularly preoccupied with human rationality and its interplay with emotion.

The tendency of the senate members to engage in rational discourse is emphasised both literally and structurally by the playwright. In this context, it is important to note the distinct and precise use that the duke and the senators make of words denoting different degrees of certainty, such as knowledge, suspicion and conjecture. They do not confuse these different levels; rather, they employ the most appropriate and precise word when referring to each particular level. In addition, the discussion in the Senate Scene is based on processes of reasoning, with sentences constructed in the 'if ... then ...' pattern:[2]

> I SENATOR: When we consider
> The importancy of Cyprus to the Turk,
> And let ourselves again but understand
> That as it more concerns the Turk than Rhodes,
> So may he with more facile question bear it,
> For that it stands not in such warlike brace,
> But altogether lacks the abilities
> That Rhodes is dressed in. If we make thought of this,
> We must not think the Turk is so unskilful
> To leave that latest which concerns him first,
> Neglecting an attempt of ease and gain
> To wake and wage a danger profitless. (I, iii, 19–30)

The conditional clause pattern is one of the prominent linguistic features of *Othello* in general; as we shall see, its prominence is not limited to the Senate Scene or to the characters participating in it. Such clauses constitute the most direct expression of the rational state of mind, which is based for the most part on the process of reasoning. The *Oxford English Dictionary* defines 'reasoning' as 'the process by which one judgement is deduced from another or others which are given'.[3] The conditional clause in the 'if ... then ...' pattern, then, is a typical, direct, explicit, and concise representation of rational thought – or of thought that *appears* rational.

3.1.2 The General Attachment to Reason in Venetian Society

While noting the central role of Reason in the Venetian government in *Othello*, scholars have overlooked the fact that the 'language of reason' found in the Senate Scene characterises not only the members of

2   In these sentences in the 'if ... then ...' pattern, and in others to be discussed below, the word 'then' does not always appear, and the 'if' element is at times represented by the word 'when'.

3   *OED*, 'reasoning', vbl., n.

the senate, but also other characters in the play. This oversight might stem from the fact that the senators display exemplary rationality, in both word and deed, whereas other Venetian characters are revealed to be manifestly irrational. The senators and the duke, as mentioned, speak the language of logic and employ the tools of rational discourse, with which they succeed both in deciphering the maritime manoeuvres of the Turks and in quenching the fire of anger that Iago seeks to ignite in the city through Brabantio. By contrast, while other Venetian characters display an idiom and a semantic field similar to those of their rulers, their rational language is nothing but the trappings and the suits of the irrational soul beneath (as elaborated upon in 3.1.3).

The worship of the rational faculty in Venice is expressed throughout the play, first and foremost in the vocabulary of the Venetian characters. The words 'reason' and 'cause' appear as frequently in the course of *Othello* as they do in *Julius Caesar* and *Hamlet*, both of which are also concerned with the interrelation of Reason and Passion in the human mind.[4] The Venetian characters in *Othello* use these words as part of their attempts to discuss reality as if it were a logical sequence of events, a series of causes and effects whose interrelationship can be grasped by one's faculty of Reason. In addition to Othello, Brabantio and Roderigo, whose language of apparent reason will be addressed in detail below, the text spoken by other Venetian characters also exhibits verbal traits that testify to a preference for rational thought processes. Thus, Lodovico and Gratiano speak a full-fledged 'language of reason' of the type we encounter in the Senate Scene. Like the senators and the duke, they engage in processes of reasoning, in the course of which they report the various facts as they perceive them, choosing words appropriate to the level of certainty of the data and of their own conclusions.[5] Even

---

4   The word 'reason' occurs 13 times in *Othello*, 15 times in *Julius Caesar* and 16 times in *Hamlet*. 'Cause' appears 15 times in *Othello*, 16 in *Julius Caesar* and 17 in *Hamlet*. Compare these rates to those in three Shakespearean tragedies in which the discussion of the faculty of reason as a theme is less fully developed: 'reason' appears 6 times in *Macbeth*, 4 times in *Anthony and Cleopatra* and 7 times in *Romeo and Juliet*; 'cause' makes 4 appearances in *Macbeth*, 6 in *Anthony and Cleopatra* and 5 in *Romeo and Juliet*.

5   See: V, i, 38, 42–44, 49, 51, 66; V, ii, 234, 253–254.

Desdemona, whose non-rational nature has been justly emphasised by scholars, at times reveals her Venetian roots: she speaks in a balanced, symmetrical pattern, very similar to that in which Shakespeare constructs Cordelia's seemingly rational and cold words to Lear;[6] she engages in such thinking processes as reasoning (III, iii, 48–50) and syllogism (III, iv, 134–142) and uses such terms as 'judgement', 'common reason' and 'cause'.[7]

3.1.3 Roderigo and Brabantio as Men of Apparent Reason

Roderigo's conduct is irrational in the extreme: conventionally characterised as 'the lover', his perspective is too narrow to contain anything but the desired Desdemona; doting on a married woman, he is deluded time and again by Iago's obviously baseless promises of help in attaining her; he sells all his land and sails in her wake to Cyprus, disregarding the possibility that he may find himself embroiled in battles with the Turks. However, a careful examination of this passion-besotted character reveals that Roderigo in fact perceives himself to be rational, receptive to rational argumentation. This can be deduced from the strategy of persuasion employed against him by Iago, the consummate psychologist and judge of human nature: it is not mere chance that, when seeking to influence Roderigo, Iago adopts a strategy that is outwardly rational, enlisting the help of syllogistic processes;[8] similarly, wishing to pacify Roderigo through flattery, Iago chooses to applaud his 'judgement' and 'wit'[9] (IV, ii, 206–207). Incited by Iago to murder Cassio, Roderigo demands 'reasons' for the deed; like Othello in the final scene and Brutus in *Julius Caesar*, Roderigo expresses a conception that uses rational tools to justify murder:

---

6   Compare *Othello* I, iii, 178–187, with *King Lear* I, i, 90–93.
7   III, iii, 50, 64; III, iv, 152.
8   Syllogism: 'reasoning from generals to the particulars' (*OED*, 'Syllogism', 2). See, e.g.: I, iii, 336–338; II, i, 216–223, 246–248.
9   Wit: 'The faculty of thinking and reasoning in general; mental capacity, understanding, intellect, reason. *arch.*' (*OED*, 'wit', n., 2a).

IAGO: ... if thou hast that in thee indeed, which I have greater reason to be-
             lieve now than ever – I mean purpose, courage and valour – this
             night show it ...
RODERIGO: Well, what is it? Is it within *reason* and compass?
             ...
             I will hear further *reason* for this.
IAGO: And you shall be satisfied. (IV, ii, 207–235; my italics)

RODERIGO: I have no great devotion to the deed,
             And yet he hath given me satisfying *reasons*. (V, i, 8–9; my italics)

Far from being rational, Roderigo seeks to impose reason on events or
on acts that are themselves completely irrational. This distinction –
between genuinely rational characters and characters who have a false
image of themselves as men of reason, who tend to rationalise reality
– is crucial to the present discussion. It will also serve the discussion
of Othello himself and of the emotional appeal that brings about his
downfall.

Brabantio, like Roderigo, is not rational at all, but is convinced
that he observes the world through the lens of rationality. From the
moment he learns of his daughter's elopement, he is moved to action
by the rage of a cheated and abandoned father; his accusations against
Othello of witchcraft and of having drugged his daughter lack a
factual basis, yet their emotional kernel, when presented to the duke,
is wrapped in a husk of supposedly logical argument, based on distinctions between the probable, the possible and the impossible in nature:

For I'll *refer* me to all things of *sense*,
If she in chains of magic were not bound ...
Judge me the world, if 'tis not gross in *sense*
That thou hast practised on her with foul charms,
Abused her delicate youth with drugs or minerals
That weaken motion. I'll have't disputed on;
'Tis probable and palpable to thinking. (I, ii, 64–76; my italics)

For nature so preposterously to err,
Being not deficient, blind, or lame of sense,
Sans witchcraft could not. (I, iii, 62–64)

122

> It is a *judgement* maimed and most imperfect
> That will confess perfection so could err
> Against all rules of nature, and must be driven
> To find out practises of cunning hell
> Why this should be. (I, iii, 99–103; my italics)

At first glance, it may come as a surprise that Brabantio and Othello exhibit similar traits. However, considering Shakespeare's subtle linkage between these two characters, the elderly senator can in fact be regarded as a caricature of the general, who also adorns himself with the language of reason, while his actions and thoughts are swayed by passions (as will be shown in detail below). The exaggerated character traits highlighted in the caricatured portrayal of Brabantio can be seen as guidelines to assist spectators in distinguishing the more subtle version of these traits in the character of Othello. The similarity between the general and the senator is suggested, among other things, by the identical language they employ, foreshadowing what turns out to be their shared tendency to be fatally agitated;[10] by their use of conditional clauses that presume to formulate a clear, definite set of rules according to which the world operates (I, ii, 98–99); and by their presumption in using apparent logic to predict future events (I, ii, 95–97; parallel expressions by Othello are presented in detail below).

3.1.4 The Appeal to Brabantio's Emotion

Thus far, this chapter has surveyed the general attachment of the Venetian characters in *Othello* to reason, and the particular tendency of certain characters to mistakenly see themselves as men of reason. We can now approach the first emotional appeal in the play, namely, Iago's attempt to incite Brabantio against Othello (I, i, 80–116). As will be shown, the play establishes a direct link between this appeal and its degree of success, Brabantio's pseudo-rational character, and the special place accorded to reason in *Othello*'s Venice.

In discussing this appeal, scholars have focused on Iago's coarse, blunt figurative language and its role in his characterisation, while

10 'With all my heart' (I, iii, 190–193, 274; IV, i, 205; V, ii, 34).

overlooking a simple fact easily noted by any reader or spectator who follows the plot: Iago fails the test of rhetoric. In other words, he does not stir the desired passion in his addressee.[11] The ancient's working assumption, as it were, is reflected in the way he instructs Roderigo to waken the senator: Iago presumes that the greater the discomfort and alarm with which Brabantio is roused from his bed, the greater will be his rage. Accordingly, Iago directs Roderigo to call out loudly and waken Brabantio 'with like timorous accent and dire yell' (I, i, 76–78). Roderigo is apparently too refined to fulfil Iago's instructions and produce the desired effect. The text does not divulge any information regarding the strength of Roderigo's call; however, since Iago takes over from Roderigo after only one line, we can conclude that the latter's shouting was, in Iago's opinion, too restrained. The vocal and emotional strength of the 'terrible summons' produced by Iago is evidenced in his massive use of rhetorical figures of repetition, such as *epizeuxis* and *ploce*: 'Thieves! Thieves! Thieves! ... Thieves! Thieves! ... Now, now, very now ... Arise, arise ...' (I, i, 80–90).

Besides vocal vehemence and emotional intensity, Iago bases his attempt to enrage Brabantio on a potent stream of hyperbole. Such hyperboles, which are sometimes classified as 'word amplifications' or 'vertical amplifications', appear in early modern rhetorical treatises as one of the central means of emotional appeal:[12]

> 'Zounds, sir, you're *robbed*; for shame, put on your gown;
> Your heart is *burst*; you have lost *half your soul*;
> Even now, now, very now, an *old black ram*
> Is tupping your *white ewe*. Arise, arise;
> Awake the snorting citizens with the bell,
> Or else *the devil* will make a grandsire of you.
> Arise, I say. (I, i, 87–93; my italics)

Iago's appeal to Brabantio's emotions can be defined as an 'emotional' emotional appeal, which seeks to agitate the addressee through

---

11   Terence Hawkes even goes so far as to base his more general assertions on the claim that Iago 'convinces Brabantio by the reasonableness' of his arguments (Hawkes is referring here directly to lines 89–90). See: Terence Hawkes, *Shakespeare and the Reason* (London: Routledge & Kegan Paul, 1968), p. 107.

12   See, e.g., Richard Sherry, *A Treatise on Schemes and Tropes* (1550), pp. 70–71.

a demonstration of urgency and vehement passion, harsh imagery, and the narrowing of his perspective by means of figures of repetition.[13] As noted, Iago's rhetorical strategy fails utterly; this failure is due to a mismatch between the rhetorical means and the specific addressee on whom these means are supposed to act. As stressed above, Brabantio has pretensions of being ruled by rational thought; the emotional nature of the speech delivered by Iago, as we shall now see, is too exaggerated to withstand the senator's 'assay of reason' and to weaken his fortifications of rationality.

Iago attempts to agitate Brabantio with the help of the phenomenon referred to in contemporary studies as 'emotional contagion', namely, the stirring up of an addressee by externalising emotion.[14] This technique is recommended in Roman and English Renaissance treatises on rhetoric elaborating on the subject of emotional appeal. Indeed, authors from the Roman Cicero to the English Wilson and Wright agree that a display of emotion is a necessary condition for agitating the addressee.[15] Yet the first task of the rhetorician is not the choice of rhetorical strategy, but the definition of the specific audience and its characteristics; it is solely on this basis that the appropriate strategy should be chosen. Brabantio, the would-be man of reason, is an exceptional addressee; from his very first words, it is clear that he is not a member of the group prone to 'emotional contagion'. The senator seeks, first of all, a logical cause for the noise that has awakened him:

What is the *reason* of this terrible summons? (I, i, 83; my italics)

---

13   On the relationship between the narrowness of perspective and the intensity of emotion, see Chapter Five, p. 220.

14   John T. Cacioppo, Elaine Hatfield and Richard L. Rapson, 'Emotional Contagion', *Current Directions in Psychological Science*, Vol. 2, No. 3 (1993), pp. 96–99.

15   See, e.g.: Cicero, *De Oratore*, II, pp. 188–192; Quintilian, *Institutio Oratoria*, 6.2, 26–36, pp. 59–65; Thomas Wilson, *The Art of Rhetoric* (1560), ed. Peter E. Medine (Philadelphia: Pennsylvania University Press, 1994), p. 163; Thomas Wright, *The Passions of the Minde in Generall* (1604), pp. 172–176.

As a senator and a respected citizen of Venice, Brabantio strives to implement the 'assay of reason' when observing the surrounding reality; this is also his attitude towards the stream of hyperboles aimed at him. Accordingly, he diagnoses his interlocutor as lacking in rationality (as mentioned, the word 'wit' was synonymous in Shakespeare's time with 'reason'):[16]

> What, have you lost your *wits*? (I, i, 93; my italics)

It is evident, based on Sherry's *A Treatise on Schemes and Tropes* (1550), that hyperbole is not an appropriate tool for manipulating characters such as Brabantio: it is a figure more suitable to the persuasion of 'the commons' or 'the rude people', whose judgement is not highly developed.[17] Indeed, the play explicitly shows Brabantio rebuffing the 'word amplifications' directed at him, through the use of a logical thought process. Iago's words do not succeed in penetrating his mind, since they fail the Venetian assay of reason:

> BRABANTIO: What tell'st thou me of robbing? This is Venice;
>   My house is not a grange. (I, i, 106–107)

After Iago hurls his last metaphor, in which he likens Desdemona and Othello's making love to a 'beast with two backs', Brabantio assails Iago with the descriptive noun 'villain'. Iago's reaction is short:

> You are a senator. (I, i, 117)

The original intention behind this sentence is not entirely clear, and the short line has garnered various interpretations. As an example, we may consider the gloss of the editor of the Cambridge edition, who provides two possible interpretations: (a) Iago intends to repay Brabantio with his own unflattering descriptive noun, but at the last

---

16   See note 9.
17   'A great part of eloquence is set in increasing and diminishing, and serveth for this purpose, that the thing should seem as great as it is indeed, lesser or greater than it seemeth to many. For the rude people have commonly a preposterous judgement, and take the worst things for the best, and the best for the worst ...'. Richard Sherry, *A Treatise on Schemes and Tropes* (1550), p. 70.

moment 'smothers' the sentence he has already begun to articulate, and completes it in a way that is inoffensive; (b) Iago pronounces the word 'senator' with ironic politeness, thereby casting doubt on the dignity of Brabantio's political position. The analysis suggested in this study offers an additional interpretation: Iago's choice of the word 'senator' is in fact an expression or admission of the failure of his rhetorical strategy. Brabantio is indeed a senator, and here, for the first time, Iago addresses him with words appropriate to the matter they are meant to reflect (to use the accepted Latin rhetorical terms, Iago closes the gap between *res* and *verba* that has characterised his appeal to Brabantio up to this moment). After this line, Iago no longer employs, either in the scene under discussion or elsewhere in the play, hyperboles for the purpose of agitating and persuading his various addressees.

Notably, it is Roderigo – whom, unlike Iago, scholars have not praised for his rhetorical skills – who takes the reins at this point and achieves the desired outcome: enraging Brabantio. Unlike Iago, he addresses the senator in a sober manner, directing his words to the addressee's rational faculty. The rational nature of Roderigo's monologue is clearly manifested in the use of conditional clauses of the 'if ... then ...' pattern, which, as shown, characterise both the rational and the would-be rational characters in the play:

> *If't* be your pleasure and most wise consent
>   ... that your fair daughter,
> At this odd-even and dull watch o' the night,
> Transported ...
> To the gross clasps of a lascivious Moor:
> *If* this be known to you, and your allowance,
> We *then* have done you bold and saucy wrongs.
> But *if* you know not this, my manners tell me,
> We have your wrong rebuke ...
> Your daughter, *if* you have not given her leave,
> I say again, hath made a gross revolt ...
> ...
> *If* she be in her chamber or your house,
> Let loose on me the justice of the state
> For thus deluding you. (I, i, 120–139; my italics)

It is precisely this moderate, unemotional appeal, seemingly directed to the addressee's rational faculty and challenging him to perform his own reasoning processes, that has an immediate impact on Brabantio, arousing in him extreme emotion.[18] His agitated state takes the textual form of short, at times fragmented sentences, whose shifting subject attests to the jerky movements of Brabantio's mind (I, i, 159–166). The explosion of anger following Roderigo's speech is also expressed metaphorically: Brabantio immediately commands his servants to 'strike on the tinder' (I, i, 139–143) and then instructs the members of the household, as they step outside carrying burning torches, to go in different directions. Iago's scheme to ignite the city with the fire of rage is about to become reality, as a result of Roderigo's unemotional emotional appeal.

The play does not indicate whether Iago is aware that he has chosen the wrong rhetorical means to agitate Brabantio, nor whether he learns from his own failure. It is also moot whether witnessing Roderigo's effective speech makes Iago realise that characters such as Brabantio are more easily agitated by means of 'rational' emotional appeals. Nevertheless, Iago does employ this same rhetorical method later in the play: like Roderigo's address to Brabantio, Iago arouses Othello's anger by appealing to his intellect, as it were, and by challenging what Othello considers to be his rational faculty. As for Roderigo, he has clearly learned nothing from his accidentally successful rhetorical experience in I, i. He subsequently fails to recognise that Iago manipulates him time and again using the same rhetorical tactic with which he himself manipulated Brabantio.

---

18   Compare: '... wise men are most moved with sound reasons & lesse with Passions: contrariwise the common people or men not of deepe judgement, are more perswaded with passions in the speakers'. Thomas Wright, *The Passions of the Minde in Generall* (1604), p. 174.

3.2 Othello's Desire for Reason

3.2.1 Othello's Compulsive Rationalisation of Reality

The ultimate expression of Othello's tendency to rationalise reality and to bind it with the chains of reason is his reference to the murder of Desdemona as the outcome of rational judgement. The motives for the murder are, of course, jealousy and anger; however, when Othello enters the bed chamber with the aim of strangling his wife, he veils these passions beneath a seemingly rational verbal exterior, describing the act he is about to perform as the implementation of justice:

> It is the *cause*, it is the *cause*, my soul ...
> ... she must die, else she'll betray more men. (V, ii, 1–6; my italics)

The repetitive use of the word 'cause' in this passage is an indication of Othello's act of rationalisation, since this word is synonymous, both today and in Shakespeare's era, with 'reason'. As mentioned at the beginning of this chapter, these two words appear frequently in the play, usually expressing the tendency of certain characters to perceive reality as a series of events linked together in a logical way. A similar use of the word 'cause' in presenting murder as an act stemming from the dictates of sober reason was discussed in the previous chapter, with reference to Brutus. His speech to the people purports from the very first line to offer a just, logical reason for murdering Caesar:

> Romans, countrymen, and lovers, hear me for my *cause*. (III, ii, 13; my italics)

Indeed, Brutus and Othello display a patently similar lack of awareness of the nature and force of the passion dwelling in them, as well as an identical certainty that they are acting in accordance with the dictates of reason.

Chapter Five will discuss the general tendency to rationalise reality as part of Man's ever-present need for security. In a similar vein, *Othello* seems to draw a direct line between the tendency to rationalise reality, and the level of self-assurance of the rationalising characters. Thus, at the beginning of the tragedy, Othello's character seems to be the embodiment of self-assurance; accordingly, he grasps reality as a series of phenomena and events that are related to one another and that can be predicted by means of reason and one's life experience:

> Let him do his spite;
> My services which I have done the signiory
> Shall out-tongue his complaints. (I, ii, 17–19)

> Not I; I must be found.
> My parts, my title, and my perfect soul
> Shall manifest me rightly. (Ibid., 30–32)

> Were it my cue to fight, I should have known it
> Without a prompter. (Ibid., 83–84)

The use in these lines of the word 'shall' is further indication of Othello's great self-confidence. As stressed throughout this study, Shakespeare frequently makes use of the semantic difference between the verbal auxiliary denoting future action, 'will', which is 'softer' in its degree of certainty, and 'shall', which expresses the presumption of knowing the future.

Othello's self-delusion, in believing that the world is familiar to him and operates logically, is also manifested in the questions that he poses at the beginning of the play. These can be divided into two categories: questions typical of a general who seeks to gather data from his subordinates in order to carry out assessments, make decisions and prepare a response to events (I, ii, 32, 36, 38); and rhetorical questions, which express his self-confidence and his presumption in predicting future events (I, ii, 84–85, 87, 88–91). These rhetorical questions are in stark contrast to those he will begin to ask in scene III, iii, when his clear, orderly worldview will begin to totter in response to the doubts and suspicions planted in his mind by Iago.

3.2.2 Structural Expressions of Othello's Desire for Reason

Othello's rationalisation of reality, like Brutus', is expressed structurally through the use, among other things, of symmetries. The symmetrical manner in which Shakespeare fashions some of the sentences uttered by Othello guides the actor to express the character's constant effort to capture reality in the pincer-like grip of a contrived balance – balance being a dominant characteristic of rational discourse. In accordance with his own tendency to fashion reality by means of symmetrical utterances, Othello reacts enthusiastically when discovering the same tendency in Iago's speech and agrees with its content. Iago employs a symmetrical pattern because he is aware of Othello's affection for symmetry; he knows that it will be rhetorically effective to address Othello in his own language:

> IAGO: Do it not with poison; strangle her in her bed, even the bed she
>   hath contaminated.
> OTHELLO: Good, good! The justice of it pleases; very good. (IV, i, 195–197)

Othello's penchant for rationalising symmetry is particularly jarring when he imposes it on matters that are utterly alien to reason, or applies it in moments of extreme passion:

> OTHELLO: She loved me for the dangers I had passed,
>   And I loved her that she did pity them. (I, iii, 166–167)

> OTHELLO: Thy bed, lust-stained, shall with lust's blood be spotted. (V, i, 36)

> OTHELLO: I kissed thee ere I killed thee: no way but this,
>   Killing myself, to die upon a kiss. (V, ii, 354–355)

As shown at the beginning of this chapter, the processes of logical discourse that characterise the Venetian government are formally expressed through the use of the 'if ... then ...' sentence pattern. As we have seen, the outward trappings of this language are also adopted by Brabantio, who cloaks his inner, irrational nature in a rational façade, and by Brutus, during his speech to the people in *Julius Caesar*.[19] Othello, who shows similarities to both these characters in terms of mental interplay between passion and reason, produces more 'if ... then ...' sentences than does any other Shakespearean character;[20] and, like his symmetries, his conditional clauses also grate on the ear when spoken in contexts unrelated to reason, or in highly emotional situations:

> If after every tempest come such calms,
> May the winds blow till they have wakened death ... (II, i, 177–178)

> If it were now to die,
> 'Twere now to be most happy ... (Ibid., 181–182)

> Perdition catch my soul
> But I do love thee; And when I love thee not,
> Chaos is come again. (III, iii, 90–92)

> I had been happy if the general camp,
> Pioners and all, had tasted her sweet body
> So I had nothing known. (III, iii, 346–348)

> If I quench thee, thou flaming minister,
> I can again thy former light restore,
> Should I repent me ... (V, ii, 8–10)

> When I have plucked the rose,
> I cannot give it vital growth again ... (Ibid., 13–14)

Othello's desire for supposedly rational activity is also expressed in Shakespeare's cunning use of the word 'satisfaction', in its various inflections. We have already seen the way in which Iago *satisfies* Roderigo's thirst for rationality when providing him with 'satisfying

---

19 '*If* any, speak; for him have I offended ... *If* any, speak; for him have I offended ... *If* any, speak; for him have I offended. I pause for a reply ... *Then* none have I offended' (*Julius Caesar*, III, ii, 25–31; my italics).
20 I, ii, 20–21; I, ii, 25–28; I, ii, 83–84; I, iii, 117–120; I, iii, 264–270; II, iii, 188–189; III, iii, 143–145; III, iii, 280; IV, i, 235–236; V, ii, 138–140; V, ii, 143–145; V, ii, 284.

reasons' for murdering Cassio.[21] Roderigo himself, in his successful emotional appeal to Brabantio, presents the senator with processes of deductive reasoning and challenges him to examine the data employed in these processes, and thus to 'straight *satisfy*' himself (I, i, 136). Othello exhibits the very same thirst, and the following lines testify that Reason satisfies a fervid need of his:

OTHELLO:	... I'll not endure it. Would I were *satisfied*!
IAGO:	I see, sir, you are eaten up with passion.
	I do repent me that I put it to you.
	You would be *satisfied*?
OTHELLO:	Would? Nay, I *will*.
IAGO:	And may. But how? How *satisfied*, my lord?
	(III, iii, 391–395; my italics)

IAGO:	What shall I say? Where's *satisfaction*?
	It is impossible you should see this,
	Were they as prime as goats, as hot as monkeys ...
	... But yet, I say,
	If imputation and strong circumstances,
	Which lead directly to the door of truth,
	Will give you *satisfaction*, you may have't.
OTHELLO:	Give me a living *reason* she's disloyal.
	(III, iii, 402–410; my italics)

3.3 Rousing Othello's Emotions

3.3.1 *The Figure of Reasoning*

In his *Treatise on Schemes and Tropes* (1550), Richard Sherry lists 'reasoning' as one of the various figures of amplification. In comparison with other types of amplification, this figure is unique in that the process of amplification that it engenders takes place mainly in the imagination of the addressee rather than in an elaborate speech spoken

---

21   IV, ii, 235–236; V, i, 9 (see 3.1.3).

by the persuader. A rhetorician who chooses to employ the figure of reasoning will pithily describe to his addressee a part, a cause, an effect or a factor of the *thing* that he seeks to amplify. The addressee will thereby be induced to complete in his imagination that same *thing*, based on his own reason and acquaintance with the laws of nature and the ways of the world:

> There is another kind of amplifying called reasoning, when of those things that either follow or go before, the hearer doth gather how great that thing is that we would to be amplified. By things that go before, as when Homer armeth Achilles, or Hector to battle, by the great preparation, we gather how sore the fight shall be. Of things that follow: How much wine Antony drank, when that having such a strong body he was not able to digest it, but showed it by the next day after. Of things joined to, as when Maro sayeth to Polyphemus: He had the body of a pineapple tree for a staff in his hand.[22]

Following are examples of Iago's versatile use of this figure. In discussing them, I shall refer to the part, the cause, or the effect of the *thing*, using the expression 'the tip of the iceberg'. The *thing* itself – that is, the whole, amplified picture that the addressee of the manipulation reconstructs in his mind – will be referred to as 'the iceberg'. The addressee, in an ongoing, lifelong process of learning, has mapped out the world, seen many icebergs and internalised their characteristics and the typical shape in which nature fashions them; accordingly, when he sees the tip of an iceberg, he 'knows', following a simple process of reasoning, the 'logical' way of reconstructing its contours concealed beneath the water. The person observing the tip of an iceberg 'knows' – based on his acquaintance with nature's ways – which shapes would be 'implausible' or 'illogical' for the submerged part of the iceberg. The term 'nature's ways' is relevant to this discussion of the process of reasoning, since characters in *Othello* persuade or are persuaded by the use of arguments based on generally accepted ideas regarding the concept of 'nature'.[23] These characters, Othello among them, regard their acquaintance with nature as a reliable body of knowledge; they do not take into account 'how nature erring from

---

22   Richard Sherry, *A Treatise on Schemes and Tropes* (1550), p. 76.
23   See, e.g.: I, iii, 61–64, 96–98, 99–103, 319–322; II, i, 222–223; III, iii, 229–235; III, iv, 137–139; IV, i, 39–40; V, ii, 42.

itself' sometimes creates icebergs whose shape is anomalous, 'unnatural' – icebergs, that is, whose visible tip is deceptive and does not relate *logically* to what is concealed below.

In light of the above, it is clear that the tendency to reconstruct a whole picture based on one piece of evidence and to consider it certain, characterises would-be rational minds. Those endowed with such a mind display a seemingly-rational thought mechanism, which appears highly developed, on the one hand, but which, on the other, is vigorously employed to the point of obsession – in other words, a rational mechanism put to exaggerated use by a non-rational force. This tendency is presented in *Othello* as early as I, iii, when Brabantio accuses Othello of drugging Desdemona: the outraged father draws false conclusions based on his 'judgement' and his acquaintance with the laws of 'nature',[24] and considers the results of his reasoning to be full-fledged facts. Based on the information supplied by Iago and Roderigo, and on the fact that the search for Desdemona within his home has failed, Brabantio concludes that his daughter has been 'stol'n'. He reconstructs the whole picture – the entire iceberg, as it were – based on his 'knowledge' that it is impossible for the blood of a chaste, white maid to be stirred by the appearance of a dark-skinned man. Therefore, the only possible conclusion is that Othello used 'drugs and minerals' in order to ferment his daughter's blood. For this purpose, he must have had recourse to special drugs and spells; drugs and spells such as these – so Brabantio has learned in the course of his life – can be obtained only from mountebanks (ll. 60–64).

Iago is well aware of the human tendency to formulate a single, absolute set of laws according to which nature operates. His rhetorical expertise stems, among other things, from his ability to understand how each of his addressees perceives this natural order; that is, what each specific addressee considers 'natural' and what for him is 'against the laws of nature'. This understanding allows Iago to present to each of his addressees an iceberg-tip that suits him personally, and according to which the addressee will reconstruct the whole iceberg desired by the manipulator.

---

24   See: I, iii, 62, 96, 99, 101.

The first character upon whom Iago implements the figure of reasoning is Roderigo. As shown above, the latter is a fitting candidate for inclusion in the category of the Rationalising Man, and is therefore an appropriate addressee for this figure. As we shall see, when Iago uses the figure of reasoning on Othello, he provides him with only minute clues, tiny tips of the iceberg, and leaves the addressee's reason-craving mind to perform the entire amplification on its own. When manipulating Roderigo, by contrast, Iago does not rely entirely on his target's rationalising abilities: instead, he leads him through a sort of 'guided' process of reasoning. Immediately following the reunion of the main characters near the port in Cyprus – following their seafaring journey – Iago seeks to persuade Roderigo that Desdemona and Cassio exhibit mutual passionate sexual attraction. Sexual attraction, particularly that which supposedly exists between Desdemona and Cassio, is of course invisible to the public eye. What Roderigo actually saw at the moment of Cassio's entrance on stage is a kiss planted by the courteous lieutenant on Desdemona's hand (or, more precisely, in accordance with the conventions of the period, Cassio kissed his own fingers that held Desdemona's hand). Iago manipulates Roderigo into seeing this kiss as the tip of the iceberg, taking pains to remind him of the law that rules nature; in other words, of the true shape of the iceberg concealed beneath the tip of a courteous kiss:

> Lechery, by this hand; an index and obscure prologue to the history of lust and foul thoughts ... when these mutualities so marshal the way, hard at hand comes the master and main exercise, the incorporate conclusion, Pish! (II, i, 243–248)

3.3.2 The Effectiveness of Reasoning in Manipulating Othello

Iago first learns of Othello's tendency to 'reconstruct icebergs' – and, therefore, of his being the ideal addressee to be stirred by the figure of reasoning – during the first night the Venetians spend in Cyprus. The general questions Iago regarding the circumstances of the fight between Cassio and Montano; in response, the ancient pretends to defend the lieutenant by means of a deductive thought process:

136

> ... surely Cassio, I believe, received
> From him that fled some strange indignity
> Which patience could not pass. (II, iii, 225–227)

Judging by what follows, Iago easily succeeds in 'transmitting' this thought pattern and 'infecting' his addressee with it. Just as intended by the manipulator, Othello perceives the mincing tone with which Iago downplays the events as the tip of an iceberg, undoubtedly suggesting Cassio's extraordinarily uncontrolled behaviour. Relying with such confidence on his powers of reason, Othello tends here to confuse suspicion and conjecture with true knowledge (as he will repeatedly do on subsequent occasions). He deludes himself that the picture seen in his mind's eye, which recreates Cassio's behaviour based on the partial data provided by Iago, is the fruit of logical thought, thus constituting an accurate reflection of a real event. He therefore considers this picture to be a valid piece of legal evidence, and judges Cassio accordingly in an expeditious procedure:

> I know, Iago,
> Thy honesty and love doth mince this matter,
> Making it light to Cassio. Cassio, I love thee,
> But never more be officer of mine. (II, iii, 227–230)

Iago will henceforth base the entire process of arousing Othello's passions on the latter's tendency to recreate icebergs from their visible tips, and to see this imaginative recreation as the product of a sound, logical thought process, with the status of fact and solid evidence.

3.3.3 The Emotional Appeal Activated by Iago

The sum total of rhetorical means by which Iago chooses to provoke Othello's anger can be defined as a series of diverse reasoning figures, each of which provides the addressee with the tip of an iceberg and leaves him to complete the picture. Thus, at the very beginning of the process:

```
IAGO:       Ha! I like not that.
OTHELLO:                       What dost thou say?
IAGO:       Nothing, my lord; or if – I know not what. (III, iii, 35–36)
```

And immediately afterwards:

```
IAGO:                          My noble lord –
OTHELLO:  What dost thou say, Iago?
IAGO:                          Did Michael Cassio,
            When you wooed my lady, Know of your love?
OTHELLO:  He did from first to last. Why dost thou ask?
IAGO:       But for a *satisfaction* of my thought;
            No further harm. (III, iii, 92–97; my italics)
```

The use of the word 'satisfaction' in line 96 has great rhetorical importance for Iago. One of his various means of persuasion is to manipulate his addressees into the mode of thinking he desires (which to some extent characterises them in any case), by exhibiting a manner of thinking similar to their own.[25] This is a familiar rhetorical tactic, based on the addressee's natural embarrassment or unease with certain of his own inclinations. From the moment the manipulator shows that he himself harbours the very same tendency or character trait, the addressee feels more comfortable in revealing it, and will exhibit it more freely. In the example above, Iago displays to Othello his supposed tendency to *satisfy* his thinking by way of completing a picture based on a shred of information. In this way, he encourages Othello to emulate him, that is, to adopt an identical thought pattern. Indeed, Othello's own desire for satisfaction of his thought intensifies, reaching a climax some three hundred lines after Iago's manipulative use of the word 'satisfaction' (see III, iii, 402–410, and pp. 132–133).

An additional means that Iago employs to incite Othello's desire for reason is to repeat the last words spoken by the latter. Iago does this at the very beginning of the process of agitation, in his first in-sinuations regarding the possible existence of secret relations between Desdemona and Cassio. From Othello's point of view, the message suggested by Iago's echoing of his own words is that Iago weighs his words before he gives them breath, not because he has nothing to say,

---

25   See, e.g.: IV, i, 67–72.

but because the things he does not say are presumably terrible. The self-restraint that Iago affects here is the tip of the iceberg in the figure of reasoning; Othello recreates the entire iceberg as a 'monster' that Iago is concealing in his thought:

IAGO: I did not think he [*CASSIO*] had been acquainted with her.
            ...
OTHELLO: ... Discern'st thou aught in that?
            Is he not honest?
IAGO: Honest, my lord?
OTHELLO: Honest? Ay, honest.
IAGO: My lord, for aught I know.
OTHELLO: What dost thou think?
IAGO: Think, my lord?
OTHELLO: Think, my lord! By heaven, he echoes me,
            As if there were some *monster* in his thought
            Too hideous to be shown. (III, iii, 98–109; my italics)

At this point, Othello cannot imagine the 'monster'. His imagination and reason still lack the information needed to complete the picture. Only later, after Iago has provided him with additional 'evidence', does it become fleshed out and real:

OTHELLO: O monstrous, monstrous! (Ibid., 428)

Iago's erotic description to Othello of Cassio's alleged dream (III, iii, 414–427) can also be classified as a figure of reasoning. From these lines, it is evident that Iago adopts a technique of agitation that is utterly different from the one he resorted to in the opening scene, when he tried to agitate Brabantio. Then, like now, his intention was to shock the addressee emotionally by evoking mental images in which the woman belonging[26] to the addressee makes love illicitly. In the opening scene, as we have seen, Iago employs hyperboles, attempting to create in Brabantio's mind the images of Othello and Desdemona as 'an old black ram' atop a 'white ewe' and as 'the beast with two backs'. Here, by contrast, Iago relies on the opposite tactic:

---

26   Prior to her marriage, Desdemona is, according to the social conventions of the period, the property of Brabantio; subsequently, she belongs to Othello.

rather than describing, in exaggerated language or in realistic detail the event that he would like to 'project' onto Othello's mind (i.e., the sexual act between Desdemona and Cassio), he describes realistically a different imagined event, based on which Othello's imagination may fill out the desired picture.

One of Othello's prominent traits is his inability to remain in a state of doubt or uncertainty (III, iii, 384–387); this inability forces him to demand that Iago supply incontestable, visible evidence – or in his words, 'ocular proof' (III, iii, 361) – of his wife's adultery. What Iago provides, fifty lines below the forceful demand, is a fictional account of Cassio dreaming a dream in which he and Desdemona share a lovers' tryst. Ironically, this description is in fact a rhetorical figure referred to in Quintilian's *Institutio Oratoria* as either *Oculos Subiectio* (Ocular Demonstration) or *Evidentia* (Proof)'.[27] The gap between the name of this figure and its true nature is analogous to the gap between what Othello demands of Iago and what he in fact receives: a rhetorician who chooses to employ the figure of *Oculos Subiectio* describes to his addressee the event in question in as detailed a manner as possible, making him visualise it 'as if he [the addressee] had himself been present and seen it in person'.[28] This is exactly what Iago does when describing the loving cries and sighs emitted by Cassio in his sleep, the way he laid his leg on Iago's thigh and the 'hard kisses' he planted on his lips. It is no accident that Iago chooses to describe an event that supposedly took place in his own bed rather than the deed itself, the act of adultery: understanding the outstanding suitability of the figure of reasoning as a means of manipulating his commander, Iago knows that Othello will construct in his own imagination the events that supposedly fed Cassio's dream, and that he will do so in a more passionate and ardent way than Iago himself could do. In order to arouse and activate the relevant mechanism in Othello's mind even further, Iago concludes his description

27 Quintilian, *Institutio Oratoria*, VIII, iii, 61; IX, ii, 40.
28 Expressions of this sort can be found again and again in the works of rhetoricians when referring to this figure. See, e.g.: *Rhetorica Ad Herennium*, IV. LV. 68 – LVI. 69, pp. 405–409; Cicero, *De Oratore*, II, 197; *De Inventione*, I. LIV, 104, pp. 155–157; Thomas Wilson, *The Art of Rhetoric* (1560), p. 161.

with a short line that challenges Othello's imagination by way of negation. The latter's reply indicates the immediate success of Iago's chosen tactic:

IAGO: Nay, this was but his dream.
OTHELLO: But this denoted a foregone conclusion. (III, iii, 428–429)

Iago's cunning use of Desdemona's handkerchief can also be defined in rhetorical terms as a typical figure of reasoning, with the handkerchief and the evidence of its presence in Cassio's possession constituting the tip of an iceberg. At the beginning of the Handkerchief Scene, we witness the skewed way in which Othello's faculty of reason operates under the influence of jealousy and anger, which have already been awakened in him:

OTHELLO: Give me your hand. This hand is moist, my lady.
DESDEMONA: It yet hath felt no age, nor known no sorrow.
OTHELLO: This *argues* fruitfulness and liberal heart:
                 Hot, hot, and moist. (III, iv, 32–35; my italics)

Othello is certain that he is drawing a logical conclusion based on the evidence before him: Desdemona's moist hand. The gap between reality and Othello's delusional self-image as a man of Reason is implied by the insertion of the word 'argues', which belongs to the semantic fields of logic. Shakespeare often uses this word – preferring it to more 'neutral' words such as 'shows' – as a kind of discordant indicator, spoken by characters who erroneously rationalise outward signs, characters who purport (without justification) to formulate an erudite logical argument, or characters who present in a manipulative manner supposedly logical conclusions.[29]

The climax of Othello's agitation is reached at the end of the 'play' that Iago 'stages' for him, during which Cassio seemingly con-

---

29   E.g.: '*Thunder ... Enter Fiends* JOAN LA PUCELLE: This speedy and quick appearance *argues* proof / Of your accustomed diligence to me' (*1 Henry VI*, V, iii, 8–9; my italics); 'FIRST CLOWN: It must be "se offendendo", it cannot be else. For here lies the point: if I drown myself wittingly, it *argues* an act: and an act hath three branches: it is, to act, to do, to perform: argal, she drowned herself wittingly' (*Hamlet*, V, i, 9–13; my italics).

fesses to intimate relations with Desdemona (IV, i, 90–161). Immediately following this 'play', Othello expresses a firm resolution to murder both Desdemona and Cassio, and in the next scene loses his self-control and strikes his wife in public. Iago's rhetorical ingeniousness is revealed when the 'play' he stages is examined in light of the familiar definitions of the various figures of amplification; this examination also reveals the great power of the emotional appeal that he – and the playwright – has created here. This elaborate appeal constitutes the high point of a series of emotional appeals that began with the opening of III, iii. What Iago does here can be defined as 'amplification within amplification', 'amplified amplification' or even 'amplification to the second power', since he combines two different types of amplification. He assembles and 'interweaves' them, so that one amplification amplifies the matter itself (i.e., the forbidden relations between Cassio and Desdemona), while the other amplification amplifies the first amplification. In line with the tactic that Iago implements throughout Othello's agitation process, one of these two amplifications is of the 'reasoning' type. The second amplification can be described as 'standard' or 'regular' amplification; it is of the type usually indicated in Roman and English Renaissance rhetorical treatises by the word 'amplification' (Latin *amplificatio*). In modern rhetorical studies this figure is sometimes called 'vertical amplification'.[30] Having clarified earlier the rhetorical term 'reasoning', I shall now describe and clarify the characteristics of 'standard' amplification. This will allow us to examine and analyse in rhetorical terms the moment when Othello observes Iago, Cassio and Bianca from his place of hiding.

In classical rhetoric, amplification is the primary means of inducing emotion. It is, essentially, 'the extension of simple statement by all such devices as tend to increase its rhetorical effect, or to add importance to things stated'.[31] The arousal and intensity of emotion depend on the degree of subjective importance that we attach to a

---

30   See: Heinrich F. Plett, 'Amplification', *Encyclopedia of Rhetoric*, ed. Thomas Slone (Oxford: Oxford University Press, 2001), pp. 25–26.
31   *OED*, 'Amplification', n., 4.

specific event or piece of information;[32] it follows that if we can cause the addressee of the emotional appeal to perceive a certain event or piece of information as significant and highly important for him, we can arouse in him more intense emotion. The central method of realising this goal is the specification of the various unique circumstances of the event in question, done with the aim of demonstrating how extraordinary and unprecedented the event is in the cruelty, baseness, shame, joy, sadness or pity, etc., associated with it.[33]

The Roman rhetoricians, as well as their English followers, provide their readers with orderly lists of topics, which are intended to assist the student of rhetoric in the preparation of a speech amplifying a certain event, whether real or imagined, in order to exercise one's rhetorical skills. Thus, the author of the *Rhetorica ad Herennium*, considered one of the most influential rhetorical treatises in Elizabethan England, provides a list of recommended topics for the composition of a speech, in defence of an accused man, designed to arouse the judges' pity. These topics include a comparison of the subject's past prosperity with his present deplorable state; a recounting of the afflictions he will undergo if the judges decide against him; an enumeration of the adversities that his parents, children and other relatives are bound to suffer; a detailing of the many good deeds he has done for others in the past, his humaneness and kindness; and an avowal that the great sorrow he feels is not for himself but for the members of his family and loved ones.[34] In *The Art of Rhetoric*, Thomas Wilson provides a similar succinct list of topics suitable for amplification intended to induce emotion in judges toward a defendant. In this case, however, the desired emotion is anger:

> In moving affections and stirring the judges ... the report must be such and the offence made so heinous, that the like hath not been seen before, and all the circumstances must thus be heaped together: the naughtiness of his nature that did

---

32 See, e.g.: Aaron Ben-Ze'ev, *The Subtlety of Emotions* (Cambridge, MA: MIT Press, 2000), pp. 13–18.

33 See, for example, the typical but particularly elaborate amplification figure, intended to arouse shame, presented by Thomas Wilson in *The Art of Rhetoric* (pp. 153–154).

34 *Rhetorica ad Herennium*, II, xxxi. 50, pp. 151–153.

the deed, the cruel ordering, the wicked dealing and malicious handling, the time, the place, the manner of his doing, and the wickedness of his will to have done more.[35]

A comparison of these precepts with Iago's instructions to Othello how to observe the scene from his hiding place and how to interpret the 'confession' that he, Iago, will elicit from Cassio, is particularly revealing. In fact, the ancient is directing his commander to organise in his mind Cassio's future reactions as a typical list of topics constituting a standard amplification:

> Do but encave yourself,
> And mark the fleers, the gibes, and notable scorns
> That dwell in every region of his face;
> For I will make him tell the tale anew,
> Where, how, how oft, how long ago, and when
> *He hath* and *is again* to cope your wife. (IV, i, 79–84; my italics)

But the figure of amplification created by Iago is not constructed in the form of a standard speech in the spirit of the rhetorical treatises, in which the speaker spells out the various topics. Othello, observing the scene from his hiding place, will take in smiles, gestures or isolated sentences, each of which will constitute, under the influence of Iago's advance instructions, one 'topic' in the entire figure of amplification. Iago's directions thus appeal to Othello's inference-craving mind, encouraging it to construct, based on these 'tips of icebergs', the icebergs themselves: the disgraceful 'events' that preceded them. In other words, Iago directs Othello to perform a process of reasoning on each of Cassio's smiles, facial expressions, gestures and words:

> IAGO: [*Aside*] As he shall smile, Othello shall go mad;
>   And his unbookish jealousy must construe
>   Poor Cassio's smiles, gestures, and light behaviours
>   Quite in the wrong. (IV, i, 98–101)

To further clarify this rhetorical assemblage: in this scene, Iago constructs a 'standard' figure of amplification, consisting of a series of

35   Thomas Wilson, *The Art of Rhetoric* (1560), p. 161.

topics that are presented to Othello as 'iceberg tips' of amplification figures of the reasoning type. In this way, Iago achieves 'amplification to the second power': he amplifies Desdemona's alleged adultery by breaking it down into topics; these topics then receive significant further amplification in Othello's mind because of his tendency to perform reasoning processes.

It is important to note that in using this staged scheme, Iago not only intensifies Othello's emotional state, but also ascertains that the intensifying passion is of the desired kind. As stressed throughout this study, anger is a highly desirable emotion from the point of view of Shakespearean manipulators, being the most intense, destructive and difficult to pacify of all the passions. The arousal of such a fervent passion will enable Iago to impair his addressees' judgement drastically and to motivate them to carry out extreme acts. In other words, passion, from the rhetorician's point of view, serves a double purpose: it impairs judgement, thereby assisting the process of persuasion, and it serves as 'fuel' motivating the addressee to take action.

Anger, as it has been defined since the days of Aristotle, is the passion aroused within us in response to what we subjectively perceive as an injury that has been unjustly inflicted upon us.[36] English sources from the end of the sixteenth and the beginning of the seventeenth centuries repeatedly emphasise, in their discussions of this passion, the great power of displays of contempt in igniting anger. Francis Bacon, in his essay 'Of Anger', observes that 'contempt is that, which putteth an edge upon anger, *as much or more than the hurt itself*. And therefore, when men are ingenious in picking out circumstances of contempt, they do kindle their anger much'.[37] Iago, who is well aware of the mechanisms of the mind and the causes of emotional reactions, takes pains to stage his 'play' in accordance with this general observation. He instructs Othello to perceive 'Cassio's smiles, gestures, and light behaviours' as referring to Desdemona, and expressing, therefore, the contempt that Cassio feels towards him. In other words, Iago stages a scene in which Othello observes 'evidence' of the offence committed against him and, *in addition*, witnesses the

36   See, e.g.: Aristotle, *Rhetoric*, II, ii.
37   Francis Bacon, 'Of Anger', *Essays* (1612), (London: Dent, 1972), pp. 166–167.

great contempt that the offender feels and publicly exhibits towards him. The fact that Iago mentions, in the passage quoted above, Othello's passion of romantic jealousy (l. 99), in no sense contradicts my claim regarding the nature of the emotion that he seeks to arouse: on the contrary, a close examination of his words reveals the extent of his mastery of emotional rhetoric. Iago refers to romantic jealousy as the specific passion that will cause Othello to 'construe quite to the wrong' the behaviour of Cassio; that is, the passion that will distort his judgement. Othello's distorted judgement will interpret Cassio's scornful gestures and isolated words as referring to him, and thereby generate the more violent passion that the ancient desires, anger ('Othello shall go mad').

As noted at the beginning of Chapter Two, the force and persistence of anger were famous in Shakespeare's time not only as common causes of hostilities between individuals, but also as the motivating force for widespread strife, even wars between kingdoms. It is, therefore, no mere coincidence that Shakespeare chooses to propel the plots of the four plays under discussion mostly through this passion: by means of anger he is able both to motivate individual characters to commit extreme acts, and to move thousands of citizens and soldiers to launch insurrections and wars. This passion is, therefore, the most appropriate choice in order to cause a character distinguished by self-control, as is Othello, to undergo such a thorough change. Shakespeare's spectators were no doubt able to recognise the protagonist's epileptic fit as the direct physical expression of his extreme rage.[38] This very passion will be the motivating force leading to Desdemona's murder itself: Othello, entering the bedchamber while uttering words that betray no emotional turmoil,[39] strangles Desdemona in an outburst of genuine rage. This outburst is brought on when Othello perceives the shocked dismay with which Desdemona receives the news of Cassio's supposed death – to him, this reaction is

---

38 Compare: '... vehement anger is often accompanied with frensinesse, and with the falling sicknesse'. Pierre de La Primaudaye, *The French Academie*, p. 498.

39 The emotion that the text suggests at this point requires an elaborate, separate discussion, involving explanations of self-persuasion and the differences between anger and hatred.

a blatant show of contempt.[40] Anger was also considered in Shakespeare's time to be the 'arch enemy' of reason: in comparison with other emotions, which only impaired the operation of reason to a certain degree, anger was said to completely 'quench the light of Reason'.[41] From the points of view of both the playwright and Iago, therefore, anger is appropriate not only for motivating Othello to action, but also for impairing his rational faculty: it enables the continued, successful implementation of emotional appeal based on the figure of reasoning.

3.4 Reasoning and Othello's Downfall

3.4.1 Free-Will and Determinism in the Tradition of Tragedy

Since the days of Classical Greece, Tragedy has offered its spectators and readers an ambiguous, puzzling world cosmos. It refrains from providing an all-encompassing, clear-cut 'message' or 'moral' that aims at resolving various existential queries; rather, it reflects life itself, with its inherent complexities and contradictions. One of the issues that tragedy tends to 'complicate' and reveal in all its subtlety, is the question of Man's role in the realisation of his fate. The protagonists of tragedies are characterised for the most part in ways that create an ambiguous impression: on the one hand, they sometimes appear as passive entities controlled by the gods, unwitting pawns in a cruel, hopeless game whose results are known in advance; on the other hand, they may seem like individuals who decide and act in accordance with their own, freely made choices. In other words, the main protagonists of the classical tragedies are presented simultaneously as passive victims of overpowering forces and circumstances

---

40 'DESDEMONA: Alas, he is betrayed, and I undone. / OTHELLO: Out, strumpet! Weep'st thou for him *to my face?*' (V, ii, 77–78; my italics).
41 See Chapter Two, pp. 81–82.

and as human beings punished for erroneous actions that they have freely decided to commit.

This traditional characteristic of the tragic cosmos is also inherent in Shakespearean tragedy. Spectators of *King Lear*, for example, might be influenced by a number of hints directing them to see the tragic occurrences as no more than the result of 'these late eclipses of the moon and stars' that afflicted Albion a short time prior to the beginning of the plot; the same catastrophes may be the result of the machinations of 'the gods', who are compared in this play to 'wanton boys' who kill flies (i.e., men) 'for their sport'. Conversely, the opening scene may encourage spectators to see the king himself, with his capricious nature and thirst for expressions of love, as the sole active agent responsible for the division of the kingdom and for his own failure to distinguish between Cordelia's love and her sisters' hypocrisy. Of course, these three viewpoints constitute only a tiny part of the much more complex picture presented by *King Lear*; they are surveyed here in a simplified manner for the sake of clarification. Shakespeare's tragic heroes, like their classical predecessors, can be placed along an axis connecting the poles from innocent victim to absolute villain, or from active decider to passive marionette.[42] The Shakespearean tragic hero will almost never be found standing squarely at one pole: during the play, spectators will receive various hints and confusing, contradictory evidence that will seemingly make the hero 'move' between poles. The spectator's ethical judgement of the hero, accordingly, will shift with the latter's peregrinations between the two poles.

3.4.2 Othello's Active Role in His Own Downfall

Othello provides an array of contradictory evidence regarding the degree of the hero's responsibility for his own fate, and the extent to which he is active in its realisation. Those who believe in the enforced

---

42 These generalisations do not contradict the fact that in comparison with Classical-world parallels, Shakespearean tragedy tends to focus on character and on the complex processes that occur in the human mind.

obedience of humans to planetary influence might trace a number of hints pointing to the cosmic circumstances that assist in bringing the catastrophe closer (V, ii, 100, 110–112, 270). Fate is also represented in the play, with Othello himself referring to it near the end as a force that man cannot control (ibid., 262–263). Iago's 'diabolic intellect' and virtuoso rhetorical and psychological skills may cause us to see Othello from the outset as lacking a true opportunity to confront the ancient's tricks. Extraordinary circumstances also 'snare' Othello over the course of the play, perhaps encouraging us to perceive him rather as a victim than as an active agent: as a military man of action, Othello is unaccustomed to the idleness imposed upon him following the sinking of the Turkish fleet; and he is certainly unaccustomed to passionate romantic agitations of the sort that grip him shortly before the beginning of the play (in early modern European thought, the transition from military life to the pacific life of love is inherently problematic, often exacting a heavy price). As opposed to these hints and circumstances, which direct spectators to discern the passive dimension in Othello's character, the play also provides a wealth of information that encourages the audience to consider Othello's personal responsibility and active participation in his own bitter end. As an example of the textual suggestions of Othello's active role, we may note the following passages, both uttered by Iago:

[*To OTHELLO*]   I do beseech you,
            ... that your wisdom then,
From one that so imperfectly conceits,
Would take no notice, nor *build yourself* a trouble
Out of his scattering and unsure observance. (III, iii, 145–152; my italics)

I told him what I thought, and told no more
Than what *he found himself* was apt and true. (V, ii, 175–176; my italics)

It is no accident that Iago, familiar with Othello's mental traits, chooses to agitate him by employing the figure of reasoning. As shown in the general presentation of this figure, the degree of its effectiveness depends on the extent to which its addressee takes an active part in quenching his thirst for 'rationality': drinking his fill of hints, rumours, bits of evidence and pseudo-evidence, and using these as a basis for reconstructing the whole iceberg, as it were. Iago's lines, quoted above, thus succinctly represent the connection between Othello's active role in his own downfall and his craving for Reason: Othello has indeed *built himself* a complete and completely wrong reconstruction 'out of ... scattering and unsure observance'. His obsessive quest to chart the world as a collection of clear, unequivocal signs has caused him to cancel the wide gap between assuming, thinking and believing, on the one hand, and knowing, on the other hand. The result is that he has 'found' the uncertain to be 'apt and true'.

It is not my intention to suggest that an analysis of the play from this point of view reveals Othello to be the main culprit of his own fate: any such attempt would imply that *Othello* should be classified as a morality play, thereby overlooking the complex tragic world presented in this play. Othello's obsession with Reason is merely one of the many factors influencing the tragic process in the play, alongside fate, the stars, Iago's diabolic traits, the extraordinary circumstances, etc. In order to avoid over-simplification, it should be noted that Othello's obsessive tendency to rationalise reality, which may be seen as the cause of his erroneous judgement, is one of the basic elements of his 'character' or 'nature'. The question of whether human beings are passive, abject slaves of their own nature, or are capable of actively overcoming that nature, is a broad philosophical issue with no single, simple answer. Shakespeare's tragedies, despite their extensive treatment of this subject, do not resolve or determine whether one's character is one's destiny, or merely one factor among many that determine the course of one's life. As in his general treatment of the question of fate versus free will, Shakespeare leaves this question open as well.

In this context, it should be noted that contemporary studies of the emotions are divided regarding the degree to which active control of emotion is possible. Some scholars consider the emotions to be full-fledged *actions*, going so far as to suggest the use of a new language that would refer to them using verbs and adverbs, and not just nouns, as is the practice today. By contrast, other scholars emphasise the passive dimension in the process of emotional arousal, contending that the individual cannot control which of his emotions will be stirred in a given situation, and which will not (i.e., emotions are 'undergone' rather than 'enacted').[43] While this issue perturbs students of emotion, its ambiguity from our point of view – that of students of theatre and drama – should by no means threaten our peace of mind: the general picture created by the various studies on this question is identical to that presented by the tragedies themselves – there are no absolute answers to the question of the protagonist's degree of responsibility for his passions and their disastrous effects.

Othello, unlike the play's spectators, readers and students, does not observe the world in which he acts from a remote, external viewpoint, nor does he discern the complex reality briefly surveyed above. He does not see his own active part in the chain of events and does not express any understanding of his own responsibility for the ensuing catastrophe; his tragic recognition in the final scene seems extremely limited. The polarity of judgements, for better or worse, passed on the play's hero marks one of the central features of the scholarly works written on *Othello*. Scholars have tended to interpret Othello's final monologue, and the degree of self-deception it displays, in accordance with their judgement of his character in general. This chapter, by contrast, does not intend to pass moral judgement on a fictional dramatic character such as Othello, nor attempts to determine the degree of self-deception that he demonstrates. Spectators and readers may see Othello – as he is portrayed on stage or realised in one's imagination at the end of the play – as the embodiment of 'Bovarysm', to use T.S. Eliot's malignant expression; they may suspend criticism and see Othello as one who exhibits, prior to his death, a profoundly human yearning for the merciful appraisal of others and for a benevolent place in their memory;[44] or they may place themselves along any point of the spectrum between these two extremes.

Whatever verdict one may pass regarding Othello's self-deception, it should be agreed that the general does not describe his part in the tragedy in the most sober or faithful manner. He presents himself in an imprecise, defensive way as 'an honourable murderer' unmoved

43   Jon Elster, *Alchemists of the Mind: Rationality and the Emotions* (Cambridge: Cambridge University Press, 1999), pp. 306–312.
44   T. S. Eliot, 'Shakespeare and the Stoicism of Seneca', *Shakespeare Othello – A Casebook*, ed. John Wain (London: Macmillan, 1971), p. 132.

by hatred (V, ii, 290–292), and as 'one that loved not wisely, but too well' (ibid., 339–340). In addition, in his last monologue, Othello makes synecdochic use of his hand in a way that suggests a will to 'brush off' direct responsibility for his actions. In shifting focus from himself to his hand, Othello seems to be saying: 'it is my hand that threw the pearl away, not I':

> ... one whose hand,
> Like the base Indian, threw a pearl away
> Richer than all his tribe ... (V, ii, 342–344)

Similarly, he uses passive language when describing the place of passion in his web of errors:

> ... one not easily jealous but, *being wrought*,
> Perplexed in the extreme ... (Ibid., 341–342; my italics)

Othello's words present him as the passive victim of emotional manipulation. This use of language completely ignores the active dimension of his craving for reason and its place in the process of his agitation.

Chapter Four
Coriolanus

'What's in a name?'
(*Romeo and Juliet*, II, ii, 43)

The Tragedy of Coriolanus is preoccupied with the human obsession with public image. Time and again Shakespeare reveals his characters' fixation with 'name' – that is, with their own reputations and those of others, as determined by society. Central characters in the play act vigorously to establish a good name for themselves; moreover, they are no less vigorous in their attempts to determine the name of fellow-characters, according to their political motives or their attitude toward these fellow-characters.

This preoccupation – epitomised in the very names of the play and of its protagonist – is strongly felt in the verbal composition of this tragedy, through Shakespeare's frequent and varied use of words like 'name' and 'report'. These words denote, directly or implicitly, a given character's public reputation.[1] The characters' intense interest in 'name' is also expressed in the unusually frequent appearance of the adjectives 'noble', 'worthy' and 'honourable':[2] gaining these epithets is a primary desire in Rome and Antium alike. This might be called a 'Roman' tendency, insofar as it is also evoked forcefully in Shakespeare's other Roman plays; in *Coriolanus*, however, this preoccupa-

---

1   *OED*, 'report', n., 1c: 'Repute, fame, reputation ...'; *OED*, 'name', n., 5–8: 'The fame or reputation involved in a well-known name ... The reputation of some character or attribute ... One's repute or reputation'. For salient examples in the play, see: V, iii, 143 (name); I, iii, 16; I, vi, 70 (report).
2   The word 'noble' and its derivatives are especially prevalent in *Coriolanus*, occurring no fewer than 86 times (in *Julius Caesar*, in which the word is also quite dominant, it appears only 44 times).

tion reaches a peak both in the intensity of the characters' obsession with their public image and in its salient position in the play's thematic design. Indeed, so significant is 'name' in the game of life as presented in *Coriolanus*, that without it one becomes 'a kind of nothing' (V, i, 11–15). The 'name' of a character can at times be of no less importance or substance than the character himself:

> VIRGILIA: But had he died in the business, madam, how then?
> VOLUMNIA: Then his good report should have been my son. I therein would
> have found issue. (I, iii, 15–17)

As a result of the weight assigned by the characters to 'name' in the game of life, *ethos*[3] becomes the dominant means of persuasion in *Coriolanus'* world, attaining primacy over the other two means, *pathos* and *logos*. 'Name' is one of the two main factors constituting one's *ethos* in a given rhetorical situation (the second factor, as noted, is the speaker's character as perceived by his audience during the speech).[4] Because the characters accord such importance to public image, *ethos* acquires a powerful influence over their minds, outweighing the impact of rational thinking and emotional sway.

This is not to say that the potency of *pathos* is dulled in *Coriolanus*, as compared to the plays surveyed thus far. Emotional appeal remains a commanding force in this tragedy, affecting the plot directly and rechanneling it at certain key moments. *Pathos*, however, is subordinated to *ethos* to a much greater degree in *Coriolanus* than in any of the other plays discussed in this book. In other words, *ethos* in this tragedy is the dominant factor in determining the nature and power of *pathos*, and emotional appeals are constructed on the foundations and building blocks of *ethos*. In seeking to agitate others, characters in *Coriolanus* make use of the 'name' of the characters involved in the rhetorical situation: their own 'name'; their addressee's 'name' as he perceives it; their addressee's desire to win a good 'name'; their addressee's 'name' in society as a whole or in a particular part thereof; and the 'name' of other characters involved in

---

3   For a definition of the term *ethos* as used in this study, see Appendix C.
4   Although these two factors might either support or contradict each other, their 'sum' determines the nature and impact of the speaker's *ethos*.

the rhetorical situation. In sum, the passion-arousing factors in the rhetorical situations of *Coriolanus* are none other than the reputations of the characters involved in those situations.

In the last part of this chapter, this broad observation will be helpful in examining the emotional appeal through which Volumnia dissuades her son from realising his desire for revenge upon Rome. Several characters in the play, like certain scholars, see this appeal as generating *pity* or *compassion*. This reading seems to me to emanate from an incomplete understanding of the mental characterisation of the protagonist, as well as from a lack of awareness of the ways in which the relevant passions were perceived in early modern England. Although it is true that Volumnia begins her speech with a typical appeal for pity, she goes on to execute a rhetorical about-face when she concludes it by vigorously 'milking' the *ethos* of the main characters involved. In so doing, she chooses in effect to enlist the most appropriate emotion for subduing her son – shame. This emotion was known in Shakespeare's time as 'a grief and a confusion', that wells up when one's good-name is threatened or lost: the Roman and Volscian characters in *Coriolanus* are so engrossed in their public image, that they are constantly exposed to shame. This is especially true of the protagonist, who frequently exhibits over-sensitivity regarding his reputation and fear of devaluation of his honour.

4.1 The Power of *Ethos* in *Coriolanus*

Ethos is an influential factor in any persuasive process; this naturally holds true of all the dramatic representations of persuasive processes discussed in previous chapters. However, in *Coriolanus* it repeatedly upstages the other means of persuasion, *logos* and *pathos*, and the playwright awards it centre stage. As will be demonstrated below, this tragedy relentlessly directs the attention of the spectators towards the *ethos* factor inherent in its various rhetorical situations, and its great persuasive force. Moreover, the rhetorical potency of *ethos* is not merely stressed in *Coriolanus*: it proves to have a greater effect than in the plays discussed heretofore. By way of comparison, in *Julius Caesar* Antony manages to stir the commons to mutiny with his speech, despite his very problematic *ethos*: this considerable rhetorical limitation of his is evident throughout the first half of the play, when, unlike Brutus, Cassius and Caesar, he is not once referred to as 'noble'. Moreover, although *ethos* proves to be a highly influential factor in this speech, it is produced by the orator from nothing, and in a very short time – in fact, Antony does this by means of a display of passion, that is, he produces his *ethos* by means of *pathos*.[5]

The tragedy *Othello*, too, allots a significant role to *ethos* in the rhetorical arena. Iago's success in arousing the passions of his general greatly depends upon his spotless reputation as an honest and frank man: this fact is repeatedly reinforced as the characters refer to him using the word 'honest' no less than fifteen times in the course of the play. But *Othello*, unlike *Coriolanus*, constantly focuses the attention of the audience on the passion-inducing means employed against the protagonist, and on the emotional process they bring about in him. Shakespeare presents in *Othello* an exceptionally long emotional appeal, encouraging the spectators to follow it closely and to note the varied emotional responses it elicits from its addressee.

4.1.1 Menenius' Dependence on Ethos

The great power of *ethos* in *Coriolanus* is demonstrated as early as the first scene of the play, during Menenius' speech to the rebellious citizens. The uniqueness of this rhetorical situation is evident if we compare it to the opening scene of *Julius Caesar*, which, as stated, emphasises the role of *pathos* in persuasive processes. In this scene, Flavius and Murellus deliver an emotional appeal to the rejoicing people, with the intention of supplanting their joy with shame. During this appeal the playwright provides no indication as to the *ethos* of the orators: the reactions of the commoners to this appeal contain not even the slightest of clues that might indicate how they perceive the char-

5   See Chapter Two, pp. 100–101.

acters of the two tribunes. A rhetorical analysis of this opening scene must therefore treat the *ethos* factor as an unknown, and focus primarily on the means and techniques of arousing emotions employed by Flavius and Murellus.

In *Coriolanus'* first speech of persuasion, by contrast, Shakespeare focuses almost entirely on *ethos*, and pushes aside the other means of persuasion. The mutinous citizens enter highly agitated, armed with staves and clubs, determined to act violently. Menenius, who arrives with the intention of restoring peace and quiet, achieves his objective by telling a 'pretty tale'. In this tale, the members of the body accuse the belly of hoarding food and withholding it from them, who toil to provide it. The belly appears to be innocent of these accusations, and kindly resolves the misunderstanding that has brought them about: indeed, being 'the storehouse ... of the whole body', it does 'receive the general food at first'; but after having received the food, the belly by no means hoards it, but rather sends it through the blood to each and every organ (ll. 113–123). Having completed his story, Menenius points to the so-called analogy between the body in his story and the Roman body-politic: in this way he attempts to convince the rebellious citizens (the body's members) that their claims against the senators of Rome (the belly) are unjust – according to him, the senators and patricians are not responsible for the people's shortage of corn,[6] but rather care for them 'like fathers' (ll. 51, 63).

---

6   It should be noted that Shakespeare's very choice of the belly as a metaphor for the senators of Rome (that is, his choosing to follow North's version in this specific case) may have generated some discord in the mind of his audience, hinting at the true quality of the senators and their rule. The belly is traditionally identified with Man's bestial instincts, and the word 'belly' used by Menenius was synonymous in early modern England with 'glutton' and 'gluttony' (*OED*, 'belly', n., c, d). The use of the belly as a metaphor for rulers of a state may be better understood if compared to a section in Edward Forset's *A comparative discourse of the bodies natural and politique* (1606): the governor of the state, wrote Forset, parallels the human soul; the seat of the soul is a subject of controversy, and Forset surveys three possible locations: 1) in the entire body, just as God is present everywhere in the world; 2) in the heart, since this sensitive organ is aware of even the slightest change in the body, and constitutes the 'fountain of life' from which the blood and the spirits flow to the organs; 3) in the head, the seat of reason and intellect, which control the body's organs from its

The logical fallacy in this analogy is obvious: in contrast to the senators of Rome, the belly does provide nourishment to all members of the body. The process of food distribution in the body is of course not visible to the eye (ll. 125–126), but its existence can be clearly proven by conducting an audit, as the belly itself suggests (l. 127). Menenius, however, does not make a similar suggestion: as in the human body, the process of distributing corn in Rome is not visible to the eye; but unlike Menenius' story, in Rome it is not visible for the simple reason that it is completely non-existent. Menenius claims that it is the gods who are responsible for the people's hardship, visiting a dearth upon Rome; yet if indeed this is the case, it can be determined whether the patricians are also lacking corn. The first citizen, more-over, enumerates concrete and visible facts that attest to the patricians' abuse of the people:

> Care for us? True, indeed, they ne'er cared for us yet. Suffer us to famish, and their storehouses crammed with grain; make edicts for usury, to support usu-rers; repeal daily any wholesome act established against the rich, and provide more piercing statutes daily to chain up and restrain the poor ... and there's all the love they bear us. (I, i, 65–70)

These accusations can of course be investigated and verified or refuted unequivocally; as long as they are not refuted, they shed a most dubi-ous light on Menenius' declarations about the 'most charitable care' of the senators for the people. Menenius, however, chooses not to re-spond directly to the accusations; instead, he diverts the discussion to the allegory of the body, effectively escaping a factual investigation based on logic. In this context, it is important to distinguish between the emotional state of the first citizen and his actual claims. While the textual structure of his accusations clearly suggests extreme anger, their content is logical for the most part: the citizen in fact forms an argument by which he rationally explains why he finds it impossible to believe that the senators care for the people. Menenius, in contrast to the enraged citizen, wraps himself in a calm, agreeable aspect, and

---

elevated position. Edward Forset, *A comparative discourse of the bodies natural and politique* (1606), pp. 23–31.

158

presents his tale in a sober manner; his manipulative analogy, however, is far from rational.

It cannot be determined whether or not the citizens are aware of the logical fallacy in this analogy, since none of them objects to it explicitly. However, it can certainly be determined that at the end of the encounter, despite the fact that Menenius' words completely fail the assay of Reason, he achieves his objective and pacifies his agitated audience. Menenius is able to accomplish his objective aided by a surprisingly limited rhetorical arsenal, which proves sufficient to cover the logical fallacy of his speech. This arsenal consists of his *ethos*, or as we shall immediately see, his two types of *ethos*. The first of these is the *ethos* referred to in previous chapters and elaborated upon in Appendix C. Menenius bases this rhetorical means primarily on his reputation in the eyes of the commons as 'one honest enough', 'that hath always loved the people' (I, i, 39–42); because of this reputation, the citizens tend to consider Menenius' declarations to be truthful and frank.

Unlike the commonly accepted meaning of the word in rhetorical contexts, '*ethos*' in Quintilian's writings indicates a different rhetorical factor. The *Institutio Oratoria* defines '*ethos*' as the moderate and genial emotion the orator externalises, giving rise to a sense of pleasure in the audience. Quintilian divides the emotions that exert an influence in a given rhetorical situation into two categories: '*pathos*', that is, vehement emotions, which he also refers to as 'violent ... powerful agents of disturbance'; and '*ethos*', those aforementioned subtle emotions that flow from the orator towards his addresses and guarantee their good will.[7] In the following pages, this rhetorical factor will be designated 'Quintilian *ethos*'. Obviously, Quintilian *ethos* can be defined plainly as one of the components of *ethos*, that is, one of the factors determining the way in which the audience perceives the character of the orator. However, examining Quintilian *ethos* in isolation proves helpful in analysing the scene in question, inasmuch as Shakespeare's characterisation of Menenius the orator is based largely on a rhetorical factor that parallels the *ethos* defined by Quintilian.

7   Quintilian, *Institutio Oratoria*, 6.2.9, p. 49.

Menenius' demeanour and the words he chooses on the occasion in question bear witness to the deliberate use he makes of his Quintilian *ethos*. The elderly manipulator externalises sympathy and amiability; he takes care not to reproach and accuse the rebellious citizens, pretending instead to enquire naively why they are carrying staves and clubs ('What work's, my countrymen, in hand?' [I, i, 42]); he eschews arrogance; he appeals to the plebeians with requests – rather than orders – and takes pains to stress his affinity with his addressees and the similarities he shares with them ('my countrymen', 'I pray you', 'masters, my good friends, mine honest neighbours', 'friends', 'my good friend', 'this most wise rebellion' [I, i, 42–141]). Using these manipulative tools is second nature to Menenius, who employs them – that is, his 'Quintilian *ethos*' – throughout the play.[8]

Menenius chooses to appeal to the people with a 'pretty tale' (l. 47), whose language and style are plain and communicative without being too common.[9] These two significant rhetorical choices are in accordance with the teachings of the *Institutio Oratoria* regarding the style of delivery best suited to externalising Quintilian *ethos*:

> The ethos which I mean, and which I want to see in a speaker, will be ... not only mild and calm, but usually attractive and polite, and pleasing and delightful to the listeners ... Hence the actual style ... should be calm and gentle. It needs no pride, and certainly no elevation or sublimity. It is enough to speak appropriately, pleasantly and credibly, and therefore the Middle Style is most suitable.[10]

Cicero, who was born some 140 years before Quintilian, naturally uses a different set of concepts; nevertheless, a number of his observations may shed light on the rhetorical tactic and the style that Menenius employs in addressing the plebeians. In *Oratore*, Cicero defines the three objectives of the orator as 'to prove, to please and

8   See, e.g.: III, i, 267–290; V, ii, 11.
9   Menenius' story is written in iambic pentameter, which is the 'proper' textual form for a patrician character. Shakespeare does not 'lower' Menenius to the level of his common audience by putting prose text in his mouth.
10   Quintilian, *Institutio Oratoria*, 6.2. 13–19, pp. 51–55.

to sway or persuade' (*'ut probet, ut delectet, ut flectat'*).[11] 'To please' means to charm or seduce the addressees by various means, such as an appeal to their natural voyeurism or the satisfaction of their esthetic appetite. Precisely like Quintilian, Cicero considers the Middle Style to be best suited to pleasing and charming the audience.[12] The use of tropes, according to him, is a salient characteristic of this style; among the different types of tropes Cicero includes allegory[13] – that is, a continuous stream of metaphors – which is, it will be recalled, the central means by which Menenius addresses the people. An historical observation made by Cicero is most relevant to the characterisation of Menenius, both as an orator and as a person: the *Oratore* directly links the Middle Style with the Sophists, whose expertise was in presenting fallacious arguments as valid; Cicero credits them as being 'the source' from which the charming, polished and highly-coloured Middle Style 'has flowed into the forum'.[14]

Menenius' strength as an appeasing orator stems from the combination of his *ethos* and his Quintilian *ethos*, which support and reinforce each other. The commons do not detect the hypocrisy behind his contrived amiability because of his firm public image as 'one honest enough' who 'hath always loved the people'; this image is strengthened by his agreeable manner, the pleasant emotions he externalises, and so forth.

As shown, Menenius' manipulates the rebellious citizens to see the belly in his story as being analogous to the Roman senators. The text of the play, on the other hand, points to the obvious analogy between the belly and Menenius himself: the belly, as an orator facing an audience, displays characteristics and techniques identical to those of Menenius, and also makes use of Quintilian *ethos*. Precisely like

---

11   Cicero, *Oratore*, xxi, 69, p. 357. Some researchers have sought to point to a parallelism between these three terms and Aristotle's *logos, ethos* and *pathos*; their attempts have met with difficulty, and it is possible that Cicero's thinking and formulation on this were aided by another conceptual system. See: Lawrence D. Green, 'Pathos', *Encyclopedia of Rhetoric*, ed. Thomas Slone (Oxford: Oxford University Press, 2001), p. 561.
12   Cicero, *Oratore*, xxi, 69, p. 357.
13   Ibid., xxvii, 94, p. 375.
14   Ibid., xxvii, 96, p. 375.

Menenius, it is amiable towards the members of the body, who address it aggressively (ll. 90–92); it eschews arrogance, stressing instead the similarities it shares with them ('my good friends', 'my incorporate friends' [ll. 113, 124]); it is not swept up in their quarrelsome mood (l. 94), but rather remains 'deliberate' (l. 93). The most aggressive of the rhetorical means employed by the belly is ridicule ('it tauntingly replied' [l. 93]). Characterising the belly in this way, Shakespeare has significantly deviated from his source: in North's version, the belly does not address the members using names that might stress similarities between itself and them, or suggest close association – rather, it even 'laughed at their follie'.[15]

In her article '*Julius Caesar* and *Coriolanus*: Shakespeare's Roman World of Words', Anne Barton examines the role of rhetoric in Shakespeare's portrayals of Rome in these two plays. The analyses in this enlightening article seem to me to attach too much weight to the words spoken in the rhetorical situations in the plays, overlooking other, no less influential factors. This tendency of Barton's, already evident in the title of the article, also prevails in her analysis of Menenius' speech, to which she refers as '... a victory achieved solely through the power of words'.[16] In light of the above discussion, it is clear that the decisive factor in Menenius' rhetorical victory is not 'the power of words', much less 'solely ... the power of words': if words

15   Compare North's 'And so the bellie, all that notwithstanding, laughed at their follie, and sayed. It is true, I first receive the meates ...' (p. 320), with Shakespeare's 'Your most grave belly was *deliberate*, / Not rash like his accusers, and thus answered: / "True is it, *my incorporate friends*," quoth he, / "That I receive the general food at first / Which you do live upon ..."' (I, i, 111–115; my italics).
16   Barton shows an identical tendency when she discusses Brutus' Orchard Soliloquy, referring to words as the beginning and the end, and viewing them as the cause of the hero's fatal error: '... Brutus extracts purpose and resolve not from the facts of the situation but from a collection of verbal nothings ... He is driven ... to kill Caesar purely on the bases of grammatical construction: a verbal emptiness which pretends to have the status of a fact'. Barton completely overlooks the existence of the hidden yet influential factor, passion, *whose existence precedes the words*: it is precisely this factor that drives Brutus to choose his words and to build grammatical constructions that do not reflect the visible facts. See: Anne Barton, '*Julius Caesar* and *Coriolanus*: Shakespeare's Roman World of Words', p. 30.

alone were the central influential factor on this occasion, the citizens would have easily discerned Menenius' logical fallacy. It is precisely the forces beyond words that affect the plebeians so strongly, causing them to overlook the logical fallacy these words create. Most dominant among these forces are the orator's *ethos* and Quintilian *ethos*: these not only precede the words he produces, but in fact determine the addressees' reaction to those words.

Menenius' rhetorical failure in V, ii clearly reveals his habit of basing his power of persuasion on the two types of *ethos* alone. Upon arriving at the Volscian camp, he attempts to persuade the sentinels to allow him to meet with their general, Coriolanus. Menenius appeals to the two on the assumption that Coriolanus has mentioned his name in their presence, and, as is his practice, oils his words with pleasantness and flattery:

> *You guard like men*; 'tis well ...
>   *... Good my friends,*
> If you have heard your general talk of Rome
> And of his friends there, it is lots to blanks
> My *name* hath touched your ears. It is Menenius. (V, ii, 3–14; my italics)

But in the Volscian camp, as Menenius will immediately discover, his powers of persuasion are entirely inadequate. Outside Rome he has no 'name', hence his *ethos* is ineffective. His Quintilian *ethos* also fails to affect the Volscian sentinels, because of its dependence upon *ethos*: as we have seen, Menenius' Roman addresses do not discern the hypocrisy in his pleasant flattery, due to the effect of his public reputation as an honest and loving man. Where his reputation does not precede him, however, the smooth manipulator from scene I, i proves to be rhetorically impotent:

> FIRST WATCH: ... go back. The virtue of your *name*
> Is not here passable. (Ibid., 15–16; my italics)

4.1.2 The Enhancement of Martius' Ethos in the Course of the War

Further evidence of the weight and potency of *ethos* in the world of *Coriolanus*, can be found in the battle scenes of the first act. The problem that faces the protagonist, as he attempts to spur his soldiers to assault the city of Corioles, is quite simply their hatred of him. The play twice reminds us that the Roman soldiers are in fact the same commoners with whom Martius frequently clashed before the war.[17] Considering this fact, as well as the fear that naturally prevails on the battlefield, it is not surprising that when Martius breaks into Corioles, not one of his soldiers follows him. The soldiers do not even express concern or sorrow for the likely fate of their commander, as he disappears through the gates of the enemy city:

> [*MARTIUS*] Enters the gates
>
> FIRST SOLDIER: Foolhardiness! Not I.
> SECOND SOLDIER: Nor I.
>
> [*MARTIUS*] *is shut in ...*
>
> FIRST SOLDIER: See, they have shut him in.
> ALL: To th'pot, I warrant him. (I, iv, 47–50)

In his attempts to spur his soldiers on to assault the city, Martius employs no rhetorical means that might compensate for his poor *ethos*. He might have used *pathos*, for example, to stir up his soldiers with potent passions such as anger or shame – as Henry V, an orator blessed with an optimal *ethos*, does. Instead, Martius causes the emotional state of his soldiers to deteriorate even further when, driven by his warlike rage, he unwittingly utters an emotional appeal that has the opposite effect to what he intends. Striving to invigorate his soldiers by means of threats, he in fact intensifies the harmful passion that already governs them – fear:

---

17   See: I, vi, 42–45; III, i, 126–128.

> Come on, my fellows!
> He that retires, I'll take him for a Volsce,
> And he shall feel mine edge. (I, iv, 28–30)

> Mend and charge home,
> Or by the fires of heaven, I'll leave the foe
> And make my wars on you! Look to't. (Ibid., 39–41)

Against all odds, Martius returns from his one-man war on Corioles. When he assaults it again, a radical change takes place. The original stage direction clearly indicates that all the soldiers follow him and enter the enemy city.[18] What, then, has changed in the short time between the two assaults? A careful examination of the events that occur during this time reveals that only one relevant factor has changed outside the walls of Corioles: the *ethos* of the hero. After Martius disappears through the gates of the city, Titus Lartius enters and is briefed on what has happened. Convinced that the great warrior is no longer among the living, he delivers a eulogy glorifying his 'name' in the presence of the soldiers (I, iv, 56–65). Immediately after this speech, the city gate opens and through it emerges Martius, covered in blood.[19] As stressed throughout the play, the sight of wounds and blood has a tremendous impact upon the people in the militant Roman society.[20] Thus, at the moment in question, three elements combine to amplify one another: Lartius' glorifying speech, the bloody figure of Martius, and of course the soldiers' awareness of his unprecedented act of heroism. This newly-earned *ethos* is so potent that it 'erases' from their consciousness the previous *ethos* of Martius, 'the people's enemy'.

Chapter Two elaborated upon the early modern concept concerning the strong emotional impact generated by the sight of blood. According to this concept, it will be recalled, the colour red inflames the blood of those who see it, infusing them with anger and blood-thirstiness. Of course, in any attempt to interpret the scene in question in terms of emotion, this notion cannot be overlooked: it appears, on

18   'They fight, and all enter the city' (I, iv, 68 SD).
19   'Enter MARTIUS, bleeding, assaulted by the enemy' (ibid., 65 SD).
20   See, e.g., I, iii, 29–32, 34–38; II, ii, 102–104.

the face of it, to provide an explanation for the abrupt reversal in the soldiers' behaviour as they see Martius' bloody image. This sight, it can be speculated, generates anger in the soldiers; the anger of the soldiers negates their fear and spurs them to assault the city. Thus, according to this possible interpretation, the soldiers' joining Martius does not necessarily arise from any change in their attitude towards him – that is, it is not related to a change, if any, in his *ethos*. However, such an interpretation meets with some difficulty, since the text does not supply the slightest hint that it is the sight of Martius' blood that brings about the change in his soldiers. Furthermore, the play as a whole, despite its frequent references to blood, does not once allude to the power of blood to arouse anger. On the other hand, as stated, *Coriolanus* repeatedly deals with the public images of its characters, even demonstrating how blood, wounds and scars can play an important role in the building of one's 'name'. It can be said, then, that the play does not encourage its spectators to view the reversal in the soldiers' behaviour as the result of anger aroused by the sight of the blood-smeared hero; on the other hand, the play's preoccupation with reputation and *ethos* most certainly encourages its spectators to interpret the events under discussion in the way suggested here.

It is possible, however, to interpret the reversal in the soldiers' behaviour from another emotional viewpoint, one that does take into account the *ethos* factor in the situation in question. While the play does not permit a glimpse into the minds of the soldiers – nor does it supply indications as to their emotional state – the events at the walls of Corioles are in line with Coeffeteau's observation regarding the qualities of shame:

> Many times she [Shame] hath made them valiant, who were faint hearted and fearful; yea, we have seen whole armies beeing amazed and terrified, have resumed courage by the presence of Casers, Alexanders, Scipioes, & other great Comanders, who have brought back their souldiers in battailes; for that the great asteeme they had of such excellent Captains, made them blush to flye before them; yea, to chuse a most cartaine death, rather to be held cowards by such *worthy* men.[21] (My italics)

21   F. N. Coeffeteau, *A Table of Humane Passions* (1621), p. 503.

166

At the beginning of the battle the soldiers did not experience shame –
at least not shame strong enough to motivate them to join Martius as
he assaults Corioles. In the absence of this emotion, they left their
general to invade the enemy city alone. One of the soldiers, furthermore, visualising in his mind's eye the fate expected to befall Martius,
appears to express malicious joy (I, iv, 50). By contrast, when the
worthy warrior emerges alive from the gates of Corioles, his newly-
earned *ethos* completely alters the rhetorical situation; this *ethos* generates in his soldiers one of the only two passions that can neutralise
fear on the battlefield. As we shall see later in this chapter, *ethos* in
Coriolanus is a fundamental rhetorical factor that dictates the nature
and intensity of *pathos*: the incident in question is only one of many
instances of this dominant dynamics in the play.

The adjectives with which characters refer to Martius provide a
clear indication of the enhancement of his *ethos* following his warlike
feats. Prior to the war with the Volsces, several characters sympathetic
to Martius referred to him as 'worthy'; following his single-handed
operation in Corioles, by contrast, he becomes 'worthiest' (I, v, 25),
and his name is exalted by all in the streets of Rome as 'renowned
Coriolanus'.[22] The power of Martius' newly-acquired *ethos* is evident
in one of the play's most expressive stage actions: in I, vi, he appeals
to his soldiers to volunteer for the attack on Aufidius' army, where-
upon the soldiers – who are, as mentioned, none other than his peace-
time enemies, the plebeians – respond with spontaneous enthusiasm:

> They all shout and wave their swords, take him up in their arms, and cast up
> their caps (I, vi, 75 SD)

4.1.3 The Deterioration of Coriolanus' Ethos after the War

Martius undergoes a process opposite to that which he experienced in
the war, when he returns to Rome and enters the political arena. Upon
returning to his city after having been awarded 'the whole name of the
war', he is treated like a god by all classes of Roman society. The hero

---

22   II, i, 139, 140. Renowned: 'covered with renown' (*OED*, 'renowned', *ppl.*, *a.*).

marching through the streets of Rome appeared to the people like Jove's statue, his posture was so graceful that it seemed 'that whatsoever god ... / Were slily crept into his human powers'.[23] This exceptionally potent *ethos* does indeed quickly realise its rhetorical potential: early in his campaign to be elected consul, Coriolanus meets in the Forum with representatives of the people; he treats them with scorn[24] and does not even display his wounds, yet they give him their voices. Even when his contempt is demonstrated most bluntly, the citizens turn a blind eye. Their verbal exchange reveals that the factor that has influenced them to ignore his insulting words and behaviour is the vivid memory of his wartime deeds:

> CORIOLANUS: Your voices! For your voices I have fought,
>   Watched for your voices; for Your voices bear
>   Of wounds two dozen odd. Battles thrice six
>   I have seen and heard of; for your voices have
>   Done many things, some less, some more. Your voices!
>   Indeed, I would be consul.
> SIXTH CITIZEN: He has *done nobly*, and cannot go without any honest
>   man's voice.
> SEVENTH CITIZEN: Therefore let him be consul. The gods give him joy, and
>   make him good friend to the people!
> ALL CITIZENS: Amen, amen. God save thee, *noble* consul!
>   (II, iii, 112–122; my italics)

As explained earlier, *ethos* is based upon two central elements: the way in which the speaker's character is perceived by the audience during his speech, and his 'reputation'. The latter component is so dominant in the event in question, that it has the power to completely cancel the negative effect of the former.

Brutus and Sicinius, who fear the election of Coriolanus as consul, act immediately to counter the people's decision to support him. This they do by delivering a series of short speeches of incitement to the representatives of the plebeians, moments after their meeting with Coriolanus:

---

23 II, i, 179–195, 235–242.
24 II, iii, 72–73, 85–91.

> Did you perceive
> He did solicit you in free *contempt*
> When he did need your loves, and do you think
> That his *contempt* shall not be bruising to you
> When he hath power to crush?
> ...
> Get you hence instantly, and tell those friends
> They have chose a consul that will from them take
> Their liberties ...
> Let them assemble,
> And on a safer judgement all revoke
> Your ignorant election. Enforce his pride
> And *his old hate unto you.*
> ... your loves,
> Thinking upon his services, took from you
> Th'apprehension of his present portance,
> Which most *gibingly*, ungravely, he did fashion
> After *the inveterate hate he bears you.* (II, iii, 185–212; my italics)

In these lines the tribunes reiterate to the citizens the jibe and contempt Coriolanus showed for them during their meeting; on the face of it, this is an obvious appeal to anger.[25] At the same time, these speeches resurrect in their addressees the memory of their meeting with Coriolanus, with one significant difference: the two tribunes modify the variable of the *ethos* of the resurrected rhetorical situation. They push aside the image of the protagonist as war hero, raising up instead neglected memories of his image as the hated enemy of the people. Anger, it will be recalled, strongly affects one's judgement; thus, when Brutus and Sicinius arouse anger in the people's representatives and simultaneously remind them of Coriolanus' old and inveterate hatred, anger causes the representatives to perceive Coriolanus' hatred as more intense and threatening. The image of Martius the spiteful, from the moment it replaces the image of Coriolanus the war

---

25 The various explanations of the cause for the arousal of anger, from Aristotle's days on, stress over and over again the subjective perception on the part of the angry individual that a wrong has been perpetrated against him. The tribunes' awareness of this is quite noticeable as they take pains – twice in the course of the lines above – to remind the citizens of their love, as it were, for Coriolanus, to which he has responded with contempt (ll. 187, 208).

hero, naturally influences the way in which the representatives perceive, in retrospect, his behaviour during their meeting in the Forum. This retroactively fuels their resentment at the contempt he showed them; their anger therefore intensifies even more, and so forth.[26]

Thus, a short while after its conclusion, the rhetorical situation in which Coriolanus and the representatives were involved is repeated, this time with opposite results. The different *ethos* of Coriolanus in the re-construed situation causes the representatives to retract their decision to give him their voices.

4.2 The Subordination of *Pathos* to *Ethos* in *Coriolanus*

Despite the intense passions they involve, the processes of persuasion examined thus far in this chapter cannot be classified strictly as emotional appeals. As shown, the dominant factor in these processes is *ethos*: the playwright focuses on this means of persuasion and consistently directs the attention of the audience to it. About the *pathos* factor, on the other hand, he supplies almost no information at all. The examples presented so far have illustrated the overwhelming dominance of *ethos* in the rhetorical battlefield of *Coriolanus*: changes in this factor bring about a drastic change in the response of the addressees. The passions, of course, exert considerable influence and supply the driving force in the three events discussed; however, they remain

---

26   In the course of their meeting with Coriolanus, the citizens' representatives are blind to the contempt he demonstrates, or at least 'suppress' it: at most, they have a general sense that his conduct is 'something odd' (II, iii, 74). The moment they leave the meeting place and are no longer mesmerised by the presence of the wonder fighter, some of them – *post factum* – begin to sense his arrogance, and reconstruct the words and gestures through which it was displayed. The two tribunes' rhetorical task is not, then, especially challenging: anger has already sprouted in the minds of their addressees, and Coriolanus' *ethos* has been somewhat diminished, even before a single word of sedition has been tossed into the air.

for the most part in the shadow of *ethos*, which determines their nature and intensity. This subordination of *pathos* to *ethos* is the central characteristic of the rhetorical processes in *Coriolanus* as a whole: as will be demonstrated below, it also governs the three emotional appeals that bring about the reversals in the plot.

4.2.1 The Emotional Appeals that Defeat Coriolanus

Coriolanus, the ultimate warrior, cannot be beaten by 'conventional' means such as direct combat. It is no coincidence, then, that his enemies from within and from without choose the indirect course, and bring about his downfall by means of emotional manipulations. An analysis of the two emotional appeals with which Brutus, Sicinius and Aufidius outsmart Coriolanus (III, iii, 66–127; V, vi, 84–132) clearly illustrates the subordination of *pathos* to *ethos* in the play. The three emotional manipulators are well aware of this subordination, and effectively turn it to their advantage. Their similar understanding of the rhetorical dynamics that governs the world of *Coriolanus* is evident in the correspondence between the emotional processes generated by their appeals. This correspondence is demonstrated below by dividing the emotional appeals in question into three stages:

I. Those desirous of destroying the hero refer to him, in a public situation, by derogatory names. In this way their rhetorical gain is twofold – they arouse his rage and degrade his image in the eyes of those present (that is, they bring about the deterioration of his *ethos*):

SCENE III, iii
SICINIUS: We charge you that you have contrived to take
          From Rome all seasoned office and to wind
          Yourself into a power tyrannical,
          For which you are a *traitor* to the people.
CORIOLANUS: How? 'Traitor'? (ll. 68–71; my italics)

SCENE V, vi
AUFIDIUS: Read it not, noble lords,
                But tell the *traitor* in the highest degree
                He hath abused your powers.
CORIOLANUS: 'Traitor'? How now?
AUFIDIUS: Ay, traitor, Martius.
CORIOLANUS: 'Martius'?
AUFIDIUS: Ay, Martius ...

                ...

CORIOLANUS: Hear'st thou, Mars?
AUFIDIUS: Name not the god, thou *boy of tears.*
CORIOLANUS: Ha? (ll. 84–103; my italics)

II. Rage overpowers Coriolanus' inhibitions and drives him to show his contempt by hurling offences at those present. In other words, the hero responds to the provocation directed at him in exactly the same coin, demeaning the 'name' of the characters he is facing:[27]

SCENE III, iii
CORIOLANUS: The fires i'th'lowest hell fold in the people!
                Call me their 'traitor', thou injurious tribune?
                ...
                                        ... I would not buy
                Their mercy at the price of one fair word,
                Nor check my courage for what they can give,
                To have't with saying 'Good morrow'.
                ...

27   One of the means by which Shakespeare increases the potency of Coriolanus' words in arousing anger, is the specific placement of the word 'I' in line V, vi, 117. This placement, for reasons of metre and syntax that cannot be detailed here, guides the actor skilled in delivering pentameter to stress the word 'I'. This emphasis amplifies the contempt that accompanies Coriolanus' words, because it sharpens the contrast that he makes between himself, the sole victor, and the many Volscians who have failed to overcome him (this contrast gains further emphasis in line 119, when the word 'I' is repeated). Shakespeare employs a similar technique when giving shape to Cordelia's words in the opening scene of *King Lear*: 'You have begot me, bred me, loved me. I / Return those duties back as are right fit' (I, i, 91–92). See: Harai Golomb, *Enjambment in Poetry: Language and Verse in Interaction, Meaning and Art* 3 (Tel Aviv: The Porter Institute, 1979).

You common cry of curs, whose breath I hate
As reek o'th'rotten fens, whose loves I prize
As the dead carcasses of unburied men
That do corrupt my air ... (ll. 73–131)

SCENE V, vi
CORIOLANUS: If you have writ your annals true, 'tis there
      That, like an eagle in a dove-cote, I
      Fluttered your Volscians in Corioles.
      Alone I did it ...
          ... O that I had him,
With six Aufidiuses, or more, his tribe,
To use my lawful sword! (ll. 116–131)

III. The offences Coriolanus utters, and the manner in which he
does so, enrage those present. At the same time, hurling these offences
brings about further deterioration in his *ethos*: not only is it detrimen-
tal to the way the people perceive his character in the present, it also
resurrects his former unfavourable reputation (before he became
'renowned Coriolanus', Martius was known to the Roman plebeians
as their chief enemy; before he became general of the Volscian army,
he was known to the people of Antium and Corioles as their great
destroyer). The emotional dynamics of the occasions in question is
identical to that generated by Brutus and Sicinius when they incite the
people's representatives against Coriolanus in II, iii (as analysed
above): the hero's former reputation, when revived by the manipulators, causes those present to perceive his contemptuous offences in a
harsher light and thus to become even more enraged; their growing
rage, in turn, affects their judgement and causes them to see
Coriolanus as even more hostile and dangerous, and so forth. This
intensifying rage allows the protagonist's enemies to realise their
scheme and deal him the final blow:

SCENE III, iii
CORIOLANUS: The fires i'th'lowest hell fold-in the people!
     ...
SICINIUS: Mark you this, people?
CITIZENS: To th'rock, to th'rock with him! (III, iii, 73–81)
     ...

SICINIUS: For that he has,
            As much as in him lies, from time to time
            Inveighed against the people, seeking means
            To pluck away their power, as now at last
            Given hostile strokes ...

                                            ... we,
            Ev'n from this instant, banish him our city ...
                ... I'th'people's name,
            I say it shall be so.
CITIZENS: It shall be so, it shall be so! Let him away!
            He's banished, and it shall be so! (ll. 100–114)

SCENE V, vi
ALL THE PEOPLE: Tear him to pieces! Do it presently! He killed my
                son! My daughter! He killed my cousin Marcus! He killed
                my father! (ll. 123–124)

To North's description of the two emotional appeals in question, Shakespeare added an original rhetorical enhancement: the enemies of Coriolanus use him as a sort of 'emotional amplifier', who makes an appeal to the emotions of the people at his own expense.[28] In North's version, the tribunes and Aufidius themselves appeal to the emotions of the citizens and arouse their rage against Coriolanus; the latter is completely passive, and helpless to amend his own situation amidst the tumult that arises.[29] In the Shakespearean version, by contrast, Coriolanus' enemies do not address their emotional appeal directly to the people: instead, they concentrate their rhetorical effort on the choleric protagonist, who, in his great rage, himself 'produces' an emotional appeal to the rage of the crowds. Thus the most inept rhetorician in all of Shakespeare's drama becomes – unwittingly, and to his enemies' advantage – the most effective of rhetoricians, arousing extreme passions in the briefest time.

This crafty tactic guarantees Brutus, Sicinius and Aufidius a number of substantial rhetorical advantages. Firstly, the passion

28   In North's version, Martius arouses the anger of the people with insults on a different occasion, corresponding to some extent to scene III, i of Shakespeare's play.
29   Thomas North, 'The Life of Caius Martius Coriolanus', pp. 340–341, 367.

aroused in the crowds will be maximal. This is true not only because Coriolanus hurls his insults directly at the people, with no mediating factor, but also because he does so whilst himself boiling with rage; thus he activates the natural mechanism of 'emotional contagion',[30] inflaming the people with his own passion. Being choleric and most intense in his passions, Coriolanus is the ideal instrument for agitating an audience through 'emotional contagion'. Secondly, the choice of this rhetorical trap – unlike the conventional emotional appeal described by North – guarantees Brutus and Sicinius minimal risk to their public image (and hence to their *ethos*). An open and sustained act of sedition might have exposed them to the people as they are revealed to the audience: as instigators and tricksters acting not for the public good but in their own self-interest. Instead, the two manipulate Coriolanus into expressing his hostility toward the people directly, more tangibly than any instigator could have done in his stead.

An additional way in which the two tribunes safeguard their *ethos* is by disguising their emotional appeal as an impartial, 'legal' discussion. They use measured and politic language and orchestrate events in a manner characteristic not of open public incitement, but rather of an ordered legal procedure governed by reason; the detonator with which they activate the emotional explosion – the word 'traitor' – appears within the framework of the reasoned discussion simply as a proper accusation in this legal procedure. At the end of the play Aufidius uses this very same detonator, but, because he does not orchestrate the event as a legal procedure as do Brutus and Sicinius, the scent of a despicable ruse reaches the noses of the lords of the city (V, vi, 134–135). Nevertheless, Aufidius' use of Coriolanus himself and his choler in order to inflame the Volscian crowd, limits the damage he brings upon his own public image:

SECOND LORD: His own [*that is, Coriolanus*] impatience
　　　　　　　Takes from Aufidius a great part of blame. (V, vi, 147–148)

30　On 'emotional contagion', see Chapter Three, 3.1.4.

4.2.2 The Uniqueness of Emotional Appeals in Coriolanus

The emotional appeals in *Coriolanus* are unique in their brevity. This differentiates them from appeals in Shakespearean drama as a whole, which tend to stretch over a long period of time or are designed as long, contrived speeches, according to the formulae of rhetorical treatises (let us recall, for example, Iago's appeal in *Othello*, which spans several days – perhaps even weeks – or the craftily-contrived passion-inducing speeches of Henry V and Antony).

The brevity of the appeals in *Coriolanus* stems from the dominance of *ethos* in the play's rhetorical arena and the characters' preoccupation with their reputations, as discussed above. Because the characters have been on a course to establish their good name for a long time, they are already charged with intense passions even before emotional manipulations are brought to bear on them. The journey on this course, which is lined with many impediments, leads to an accumulation of the emotions of anger, shame and pride; for this reason, a single word pertaining to a character's 'name' – uttered at the right moment and in the right place – often suffices to unleash a powerful emotional outburst.[31] This dynamics is entirely different from what we found in emotional appeals in *Henry V*, *Julius Caesar* and *Othello*. The addressees of the appeals in these three plays are not charged in advance with the passions the manipulator is seeking to arouse in them: he must first neutralise existing emotions, then stir up the emotions he wishes to induce; such a process, of course, demands time. Thus, as demonstrated, Henry's soldiers are extremely agitated during their attempts to assault the walls of Harfleur, but the emotion that sways them – fear – is less suited to achieving their mission; the king must quench it and arouse their anger. Similarly, in *Julius Caesar* III, ii, the commons express their great enthusiasm for Brutus and his speech, and most certainly are not enraged;[32] Antony must devote a

---

31   Compare: '... the better that a man thinkes of himselfe, the sooner he is offended at euery thing, and the readier he is to be mooued to anger, as taking himselfe to be despised'. Pierre de La Primaudaye, *The French Academie*, p. 497.

32   As argued in Chapter Two, Brutus unwittingly infuses the commons with anger by means of his bloody hands. However, as the enthusiastic reactions of the

great deal of time, words and rhetorical devices to arousing in them the intense passion that will enable him to generate the havoc he desires. Othello harbours no jealousy regarding Desdemona, nor anger towards Cassio, until scene III, iii. Iago himself must plant, fertilise and nurture these passions from nothing.

On the face of it, the emotional appeal by which Volumnia persuades her son to spare Rome does not fit the above generalisation. This speech, to which the remainder of the chapter will be devoted, is prolonged, not only by the standards of *Coriolanus*, but in comparison with any other Shakespearean play. In fact, Volumnia's appeal conforms very well to the generalisation in question: as will be shown, this speech does not exploit, through most of its stages, the great potential of *ethos* inherent in the rhetorical situation; it is only toward its end, when Volumnia changes her rhetorical tactics and fully exploits *ethos*, that she achieves her goal – and that within a very brief time.

4.3 Coriolanus' Capitulation to his Mother

Volumnia's emotional appeal to her son, which saves Rome from the rod of his wrath, is one of the play's numerous enigmas. The way in which this appeal influences its addressee, and the exact emotional responses it generates in him, cannot be deduced from Shakespeare's elusive text. This lengthy and diversified appeal is perplexing in the extreme to anyone attempting to outline the emotional process it arouses in the protagonist: various rhetorical means are brought to bear upon Coriolanus, yet the play gives no indication of a hierarchy among them in terms of their emotional impact. Confronted by the eloquent Volumnia, Coriolanus has been given but few lines in this scene. The dearth of replies on his part hinders any attempt to recon-

---

citizens to his speech clearly indicate, this anger is not yet intense enough to be manifested outwardly.

struct the effects of his mother's manipulations, and to outline the emotional path along which he is being steered.[33]

The analysis proposed below does not pretend to completely uncover the mystery of these key moments. Rather, it will point out the plausibly central role of shame in Volumnia's rhetorical triumph, and its correlation with the general dominance of *ethos* in the play's rhetorical situations. It is my impression that scholars have tended to ignore the central place of shame in Coriolanus' fatal capitulation, overlooking the following substantial facts: 1) shame is explicitly mentioned twice in the course of this scene; 2) in the final, apparently most influential part of her emotional appeal, Volumnia refers to this passion, expressing her intention to infuse her son with it; 3) shame holds a very important position in the array of emotional forces of *Coriolanus*; it is an ever-present factor of which the characters are well aware, and which they shun – being so concerned with their good-name and honour, it is only natural that they should be no less preoccupied with the threatening opposite, shame.[34]

4.3.1 The Difficulty in Classifying Volumnia's Speech

The scene in which Volumnia subdues Coriolanus has not, to my knowledge, been analysed by isolating the emotional factor. Most scholarly references to this factor appear to be based on a number of

33   The technique that Shakespeare employs in this scene is inherently different from those he has chosen in portraying other lengthy and ongoing emotional processes of persuasion. The Forum speeches of *Julius Caesar*, for example, are interspersed throughout with the responses of the citizens, enabling the audience to follow their changing emotional state. So too in the process of Othello's downfall, the protagonist's frequent responses to Iago's rhetoric make it possible to follow closely his emotional transformation.

34   On the over-vulnerability to shame of those who pursue honour, see below, note 61. Throughout *Coriolanus*, characters are preoccupied with the devaluation of their own and their dear ones' honour, and with the emotion of shame accompanying such devaluation. See, e.g.: I, i, 77–78; I, iv, 31–39; I, viii, 8–15; I, ix, 67–69; II, ii, 61–62, 139–141; III, i, 59–62; III, ii, 59–62, 124–126; III, iii, 62–65; IV, ii, 18–19; IV, v, 81–85, 95–98; IV, vi, 4–5, 87, 114, 120–122; V, iii, 40–42; V, vi, 79–81, 100–102, 118–120, 134–135.

misleading clues that Shakespeare has cunningly scattered: as the climactic scene approaches, several characters refer to 'pity', 'compassion' and 'mercy'[35] as the proper passions that will dissuade Coriolanus from exacting his vengeance.[36] The characters mention these passions when referring to all three emotional appeals addressed to Coriolanus, as he camps with the Volscian army near Rome; they seem unaware of the significant difference between the first two appeals and the third. The speeches uttered by Cominius and Menenius are indeed typical appeals for pity. This can be seen from the content of the latter[37] and from the central rhetorical devices used in both, such as shedding of tears and kneeling – perhaps the two most stereotypic characteristics of an appeal for pity.[38] Naturally, it is tempting to classify Volumnia's appeal as the third in a sequence of identical rhetorical efforts,[39] especially considering that she too kneels

---

35 It should be noted that in Shakespeare's time the noun 'mercy' was synonymous with (the emotion of) 'pity'.

36 IV, vi, 112–113; V, i, 71–74; V, iii, 201–202; V, iv, 14–20.

37 The first appeal, Cominius', is not seen on stage; he describes it only in part to Menenius and the tribunes (V, i, 9–28).

38 Cominius, as he himself testifies, knelt before Coriolanus (V, i, 66); Menenius, in the course of his appeal, calls the attention of his addressee to the tears that he sheds (V, ii, 67–68). Despite the absence of stage directions stating that Menenius, like Cominius, kneels while speaking to Coriolanus, this gesture is very plausible for two main reasons. First, the content and prosodic structure of the text he delivers bear witness to an outbreak of strong and sudden emotion from line 65 on – a drastic gesture such as kneeling is appropriate for a sharp emotional transition like this one, and makes it easier for the actor to execute. Second, when Menenius mockingly suggests that Brutus and Sicinius themselves try appealing to Coriolanus' mercy, he naturally assumes that this appeal would be based on the gesture of kneeling: 'Go, you that banished him; / A mile before his tent fall down, and *knee* / The way into his *mercy* ...' (V, i, 4–6; my italics).

39 Thus the influential E. A. J. Honigmann judges severely the emotional impact of the entire scene, based on a one-dimensional perception of Volumnia's diversified speech: 'In *Coriolanus* the ladies appeal to the hero's compassion – "How more unfortunate than all living women / Are we come heather" – yet the scene's emotional pressure cannot compare with that of the most moving scenes in *Othello* and *King Lear*, if only because Volumnia talks of pity from afar and scarcely understands it'. E. A. J. Honigmann, *Shakespeare: Seven Tragedies: the Dramatist's Manipulation of Response* (London: Macmillan, 1976), p. 189.

before Coriolanus and employs several means that are typical of appeals for pity. As will be shown, however, during the second part of her speech she utilises several persuasive means far removed from the rhetoric of pity and compassion. These means enable her to exploit the unique characteristics of the rhetorical situation in which she is acting – a situation inherently different from that in which Cominius and Menenius present their appeals. Thus, what first appears to be an obvious appeal to pity, ultimately proves to be an entirely different rhetorical device, aimed at arousing an entirely different passion.

4.3.2 Coriolanus' Immunity to Pity

The anger of the choleric Coriolanus grows to extreme proportions after his exile from Rome. While this passion is not evident when he takes leave of his family and friends – in this parting scene he puts on a 'stoic' disposition – it is most certainly evident in his subsequent actions: entering an alliance with the Volsces in a military campaign of vengeance against Rome. This campaign is not presented to the audience on stage, but its furious nature is illustrated by means of two different verbal descriptions: leading the Volscian army, Coriolanus begins to realise his desire for revenge, as he destroys and burns settlements in the advance on Rome (IV, vi, 41–44, 78–82).

In the absence of textual evidence that could shed light on the 'stoic' semblance of the hero as he goes into exile (IV, i, 25–27), consideration may be given to Thomas North's account of the same event. North's characterisation of Coriolanus as he leaves his city is similar to that in the Shakespearean dramatic adaptation: the exiled hero 'dyd outwardly shewe no manner of passion'. Yet Shakespeare's primary source adds an interpretative comment that explains the cause of this outward appearance and reveals the agitated reality beneath it:

> Not that he [Coriolanus] dyd patiently beare and temper his good happe ... but because he was so carried awaye with the vehemencie of anger and desire of revenge that he had no sense nor feeling of the hard state he was in ...[40]

A comparison between Coriolanus as he exits the gates of Rome and Othello as he enters his bedchamber may also prove helpful in understanding the moment in question. In *Othello*, written several years before *Coriolanus*, Shakespeare first portrayed such a seeming emotional paradox, assigning his protagonist an 'outward action' that does not 'demonstrate the figure' of his heart. In the beginning of V, i, Othello appears on stage with a semblance of tranquil resolution immediately before he discharges his great anger and takes his revenge.

Coriolanus' mighty inner anger is externally manifested later, as his vengeful plan draws near its fulfilment. This implacable passion is illustrated to the audience through Cominius' verbal description of his brief visit to the Volscian camp:

> ... he does sit in gold, his eye
> Red as 'twould burn Rome, and his injury
> The gaoler to his pity. (V, i, 64–66)

According to Thomas Wright, red eyes are a clear sign of anger brooding within the soul hidden behind them;[41] Thomas Newton, in *The Touchstone of Complexions* (1581), lists the physical changes that this passion brings about in the body, including 'fiery eyes'.[42] In addition, this description by Cominius portrays Coriolanus' anger by means of imagery: the gold of the throne upon which he sits and the red in his eyes suggest the colours of flames – as repeatedly pointed out in this study, anger was known in Shakespeare's time as the passion that enflames the blood and sets the inner body on fire.

---

40 Luis Pujante was the first to examine these lines in an effort to interpret Coriolanus' emotional state in this scene. See: Thomas North, 'The Life of Caius Martius Coriolanus' (1579), p. 342; Luis A. Pujante, 'No Sense nor Feeling: A Note on *Coriolanus* IV, I', *Shakespeare Quarterly* 41 (1990), p. 489.

41 Thomas Wright, *The Passions of the Minde in Generall* (1604), p. 132.

42 Thomas Newton, *The Touchstone of Complexions* (1581), p. 86. Cited in Lily B. Campbell, *Shakespeare's Tragic Heroes: Slaves of Passion*, p. 180. Compare *King John*, IV, ii, 163: 'With eyes as red as new enkindled fire'.

The extreme nature of Coriolanus' passion, as he camps outside Rome, was stressed above because of its crucial relevance to the emotional appeals addressed to him by Cominius, Menenius and Volumnia. Anger, even more so mighty anger, drastically reduces Coriolanus' capacity for feeling compassion. Shakespeare's play is in complete accord with other writings of his time with regard to the power of anger to negate pity:

> This [anger] is a very vehement and violent affection. For it ouerthroweth very often the whole minde and soule, for that it forgetteth all right, iustice and equitie, all good will and amitie, and pardoneth not, no not women or children, neither yet kinsfolkes or friends ... Now, when the heart is hardened with reuenge, it is turned into crueltie, which is a priuation of pitie & compassion. For when offense and anger are set on fire, they exclude all good thoughts out of the minde, and perswade to all kinde of crueltie ...[43]

> But they that are transported with a violent Passion of Courage, Choller, or Hardinesse, *are nothing moved [to pity]; for that the heate of their blood*, and the excesse of their Passion will not suffer them to think seriously of these things ...[44] (My italics)

> CORIOLANUS: I sometime lay here in Corioles
>   At a poor man's house. He used me kindly.
>   He cried to me; I saw him prisoner,
>   But then Aufidius was with in my view,
>   And *wrath o'erwhelmed my pity*. (I, ix, 81–85; my italics)

It is possible that in Cominius' description of the red-eyed Coriolanus, cited above, there exists a further indication that the hero's anger negates his pity. Several spellings of the word 'gaoler' common in early modern English are similar to those of the word 'galler' (he who galls or irritates: this adjective is derived from the noun 'gall').[45]

---

43   Pierre de La Primaudaye, *The French Academie*, pp. 497, 506.

44   F. N. Coeffeteau, *A Table of Humane Passions* (1621), pp. 363–364. Compare a similar statement: 'Of this affection cometh ... losse of charitie'. Thomas Elyot, *The Castel of Helthe* (1539), p. 62.

45   *OED*, 'galler'. The *OED* supplies only one form of spelling for the word 'galler'. The following ways of spelling the word 'gaoler' hint, perhaps, at the possibility that the two words were pronounced similarly in the period in question: gaoler, goaler, gaylere, gayler, gailer.

It is therefore possible that the two words were pronounced similarly, or even identically, in Shakespeare's day. If this is the case, Cominius' words carry an additional meaning: the injury within Coriolanus' soul 'angers his pity', or 'transforms his pity to anger'.

A further characteristic of Coriolanus' that makes it difficult to arouse his pity, is his relative inability to identify with others. In *A Table of Humane Passions*, Coeffeteau explains that identification of oneself with others is a principal and essential condition for the arousal of pity: compassion is aroused when one is aware that the misfortunes that have befallen another might just as easily befall him or his loved ones.[46] *The French Academie* expresses a similar view, referring to the capacity of identifying with others as the very root of pity.[47] Coriolanus is characterised as completely lacking in such a capacity. This is obvious whenever he comes into contact with the commoners or refers to them in his speech: not only does he make no attempt to understand the reasons for their behaviour and actions, he does not even consider the possibility that they may indeed be suffering from hunger.[48]

In this regard, note should be taken of the observations by a number of scholars who insist on wringing from the text a hero sensitive to the suffering and feelings of others. These scholars extract their 'empathic' Coriolanus from two brief moments in which he speaks of the Volscian widows and of the losses he has brought upon his enemies:[49]

---

46   F. N. Coeffeteau, *A Table of Humane Passions* (1621), p. 357.

47   Pierre de La Primaudaye, *The French Academie*, p. 493.

48   See, for example, I, i, 180–183. Later in this scene, Shakespeare brings to a climax his protagonist's inability to identify with others when, of all the degrading names in the world, he chooses to call the starving citizens, to their faces, 'fragments' – that is, scraps of uneaten food (I, i, 206).

49   It seems that researchers rely in this matter on the authority of Brian Vickers, who was one of the first to trace, as it were, expressions of empathy in IV, iv, 1–4: 'This quality ... hardly commented on by any student of the play ... is Coriolanus' sensitivity to the feelings, and especially the suffering of others'. Brian Vickers, *Shakespeare: Coriolanus*, *Studies in English Literature* 58 (London: Edward Arnold, 1976), p. 38.

[*To VIRGILIA*]   My gracious silence, hail!
Wouldst thou have laughed had I come coffined home,
That weep'st to see me triumph? Ah, my dear,
Such eyes the widows in Corioles wear,
And mothers that lack sons. (II, i, 148–152)

A goodly city is this Antium. City,
'Tis I that made thy widows. Many an heir
Of these fair edifices 'fore my wars
Have I heard groan and drop. Then know me not,
Lest that thy wives with spits and boys with stones
In puny battle slay me. (IV, iv, 1–6)

These lines in themselves, however, express no empathy or compassion at all; in this respect they are completely neutral and dependent upon their subtext during performance. The actor may express through them compassion and empathy, or may, by the same token, externalise pride, malicious pleasure, or any other emotional attitude he considers appropriate for his interpretation.

The chief Roman characters of *Coriolanus*, seeking ways to escape calamity, display a complete unawareness of the contradiction between the anger of Martius and the pity they hope to arouse in him. Their faulty understanding of the emotional factors upon which the safety of Rome depends, can be seen in the rationalisation performed by Menenius a moment after he decides to appeal to Coriolanus' pity. At this stage, one appeal to the hero's compassion has already failed – that by Cominius, his former commander and close friend. Discussing possible future efforts, Menenius tries to persuade Cominius and the two tribunes – and perhaps above all himself – that the first appeal failed simply because of poor timing. Cominius met Coriolanus before the latter had dined, and this, according to Menenius, hindered his appeal: after fasting all night, 'the veins [are] unfilled', and for this reason 'our blood is cold', our mood sour, and we 'are unapt / To give or to forgive'; after dining, however, 'when we have stuffed / These and these conveyances of our blood / With wine and feeding, we have suppler souls' (V, i, 51–57). Menenius is therefore determined to present his appeal for pity only after Coriolanus has eaten and drunk his fill. However, he is mistaken in both the diagnosis and the treatment he suggests: as Coriolanus' red eyes clearly indicated, his

184

blood was by no means cold during Cominius' visit, and he was 'unapt to give or to forgive' precisely because his blood was boiling; moreover, serving wine to a man in the grips of anger, particularly to a man choleric by nature, is a grave mistake, as 'wine enflames the blood',[50] and thus will but increase his anger. Elyot's *The Castel of Helthe*, for example, refers to wine as one of the foods and beverages that stimulate the secretion of the red-orange humour (choler).[51]

4.3.3 The Opening of Volumnia's Speech: the Appeal to Pity

Of the three characters who seek to save Rome by appealing to the emotions of Coriolanus, only Volumnia understands that attempting to arouse his pity is a completely futile rhetorical tactic. However, she seems to arrive at this understanding only during the course of her speech, after various attempts to stir her son to compassion. Before discussing the rhetorical about-face she performs in the wake of this insight, it would be useful to see how Shakespeare characterises the first part of the speech (V, iii, 94–125) as a typical appeal for pity.

The most conspicuous element in the appearance of Volumnia, Virgilia and Valeria in the Volscian camp is their apparel. The original stage direction describing the entrance of the women makes no note of their clothing. Several editors have adopted the stage direction from Theobald's edition (1726), which notes that the ladies and their attendants enter 'all in mourning';[52] others believe it makes more dramatic sense for the women to wear clothing identical in character to that worn by Coriolanus upon his arrival in Antium in IV, iv – the original stage direction marking his entrance in this scene specifies 'mean apparel'.[53] Of course, no decisive answer is possible in this matter, particularly as the terms 'mourning (weeds)' and 'mean apparel' are open to a broad range of interpretations. What is clear, from the

---

50   F. N. Coeffeteau, *A Table of Humane Passions* (1621), p. 424.
51   Thomas Elyot, *The Castel of Helthe* (1539), p. 11.
52   Cit. at: Lee Bliss, 'Notes to *Coriolanus*', *Coriolanus*, ed. Lee Bliss (Cambridge, New York and Melbourne: Cambridge University Press, 2000).
53   'Enter Coriolanus in mean apparel, disguised, and muffled' (IV, iv, 0, SD).

opening lines of Volumnia's speech, is that the ladies do not enter wearing everyday clothing:

> Should we be silent and not speak, our raiment
> And state of bodies would bewray what life
> We have led since thy exile. (V, iii, 94–96)

These words imply the conscious use of a rhetorical tactic described in Roman rhetorical treatises, echoes of which can be found in English writings of Shakespeare's time:

> Wherefore in old time the Romans to moue the magistrates to *Mercy*, striued to make a more sensible impression of their miseries, by causing their wives, children, and families to come desolately unto the place of iustice: And as for theirselues they appeared in judgement with garments befitting their fortune, all filthy and torne ...[54]

Befitting her garments, the first part of Volumnia's speech employs additional means specified in the Roman formulae regarding pleas for pity. The most obvious of these is her attempt to exploit her son's sense of sight, that is, to stir his emotions by presenting him with tangible evidence.[55] Volumnia arouses Coriolanus' awareness of what he sees before him, not only by instructing him explicitly to look at her and her delegation (V, iii, 94–96), but also by implicit means – she describes to him how passions have been aroused and will be aroused in her, Valeria, Virgilia and young Martius, by what their eyes behold:

---

54 F. N. Coeffeteau, *A Table of Humane Passions* (1621), pp. 371–372. On the use of dirty and torn clothes in appealing to the pity of Roman judges, see also: Cicero, *De Oratore*, II, 195, pp. 174–175; Quintilian, *Institutio Oratoria*, 6.1, 31–35, pp. 32–35; Plutarch, *Caesar*, 68, *Brutus*, 20; and Suetonius, *Divus Iulius*, 84.

55 '... the bloody sword, the bits of bone taken from the wound, the blood bespattered clothing, the unbandaging of the wounds, the stripped bodies with the marks of the scourge. These things commonly make an enormous impression, because they confront people's minds directly with the facts'. Quintilian, *Institutio Oratoria*, 6.1, 30–31, pp. 32–33.

>   ... thy sight, which should
> Make our eyes flow with joy, hearts dance with comforts,
> Constrains them weep and shake with fear and sorrow,
> Making the mother, wife and child to see
> The son, the husband, and the father tearing
> His country's bowels out. (Ibid., 98–103)

According to Cicero, the principal task of one who pleads for mercy is to present himself as having become miserable through misfortune.[56] This is precisely the tactic Volumnia chooses in the first part of her speech; she constantly focuses her son's attention on herself and on the other members of her delegation, elaborating upon the fate they will suffer should he realise his intention of vengeance: 'How more unfortunate ... are *we* ... *our* eyes ... weep ... and shake with fear and sorrow ... poor *we* ... how can *we* ... Whereto *we* are bound ... *we* must loose ... *we* must find / An evident calamity ...' (ll. 97–112; my italics).

Another typical means of pleading for mercy is the figure of repetition in its various forms. By repeating a word or a combination of words, the speaker expresses his troubled state of mind; the repetition also allows him to forcefully externalise his passion and thus 'contaminate' his audience with it.[57] In the opening lines of her speech, Volumnia makes double use of this figure:

>   For how can we –
> Alas! How can we for our country pray,
> Whereto we are bound, together with thy victory,
> Whereto we are bound? Alack ... (Ibid., 106–109)

In the notes to his edition of the play, A. H. Gomme regards the second of these two repetition figures as an indication that the text of *Coriolanus* has been corrupted. Such repetition, according to Gomme, cannot be Shakespeare's original writing, because it 'obstructs the

---

56   Cicero, *De Inventione*, I, liv, 106–109, pp. 157–163. Compare: 'We shall stir Pity in our hearers by recalling the vicissitudes of fortune ...' (*Rhetorica ad Herennium*, II, xxxi, 50, pp. 150–151).

57   Ibid., IV, xxviii, 38, pp. 324–325.

flow of the lines'.[58] However, it can be assumed that Shakespeare's central objective in composing this dramatic moment was not to please the ear with flowing text, but rather to put into Volumnia's mouth a text whose structural arrangement would serve her specific rhetorical purpose. If this is so, the two repetition figures can be seen as an integral part of the first part of Volumnia's appeal: they are completely congruous with the other rhetorical means it employs, all of which seek to awaken the addressee's pity.

In the course of the first part of her speech, Volumnia threatens to lie down in the path of the Volscian army as it advances on Rome, and be trampled by her son's feet. This too is but a means for arousing pity, as specified in the Roman rhetorical treatises: Cicero, listing topics for such pleas, states that the supplicant must create a virtuous and high-minded impression on his addresses; this he will achieve by showing that he is not lamenting his own ill fortune, but rather that of his loved ones, and that he is not afraid of further misfortunes the future may hold for him.[59]

4.3.4 The Rhetorical About-Face: The Appeal to Shame

The nature of Volumnia's appeal changes significantly after Coriolanus voices his intention of leaving the scene (V, iii, 129–131). His words indicate his intense emotional state and his concern that any further intensification will lead to his capitulation; however, the possibility that her son will leave the scene without capitulating leads Volumnia to seek more effective means than she has used up to that point. It is possible that the new emotional tactic she subsequently adopts is inspired by the threat just uttered by Virgilia, alluding to Coriolanus' future reputation:

58   A. H. Gomme, 'Notes to *Coriolanus*', *Coriolanus*, ed. A. H. Gomme (New York: Shakespeare Workshop, 1969).

59   Cicero, *De Inventione*, I, LVI. 109, p. 161. Compare: 'Most piteous of all is it when, in such times of trial, the victims are persons of noble character: whenever they are so, our pity is especially excited ...' (Aristotle, *Rhetoric*, II, 8, 386b).

```
VOLUMNIA: [To Coriolanus]    ... thou shalt no sooner
                 March to assault thy country than to tread ...
                 ... on thy mother's womb,
                 That brought thee to this world.
VIRGILIA:                              Ay, and mine,
                 That brought you forth this boy to keep your name
                 Living to time. (V, iii, 122–127; my italics)
```

While there is no textual evidence that Volumnia is influenced by this sentence, the topic around which her appeal is reorganised is a direct continuation of Virgilia's closing words. Up to this point, she has kept her son's attention focussed on *her and her companions*, and their anticipated ill fate (thus carrying out a typical appeal for pity); from this moment on, however, she directs his thoughts to *himself* and his own reputation (V, iii, 131–153). Volumnia describes to Coriolanus the two options he faces, and elaborates upon the 'name' (l. 143) that each option will earn for him in the 'chronicle' (l. 145): he may be blessed in the future for having brought peace to the Romans and the Volsces, but should he decide to conquer Rome, he will earn 'Such a *name* / Whose repetition will be dogged with curses' and will be remembered as the man whose '*name* remains / To the ensuing age abhorred' (ll. 136–148). Volumnia thus clearly appeals to her son's shame, inasmuch as this emotion was defined in the period in question as distress arising from an imminent or future threat to one's reputation.[60]

Considering the specific addressee Volumnia faces, an appeal to shame is far more appropriate in this situation than an appeal for pity. Coriolanus, as the play shows, is highly vulnerable to shame because of his great sensitivity regarding his good-name and his constant fear of injury to his honour.[61] His choleric disposition, particularly his

---

60 'Shame then is, a grief and a confusion, which grows from the apprehension of some crosses, which may make man infamous: And under this kinde we comprehend those calamities which are present, past, or yet to come ...'. F. N. Coeffeteau, *A Table of Humane Passions*, (1621), p. 473.

61 See: I, viii, 5–7; II, ii, 139–141; III, ii, 121–124; III, iii, 62–65; V, iii, 40–42. *The French Academie* clearly points to the vulnerability of honour-seekers to shame: '... as much therefore as Shame is a feare of dishonour, it is of great force in them that loue honour'. Pierre de La Primaudaye, *The French Academie*, p. 507.

mighty anger following his exile, makes him even more vulnerable to shame. In Shakespeare's time, anger and shame were considered to be inextricably joined, with the latter invariably appearing after the former has faded:

> Wrathe leadeth shame in a lease ... shame ... is follower and ende of anger, and there-fore joined inseperablye, even as the shadowe foloweth the body ...[62]

Coriolanus does not respond immediately to this new rhetorical tactic but rather keeps his silence (ll. 153–158). Volumnia therefore plays her trump card, amplifying the potential of her appeal to awaken shame: she continues to draw her son's attention to his name, but instead of a theoretical threat to his future reputation, she describes the danger as clear and present (V, iii, 155–182). In these lines, the mother accuses her son of faults considered most grave in Shakespeare's day, as well as in his plays – filial ingratitude and the violation of the natural bond of kinship:[63]

> There's no man in the world
> More bound to's mother ...
> Thou hast never in thy life
> Showed thy dear mother any courtesy ...
> Say my request's unjust,
> And spurn me back. But if it be not so,
> Thou art not honest, and the gods will plague thee
> That thou restrain'st from me the duty which
> To a mother's part belongs.
> ... Come, let us go.
> This fellow had a Volscian to his mother;
> His wife is in Corioles, and his child
> Like him by chance. (V, iii, 158–180)

---

62 William Baldwin, *A Treatise of Morall Philosophie*, 1547. Section II, note 2 on p. 49, ante. Cit. at: Lily B. Campbell, *Shakespeare's Tragic Heroes: Slaves of Passion*, p. 175.

63 '... we are ashamed to see our selues destitute of all honest qualities, which recommend all our equals generally ...'. F. N. Coeffeteau, *A Table of Humane Passions* (1621), pp. 479–480.

According to Coeffeteau, we experience particularly strong shame when our reputation is damaged in a public situation;[64] this passion is intensified even more when the audience present is composed of people we honour and whose criticism we fear, or of our rivals for a goal such as garnering honours.[65] In light of this, it is clear that among the characters of the play no two have an *ethos* better suited to arousing shame in Coriolanus than those present on the occasion in question: Volumnia, 'the most noble mother of the world' (V, iii, 49); and Aufidius, 'the second name of men' (IV, vi, 130).

The central role of shame in the hero's capitulation is indicated ironically even before Volumnia begins her emotional appeal, in the twofold meaning of Coriolanus' greeting to his son:

> The god of soldiers,
> With the consent of supreme Jove, inform
> Thy thoughts with nobleness, that thou mayst prove
> To shame unvulnerable and stick i'th'wars
> Like a great sea-mark, standing every flaw
> And saving those that eye thee! (V, iii, 70–75)

Literally, this greeting is yet another indication of Coriolanus' preoccupation with the emotion of shame. He wishes for Jupiter and Mars to assure that his son, Rome's future warrior, will not disgrace himself in the battles that await him; Coriolanus hopes instead that the younger Martius will prove an example of courage and a source of inspiration to his soldiers, who will look up to him (just as the Roman soldiers looked up to his inspiring father during the battles of Corioles). The secondary meaning of this wish, however, suggests that the younger Martius will 'stick i'the wars' as long as he proves 'To shame invulnerable' (that is, that the moment in which he ceases his wars and the moment in which he experiences shame are in fact one and the same). This secondary meaning applies with painful accuracy to the speaker himself, who, shortly after uttering this wish, in fact proves vulnerable to shame, and does not stick in his wars.

---

64   Ibid., p. 493.
65   Ibid., pp. 485–487.

Volumnia completes her appeal with the act of kneeling. She supports this gesture with what can be referred to as 'simultaneous commentary', shedding light on her rhetorical move:

Down, ladies. Let us shame him with our knees.
To his surname Coriolanus longs more pride
Than pity to our prayers. (V, iii, 169–171)

This remark of Volumnia's should not be regarded as a mere utterance of frustration, denouncing Coriolanus' lack of pity and excessive pride; it is also a straightforward explanation of the cause behind her rhetorical about-face: since proud men are known to be immune to pity[66] and vulnerable to shame, and since her son is evidently proud, the proper way to subdue him emotionally is to appeal to his shame.

These lines, however, do not merely interpret the unfolding drama to the audience. Within the fictional world, from Volumnia's point of view, they serve a specific rhetorical purpose: through them she is guiding Coriolanus to realise that the events he is experiencing at present are meant to arouse him to shame. Since the first part of her speech was an unmistakable appeal to pity, Coriolanus is liable to interpret the remainder as a further effort to arouse his compassion; to avoid this, and because shame is most likely to be aroused when the addressee is aware that he is expected to be ashamed,[67] Volumnia must make her son aware of the fact that she is now appealing to his shame. It is all the more crucial for Volumnia to 'update' Coriolanus' awareness because the physical gesture by which she appeals to his shame is perhaps the most unmistakable means of appealing for pity.

This rhetorical switch performed by Volumnia, exploiting to the maximum the *ethos* factor inherent in the given rhetorical situation, has not been discussed, to my knowledge, in the research literature. Vickers rightly observes that the appeals of Cominius, Menenius and Volumnia follow one another in an ascending hierarchy of the ap-

---

66 According to Coeffeteau, pride counteracts pity. F. N. Coeffeteau, *A Table of Humane Passions* (1621), p. 363.
67 The validity of this generalisation is evident from the proved effectiveness of the timeless emotional appeal '*Shame* on you!'.

pealer's degree of intimacy with Coriolanus;[68] however, this diagnosis is not complete, because Volumnia has a blood relationship with the addressee, whereas her two predecessors do not. Cominius is a former commander and a loving friend (IV, i, 38–44), and Menenius is his 'father' only in a forced, figurative sense.[69] Isolating the *ethos* factor and examining its effect on *pathos* thus clarifies the fundamental difference between the first two appeals to Coriolanus and the last: when Menenius and Cominius kneel, the result is an appeal for pity; when a mother kneels – an appeal to shame.

Shakespeare's dramatisation of Volumnia's speech closely follows North's version, at times even borrowing the exact language of the source. A few seemingly minor modifications and additions by the playwright, however, link this emotional appeal to the diverse themes of the play, making it a high point in their development and an integral part of the play's intricate totality. The three stages of the speech and the rhetorical objective of each, as discussed above (the appeal for pity; the appeal to shame by referring to Coriolanus' future reputation; and the appeal to shame by referring to his present reputation), are taken directly from North. Unlike North, however, Shakespeare shows an awareness of the rhetorical changes that Volumnia performs during the appeal, and sharpens them in various ways. For example, he intensifies the appeal for pity at the beginning of the speech by adding various rhetorical devices, such as the repetition figures quoted above – of which there is no trace in North's version – or metaphors and imagery far more powerful than those of the source.[70] The reinforcement of the first part of the speech not only helps the spectator to recognise the typical appeal for pity, it also sharpens the boundary between it

68   Brian Vickers, *Shakespeare: Coriolanus*, p. 43.
69   See V, ii, 66; V, iii, 8–9. Darkening Menenius' pretension to be Coriolanus' 'father' is his cynical manipulative use of this word while appeasing the mutinous citizens: '... Alack, / You are transported by calamity / ... and you slander / The helms o'th'state, who care for you like fathers ...' (I, i, 60–63).
70   Compare, for example, Shakespeare's 'The son, the husband and the father tearing / His country's bowels out' (V, iii, 102–103), with North's '... making my selfe to see my sonne, and my daughter here, her husband, besieging the walles of his native countrie'. Thomas North, 'The Life of Caius Martius Coriolanus' (1579), p. 361.

and the appeals to shame that follow. In North's version it is difficult to distinguish the thematic and rhetorical transitions in this speech, which seems like an arbitrary collection of arguments being hurled by a mother at her son, with no apparent rhetorical awareness.

The most conspicuous difference between North's account of the speech and Shakespeare's dramatic adaptation thereof can be found in its conclusion. North's version lacks Volumnia's explicit instruction to her son (and to the audience) to see the final act of kneeling as a means of arousing shame. Unlike Shakespeare's Volumnia, North's does not mention this emotion at all during her speech; rather, in a margin note beside the paragraph in which the appeal ends, North, or his publisher, glosses: 'Coriolanus' compassion of his mother'.

Shakespeare links the act of kneeling, which he drew from North's account, to the thematic fabric of his play. This kneeling, in *Coriolanus*, brings to a head the broad discussion of the balance of power between *word* and *action*, the two basic means of persuasion and arousing emotion.[71] In early modern English, the noun 'action' belonged to the semantic fields of rhetoric and theatrical acting; in these contexts, it indicated the non-verbal means employed by the orator and the actor – such as voice, gesture, posture, mimicry, and eye-expression.[72] Traditionally, action was held to be the orator's most effective means of persuasion,[73] particularly with regard to

71 In the course of the play, several characters draw the audience's attention to the fact that visual stimulation is at times the most stirring and persuasive factor (I. i, 10, 46–47; II, ii, 20–23; III, i, 133–136; IV, v, 203–205; V, iii, 129–131). Alongside these utterances, the play presents processes of persuasion and agitation in which the words play a significant part, both in volume and in effect. In most cases, however, word and action work jointly, reinforcing one another, and it is clearly not possible to discuss them in isolation or to give one precedence over the other.

72 See: Cicero, *Oratore*, xvii, 55–xviii, 60, pp. 346–350; *Rhetorica ad Herennium*, III, xi, 19–xv, 27, pp. 188–205; Quintilian, *Institutio Oratoria*, XI, iii, pp. 85–183.

73 See, e.g.: 'It is a trivial grammar-school text, but yet worthy a wise man's consideration. Question was asked of Demosthenes, *what was the chief part of an orator?* He answered, *action*: what next? *Action*: what next again? *Action.* He said it that knew it best ...'. Francis Bacon, 'Of Boldness', *Essays* (1612), p. 35. See also: Cicero, *Oratore*, xvii, 56, p. 346. Compare: 'TAMORA: Titus, I am come to talk with thee. TITUS: No, not a word; how can I grace my talk, /

commoners, whose ability to follow logical argumentation was considered to be limited. This ancient perception is expressed in III, ii, when Volumnia attempts to persuade Coriolanus to face the tribunes and the people in the market place:

> VOLUMNIA: Go to them, with this bonnet in thy hand,
>   And thus far having stretched it – here be with them –
>   Thy knee bussing the stones – for in such business
>   *Action is eloquence*, and the eyes of the ignorant
>   More learned than the ears ... (III, ii, 74–78; my italics)

Thus, when Volumnia kneels before Coriolanus in the Volscian camp, her wheel is come full circle: the theoretical lesson in rhetoric she has tried to impart to her son, and which he has failed to implement, she puts into practice, thereby subduing her ignorant pupil.

The thematic treatment of the balance of power between word and action in *Coriolanus* is not, however, limited to narrow matters of rhetorical practice. In fact, the play as a whole can be seen as a theatrical examination of the saying 'action is eloquence': it presents a protagonist characterised as a typical man of action, whose relationship with the spoken word is most problematic; this protagonist shows his greatness and establishes his name by virtue of his actions, and loses it by virtue of his words. The play itself, in its linguistic simplicity and its avoidance of rhetorical artificiality, resembles its 'plain' hero: as mentioned above, *Coriolanus* contains very few contrived speeches and formal, elaborate rhetorical devices; its language creates an initial impression of being simple, even 'primitive', and it draws great strength – compared to other Shakespearean plays – from gestures, stage actions and images, and Tableaux.

One such typical moment, in which action takes centre stage, occurs immediately following Volumnia's kneeling, a moment before Coriolanus' capitulation. The original stage direction aims to ensure that the action will receive the centrality it deserves; having the power

---

Wanting a hand to give it action? / Thou hast the odds of me; therefore no more'
(*Titus Andronicus*, V, ii, 16–19).

to impart meanings and intensities beyond the range of spoken language, it must not be sullied with words:

> Holds her by the hand, silent (V, iii, 182 SD)

This enigmatic moment culminates the deliberate blurring of the emotional process Coriolanus undergoes in this scene. The pithy stage direction suggests a relatively long, static pause, devoid of gestures – which, in the absence of words, might have provided an external indication of his inner state. As demonstrated, the rhetorical means Volumnia employs in the second part of her appeal are unquestionably designed to subdue her son with shame; it is also evident that the playwright is directing his audience to consider the role of this emotion in breaking Coriolanus' vindictive resolution. However, enveloping this key moment in mysterious, motionless silence, opens the hero's capitulation to numerous possible interpretations, in keeping with the spectator's individual perception of the drama, and the emotions stirred in him by Shakespeare's rhetoric.

Chapter Five
Shakespeare's Emotional Appeals
and Modern Theories of the Emotions

CLOUSEAU: Facts, Hercule, facts. Nothing matters but the facts.
Without them, the science of criminal investigation
is nothing more than a guessing game ... Now, then,
Hercule, what is the inescapable conclusion?
HERCULE: Maria Gambrelli killed the chauffeur.
CLOUSEAU: What? You idiot! Impossible! She is protecting
someone!
HERCULE: How do you know that?
CLOUSEAU: Instinct.

(*A Shot in the Dark*)

Historical, philosophical and literary studies have always tended to
consider that the 'traditional' Western worldview – dominant since
classical antiquity – holds Passion to be the primary enemy of the
soul. Scholars have generalised that this tradition places Passion in
polar opposition to Reason and preaches neutralising the emotions and
seeking purely rational modes of thinking. As Richard Strier shows,
this generalisation belies reality and represses numerous voices from
classical and early modern writings. These voices extol emotion as
defining the human being and the human experience, and as instructing and inspiring humans to spiritual belief, virtuous deeds, and the
achievement of creative heights. This 'anti-stoic' tradition – as expressed, for example, in the writings of Luther – sees the exhortation
to pursue the rule of reason as unrealistic and leading to misery and
desperation: the challenge it presents is impossible, since there are no
human beings whose emotions do not erupt from time to time; even if

there were, they should not be considered humans, but monsters.[1] Strier also points to several expressions of this 'untraditional tradition' in two Shakespearean plays, *The Comedy of Errors* and *King Lear*.

The dominant voices in modern research of the emotions can be considered the direct continuation of the 'Praise of Passion' tradition Strier investigates. Contemporary studies do not see the aspiration to neutralise the emotional mind and its influence on the faculty of reason as merely an idle, frustrating and absurd presumption: they consider it harmful. Our rational faculty has in fact many limitations, and cannot function adequately on its own. Emotion serves, among other things, as a complementary mechanism, compensating for the limitations of the intellect ('rational thought', 'Reason'). Any attempt to suspend emotion and become 'purely rational' must therefore lead to a serious impairment in processes of thought and decision-making, and is therefore manifestly irrational.

As this chapter will show, the contemporary world view summarised above is identical to the world view that emerges from the four plays examined in this study. In the fictional worlds of these plays, emotion is a constant and dominant force that cannot be denied without catastrophic results. Several characters in the plays display a 'traditional' approach to emotions, obstinately perceiving and presenting themselves as purely rational entities: they untiringly aspire towards modes of thought based on intellect alone, and they view and portray their actions as the outcome of rational judgement. However, the plays expose this pretension as one doomed to failure, and it is precisely these emotion-denying characters who eventually fall victim to intense emotional stimuli. Shakespeare contrasts these pseudo-rational characters with others who, far from refusing to acknowledge emotion, display a sober awareness of its impact on them and on Man in general. These characters understand that the emotional variable is persistent and influential, and must therefore always be taken into account. In fact, the playwright equips these characters with the same

---

1   Richard Strier, 'Against the Rule of Reason: Praise of Passion from Petrarch to Luther to Shakespeare to Herbert', *Reading the Early Modern Passions: Essays in the Cultural History of Emotion*, ed. Gail Kern Paster, Katherine Rowe and Mary Floyd-Wilson (Philadelphia: University of Pennsylvania Press, 2004), pp. 23–42.

skills that contemporary thought views as aspects of *emotional intelligence*: they know how to balance reason with passion, how to think with their 'hearts' and 'heads' alike, and they can identify and appraise their own as well as others' emotions as they arise. On the solid basis of these two abilities, the emotionally-gifted characters develop additional skills, such as the regulation of emotion in themselves and in others – using varied forms of emotional appeal. These characters understand that emotion is a phenomenon subject to rules, and that it is possible, with some degree of accuracy, to predict other characters' probable emotional responses in given circumstances. This understanding enables them to arouse and channel the emotions of others, and to manipulate them for their own benefit.

Current thinking views emotional intelligence as an essential trait that helps humans deal optimally with the complex situations occurring in their lives. In the Western-capitalist jargon employed in the bestseller that popularised this idea, people with high emotional intelligence are destined for 'life success'.[2] Precisely the same is true of the Shakespearean worlds examined in this study, and at the end of each play we find that those characters endowed with high 'emotional intelligence' indeed emerge on top.[3]

---

2   Daniel Goleman, *Emotional Intelligence* (New York: Bantam Books, 1995), pp. xi–xiii, 37–42.

3   Some readers might question whether Iago does indeed 'emerge on top' at the end of *Othello*. Limitations of space do not allow a detailed discussion of this question; suffice it to say that there are several hints in the play linking Iago to the Devil (e. g., I, i, 66; V, ii, 283) and suggesting that, even at the play's end, he has not been totally neutralised and that the 'Iago problem' has by no means been resolved. The very fact that he survives Othello's attempt to kill him – emphasised by his own words, 'I bleed, sir; but not killed', as well as Othello's 'If that thou be'st a devil, I cannot kill thee' – is highly significant, especially if we bear in mind that in Shakespeare's source for this play, Cinthio's *Hecatommithi*, the Moor's Ensign does die.

5.1 Shakespeare's Characters and *Emotional Intelligence*

5.1.1 The five basic skills of emotional intelligence

The concept of emotional intelligence is a new one. In 1983 Howard Gardner fired what is considered the opening shot in the race to define the types of 'intelligence' that are alternatives to the traditional IQ. In his book *Frames of Mind*, he first expressed the need to define human skills other than the 'academic' verbal and mathematical. As a basis for discussion and development of this idea, Gardner proposed five basic abilities: spatial, kinesthetic, musical, intrapsychic, and interpersonal.[4] The last two are the most relevant to our subject, and in *Multiple Intelligence*, published ten years later, he explicitly designates them 'intelligences' and supplies concise definitions: 'interpersonal intelligence' is the ability to understand the character of one's fellow human beings, their feelings, moods, desires, and motives, and to act appropriately;[5] 'intrapersonal intelligence' involves the same characteristics, differing only in that the ability to identify and understand is turned inward towards one's own psyche. Gardner defines intrapersonal intelligence as the degree of the subject's ability to create an accurate and truthful model of himself, and to use this model to guide his behaviour and conduct.[6]

The term 'emotional intelligence' was first officially coined in 1990, in an article of the same name. The authors of the article, Peter Salovey and John D. Mayer, define emotional intelligence as 'the ability to monitor one's own and others' feelings and emotions, to discriminate among them and to use this information to guide one's thinking and actions'.[7] The echo of Gardner's two 'personal intelligences' is discernable in this definition. Salovey and Mayer divide emotional intelligence into five component skills:[8]

---

4   Howard Gardner, *Frames of Mind* (New York: Basic Books, 1983).
5   Howard Gardner, *Multiple Intelligence: The Theory in Practice*, p. 9.
6   Ibid.
7   Peter Salovey and John D. Mayer, 'Emotional Intelligence', p. 189.
8   Ibid., pp. 189–200.

1. *Appraisal and expression of emotion in the self.* This is the cornerstone of the emotional intelligence of each and every human being. An individual endowed with this skill is able to truthfully and accurately perceive the nature and force of his emotions as they occur, and to follow the changes they undergo. Emotional self-appraisal is of course among the factors that affect one's ability to express emotion, verbally or non-verbally, and thus to communicate with others on an emotional level.

2. *Perceiving and appraising others' emotional reactions.* Salovey and Mayer point to developmental perspectives suggesting that the fundamental condition for the existence of this skill is the existence of skill no. 1, the ability to appraise one's own emotions. In effect, it would appear that neither of the first two components of emotional intelligence can exist without the other: people who have difficulty identifying their own emotions have difficulty identifying the emotional messages transmitted by those around them, and vice versa. Similarly, many of those who correctly evaluate the nature and force of their own emotions, are also able to recognise the emotional states of people with whom they come in contact.

3. *Regulation of emotion in the self.* This ability depends, of course, on the first skill of emotional intelligence, since it is impossible to control and regulate emotions without first being able to identify and appraise them.

4. *Regulation of emotion in others.* Salovey and Mayer emphasise the potential consequences of this skill – positive as well as negative: a person with high emotional intelligence can improve the mood of those around him, and even use personal charisma to regulate and channel the emotions of others in order to realise good and beneficial goals; on the other hand, these abilities to regulate and channel can also be harnessed to further evil goals by means of deceptive emotional manipulation, in the manner of the great Shakespearean villains. The ability to regulate the emotions of others is conditional upon the existence of skills 1 and 2, since in order to channel another's emotions along the desired path, that person's present emotions must first be recognised and appraised (2), and the ability to do this is conditional upon the ability to appraise emotion in the self (1). Furthermore, in order to regulate another's emotions, the

regulator must control his or her own emotions (3) and their outward expression, because they are likely to have a direct effect on anyone whom he or she encounters. This can be accomplished, as mentioned, only by those endowed with the first skill of emotional intelligence.

5. *Utilisation of emotion.* Emotion is a mechanism whose function includes exerting a positive influence on thought processes by making them more efficient. For this reason, those who use emotion 'intelligently' can utilise it to increase their power of concentration; to focus their thinking on immediate, urgent matters; to help in solving problems; and to organise their memory so that it functions more efficiently. Well directed emotions can improve the individual's mental and physical performance, and provide the motivation to realise specific goals. This does not mean only those emotions usually considered 'positive', such as joy or love: the often angry face of Michael Jordan reflected the nature and force of the emotion that motivated him to overcome obstacles placed in his path to glory (by rivals and team mates alike). Similarly, an emotion such as anxiety, usually considered undesirable, can motivate individuals to realise lofty objectives with which it has no apparent connection, such as publishing a study on Shakespearean drama.

This brief survey reveals a fact very significant to the matter at hand, and one of which I shall make use in examining the 'emotional abilities' of the Shakespearean characters under discussion: skills 3 and 5 of 'emotional intelligence' rely on skill 1; skill 4 depends on skill 2, which is in turn dependent on no. 1. In other words, the first and necessary condition for emotional intelligence is the existence of the ability to appraise emotion in the self. Any analysis or diagnosis that makes use of the tools of emotional intelligence must, therefore, first examine the subject's ability to observe and properly understand his own emotions. Only then can his ability to regulate his own emotions, motivate himself, appraise and regulate the emotions of others, and make correct, successful social decisions, be examined.

Before investigating in detail the 'emotional abilities' of key characters discussed here in light of Salovey and Mayer's insights and definitions, two examples will be examined. These examples illustrate how, in the Shakespearean world, there sometimes exists a significant link between the quality of the most basic of the skills of emotional intelligence – appraisal of emotion in the self – and the existence and quality of additional skills. Shakespeare sometimes demonstrates the inability of a certain character at a given moment to 'read' his own emotions or mental state, and with conspicuous proximity, his failure to read the emotions of others. This he does explicitly in the opening scene of *King Lear*,[9] as well as in *Julius Caesar*, as I shall demonstrate below. In *Coriolanus*, too, he creates such a moment, indicating the fundamental affinity between the two basic skills. I am referring to the emotionally charged moment in which Coriolanus gives in to his mother's persuasive speech: as shown in Chapter Four, the emotion of shame plays an important, if not central, part in his acquiescence. Coriolanus, however, the Shakespearean hero most limited in powers of self-observation,[10] shows no awareness whatsoever of this fact as he speaks to Aufidius; instead, he expresses his belief that the emotion flooding him is *compassion* (as explained, compassion is the emotion least likely to be generated in Coriolanus in this scene, in light of his generally choleric nature and his extreme rage at being banished from Rome). Accordingly, and in close proximity to his emotional self-misinterpretation, Coriolanus fails to recognise the emotions and true intentions of Aufidius:

CORIOLANUS: ... Now, good Aufidius,
              Were you in my stead, would you have heard
              A mother less? Or granted less, Aufidius?
AUFIDIUS: *I was moved withal.*

9   Regan, one of those Shakespearean villains who excel in their powers of 'psychological diagnosis', directly links her father's limited self-knowledge with his inability to recognise the authentic emotions of other characters in the opening scene: 'GONERIL: He always loved our sister most, and with what poor judgement he hath now cast her off appears too grossly. REGAN: 'Tis the infirmity of his age; yet he hath ever but slenderly known himself' (I, i, 281–285).

10   Coriolanus' tendency to avoid looking inward is manifested clearly in his longest soliloquy (IV, iv, 12–24): after the emotional shocks and the dramatic reversals he experiences after his return from the war – which were, to a considerable degree, generated by his own fierce disposition – he ponders the 'slippery turns' occurring in the 'world', and does not reveal even a trace of introspection.

CORIOLANUS: *I dare be sworn you were.*
                 And, sir, it is no little thing to make
                 Mine eyes to sweat *compassion*. (V, iii, 192–197; my italics)

Coriolanus' deficiency in the two basic emotional skills leaves very meagre ground for the growth of additional emotional abilities: he is particularly deficient in regulating and utilising his own emotions (skills 3 and 5), as can be observed repeatedly in his public outbursts in civilian life. These uncontrolled outbursts often cause the characters towards whom they are directed to develop negative emotions and act against him – in other words, Coriolanus is also completely lacking in skill no. 4, the ability to regulate the emotions of others.

An opposite example can be found in the characterisation of Iago. Traditionally, students of the play have referred to the ancient's proclamations of hatred and thirst for revenge as evidence of the feebleness of his declared motives;[11] to the best of my knowledge, scholars have not noted the fact that these proclamations reveal an impressive emotional self-awareness on his part. The following quotations, which appear in a variety of discussions on Iago's problematic motives, reveal his genuine awareness of his emotions and the true reason for their arousal:

> I hate the Moor,
> And it is thought abroad that 'twixt my sheets
> He has done my office. I know not if't be true
> Yet I, for mere suspicion in that kind,
> Will do as if for surety. (I, iii, 368–372)

> I'll have our Michael Cassio on the hip,
> Abuse him to the Moor in the rank garb –
> For I fear Cassio with my night-cap too ... (II, i, 286–288)

The choice of words in these lines indicates that not only does Iago know how to recognise the true emotion that sways him, he is also

---

11   See, e.g.: Robert B. Heilman, *Magic in the Web: Action and Language in Othello* (Lexington: University of Kentucky Press, 1965), pp. 30–32; E. A. J. Honigmann, 'Secret Motives in *Othello*', *Shakespeare: Seven Tragedies: The Dramatist's Manipulation of Response*, pp. 85–88.

quite aware that this emotion has been awakened only because of *suspicion*, rather than *knowledge* of solid facts. In this respect he differs significantly from Othello, who is entirely convinced that the hatred he proclaims for Desdemona and Cassio arises from an absolute *knowledge* of proven facts. These precise and realistic statements of Iago's show the degree of his emotional complexity and his capacity for self-examination. His verbal references to the lack of certainty about his wife's alleged love affairs with Othello and Cassio, show that he is not rationalising his emotions or trying to justify them ('justify' in the usual sense of showing them to be 'logical'). Shakespeare directs his audience to draw a comparison between the ancient and his commander, in whose mouth he often puts words that express certainty.[12] Iago's ability to know his emotions is a result of his not trying, like Othello, to fuse the fields of logic and emotion and resolve their alleged incompatibility, but of acknowledging instead the separate and legitimate existence of each. This self-awareness allows him to recognise its complete absence from the mind of Othello, and thus to choose the most appropriate emotional strategy for bringing him down.

5.1.2 Antony and Brutus

Antony is perhaps the Shakespearean character whose emotional skills are depicted in the greatest detail. As I shall now show, *Julius Caesar* gives us specific indications that Antony possesses the two levels of awareness essential for well-developed 'emotional intelligence': he is aware of the quality of his emotions as they occur; and he is able to recognise and appraise the emotions of others. Shakespeare's tragedy is in line here with Salovey and Mayer's contemporary definitions of emotional intelligence: Antony's two levels of awareness are the basis for additional emotional skills, among them impressive emotional self-control and the equally impressive ability to regulate and channel the emotions of fellow characters.

---

12   See below, pp. 255–257.

One of Antony's most noteworthy characteristics is his attraction to excitement and experiences that stimulate the senses and the passions. It was apparently important to the playwright that his audience be well aware of this characteristic, as he takes pains to have the characters mention it no fewer than five times in the course of the play.[13] For our purposes, Antony can be defined as a character who 'knows how to be emotional', that is, one who experiences emotions without denying or suppressing them, as opposed to characters such as Caesar or Brutus, who 'do not know how to be emotional': the play draws the attention of the audience to the fact that all its central characters are subject at various times and in various circumstances to strong passions; a character who 'knows how to be emotional' is aware of how emotion affects him and does not try to delude himself or others that he is immune to it;[14] characters who 'do not know how to be emotional', on the other hand, deny and suppress the strong passions they experience.

In the course of the encounter between Antony and the servant of Octavius, as Caesar's corpse lies at their feet, Shakespeare points out Antony's simultaneous awareness of both his own emotions and those of the character with whom he is engaged:

> ANTONY: Thy heart is big, get thee apart and weep.
> Passion, I see, is catching, for mine eyes,
> Seeing those beads of sorrow stand in thine,
> Began to water. (III, i, 282–285)

As stressed above, these two basic skills constitute the essential source from which additional skills can develop; indeed, Antony identifies the nature of the relationship between his passions and those of the

---

13 I, ii, 28–29, 203–204; II, i, 188–189; II, ii, 116–117; V, i, 62.
14 Antony, for example, reveals such sober awareness while negotiating with the conspirators over Caesar's dead body: 'Therefore I took your hands, but was indeed / *Swayed* from the point by looking down on Caesar' (III, i, 218–219; my italics). In two instances elsewhere in the play, the verb 'sway' denotes the channelling force or influence of the passions (II, i, 20, 203). Antony, then, does not deny that he is affected by his passions, and does not attempt – as Brutus does in reference to the death of Portia – to present himself as a 'stoic', affected only minimally by the death of someone close to him.

servant (he defines the nature of this relationship by means of a general comment regarding the contagious nature of emotion). Using his two basic emotional skills and the insight he gains through them, he is ready to channel the emotions of the Romans in the Forum by 'contaminating' them with the intense passions he chooses to externalise. In the terminology of Salovey and Mayer, Antony demonstrates perfectly in his speech the fourth skill of emotional intelligence: the ability to regulate emotion in others. This skill, as we have seen, is conditional upon the existence of the other four basic skills; thus, the planning and execution of the speech are a comprehensive and impressive demonstration of fully developed 'emotional intelligence' (This will be enlarged upon below, in a discussion of the connection between Antony's 'emotional intelligence' and his 'acting' abilities).

Opposite the stirred and stirring Antony, the play sets Brutus. The absolute contrast between the abilities and willingness of these two characters to experience emotion is stressed from the beginning of the play: I, ii opens with an exposition of Antony the athlete, preparing for the holy chase, and Brutus, whose seemingly sober nature is revealed in the very first line he utters.[15] A succinct statement from the mouth of Brutus encourages the audience to follow the continuous onstage comparison between the two characters; this statement also encourages further consideration of the emotional difference between Brutus and Antony, and its implications:

> I am not gamesome: I do lack some part
> Of that quick spirit that is in Antony. (I, ii, 28–29)

The immense gap between the attitudes of Brutus and Antony towards the passions parallels the gap between their emotional skills – or, in the terminology of this chapter, their 'emotional intelligence'. Just as Shakespeare invites his audience to take note of the connection between Antony's ability to recognise his own emotions and his ability to interpret the emotions of others, so, inversely, Brutus' inability to identify his own emotions is closely tied to his failure to identify the emotions of those around him. The playwright hints at the connec-

---

15   See Chapter Two, note 3.

tion between these two limitations of the hero's by staging two incidents in which Brutus makes critical errors in recognising emotions, and by linking these two incidents through symmetry. The first incident reveals Brutus' defective appraisal of emotion in himself. In the Orchard Scene, after Shakespeare has given us various hints about the anger flaming in his heart, and after Portia has described the anger he displayed inside their house, Brutus *twice* testifies to his sadness:

> You are my true and honourable wife,
> As dear to me as are the ruddy drops
> That visit my sad heart. (II, i, 290)

> All my engagements I will construe to thee,
> All the charactery of my sad brows. (Ibid., 307)

The second incident reveals Brutus' failure to perceive and appraise others' emotional reactions. In scene I, ii, following the long speech in which Cassius tries to incite Brutus against Caesar, the latter enters the stage accompanied by his entourage and other characters. Brutus observes them and reports to Cassius that the prominent part of Caesar's forehead, to which he refers as his 'angry spot', is glowing (l. 83). Later in the scene he *twice* conveys his impression that the emotion that Caesar felt at the moment in question was sadness:

> Ay, Casca, tell us what hath chanced today
> That Caesar looks so sad. (I, ii, 216–217)

> And after that he came thus sad away? (I, ii, 266)

The expression 'angry spot', then, is for Brutus merely a noun indicating a part of the body; in his mind, this noun has lost all connection with its original emotional referent.

The two incidents surveyed above are linked through threefold symmetry: the character whose emotional state Brutus is interpreting is in both cases angry; in both cases Brutus in fact interprets the emotional state of the character in question as sadness; and in both cases Brutus utters his erroneous interpretation twice. This threefold linkage between the two incidents suggests that Brutus' limitations in perceiving and appraising his own and others' emotions are consistent, deeply rooted, and interconnected.

Brutus' defective 'emotional intelligence' is manifested in one of the fatal mistakes – perhaps the most fatal – that he makes during the play: giving the pulpit to Antony, the stirring orator. In this context Shakespeare makes a direct comparison contrasting his two major characters: just as Antony is aware of the contagious quality of emotion, the play indicates Brutus' complete lack of it. This lack of awareness is the central cause of the fatal mistake, and is revealed ironically in the exchange between Brutus and Antony over the warm corpse of Caesar. As they test each other's intentions, Brutus tries to explain the motive for the assassination and the emotional state of the assassins at present. He finds it fitting to make these clarifications because intentions and emotions are concealed, whereas the blood-smeared hands of the assassins are all too visible to Antony's eyes:

> Our hearts you see not, they are pitiful;
> And pity to the general wrong of Rome –
> As *fire drives out fire*, so pity pity –
> Hath done this deed on Caesar. (III, i, 169–172; my italics)

The editors of the major editions of *Julius Caesar* compare the two proverbs interwoven in Brutus' statement to various early modern parallels, all of which express the capacity of one instance from within a whole to override another, identical instance from within the same whole. I believe the more relevant object of comparison – considering the timing of these words and the problematic relationship of the speaker with emotion and the rhetoric of emotion – is not this proverb or another, but a dictum repeated again and again in Roman and Elizabethan treatises on rhetoric. In contrast to the proverbs cited by the editors of the play, this traditional dictum essentially contradicts Brutus' words. The writers of rhetorical treatises usually employ it to illustrate and reinforce their generalisations regarding the contagiousness of emotion and the first necessary condition for stirring up the audience:

The heart of the matter as regards arousing emotions, so far as I can see, lies in being moved by them oneself ... Nothing but fire can burn, nothing but water can make us wet, and 'nothing gives colour but what colour has'.[16]

There is no substance of itself that will take fire except ye put fire to it. Likewise, no man's nature is so apt straight to be heated except the orator himself be on fire and bring his heat with him ... he that is heated with zeal and godliness shall set others on fire with like affection ...[17]

Firstly, with no direct connection to the latter quotation, taken from Thomas Wilson's treatise, Brutus' comment to Antony constitutes one of the many expressions found in the play of its protagonist's tendency to rationalise the emotions. Brutus perceives the passions as qualities that can be measured and compared; he is convinced that decisions can be made and actions justified by calculating them arithmetically.[18] Secondly, in light of Wilson's traditional assertion and the specific moment at which Brutus employs the proverbs quoted above, his words to Antony carry a heavy irony and indicate abysmal emotional ignorance: they are spoken precisely at the critical moments when the process of Italy's inflammation has passed the point of no return, and the fire of anger that was hidden within him, and which has now erupted in the act of murder, does not 'drive out fire', but rather generates another fire. As elaborated in Chapter Two, *Julius Caesar* constitutes a theatrical illustration that fire does not eliminate fire, but rather brings about a rapid and widespread conflagration. Moreover, of all the characters of the play, Brutus chooses to voice his erroneous insight to precisely that character who is well aware of the real qualities of 'fire'. In just a few moments the protagonist will grant his antagonist the right to speak publicly, thus enabling him to enflame all of Rome and demonstrate most convincingly that 'fire drives out fire' only in proverbs.

A phenomenon repeatedly emphasised in *Julius Caesar*, and one that has received considerable attention from scholars, is the central characters' reference to themselves in the third person. This trend is

16   Quintilian, *Institutio Oratoria*, 6.2.26–28, p. 59.
17   Thomas Wilson, *The Art of Rhetoric* (1560), p. 163.
18   The best example of this is Brutus' justification for the assassination of Caesar: 'Not that I loved Caesar less, but that I loved Rome more' (III, ii, 19–20).

210

highlighted as early as in the first appearance of Caesar, Brutus and Cassius (I, ii), who repeatedly refer to themselves by their own name. Later in the play the central characters continue this practice, which appears more frequently in *Julius Caesar* than in any other Shakespearean play. It seems that this phenomenon is connected directly to the matter at hand and to the play's concern with the 'emotional intelligence' of its characters. Not only does it express the exaggerated sense of self-importance of certain characters, or their political ambitions:[19] it is also symptomatic of a way of thinking that leads to deficient self-observation, hence to weak 'emotional intelligence'. The word 'name', in the language of the play, indicates among other things the public image of a given character, that is, the way in which that character is perceived by the public (as for example in *Coriolanus*).[20] The tendency of the characters in question to refer to themselves by their own names, then, reveals their inclination to exchange inner self-observation for outward observation. In other words, these characters tend to avoid observing themselves directly, and see themselves instead as society sees them, or, rather, as they would like society to see them.

As Alexander Leggatt points out, most of the central characters in *Julius Caesar* are intensely concerned with their public reputation and allot considerable resources to establishing for themselves an impressive image. Leggatt interprets this phenomenon as arising from the interdependence between the power of the individual in the society of the play, and his public image – as opposed to his official position or his place in the political hierarchy.[21] Following this excellent observation, Shakespeare's Rome can be seen as a society that systematically shapes individuals with low 'emotional intelligence': the game of life that dominates there encourages them to refrain from self-observation[22] and become enslaved instead to their public image,

---

19   Anne Barton, '*Julius Caesar* and *Coriolanus*: Shakespeare's Roman World of Words', p. 44.
20   See, e.g.: *Julius Caesar* I, ii, 308.
21   Alexander Leggatt, *Shakespeare's Political Drama*, pp. 141–142.
22   An ironic instance of this can be found in the first dialogue between Cassius and Brutus; Shakespeare chooses to put it in the mouth of the latter, who is the embodiment of enslavement to public images: 'CASSIUS: ... Tell me, good

that is, to their 'name'. Caesar, as the ruler of this society, is the embodiment in the extreme of this general phenomenon:

> CAESAR: Would he [*CASSIUS*] were fatter! But I fear him not.
> Yet if *my name* were liable to fear
> I do not know the man I should avoid
> So soon as that spare Cassius. (I, ii, 198–201; my italics)

Caesar's inability to recognise his emotions – and his deficient self-knowledge as a whole – is revealed here, ironically, precisely because his declaration is completely correct, literally: his 'name', that is, the word the Romans use to indicate the man who is their ruler, is indeed not subject to the rule of his passions; but Caesar himself – as opposed to his name and as the play takes pains to demonstrate – is most certainly subject to it.

It is interesting to note that Antony, who differs from the characters around him in his skill at emotional self-observation, is the only one not affected by the habit in question: in effect, he refers to himself by his own name only once, and even then his use of his name is intrinsically different from that of the other main characters.[23]

5.1.3 Antony as 'Actor', 'Director' and 'Playwright'

The 'emotional intelligence' of Antony and Henry V can be directly linked to their specific characterisation as gifted 'men of the theatre', that is, they are endowed with 'acting', 'directing' and even 'writing' skills. These skills facilitate their ability to communicate on an emotional level with their fellow characters, and to channel their emotional state at will. The term 'role-playing characters' is inadequate in discussing Henry and Antony, because they cannot make do with the

---

Brutus, can you see your face? BRUTUS: No, Cassius, for the eye sees not itself, / But by reflection, by some other things' (I, ii, 51–53).

23 Antony refers to himself by his own name for the sake of describing a hypothetical situation in which 'I Brutus and Brutus Antony' (III, ii, 216–218); yet even in this exception, as it were, he opens this description referring to himself as 'I'.

status of performer, but also 'stage' the various situations in which they are involved; at times, they even 'compose' in advance the 'text' that will be performed on these occasions, as will be shown.

Antony's high 'emotional intelligence' is manifested in a variety of abilities that can be considered 'theatrical' skills. These abilities are quite apparent even on a first reading of his great speech; for this reason I shall point to their first harbingers, subtly sprouting several moments before the glorious rhetorical tour de force. Antony's ability as 'playwright' and 'director' is seen in the way he instructs his servant to approach Brutus immediately following Caesar's assassination. He directs him to kneel (this fact is stressed twice: III, i, 123, 125), and to speak in the style most suited to the addressee: in fact, the language of the servant as he delivers the text his master has composed (l. 125), is the very language of the addressee himself, that is, Brutus' formal and contrived 'language of reason'. Ironically, Antony presents us with the essential characteristics of Brutus' oratorical language even before we have heard them from the source himself; this is evident when we compare the servant's form and style of speaking with that of Brutus in his speech to the people:

SERVANT:
Brutus is noble, wise, valiant, and honest; / Caesar was mighty, bold, royal, and loving. / Say I love Brutus, and I honour him; / Say I feared Caesar, honoured him, and loved him.
(III, i, 126–129)

BRUTUS:
As Caesar loved me, I weep for him; as he was fortunate, I rejoice at it; as he was valiant, I honour him; but, as he was ambitious, I slew him. There is tears for his love, joy for his fortune, honour for his valour, and death for his ambition.
(III, ii, 21–25)

If Brutus will vouchsafe that Antony / May safely come to him and be re-solved / How Caesar hath deserved to lie in death ...
(Ibid., 130–132)

If there be any in this assembly, any dear friend of Caesar's, to him I say, that Brutus' love to Caesar was no less than his. If them that friend demand why Brutus rose against Caesar, this is my answer: not that I

loved Caesar less, but that I loved
Rome more.[24]
(Ibid., 16–20)

Mark Antony shall not love Caesar dead / So well as Brutus living ... (Ibid., 132–133)	Had you rather Caesar were living, and die all slaves, than that Caesar were dead, to live all free men? (Ibid., 20–21)

The language in which Antony chooses to compose this appeal to Brutus proves most effective in terms of its result, and the latter is convinced that he and his fellow conspirators 'shall have him [Antony] well to friend' (l. 143).

Following the initial contact made through his servant, Antony arrives at the scene of the murder with the intention of examining the circumstances and possible courses of action. During his meeting with the assassins he continues to address Brutus in Brutus's own language; this language reflects a world-view according to which emotions arise for logical reasons, and, using such reasons, it is possible to justify murder:[25]

> ANTONY: Friends am I with you all, and *love* you all,
> Upon this hope, that you shall give me *reasons*
> Why and wherein Caesar was dangerous.
> (III, i, 220–222; my italics)

The already jarring use Antony makes here of the word 'reason', of which his addressee is so fond, is all the more jarring due to its timing: it follows the sequence of impassioned words Antony directs toward the body of Caesar, punning on 'heart' and 'hart'; the heart, it will be recalled, is the seat of the passions, yet Brutus, hearing Antony speak in such rapid sequence both the language of the heart and the language of Reason, does not appear to sense any discord.

24 Lines 130–134, spoken by the servant, constitute a conditional clause which confines emotional contents within a contrived structure typical of 'the language of Reason', in the same manner as do Brutus' conditional sentences (III, ii, 16–20, 25–31).

25 Compare these lines to Brutus' in the Orchard Scene: 'He *loves* me well, and I have given him *reason*' (II, i, 219; my italics).

Antony also makes use of Brutus' style of speaking in his great speech in the Forum. He ascends to the pulpit after his rival's successful speech has aroused an enthusiastic response from the citizens; as a wise rhetorician, and for the sake of avoiding the initial resistance of his audience, he does not attempt to force a new and different style of speaking. Instead of trying to break with the rhetorical and linguistic norm set by his predecessor, he takes advantage of it and rides on its momentum at the beginning of his own speech. Scholarly references and rhetorical analyses comparing the speeches of Brutus and Antony invariably focus on the significant differences between them (Brutus' 'cold' and 'logical' speech; Antony's emotional speech) and characterise Antony's as a single unity of passionate and sweeping oratory. Of course there is nothing unacceptable in this generalisation because, like most scholarly generalisations, it provides a first step, so to speak, without which it is not possible to proceed to the subsequent ones; it is important, however, to discern that the first part of the stirring oration over the body of Caesar is similar, not to what follows, but to what precedes it, that is, to Brutus' speech. Antony's opening section (lines 65–99), although written in iambic pentameter, is in fact an unmistakable imitation of Brutus' rigid and contrived prose, approaching at times the realm of parody.[26]

This observation has a significant theatrical implication. Shakespeare has built into his dramatic texts a variety of means to assist and direct actors in portraying the specific characters and situations they are to represent; the actor playing the role of Antony must not ignore the typical 'Brutus-like' formal structure of the opening lines of his great speech – this structure is an obvious Shakespearean 'instruction', and dictates the general manner in which the lines in question are to be delivered. At the beginning of the speech Antony enacts, not himself, but his rival, and for this reason uses repetitive figures, symmetry, inverse symmetry, and frequent emphasis of words. As

26   For example, he imitates Brutus' practice of employing linguistic symmetry in an attempt to present a correlation between cause and effect (and specifically, as in the following citation, between crime and punishment): 'If it were so, it was a *grievous* fault, / And *grievously* hath Caesar answered it' (III, ii, 71–72; my italics).

stressed in Chapter Two, the meticulous and rigid structure of Brutus' Forum speech should be reflected in the body language of the actor delivering it. Similarly, in the opening lines of his great speech Antony imitates Brutus not only in the content and form of his words, but also in their physical manifestation – that is, in body language. Thus Antony adopts Brutus' very gestures, which, it will be recalled, serve to demonstrate the 'rationality' of his words, and by means of this imitation demonstrates to the citizens the failed logic of the speaker who preceded him.

This tactic of mimicry allows Antony to undermine Brutus' purportedly logical argumentation, using the latter's own tools. The citizens respond accordingly, and in a seemingly logical exchange of opinions express their understanding that the argument they accepted a moment earlier has been revealed as invalid (III, ii, 100–106). This conclusion leads them to the further conclusion that 'Caesar has had great wrong', and their anger begins to mount.[27] It should be noted that Antony's hands, like those of Brutus, are tainted with blood, since only a few moments earlier he shook the bloody hands of the conspirators. Thus, while employing 'the language of Reason' at the beginning of his speech, he simultaneously continues to enflame the anger unwittingly awakened through Brutus' bloody hands (see Chapter Two, 2.3.3). Once the anger of the citizens has grown and become focused on Brutus and the other conspirators, Antony is free to abandon the cumbersome language of Reason, and can now turn to the flowing style of speech upon which he will base the remainder of his emotional appeal. This fluent style will enable him to present, as he speaks, emotionally charged objects such as Caesar's vesture and wounds. This style is also the rhetorical tool most suited to externalising strong passion, which, as we have seen, is an important condition to moving an audience.

Antony's potency as an 'actor' arises not only from his skills as a mimic and one capable of expressing emotion, but also from his ability to regulate his emotions and to utilise them for specific ends

---

27 As shown in Chapter Two, when Antony begins his speech the citizens are already aroused to some degree of anger, which Brutus has unwittingly awakened in them.

(the third and fifth skills in Salovey and Mayer's contemporary definitions). In order to overcome the extreme situations he faces throughout the play, Antony requires extraordinary emotional self-control: in scenes III, i and III, ii, he finds himself in new circumstances in which uncertainty reigns, and his life is endangered by agents of whose true intentions he is ignorant; to the emotional agitation such a situation entails is added the emotion caused by the death of someone close – the intimate soliloquy Antony delivers over Caesar's body (III, i, 254–275) clearly testifies that he admired and loved Caesar. Antony, however, must regulate and channel his emotions according to the circumstances, hiding them at times, expressing them at others in a considered, judicious manner, and using them as a motivating force for his speech and his actions. Ironically, the use he makes of his emotions completely belies Brutus' prediction that Antony's grief following the death of Caesar would infuse him with melancholy, and perhaps even lead to his death.

It is interesting to note that Shakespeare, just as he characterises Antony and other 'emotionally intelligent' characters as the best 'actors', characterises Coriolanus – who might be described in today's politically correct jargon as 'challenged' in the area of emotional intelligence – as the worst 'actor'.

5.1.4 Henry V

Henry is Antony's chief rival for the crown of moving oratory. In light of the traditional rhetorical observation that one cannot stir without being stirred, it is apparently no accident that Shakespeare has given these two characters similar 'emotional biographies'. Just as there is a direct connection between Antony's ability to arouse passions in others and his tendency to pursue emotional stimuli, so can a connection be made between Henry's oratorical prowess and his wild youth, as presented in the two parts of *Henry IV*. This biographical background is mentioned explicitly at the beginning of *Henry V*, stressing Henry's former penchant for 'riots', 'banquets' and 'sports'.[28] From

---

28   I, i, 54–56, 64; I, ii, 268, 272.

this study's point of view, his days as a hedonistic prince can be seen as a sort of apprenticeship, during which he learned the mystery of the emotions. Prior to his coronation, Prince Hal could allow himself to drink to excess, keep company with the likes of John Falstaff, and experience a variety of extreme emotional conditions. Once he becomes king he must adopt the persona of the revered ruler, level-headed and not governed by his passions; his past experiences, however, are engraved in his mind, and he makes use of the essential emotional knowledge they contain during his reign.

It seems that this characteristic – the ability to experience emotion – constitutes in the four plays under discussion the most basic condition for the existence of developed emotional skills. It can be conceived as a sort of nourishing ground for the growth of the skill defined by Salovey and Mayer as the basic skill of emotional intelligence, namely, the appraisal and expression of emotion in the self. The Night Scene in *Henry V* supplies a number of salient hints regarding the king's ability to truthfully observe his own emotions. For example, Henry, alone onstage, describes the emotional state of the ruler who is forced to instil fear in his subjects in order to enforce his authority:

> Art thou aught else but place, degree and form,
> Creating awe and fear in other men,
> Wherein thou art less happy, being feared,
> Than they in fearing? (IV, i, 243–246)

Since there are no other characters on stage at that moment, it is obvious that Henry's words lack any manipulative purpose, hence they reflect his true thoughts. Some few moments earlier, debating with his soldiers Williams, Bates and Court, Henry had described the tendency of the king's emotions to swoop downwards like those of any man (ll. 106–108); he commented that the king, discerning something fearsome, is also afraid, and that the 'relish' that accompanies his fear is identical to that of any man in similar circumstances (ll. 108–112).[29]

---

29 It should be noted that in keeping with the remarkably ambiguous nature of *Henry V*, these lines too are much more evasive than they seem at first glance: unlike the soliloquy he delivers later, Henry's words are addressed to those he is attempting

Interestingly, the text provides no clear indication of Henry's ability to perceive and appraise others' emotional reactions (skill no. 2 as defined by Salovey and Mayer). Instead, the play 'skips' a stage and demonstrates that the king is endowed with the skill based upon it, namely the ability to regulate emotion in others (skill no. 4). This can be seen unambiguously in the strong emotional impact he has on his soldiers during the assault on the wall of Harfleur, when through the power of speech he manages to abolish the fear that has driven them to retreat, and to incite them to renewed attack. Alongside this skill, the play demonstrates Henry's ability to regulate his own emotions and harness them to his advantage (skills no. 3 and 5). His extraordinary self-control[30] is particularly conspicuous in light of the extreme, hardship-ridden situations in which the playwright places him, above all the battlefield. Prominent here are Henry's efforts to arouse anger in his soldiers in order to improve their performance as warriors, at a time when he himself is far removed from the influence of this passion. Within the context of the great Shakespearean warriors, traditionally characterised as choleric or 'sudden and quick in quarrel', it may seem surprising that Henry, the legendary conqueror of France, is characterised so differently. In effect, Henry's relative immunity to anger fits well with his military achievements: according to an observation made by Aristotle, echoes of which can be found in early modern English sources, 'true' courage stems not from passion, but from sober rationality. A courageous man (as opposed to an angry man, who only appears to be courageous) draws his self-confidence from *wisdom*, and is not tempted to perform acts beyond his power; he accurately gauges his strength and abilities and does nothing beyond the limitations of *reason*. Thus he does not encounter trouble or unforeseen developments. Such unforeseen developments are in fact the principal generators of fear on the battlefield; because the rational

---

to influence, that is, they are designed for a manipulative purpose. Furthermore, the king is not speaking as himself here, but is portraying a character: his words reflect first and foremost the 'thoughts' of that character, which do not necessarily duplicate his own.

30   See, e.g.: '... now he weighs time / Even to the utmost grain' (II, iv, 137–138).

man of war does not encounter them, he is not subject to this passion, hence his performance improves as the battle progresses.[31] Henry's ability to avoid anger is particularly impressive in light of the fact that Shakespeare places him in circumstances in which this emotion is particularly likely to be aroused. The tendency of anger to arise in the face of impediments, and its role of spurring one to overcome them, are emphasised not only in contemporary theories of emotion but also in Shakespeare's drama and in other writings of the time.[32] The play, by means of frequent repetition of words indicating impediments or inhibitions that separate Henry from the French crown, thus demonstrates the great circumstantial potential for the kindling of his anger.[33]

Henry's ability to avoid immoderate passions can also be viewed in terms of his broad perspective. One characteristic of emotions is their tendency to 'narrow' and 'fragment' our perspective: emotion focuses our attention on extremely limited factors, causing us to concentrate on a limited amount of data while excluding other data.[34] This phenomenon is related to the role of the emotions in mobilising those resources that enable us to adapt to changing circumstances, to overcome hardship, and to prepare for action that is aimed at achieving specific goals: when an emotion occurs, our 'mental spotlight' suddenly contracts, focusing on only what is directly relevant to the task at hand, to the exclusion of anything that might distract and prevent us from realising our goals.[35] These observations are by no means new; Wright, for example, has formulated his insights in a similar vein:

---

31   F. N. Coeffeteau, *A Table of Humane Passions with their Causes and Effects* (1621), pp. 426–427.

32   See, e.g.: *King John*, II, i, 334–340; Thomas Wright, *The Passions of the Minde in Generall* (1604), pp. 19–21; K. Oatley and J. M. Jenkins, *Understanding Emotions*, p. 260.

33   Impediment (I, i, 90; V, ii, 33); bar (I, ii, 12, 35, 42, 92; III, v, 48; V, ii, 27); in/on our/my/the way (II, ii, 187, 189; III, vi, 157; V, ii, 315, 322); hinder (II, ii, 188; III, vi, 159); rub (II, ii, 189; V, ii, 33).

34   Aaron Ben-Ze'ev, *The Subtlety of Emotions*, pp. 35–38.

35   See: Dylan Evans, *Emotion: A Very Short Introduction* (New York: Oxford University Press, 2003), pp. 76–79; K. Oatley and J. M. Jenkins, *Understanding Emotions*, pp. 96–98.

For the passion delighting or afflicting the minde, causeth the judgement to thinke, invent, devise all means possible, eyther to enjoy the Passion of delight, or to avoyde the molestation of sadnesse and feare ... Ire, Ambition, &c. All which passions consisting in prosecution of some thing desired, and bringing with them a certaine sence of delight, enforce the minde (for fostering and continuing that pleasure) to excogitate new means and ways for the performance thereof ... so, he that once apprehendeth the pleasure of the passion, ordinarily followeth it, and the passion increaseth the imagination thereof, and the stronger imagination rendereth the passion more vehement, so that oftentimes they enter but with an inch, and encrease an ell ... that men, in great payne, or exeding pleasure, can scarce speake, see, heare, or thinke of any thing, which concerneth not their passion[36]

Henry's conduct in the course of the play attests repeatedly to the breadth of his perspective: while in the midst of intense, charged situations, he is able to calculate the future implications and effects of actions and events occurring here and now.[37] The king's relatively broad perspective in evident from Shakespeare's implied comparison between him and the youth of England as, like him, they prepare for war:

CHORUS: Now all the youth of England are on fire ...
            Now thrive the armourers, and honour's thought
            Reigns *solely* in the breast of every man.
            (II, Chorus, 1–4; my italics)

KING HENRY: For we have now *no thought in us but France*,
            Save those to God that run before our business.
            (I, ii, 303–304; my italics)

36   Thomas Wright, *The Passions of the Minde in Generall* (1604), pp. 52–57.
37   An example of a Shakespearean indication of Henry's exceptional ability to function in the intensive present while constantly considering future implications is the king's choice of words when responding to the hanging of Bardolph (see Chapter One, p. 64). An additional example is the exchange of gloves with the soldier Williams, which Henry initiates the night before the battle at Agincourt: the king is not acting in anger (this can be deduced from lines IV, i, 201–202 and IV, vii, 54–55) but rather equanimously looking ahead, composing a 'play', which he will 'stage' in the end of the battle; this 'play' is designed to reestablish his authority as a ruler who arouses in his subjects both love and fear (similar to the 'play' he staged at Southampton, before the departure for France [see Chapter One, pp. 28–31; and Appendix B, pp. 297–299]).

This remains true even if we choose to interpret Henry's declaration in the above quotation as false and cynical: throughout the many difficult situations in which he finds himself, he must be consistent in his pretence that he is a modest, God-fearing king; such consistent pretence does not allow a single-minded concentration on the difficulties of the military and political campaigns, but rather demands simultaneous concentration on the 'theatrical' mission as well. Henry is one of Shakespeare's prominent role-playing characters, and even interpretative readings that seek a 'moral' king in the play – that is, one who does not tend to hypocrisy or cynical pretence – cannot ignore the way in which Henry plays many parts in order to achieve his goals.[38] It can be argued that one of the essential characteristics of a role-playing character – such as Antony, Richard III, Iago and Edmund – is a broad mental perspective: the art of acting obliges the actor, while in a highly emotional situation (being the focus of the audience's attention), to externalise emotions essentially different from the emotions he is actually experiencing; moreover, under the emotional veil he externalises, the actor must employ his cold rationality, coordinating his actions with numerous factors such as technical constraints, interaction with the other actors present, and reactions of the audience.

In the spirit of these observations regarding Henry's ability to regulate his emotions in keeping with the circumstances and the time, an explanation can be put forward that touches upon one of the more problematic events for interpreters of the play. The event in question is Henry's instruction to his soldiers, in the middle of the battle of Agincourt, to execute the French prisoners. This command perplexes scholars because of its proximity to the moment in which a 'humane' aspect of Henry's character is revealed, following Exeter's moving account of the death of York and Suffolk:

---

38   For example, the speech threatening Harfleur: for the sake of advancing a goal that has the appearance of being moral – prevention of further bloodshed – Henry delivers a particularly 'cruel' speech, designed to frighten the governor of the town into an immediate surrender.

```
EXETER:      ... I had not so much of man in me,
             And all my mother came into mine eyes
             And gave me up to tears.
KING HENRY:                  I blame you not,
             For hearing this I must perforce compound
             With my full eyes, or they will issue too.
                  Alarum
             But, hark, what new alarum is this same?
             The French have reinforced their scattered men.
             Then every soldier kill his prisoners!
             Give the word through. (IV, vi, 30–38)
```

Because of what might appear to be a sudden break in emotional continuity, some scholars tend to treat Henry's show of compassion and empathy as mere pretence – it is impossible, in their view, that authentic emotions bringing a man to the brink of tears can fade so fast and give way to cold cruelty. From such a viewpoint, furthermore, it is difficult to see how a character capable of empathy can turn into a mass murderer in the blink of an eye. However, when we consider that Henry's extraordinary ability to regulate his emotions is stressed throughout the play, this display of compassion can be interpreted as entirely genuine: the lull in the fighting has allowed him to devote his attention to Exeter's account and be moved; however, the moment the French trumpet is sounded and circumstances change, his emotional control allows him to swiftly refocus on the events at hand, examine them soberly, and issue the order for action most likely to bring about victory. Henry understands that the attention his soldiers are diverting to the prisoners will prevent them from functioning properly in the face of the renewed French attack; hence he orders the only practical measure that will prevent heavy losses or even a defeat in battle.

5.1.5 Volumnia

Volumnia is a unique phenomenon in our discussion of the emotional skills of Shakespearean characters. On the one hand, she channels the emotions of the protagonist and thus exerts a far-reaching influence on the course of events; on the other hand, unlike Shakespeare's treatment of other emotional manipulators, here the text does not allow us to determine to what degree, if any, she is endowed with a well-developed 'emotional intelligence'. The play provides no clear-cut indication regarding the quality of Volumnia's various emotional skills, and from a general glance at the scant evidence it would appear that these skills are not particularly well developed. For example, like her son, she lacks – to put it mildly – the ability to comprehend another's feelings and to re-experience them herself (empathy), which is considered a central characteristic of emotionally intelligent behaviour.[39] Even with regard to more basic skills – the appraisal and regulation of emotion in the self (skills no. 1 and 3)[40] and appraising others' emotional reactions (2) – Shakespeare does not supply any special clues that might indicate developed abilities (as he most certainly does with regard to other characters who channel the plots of his plays through emotional appeals). The fact that Volumnia demonstrates awareness of a traditional rhetorical insight regarding persuasion of the masses ('action is eloquence', III, ii, 76–78), does not

39   Volumnia displays an obvious lack of empathy in scene I, iii, when she belittles Virgilia's desire to avoid social encounters. The latter is in a sensitive emotional state, completely absorbed in concern for her husband, who is on the battlefield. This emotional state is completely alien to Volumnia, and for this reason she considers the wish of her daughter-in-law to be improper (ll. 22–23, 62–66, 94–95).

40   Volumnia demonstrates awareness of the strong anger she feels after the banishment of her son and her chance meeting with the tribunes in the street (IV, ii, 54–55); however, there is nothing in this demonstration of awareness to indicate an exceptional ability to recognise her own emotions, particularly as her words smack of self-dramatisation. From her rebuke of Coriolanus for his supposed *pride*, which is preventing the resolution of his dispute with the people (III, ii, 130–131), it is evident that she believes herself immune to this emotion. Although her characterisation as a proud matron is obvious in a first exposure to the play, her rebuke cannot be considered a clear manifestation of defective emotional self-awareness: the purpose of this rebuke is primarily manipulative, and thus should not be treated as a candid statement. Regarding her ability to regulate and direct her emotions: in her attempt to moderate her son's anger, Volumnia refers to herself as a model worthy of imitation because of her ability to use the 'brain' to guide the 'heart', thus putting her anger to good use ('I have a heart ... / But yet a brain that leads my use of anger' [III, ii, 29–32]); however, this self-appraisal receives no real textual support.

indicate a deep understanding of the mechanisms of human emotion so much as some familiarity with basic and well-known principles of rhetoric.

How is it, then, that this particular character accomplishes the task of saving Rome through the use of emotional manipulation? It seems that the answer to this question lies in the specific circumstances unique to the emotional appeal in question, namely, the kinship and special relationship shared by manipulator and addressee. The similar characterisation of Volumnia and Coriolanus is noticeable even in a first exposure to the play. Particularly conspicuous is the similarity in the 'emotional profiles' of the two: just like her son, Volumnia is outstanding in her raging and quarrelsome disposition;[41] this shared characteristic is reinforced by the identical structural design of their sudden bursts of rage,[42] and by the identical way in which they express their hatred of the plebeians.[43] The similarity between the two is not merely a matter of 'genetics', but stems in large part from Volumnia's active and conscious moulding of her son from his youth: Martius is for his mother a means to realise her 'very wishes / And the buildings of [her] fancy' (II, i, 173–175); she sees herself a partner in fashioning him as a warrior (V, iii, 62–63), having 'suckled' him with 'valiantness' (III, ii, 130). Volumnia is '... the honoured mould / Wherein this [Martius'] trunk was framed' (V, iii, 22–23). The moulding and the fashioning of Martius have proved so successful, that there exists a 'telepathic' connection between the mother and her son:

41   See, e.g.: I, iii, 66–67; IV, ii, 52–55.
42   One of the ways Shakespeare characterises Coriolanus' quick temper is by his tendency to repeat words addressed to him that have incurred his wrath (I, i, 172–173; II, iii, 48–50; III, i, 76, 84–85, 91–107; III, ii, 71–74; V, vi, 84–87, 88–89, 103–119). Volumnia (IV, ii, 32–53), Virgilia (IV, ii, 27) and Aufidius (I, x, 1–7) display a similar tendency, although in lesser measure. The fact that this idiosyncratic form of expression is shared by all four seems an indication of their common emotional characterisation.
43   See: III, ii, 8–14, 24–25.

VOLUMNIA:	MARTIUS:
Methinks I hear your husband's drum; / See him pluck Aufidius down by the hair; / As children from a bear, the Volsces shunning him. / Methinks I see him stamp thus, and call thus: / 'Come on, you cowards! You were got in fear, / Though you were born in Rome'. (I, iii, 24–29)	All the contagion of the south light on you, / You shames of Rome! you herd of – Boils and plagues / Plaster you o'er, that you may be abhorred / Further than seen, and one infect another / Against the wind a mile! You souls of geese / That bear the shapes of men, how have you run / From slaves that apes would beat! Pluto and hell! / All hurt behind: backs red, and faces pale / With flight and agued fear! (I, iv, 31–39)

Because of this likeness between 'the honoured mould' and the famed reproduction, Volumnia, when emotionally manipulating Coriolanus, has no need of skill in appraising others' emotions: she knows full well that the aspiration to a good name constantly burns within her son's mind, because so it is in her own mind, and that is how she has fashioned him (I, iii, 4–17). Built into this aspiration is the fear of a possible diminution of good name, that is, the great vulnerability to shame; as shown in Chapter Four, Volumnia exploits this vulnerability at the end of her long speech, thus succeeding where Cominius and Menenius have failed. In this particular rhetorical-emotional situation, then, the manipulator requires only the most superficial emotional self-knowledge in order to know the emotional profile of her addressee.

The clearest evidence that Volumnia is not endowed with a special ability to interpret and regulate others' emotions, is the fact that throughout the play she performs emotional manipulations only on Martius. Not once does she try to resolve the crises that befall by manipulating other characters; in two critical moments of crisis, in an attempt to influence the course of events, she appeals to her son's emotions, and in both she makes use of the very same passion.[44]

---

44 Volumnia first took advantage of the emotion of shame in scene III, ii, when she succeeded in changing her son's decision not to appear before the people and the tribunes in the market-place (ll. 124–131).

5.2 Mastering the 'Laws of Emotion'

5.2.1 The Benefit of Applying the 'Laws of Emotion'

The accepted definitions of the skills of emotional intelligence do not take into consideration the subject's ability to foresee and plan emotional reactions in advance, as based on predicted circumstances. Salovey and Mayer, for example, consistently refer to emotional self-appraisal and appraisal of others' emotions in the present, that is, at the time they occur. This seems inadequate, since situations are liable to arise in which an undesired emotion is awakened in oneself or in others, when circumstances do not allow even the most emotionally skilled individual to quell the emotion or to channel it in a different direction. An individual's ability to predict approximately how he will react emotionally to the anticipated circumstances, will enable him to avoid becoming involved in situations with which his emotional skills are unable to cope; his ability to predict the emotional reactions of others enables him to plan effective manipulations and to influence the judgement and actions of others to his advantage. For this reason – which is highly relevant to the analysis of the plays under discussion – this study suggests defining *the ability to predict emotional reactions*, as one of the elements of emotional intelligence as a whole. To this theoretical skill must, of course, be added the practical skill to utilise these emotional predictions.

A basic condition for the existence of these two additional skills is the awareness that emotions arise and undergo changes in keeping with certain laws: phenomena that are not controlled by laws are of necessity governed by chance, which, by definition, cannot be predicted. The idea of systematically discussing emotions as a phenomenon that obeys laws is relatively recent. It was first advanced by N. H. Frijda,[45] who attempts to refute what he calls 'the romantic approach to the emotions', which tends to wrap them in a mystical glow or see them as an expression of human freedom (the freedom supposedly

---

45   N. H. Frijda, 'The Laws of Emotion', *American Psychologist*, 43 (1988), pp. 349–358.

bestowed upon every human being to experience sensations and feelings according to his own free will). This view, according to Frijda, is an illusion: the emotions are subordinate neither to one's free will[46] nor to chance, but to a system of laws, which can be formulated. Frijda suggests a preliminary set of nine such laws; this system helps him demonstrate how a number of simple and universal forces are at work behind the complex, subtle and idiosyncratic emotional changes we witness in our lives.

This section will examine the emotional skills of Henry V and Antony by testing the degree of their 'familiarity' with these laws and the benefit they derive from them. In other words, we shall examine the ability of these characters to identify the principles behind emotional changes, and their practical skill in translating these 'theoretical' insights into the manipulative channelling of others.

5.2.2 Henry V and the Laws of Emotion

The faculties of appraisal and comparison have an important place in present-day discussions of the phenomenon of emotion. In particular, these faculties are frequently referred to in models that attempt to reconstruct processes of emotional arousal.[47] The recognition that the element of comparison is a factor in the arousal of emotions is by no means a new insight: for example, this notion clearly guided Thomas Wilson in constructing the exemplary amplification figure, intended to arouse shame, which he presents in *The Art of Rhetoric*.[48] The speaker who employs this figure repeatedly illustrates to his addressee the great disparity between the circumstances in which he vomited, and a variety of other possible, less shameful, circumstances. The speaker's continuous comparisons are meant to cause the addressee to grasp the

---

46 Frijda does not, of course, claim that one's free will has no effect on one's emotions, but rather that it should not be considered the only factor involved.
47 See, e.g.: Aaron Ben-Ze'ev, *The Subtlety of Emotions*, pp. 18–29; K. Oatley and J. M. Jenkins, *Understanding Emotions*, p. 98.
48 Thomas Wilson, *The Art of Rhetoric* (1560), pp. 153–154.

enormity of this disparity, and, accordingly, generate in him enormous shame.

Henry V also points to the direct linkage between processes of appraisal and comparison, and the arousal and intensity of emotion; this play often links various quantitative and qualitative data with emotions that are aroused or likely to be aroused in the characters or the audience, after having been cognitively processed. Shakespeare's interest in focussing the attention of the audience on this theme is evident from the speeches of the Chorus: this character obsessively compares the stage spectacle with the 'real' past events it is supposed to represent, and expresses concern that the considerable disparity between them will generate negative emotions in the audience.[49] This disparity exists in both size and quantity, and the Chorus is concerned about the immense discrepancy between the little theatre and the 'vasty fields of France', and between the few actors with their 'four or five most vile and ragged foils' and the great armies that fought each other in 'historical reality'. In order for the play to succeed, the Chorus asks the spectators to assist by activating their imagination, which has the power to neutralise the proportional and numerical gaps between the stage presentation and the original it is meant to represent.[50]

As demonstrated in Chapter One, Shakespeare repeatedly reveals the emotions that dominate the English and French camps, and stresses their decisive role in the balance of power. At the same time, he exposes the mental mechanisms of reckoning and appraisal, which trigger these dominating emotions and determine their nature and intensity. For example, the play directly links the faculties of appraisal and comparison of the French to their pride, presenting them as cause and effect:

> CONSTABLE: This becomes the great.
> Sorry am I his numbers are so few,
> His soldiers sick and famished in their march,
> For I am sure when he shall see our army
> He'll drop his heart into the sink of fear ... (III, v, 55–59)

---

49   See: I, Chorus, 8–15; II, Chorus, 31–32; and IV, Chorus, 48–52.
50   See: I, Chorus, 23–25; III, Chorus, 34–35; and V, Chorus, 1–6.

CHORUS: Proud of their numbers and secure in soul,
            The confident and over-lusty French
            Do the low-rated English play at dice ... (IV, Chorus, 17–19)

The awareness of the existence and working of these mental mechanisms is by no means limited to the playwright: a number of characters express it explicitly. In the Night Scene, for example, the commanders of the French army attribute the seeming absence of fear in the opposing army to a lack of intellect, characteristic of the English soldiers – a defect that prevents them from grasping the obvious quantitative and qualitative differences between them and the superior French:

CONSTABLE: If the English had any apprehension they would run away.
ORLEANS: That they lack, for if their heads had any intellectual armour
           they could never wear such heavy headpieces. (III, vii, 135–139)

ORLEANS: Foolish curs, that run winking into the mouth of a Russian bear
           and have their heads crushed like rotten apples. You may as well
           say that's a valiant flea that dare eat his breakfast on the lip of a
           lion.
CONSTABLE: Just, just; and the men do sympathize with the mastiffs in
           robustious and rough coming on, leaving their *wits* with their
           wives. (Ibid., 142–148; my italics)

A similar awareness of the role of appraisal and comparison in the emotional mechanism can be found in the opposing camp: knowing that his chief enemy is not the French army, but his soldiers' fear, Henry asks the help of Mars in preventing this emotion from possessing his army. The king's words imply that the god of war can fulfil this wish by affecting the soldiers in two different ways – physical and mental:

O God of battles, *steel my soldiers' hearts*;
Possess them not with fear. *Take from them now*
The sense of reckoning,[51] if th'opposed numbers
Pluck their hearts from them. (IV, i, 286–289; my italics)

51   It is possible that Henry's awareness of the appraisal mechanism and its influence
     on the emotions, as well as the reason for the use he makes of the verb 'reckon',
     were planted somewhat earlier by the soldier Bates: 'Be friends, you English
     fools, be friends! We have / French quarrels enough, if you could tell how to
     reckon' (IV, i, 219–221).

But Mars, so it emerges, does not answer this prayer. Eavesdropping on his peers on the morning of the battle, Henry discovers that their faculties of appraisal and comparison have not been suspended, nor has their effect on the emotional mechanism:

WESTMORLAND: Of fighting men they have full three score thousand.
EXETER: *There's five to one*; besides, they all are fresh.
SALISBURY: God's arm strike with us! 'tis a *fearful* odds.
        (IV, iii, 3–5; my italics)

In the absence of help from the heavens, the king must deal with the harmful passion by himself. In the corresponding event in Hall's account, Henry does so in an entirely conventional manner: he charges his soldiers to put their faith in God and in the justice of the cause for which they are fighting, and thus prevent the greater numbers of French from inspiring fear in their hearts.[52] It can be said that Hall's Henry does not deal with the 'heart' of the problem, that is, with the mechanism that arouses the soldiers' fear: instead, he tries to bypass this mechanism and cause his men to 'suppress' the data that are feeding it. Shakespeare's Henry, by contrast, uses an original and sophisticated rhetorical solution, and it can be said that he is endowed with 'emotional intelligence' superior to that of Hall's Henry: instead of instructing his soldiers to ignore the un-ignorable clear facts (the imbalance between the armies in numbers and physical condition stands out – or will soon stand out when the two armies face each other), he delivers a speech devoted almost entirely to stimulating desire for honour, which distils and amplifies the dram of good in their bad situation.[53] The central argument of this speech is based on a

---

52   'Therfore puttyng your only trust in hym [God], let not their multitude feare your hearts, nor their great numbre abate your courage'. Edward Hall, *The Union of the Two Noble and Illustre Families of Lancaster and York*, p. 67.

53   As demonstrated above, Shakespeare presents on stage the very moment of Antony's insight into the existence of 'emotional contagion', shortly before he applies it in his great speech. Similarly, the playwright reveals the moment in which Henry shows his awareness of the principle upon which the St Crispin speech will be based: 'KING: There is some soul of goodness in things evil, / Would men observingly distil it out ... / Thus may we gather honey from the weed / And make a moral of the devil himself' (VI, i, 4–12).

'positive paradox', that is, on an emphasis of the potential benefit and gain in a situation that appears desperate: the greater the numerical advantage of the French, the greater the share of honour for one who fights them.[54] Just as the numerical imbalance between the armies is liable to cause excess pride among the French and strong fear among the English, so too, with the help of the appropriate manipulation, it may arouse the latter 'to covet honour'. Henry's rhetorical tactic thus takes advantage of the very same principle formulated in Frijda's 'The Law of Situational Meaning':

> Emotions arise in response to the meaning structures of given situations: different emotions arise in response to different meaning structures ... Emotions change when meaning change. Emotions are changed when events are viewed differently. Input is changed, and output changes accordingly.[55]

From these remarks it is clear that the emotional state of an addressee can be altered in two different ways. The first is by *changing the circumstances*; this would be very difficult to achieve in the present case, as presented in *Henry V*. The rhetorical tactic Henry chooses in Hall's version is a variation of this possibility: ignoring given circumstances is an attempt to banish them from the consciousness. The second way is by changing the *significance* of the circumstances, from the viewpoint of the addressee, as Shakespeare's Henry does.

A similar exploitation of the law of situational meaning by a Shakespearean character was introduced in Chapter Four, albeit without prematurely applying it to the modern system of concepts. Volumnia, in a final effort to persuade her son to refrain from attacking Rome, brings about an emotional change in him by giving new

---

54   It is possible that the basic idea for this rhetorical tactic of amplifying the advantage-within-the-disadvantage was suggested to Shakespeare by his source material. In Hall's work Henry presents to his soldiers an argument he attributes to his valiant ancestors, according to which the larger an army is, the less knowledgeable are the masses that make it up in the ways of military practice. Hall's Henry does not develop the subject further, but rather bases his speech on the just cause of the war, and on the common assumption that God assists those who follow a just cause. Edward Hall, *The Union of the Two Noble and Illustre Families of Lancaster and York*, p. 67.

55   N. H. Frijda, 'The Laws of Emotion', pp. 349–350.

significance to the same rhetorical situation: the ladies' ragged garments, their physical and emotional condition, and the desolation that awaits them, cease toward the end of the speech to function as facts meant to testify to their misery and arouse pity in Coriolanus; with Volumnia's direction and commentary, reinforced by the ladies' kneeling, they become a testimony to the unnatural ingratitude of the son, the husband and the father, and thus arouse shame.

5.2.3 Antony and the Laws of Emotion

Antony's prodigious 'emotional intelligence', as detailed above, is also evident in his mastery and practical use of the 'laws of emotion'. His rhetorical-emotional skills are intensely expressed, as has been mentioned, in his great speech; one of the most conspicuous characteristics of this speech, and one of the principal keys to its success, is what might be termed its 'realism': like the great Roman orators, as well as proven Shakespearean rhetoricians such as Iago and Edmond, Antony understands that the intensity of the addressee's passion depends on the degree to which he perceives the facts presented to him as genuine and palpable.[56] This is precisely the insight behind Frijda's 'law of apparent reality':

> Emotions are elicited by events appraised as real, and their intensity corresponds to the degree to which this is the case.[57]

In the course of his speech Antony utilises extremely vivid, detailed, and sensuous descriptions. He makes extensive use of the sight of blood, which – as explained in Chapter Two – was thought to arouse anger: Antony not only draws the attention of the citizens directly to Caesar's blood, by displaying his stained vesture and his wounds; he also attempts, when his speech is not focussing their gaze on the body, to evoke bloody images in their imagination by means of realistic verbal descriptions (III, ii, 122–125, 181–184). But the

---

56   See for example: Cicero, *De Inventione*, I, LIV, 104; LV, 107, pp. 154–159.
      Quintilian, *Institutio Oratoria*, 6.2.32, pp. 61–63.
57   N. H. Frijda, 'The Laws of Emotion', p. 352.

average human imagination is weak and prone to a degree of laziness, and it appears that for this reason Antony does not base his speech on the evocative power of words: instead, he relies first and foremost on concrete exhibits, which he presents throughout his speech; these exhibits are the means to both stimulate and support the imagination of his audience, a sort of 'solid material base' upon which the imagination can reconstruct the supposed events described by the orator. For example, Antony takes pains to produce before the eyes of the citizens Caesar's 'genuine' will, and twice to point out its 'original' seal (ll. 120, 230). He carries out his presentation of tangible exhibits in a hierarchical order, affecting the imagination of his audience in a manner similar to 'zooming-in' with a camera – gradually getting closer to the object, revealing further details, advancing in the scale of realism: Caesar, lying dead before the eyes of the citizens (ll. 65–99); Caesar's vesture (ll. 161–164); the rents in this vesture (ll. 165–174); Caesar's bare body (l. 188); his exposed, bleeding wounds (ll. 218–219).

The 'realism' to which Antony strives is also expressed through the language and style in which he addresses the citizens. It should be noted that from the point of view of the audience in the Elizabethan theatre, Antony's speech – compared to that of Brutus – was most certainly perceived as more genuine and 'realistic', precisely because it is written in iambic pentameter, so different from the contrived and constrained constructions of Brutus' prose. From the point of view of the modern spectator this claim might seem surprising, but it should be remembered that for Shakespeare's audience, prose was an exception to the norm for plays, the vast majority of which were based on pentameter. As Brian Vickers argues, the transition into prose during the course of a play would have been conspicuous to the ears of Elizabethan playgoers, who were accustomed to the norm of iambic pentameter.[58] The degree of 'realism' in Antony's speech is even higher, due to the flowing nature of its lines and to the orator's simple language, which strengthens the naïve persona behind which he hides: a 'plain, blunt man' who is 'no orator' but is simply passing on the bare facts as known to him and to those present (ll. 207–213). The

---

58   Brian Vickers, *The Artistry of Shakespeare's Prose*, pp. 1–18.

oration grows in fluency as it progresses, and the various articulation impediments that are built into the opening lines gradually disappear. The beginning of the speech (ll. 65–99), as has been shown, is merely a pentameter version of Brutus' prose, and as a faithful copy it is full of those impediments in articulation that are characteristic of the rhetorical schemes upon which logical argumentation is based. As Antony enters deeper into the task of arousing the Romans' passions, the flow of the lines he utters becomes ever freer; this flow enables the increasingly intense externalisation of passion and its direct induction in the people trough 'emotional contamination'.

The rhetorical use of 'Caesar's will' requires an additional and separate reference, because it reveals Antony's intuitive understanding of the principle formulated in Frijda's 'Law of Concern':

> Emotions arise in response to events that are important to the individual's goals, motives, or concerns.[59]

The use of the 'will' testifies to Antony's awareness that the 'great wrong' done to Caesar has the power to arouse only limited wrath on the part of the citizens; this wrong cannot arouse *intense* and *ongoing* passion, because of the limited personal concern it holds for each of them; Antony has need of such intense and ongoing passion in order to create the violent riots that will enable him to immediately neutralise the conspirators. Shakespeare takes pains from the very beginning of the play to show in the clearest possible fashion that the emotions of the people are easily and quickly swayed (I, i, 31–59); Antony must therefore charge the citizens with passion of such an intensity that it will not soon wane, or that will prevent his enemies from quenching it using emotional countermeasures. Anger, it will be remembered, is awakened as the result of one's subjective perception that a wrong has been committed towards oneself or one's loved ones. For this reason, it will not suffice for Antony to base his emotional rhetoric solely on the love of the Romans to Caesar: the vast majority of the citizens, naturally, were not in familiar terms with this imperious figure. Of course, in their shock at the assassination, they may have perceived

---

59   N. H. Frijda, 'The Laws of Emotion', p. 351.

themselves to be closer and more intimate with the victim than they were in reality, nevertheless, this perception would be subject to fluid subjectivity and the passage of time, and a wise rhetorician would not establish his tactics on such fickle ground. At the beginning of the speech Antony takes pains to arouse the citizens' love for Caesar (ll. 80–83, 94), with the intention of proportionally arousing their anger against the conspirators; this, however, is not enough, and he therefore chooses to end his speech with a reading of 'the will' – thus demonstrating that the assassination is in fact a wrong that has been perpetrated against each and every one of them:

> To *every Roman citizen* he [Caesar] gives,
> To *every several man*, seventy-five drachmas
> ...
> Moreover, he hath left you all his walks,
> His private arbours and new-planted orchards,
> On this side Tiber; he hath left them *you,*
> *And to your heirs* for ever ... (III, ii, 231–240; my italics)

Antony's awareness of the principles that govern human emotions is central to the structure of his speech. The lion's share is devoted to arousing the passions of the people by showing the body, wounds and blood (a direct, sensual, emotional appeal), which he reinforces through verbal descriptions (that is, an emotional appeal to the cognitive faculties of his addressees). Lastly, once he has inflamed their blood and ruffled up their spirits by combining these two means, he fatally adjusts the 'thermostat' by employing 'The Law of Concern' – as described above. The Romans are thus launched into the streets having been heated to the maximum.[60] Antony's intention at this stage is to create general havoc; unlike an orator who stirs his au-

---

60　Thus Shakespeare altered significantly the course of events described in North's translation of Plutarch: in that version, the will is first read to the citizens, arousing their love and sorrow; following this Caesar's body is brought to the marketplace, and Antony delivers an eulogy; when he discerns that his words have awakened the compassion of the people, he changes his rhetorical tactic, takes Caesar's blood-soaked mantle in his hand and holds it up for all to see, with its many rents; influenced by this action the anger of the citizens is aroused and they begin their rampage.

dience to pursue a certain desired course, he does not have to avoid charging the citizens with excess passion that hinders their capacity to focus on a defined goal:

ANTONY: Now let it work. Mischief, thou art afoot,
Take thou what course thou wilt! (Ibid., 250–251)

5.3 Harmonising Reason and Passion

5.3.1 Othello and the 'Intellect'

A number of critics see Othello's falling into the trap of emotional appeal as the consequence of what they refer to as his 'flawed intellect'.[61] Paul Jorgensen, who in this context contrasts Othello with the intellectually-endowed Brutus and Hamlet, expresses a particularly denigrating view of the black general's noetic abilities:

... a strong, impressive, but not a thoughtful man ... He is not intellectually equipped to enlarge by his own sense of tragedy upon man's plight in general.[62]

Jorgensen, who draws a direct connection between what he sees as the limited thinking capacities of the hero and his tragic mistakes,[63] is following an earlier observation by Terence Hawkes. According to Hawkes, Othello's life can be divided into two main chapters, characterised by the different modes of thinking he employs in each: during his life as a military leader, until he falls in love with Desdemona and

61   M. R. Ridley expresses this approach in an explicit manner: 'In the first place, his intellectual power is nowhere near on a par with his other qualities. Whenever he thinks, he is a child, and not even a very intelligent child'. M. R. Ridley, 'Introduction to *Othello*', *Othello*, ed. M. R. Ridley (London: The Arden Edition, Methuen, 1984), p. liv.
62   Paul A. Jorgensen, 'Perplex'd in the Extreme: The Role of Thought in *Othello*', *Shakespeare Quarterly* 15 (1964), p. 265.
63   '... the burden of real thought is put [in *Othello*] upon a man who is unaccustomed to it and cannot long endure the ordeal' (ibid., p. 275).

marries her, Othello is aided by what Hawkes calls 'intuition' or '*ratio superior*', which does not involve analytical, rational thought processes.[64] This mode of thinking allowed him during his military career to make the quick decisions essential to success on the battlefield. Such 'higher reason' proves unsuited to the world Othello enters at the beginning of the play: when he opens the next chapter of his life, the 'civil' chapter, in which he falls in love, marries, and is militarily inactive after the drowning of the Turks, he must make use of fundamentally different modes of thinking – which, argues Hawkes, are based on the very intellect that Othello lacks. Philip McGuire attempts to show that Iago succeeds in leading Othello's thoughts astray by changing his perception of reality; the tragedy of *Othello*, according to him, is a document about 'abuse of intelligence': the protagonist fails to discern that the intellectually endowed villain is distorting the facts before his very eyes.[65]

These observations are in my view problematic, and ignore the complex interrelationship of Reason and Passion in *Othello*. First, there is no real indication in the play that in his past Othello made use of his 'intuition' to analyse circumstances and make decisions; Hawkes bases this observation on the general's numerous displays of self-confidence in the first act, which he sees as arising from an intuitive, rather than a rational, thought process. For example, he quotes the following sentence in support of his claim:[66]

> Not I; I must be found.
> My parts, my title, and my perfect soul
> Shall manifest me rightly. (I, ii, 30–32)

It is difficult to see how Hawkes fails to discern the logical process of appraisal upon which this proclamation is based, as well as the clear textual structure so typical of rational argumentation. Jorgensen, supporting Hawkes' line of approach, cites as an example Othello's words to the vengeful Brabantio:

---

64   Terence Hawkes, *Shakespeare and the Reason*, pp. 67, 110–111.
65   Philip C. McGuire, '*Othello* as an "Assay of Reason"', *Shakespeare Quarterly* 24 (2), (1973), p. 206.
66   Terence Hawkes, *Shakespeare and the Reason*, pp. 110–111.

> Were it my cue to fight, I should have known it
> Without a prompter. (I, ii, 83–84)

This confident declaration, however, does not indicate an intuitive thought process, but rather one based on intellect. 'The military world', that is, the world in which Othello has so excelled and benefited until the plot opens, is characterised as a paradise for rational thinkers: the inhabitants of this comprehensible world have no need for modes of thinking other than those based on the intellect, namely, on processes involving *knowledge, argumentation, and drawing conclusions.*[67] The need for intuitive skills does not arise in such a world, since it is completely lacking in deceptive outward appearances, and the data with which it feeds the thinking of the military man are clear and unequivocal: the enemy can be identified by his dress, the ships in which he sails and the symbols borne by the ancient, whose task it is to accompany his commander throughout the battle (the ancient, in this simple world, is of necessity the commander's friend and not his enemy, and the outward signs he bears do match 'The native act and figure of [his] heart / In compliment extern'). Moreover, the modes of 'military' thinking we encounter in the play, including those implied in references to Othello's past, involve appraisals, estimations and calculations based on just such clear and unequivocal facts. During the Senate Scene, for example, the duke and the senators evaluate the military situation in the Mediterranean based on data that are quite free of ambiguity: the Turkish enemy is defined and familiar, his sinister intentions are undoubted, and the place, quality and military importance of the citadels in Cyprus and Rhodes are known and agreed upon by all. On the basis of these known and clear facts, the likelihood of various scenarios can be estimated, taking into account other data that are not certain, such as the exact number of Turkish galleys and the direction in which they are sailing.

In light of the above, we can understand why Othello strives obsessively throughout the play for indisputable, conclusive knowl-

---

67   Intellect: 'That faculty, or sum of faculties, of the mind or soul by which one knows and reasons (excluding sensation, and sometimes imagination; distinguished from feeling and will) ...' (*OED*, 'intellect', n., 1).

edge of the facts: this practice served him well during his life as a military leader, when he encountered an abundance of outward signs and unambiguous data; such signs and data enabled him to reach quick conclusions in intellect-based thought processes, and to act upon them. In the military world, as presented in *Othello*, a turbaned man who traduces Venice is an enemy, and therefore must be killed (V, ii, 349); similarly, a friend, in that simple world, is immediately recognised by virtue of perfectly clear and reliable signs:

A shot [*is heard within*].
2 GENTLEMAN: They do discharge their shot of courtesy;
          Our friends at least. (II, i, 56–57)

[*A shout*] *within, 'A sail, a sail!'* [*A shot is heard.*]
CASSIO: ...   But hark, a sail!
2 GENTLEMAN: They give their greeting to the citadel:
          This likewise is a friend. (Ibid., 93–95)

The ultimate instance of the intellect-based mode of thinking of the high-ranking military man is found in *Coriolanus*. In scene III, i, the tribunes Brutus and Sicinius succeed in agitating the people and the choleric hero, and a street brawl takes place; Cominius evaluates the situation and, accordingly, advises the battle-hungry Coriolanus to retreat:

CORIOLANUS: On fair ground
          I could beat forty of them.
MENENIUS: I could myself
          Take up a brace o'th'best of them, yea, the two tribunes.
COMINIUS: But now 'tis odds *beyond arithmetic*,
          And manhood is called foolery when it stands
          Against a falling fabric. Will you hence,
          Before the tag return ...? (III, i, 244–250; my italics)

This manner of thinking is essential to a high-ranking military officer like Cominius, who leads soldiers into the battlefield and must be endowed with the ability to evaluate the overall picture of the battle; the various data and the senior officer's own faculty of reason guide him in certain instances to realise that retreat may be the necessary tactical move, more effective, in an all-encompassing view, than attack.[68] It is no accident that Shakespeare takes pains on numerous occasions to attach the title 'General' to Cominius' name: this word reflects the 'general' – that is, comprehensive – responsibilities of this military position,[69] thus indicating that a broad perspective is essential to someone who holds such a post (this is a deliberate choice on the part of the playwright: in North's version he is for the most part called 'Consul').

Coriolanus, unlike Cominius, despite his high place in the military hierarchy, is not once referred to as 'general' while serving in the Roman Army; he is so entitled only after his defection to the Volscian army, a fact that is strongly emphasised in Shakespeare's text.[70] The narrow mental perspective resulting from his choleric nature is unsuitable to the position of general, and indeed, the play does not show its hero occupied with the broad matters relevant to his high position: he is not at all concerned with evaluating the balance of forces or with strategic and tactical considerations;[71] accordingly, he cannot understand why Cominius has ordered his troops to withdraw in order to regroup for a renewed attack on the Volscians – for him, attack is the only valid move on the battlefield.[72] It can be said that for Rome, Coriolanus is less a commander than a miraculous warrior, a one-man military unit motivated by intense anger. A comparison between Cominius and Coriolanus thus sharpens the following general distinction: the weapon of the warrior, who is totally absorbed in face-to-face

---

68   See also: *Coriolanus* I, vi, 1–4; I, vi, 49–50.
69   General: 'Including, participated in by, involving, or affecting, all, or nearly all, the parts of a specified whole, or the persons or things to which there is an implied reference; completely or approximately universal within implied limits; opposed to *partial* or *particular*' (*OED*, 'general', adj., 1a).
70   During scene V, ii, in which Coriolanus is first called 'general', various characters refer to him thus no fewer than 11 times.
71   This tendency of the hero is implied in his words to Aufidius as they fight each other on the battlefield – Martius is not at all concerned about the balance of forces or achieving military objectives in accordance with logical strategy: 'I'll fight with none but thee, for I do hate thee / Worse than a promise-breaker' (I, viii, 1–2).
72   'MARTIUS: Where is the enemy? Are you lords o'th'field? / If not, why cease you till you are so?' (I, vi, 47–48).

combat, is passion, whereas the weapon of the general, whose objective is victory in the entire campaign, is the intellect.

In light of the above, it can be appreciated that Othello's glorious past achievements as a military leader stemmed from his ultimate mental suitability to the position of 'general'; indeed, this title is attached to his name no less than twenty-six times during the play. His problematic condition as presented in the play can be seen to have arisen from the changed circumstances in which he finds himself, together with his unchanged mode of thinking: after many years in the 'military' world described above, he now faces, in his 'civil life', a world less clear and intelligible, in which it is difficult to distinguish between friend and foe on the basis of simple external signs. In this new world, it is actually wise to ignore external signs, or at least to regard them with suspicion; for this reason it is impossible to carry out reliable processes of evaluation and reasoning based solely on the intellect. In this civilian world that Othello enters before the beginning of the play, new modes of thinking must be adopted; here he must make use of those levels of thought that are not 'rational' (in the traditional meaning of this word), but rather those by which one may 'feel', 'smell' or 'divine' the quality, intentions and emotions of others. In the civilian world, emotions constitute, as we shall see, a significant factor that must be acknowledged and taken into consideration; but Othello, who has learned to suppress their effect in order to preserve the discretion and courage required of a military leader (III, iv, 128–131), continues his practice of suppressing and denying emotions in a world where they are no longer enemies, but, rather, helpful and essential tools.

It is therefore problematic to regard Othello's allegedly 'flawed intellect' as the reason that he falls into the trap of emotional appeal. The crux of the matter, as explained, is not Othello's 'flawed intellect' – it has served him well in the past and has enabled him to rise from lowly origins to the highest rank in the Venetian army – but rather his stubborn adherence to it, even in situations in which it is not viable.

5.3.2 Othello and the Balance of Reason and Passion

Just as the concept 'emotion' has a variety of definitions, so, naturally, does the related concept, 'emotional intelligence'. Thus far we have evaluated the 'emotional intelligence' of several key Shakespearean characters from two perspectives: first, in accordance with Salovey and Mayer's definitions of the five basic skills; second, by assessing the degree of 'mastery' of the 'Laws of Emotion' these characters demonstrate. In the following discussion, the 'emotional intelligence' of Othello will be evaluated in light of a different, broader definition: *the ability to optimally integrate the emotional and intellectual systems.*[73]

This contemporary definition is of special relevance to the matter at hand, exactly because Shakespeare employed medieval dramatic conventions in composing *Othello*. The play presents a hero, characterised in the tradition of the morality plays, in whose mind a war is taking place between entities that are perceived to be opposing. In the medieval morality plays, which depict the world as simple and easily comprehended, the desired outcome is the victory of the 'good' entities over their 'evil' counterparts. By contrast, the cosmos presented in *Othello* is far more complex and entangled: although, like a typical morality play, it is constructed as a collection of polar opposites,[74] the remedy for the hero's predicament is by no means a *psychomachia* between 'good' and 'evil', ending in the defeat of the latter; instead, the optimal solution would be the integration of the various opposing entities into a harmonious balance.[75] The most conspicuous pair of such opposing entities in *Othello*'s world is of course Reason vs. Passion.[76] As shown below, Othello's predicament stems not from the failure of his intellect to subdue his emotion, but from his very attempt to do so. Instead of harmonising his rational and emotional modes of

---

73   See, e.g.: Aaron Ben-Ze'ev, *The Subtlety of Emotions*, pp. 175–181; Dylan Evans, *Emotion: A Very Short Introduction*, pp. xiv, 98.
74   Alvin Kernan, 'Introduction to *Othello*', *Othello*, ed. Alvin Kernan (New York: The New American Library, 1963), pp. xxv–xxxv.
75   Thomas McAlindon, *Shakespeare's Tragic Cosmos*, pp. 135–140.
76   See, e.g.: I, iii, 319–324; II, iii, 185–188.

thinking, Othello seeks to completely eliminate the latter mode; yet precisely by doing so, he fatally sabotages the healthy operation of his rational thinking, resulting in the sequence of erroneous judgements and decisions he subsequently makes.

In the following examination of Othello's fatal inability to harmonise his emotional and intellectual systems, the broad definition above of the term 'emotional intelligence' will be divided into two secondary definitions:

a) the ability to use emotion in problem-solving, and as a complement to rational thinking (sections 5.3.3 and 5.3.4);

b) the ability to make use, in keeping with the need and circumstances, of two types of logic: noetic logic, and 'the logic of emotion' (sections 5.3.5 and 5.3.6).

5.3.3 The Ability to Use Emotion in Problem-Solving

Modern research sees the emotional system as a purposeful mechanism with a variety of functions, both physical and mental. One such function is to assist noetic thinking and to provide solutions for its limitations: psychological and neurological experiments conducted in the past twenty years have shown that without the active intervention and assistance of emotion, the logical mechanisms of thought would become entrapped in endless evaluations and calculations. What appear to be the simplest processes of logical calculation, such as the decision about whether or not to leave home armed with an umbrella on a cloudy morning, are influenced by much more data than first appears. These include the media weather forecasts; how reliable we deem the forecasters to be, based on the accuracy of their previous forecasts; the capacity of our clothing to withstand the rain and to dry quickly; our current hairstyle and its vulnerability to various intensities of rain; the inconvenience of carrying an umbrella as opposed to the discomfort of wet clothing; the time and place required to dry the umbrella during the day; and so forth. The process of reaching a logical decision taking into account all the data that may have bearing on the matter, may therefore be long, and in human terms, even endless. Emotion is a helpful factor, intervening in the decision-making process and directing us as we choose among the countless data before us, to enable more streamlined decision-making.[77] On occasion, 'rational' thinking encounters the opposite problem: instead of the confusing surplus of data that cannot be processed or sorted, we are faced with a lack of data essential to the completion of a logical, continuous process; in such cases, emotion intervenes, taking the place of the missing data and thereby enabling us to reach a decision.[78]

Man is a creature who must act in order to survive. Without the essential intervention of emotion, his survival would be impossible: whenever the need arose to make a decision about a course of action, he would sink into endless calculations, or, alternately, reach an impasse because of lack of data essential to the process of logical deliberation. In fact, there are few instances in daily life in which we can carry out entire processes of rational thought without recourse to the complementary intervention of emotion: being human – that is, being bound to a specific time and place – we have access to a limited amount of data; in making most decisions we require essential information from other times and places, yet our human state itself prevents us from obtaining it.[79] Absolute rationality in our lives is impossible, furthermore, because of the fact that they are full of contradictions that logic cannot resolve. Our professional lives, for example, are sometimes at odds with our personal lives (the classic example is that of a man and a woman who fall in love while both are employed at different levels of the same hierarchical system). Because

77   Ronald De Sousa, *The Rationality of Emotions*, Cambridge, MA: MIT Press, 1990, p. 194; Antonio Damasio, *Descartes' Error*, pp. 191–201.

78   This very capacity of emotion – to guide thought through oceans of myriad data and to compensate for missing information – is exploited by the rhetoric of emotional appeal. The emotional manipulator leads his addressees to form decisions and judgements, even though essential information is usually missing: either the addressees do not have access to all the relevant facts, or the manipulator himself hides those facts liable to harm his case. The manipulator generates in his addressees the desired emotion, which causes them to bridge the gaps of the missing data and reach the desired conclusion. See: K. Oatley and J. M. Jenkins, *Understanding Emotions*, pp. 252–258, 280–283.

79   H. A. Simon, 'Motivational and Emotional Controls of Cognition', *Psychological Review* 74 (1), (1967), pp. 29–39.

our lives are a sequence of interactions with other human beings, we find ourselves day after day facing contradictions between our desires and the desires of others, or even between different desires of our own. The multiplicity of desires and contradictions in life cannot be resolved by intellectual means; without the decisive intervention of the emotions, we would be unable to exist and act as individuals in society.[80] This observation has led Keith Oatley and Jennifer M. Jenkins to define the emotions first and foremost as a means bestowed upon us in order to assist us in our social interactions:

> What emotions really are, therefore, are the guiding structures of our lives – especially of our relations with others.[81]

In light of the brief summary above, the notion that reason and passion exist in a state of conflict is incompatible with contemporary thinking. Emotion is by no means the enemy of rational thought – it is perhaps its best friend, since without it our thinking would be limited to the point of impotence; like a true friend, emotion complements rational thought and makes up for its limitations.

5.3.4 Othello's Denial of Emotion as a Component of Thought

Othello can be seen as a character endowed with a 'stoic' or 'traditional' view of the place of emotion in the human psyche. As demonstrated in Chapter Three, his pretension of implementing purely rational modes of thinking is evident throughout the play. From the selected quotations below, we can deduce that Othello rejects emotion as a legitimate factor in processes of judgement and consideration: the proper mode of thinking, according to him, is one that is not affected by passions and does not take into account the emotional variable. Man's best instructor is, for Othello, his faculty of Reason, which functions properly only when not influenced by Passion:

---

80   K. Oatley, *Best Laid Schemes – The Psychology of Emotions* (Cambridge: Cambridge University Press, 1992), pp. 44–68.
81   K. Oatley and J. M. Jenkins, *Understanding Emotions*, p. 124.

OTHELLO: Now by heaven,
My blood begins my *safer guides* to rule,
And passion, having my *best judgement* collied,
Assays to lead the way ... (II, iii, 185–188; my italics)

EMILIA: The Moor replies
                    ... that in *wholesome wisdom*
He might not but refuse you; but he protests he loves you,
And needs no other suitor but his likings ...
To bring you in again. (III, i, 42–48; my italics)

As explained above, contemporary studies see emotion as assisting in a world in which the tools of logic are insufficient. If we examine Othello's conduct throughout the play from this perspective, his fundamental, recurrent error can be characterised as follows: since he is 'human', and is hence limited by place and time, he is incapable of gathering all the data relevant to an examination of Iago's accusations; this lack of essential data precludes an assaying of the accusations solely through rational tools. Beginning in III, iii, Othello seeks to conduct a completely logical inquiry, based on the search for *unequivocal* proof that could remove *all doubt* regarding Desdemona's infidelity (III, iii, 365–367). This pretension is of course absurd, since it is impossible for him, even in theory, to obtain data that would enable him to form a valid line of argumentation, proving either that Desdemona has betrayed him or that she has remained faithful: he cannot, for example, be present in those places and times in which she allegedly 'lay' with Cassio, or the moment in which she supposedly gave him her handkerchief as a love-token.

An intellect-based investigation, such as that Othello purports to conduct, is outside the realm of the possible for an additional significant reason: the objects of Othello's investigation are human; the true thoughts and intentions of humans are always concealed from others, and Othello cannot know with certainty what is in the hearts of Desdemona, Cassio, Iago, and Emilia. In the game of life, in which we must decide and act according to our understanding of the human factors surrounding us, we often fail due to misinterpretation of the intentions, desires and thoughts of others. As mentioned above, in order to compensate for this shortcoming, nature has provided us with emotions; making use of emotional intelligence to 'smell' others' intentions is not, of course, an absolute solution to this general problem, and is not always on target, but in the test of evolution it has proven superior to random guessing or prolonged and passive logical calculations.[82] Othello, who relies solely on his intellectual faculties and ignores the guiding voice of his love for Desdemona, errs in his pretension *to know* (as opposed to assume, guess, feel, divine, believe, etc.) the thoughts of others. Iago himself points out to him this fundamental error – quite harshly and explicitly – but Othello does not assimilate the implications of his words:

> OTHELLO: By heaven, I'll know thy thoughts.
> IAGO: You cannot, if my heart were in your hand,
>   Nor shall not, whilst 'tis in my custody. (III, iii, 163–165)

Critics often mention the Handkerchief Scene as a significant reference point marking the beginning of Othello's return to the 'barbarian' core of his nature. A moment before he begins the 'juridical' investigation of evidence and demands that Desdemona show him the handkerchief, he takes her hand:

> OTHELLO: Give me your hand. This hand is moist, my lady. (III, iv, 32)

It is customary to see this gesture and these words as the first signs of the savage that will later seize Othello entirely, as he abandons the conventions of cultural behaviour and seems to give reign to his instincts. Indeed, this may appear to be a moment in which he suspends his rational thought and performs an act called in the language of the time 'to smell', that is, to discern or feel instinctively another's intentions.[83] For an additional examination of this theatrical moment we shall turn for a moment to the tragedy *King Lear* and the learning process undergone by its protagonist. At the beginning of the play, Lear shows no awareness of any means of communication other than the verbal, and for this reason he misinterprets the emotional attitudes of Goneril, Regan, Cordelia and Kent towards him. Towards the end

82   Ibid., pp. 123, 252–253.
83   *OED*, 'smell', v., 2a.

of the play, he develops additional channels of communication: for example, he shows an awareness of non-verbal signs, claiming to have 'smelt' the true quality and intentions of insincere characters.[84] In contrast to this tragedy, notable for its protagonist who undergoes a drastic learning experience and a significant change of character, the picture we encounter in *Othello* is entirely different: Othello develops no skills whatsoever for 'smelling' others as the plot progresses; he only learns factually, retrospectively, near his death, of his misjudgement of the real inner qualities of Iago, Cassio and Desdemona. The moment under discussion, in which he seemingly uses his instincts while feeling the hand of his wife, is in fact one more manifestation among many in the play of his inexhaustible striving to rationalise the dictates of his passions: a hand may be moist for a variety of reasons, including, as Desdemona herself says, youth and a life free of sorrow (l. 33). But Othello, who at this point already 'knows' that his wife is guilty, chooses the explanation that will best confirm the logic that has led him to this 'knowledge' – Desdemona is governed by the reproductive drive and a permissive nature, hence her hand is hot and moist:

OTHELLO: This *argues* fruitfulness and liberal heart.
              Hot, hot, and moist. (III, iv, 34–35; my italics)

The discordant intrusion into Othello's speech of the word 'argues' – a word that is both salient in the semantic field of logic and synonymous with the verb 'reason' – exposes his act of rationalisation.

Of course, it would not be invalid to regard this instance as indicative of the start of Othello's reversion to the savage within him. Nevertheless, this scene must be viewed in all its complexity: alongside this glimpse of 'bestiality' (and other glimpses to come), Othello continues to preserve his obsessive penchant for Reason and the rationalisation of reality. As we have already seen, it is precisely this obsessive penchant that exposes him to Iago's emotional appeal.

---

84   'LEAR: When the rain came to / wet me once and the wind to make me chatter, when / the thunder would not peace at my bidding, there I / found 'em, there I smelt 'em out. Go to, they are / not men o' their words' (IV, v, 97–101).

There is, however, one moment during the play in which Othello's emotions manage to completely overwhelm his tireless attempts at rational thinking. This is the moment when he recovers from his severe emotional seizure in IV, i. It is precisely in this moment – paradoxically, as it were – that Othello comes close to discovering the truth, and reveals an ability to 'smell' the hidden intentions of others. The extreme passion that brings on the seizure is expressed theatrically by Othello falling to the ground, and at the textual-structural level, by his 'falling' from pentameter into prose. This prose consists of a confused collection of sentence fragments in which he rapidly shifts from subject to subject. In the framework of the theatrical conventions of the time, such a text usually served to indicate a temporary or permanent state of madness;[85] the madman is distinguished from the sane person by the lack of reason in his thought processes – hence his words are not combined in a way that reason can grasp:

> Lie with her! Zounds, that's fulsome! Handkerchief – confessions – handkerchief! To confess and be hanged for his labour. First to be hanged and then to confess. I tremble at it. Nature would not invest herself in such shadowing passion without some instruction. It is not words that shake me thus. Pish! Noses, ears, and lips. Is't possible? – Confess? Handkerchief? O devil!
> [*He*] *falls in a trance.* (IV, i, 36–41)

Yet precisely as Othello is awakening from his seizure, before he has fully regained 'himself', he utters a short line that accurately reflects what Iago is doing to him:

> Dost thou mock[86] me? (Ibid., l. 58)

It seems that Othello touches on the truth here precisely because his 'pales and forts of reason' have just completely collapsed, during the passionate fit, and he has not yet regained his usual mental state, fortifying himself once again behind them. At this unique moment his instinct, his ability to 'smell' – or in contemporary terms, his 'emotional intelligence' – is not suppressed by his ceaseless desire for

85 For example, Shakespeare uses such prose to characterise Lear's temporary madness and Edgar's crafty madness (*King Lear*, III, iv, 43–105; IV, v, 82–100).

86 Mock (trans.): 'to deceive ... to delude, befool ...' (*OED*, 'mock', v., 3a).

250

Reason, and he 'smells' the truth. Immediately afterwards, upon his recovery, Othello reverts to the obsessive adherence to his 'intellect', thus continuing to err and to fall prey to Iago's emotional appeal.

Othello, during his would-be juridical investigation, rejects emotion and the heuristic benefits it offers in processes of judgement and decision-making. Specifically, he ignores the guidance of love, which would have induced him to believe his wife. This rejection is fatally erroneous not only because the faculty of reason is not a valid tool in the specific circumstances in which he finds himself: the central problem is that the influence of emotion upon thinking cannot be suspended at will; the emotional mechanism is rooted in each and every one of us and its activation is not susceptible to willpower. Indeed, despite his pretension, Othello does not neutralise the influence of his emotions: were he able to suspend them and conduct an investigation based on noetic rationality alone, at some point he would inevitably 'get stuck' in the sequence of argumentation, due to lack of essential data. In other words, although Othello attempts to neutralise the intervention of emotions in his thinking, he cannot choose whether or not to be affected by them; the only choice before him is whether to heed the guidance of love, or the guidance of jealousy, hatred and anger. Love would have guided him, long before he became 'perplexed in the extreme', to believe Desdemona and interpret the evidence to her advantage; jealousy, hatred and anger ultimately guide him to see the scant data and outward appearances Iago presents to him as solid and unequivocal proof of his wife's guilt.

5.3.5 The Logic of the Emotions

The concepts of 'intellect' and 'logic' are traditionally joined in a bond that is not easily undone: we tend to attach the label 'logical' to conclusions, decisions, and actions that stem from a process of sequential and sound deliberation by the intellect. Modern research into the emotions undermines this conceptual fixation, asserting that adherence to the dictates of the intellect is not necessarily, in all circumstances, the logical choice, and that obedience to the dictates of emotion can also at times be logical. In other words: scholars of the emotions today are inclined to view the emotions as having their own logic, and are searching for new ways to define and characterise this 'rationality of emotions'.[87]

Aaron Ben-Ze'ev distinguishes between two different types of logic: the descriptive and the normative. He claims that thinkers over the generations have tended to see the two as one and the same, and have not discerned the significant difference between them. According to Ben Ze'ev, we can consider something to be logical in the *descriptive* sense if it results from a process of deliberation by the intellect, and in the *normative* sense if it constitutes the best possible response in a given set of circumstances.[88] Indeed, noetic rationality – the logic of the intellect – is in some cases quite likely to guide us, after a logical process of deliberation, to respond in the most appropriate manner (that is, descriptive logic can at times also be normative). However, there are many cases in which this does not happen, as in the instances mentioned above, when data that are vital to the completion of a sequential logical process are lacking. Similarly, there are cases in which the possibility of carrying out a complete and proper intellectual thought process does not exist, such as moments of extreme emotion, or situations in which there is not ample time to evaluate the relevant data. Were we suddenly to come across a lion, it would not be logical (in the normative sense) to turn to our intellectual descriptive logic and weigh all the circumstances and prospects for an appropriate response. In such a case, the logical action would be immediate flight to a safe shelter. Flight is the appropriate response, and it is dictated to us by the emotion of fear. Emotion, in this specific situation, is *logical*: obedience to its imperatives (along with suspension of the intellect) is in this case the logical response. Scholars who examine emotion and its role from an evolutionary point of view, see it as Nature's solution to the limitations of human thinking: it directs us to a quick solution that has proven effective in the course of evolution.[89]

---

87   See, e.g., Dylan Evans, *Emotion: A Very Short Introduction*, pp. 121–124.
88   Aaron Ben-Ze'ev, 'The Logic of Emotions', *Philosophy and the Emotions*, ed. Anthony Hatzimoysis (Cambridge: Cambridge University Press, 2003), p. 150.
89   J. Le Doux, *The Emotional Brain*, p. 196.

5.3.6 Othello's Illogical Attachment to Descriptive Logic

As inferred above from III, i, 42–48, the 'wholesome' way of thinking, according to Othello, is that in which emotion plays no part. The
type of logic he tries repeatedly to apply is intellectual *descriptive*
logic (manifested, as we have seen, in his excessive use of conditional
clauses and reasoning); Othello adheres to this logic and attempts to
use it in dealing with the situation he faces, by discovering evidence
and proof that will clarify beyond a doubt that Desdemona is an adul-
teress. His situation, however, is one in which descriptive, intellectual,
logic is useless. Firstly, decisive, unambiguous proof for good or for
ill cannot be supplied because, as indicated, Othello cannot visit the
past in order to gather proof of deeds committed. Furthermore, as Iago
himself says, Cassio and Desdemona cannot be caused to have sexual
relations at a place and time in which Othello can be present and see
them with his own eyes. Iago states this explicitly to Othello, thus
showing him that the alleged betrayal cannot be proven 'descrip-
tively', beyond a shadow of a doubt (III, iii, 398–406). Nor is proof of
the opposite a possibility, since no unequivocal evidence can be provided that Desdemona did not lie with Cassio. Secondly, Othello is in
an extreme emotional state, caused by his falling in love with Desdemona, his lack of military activity following the sinking of the Turkish
fleet, and of course Iago's emotional appeals. Such a state disrupts the
workings of the intellect and turns it into a flawed tool, and the use of
a flawed tool is not logical in the normative sense. In other words, in
Othello's circumstances in the play, it is entirely illogical on his part
(in the normative sense) to employ his descriptive logic, because in
such circumstances it becomes a damaged tool. On the other hand, it
would have been quite logical on his part (again, in the normative
sense) to allow his emotion of love to guide him to the response appropriate to the circumstances.

The discourses of the Senate Scene were presented in Chapter
Three as an example of the use made by Venetian characters of 'the
language of Reason'. It was pointed out that the discussions conducted
by the duke regarding the Turkish fleet and Brabantio's accusations,
are based on purely logical thinking: the language employed by the
duke and the senators is not a mere construction of words typical of

rational argumentation, but is actually a faithful reflection of the true rationality of those who speak it. It is now time to disclose more of the subtlety within the Senate Scene, and to show that the sound governance of Venice is not characterised only by use of intellectual, 'descriptive' rationality: a careful examination of the verbal nuances reveals that the senate, in addition to its ability to make profitable use of the dictates of the 'head', knows how to complement it by heeding the dictates of the 'heart'.

The senate's emergency night council is held in Venice; thus, the brief military reports regarding the Turkish fleet, arriving from afar, cannot be considered certain: they should be treated as conjecture, and those present on the occasion are well aware of this. Use of intellectual logic in such a case cannot lead to final and decisive conclusions, because in addition to facts known with certainty (such as the malicious intent of the Turks and the degree of strength and military importance of the fortresses of Cyprus and Rhodes), the council also faces evasive and indefinite variables. This is stressed by the playwright, who directs our attention to the contradictions among the different reports reaching the senate with regard to the number of Turkish vessels and the direction in which they are sailing. Such evasive and indefinite variables do not permit the formation of a continuous and complete sequence of reasoning, and cannot therefore be digested by the intellect alone.

Because the senators and the duke employ an exemplary 'language of Reason', they may appear to be engaged in a process of reasoning based solely on descriptive logic, and to have suspended all other modes of thinking. The true picture, however, is in fact somewhat more complex, and scholars who refer to the exemplary rationality demonstrated by those present,[90] ignore the deliberate choice of words made by history's greatest chooser of words. Following a descriptive-logical analysis of information delivered by several messengers, the duke and the senators reach a conclusion: it is highly probable that the enemy intends to assault not Rhodes, but Cyprus, and that his sailing to Rhodes is merely an attempt at deception. The degree of certainty of this conclusion is defined by the duke as 'in all confi-

90   See, e.g.: Philip C. McGuire, '*Othello* as an "Assay of Reason"', pp. 199–200.

dence' (I, iii, 31). Immediately following this line, however, yet another messenger enters, sent by Montano, governor of Cyprus. Like his predecessor, this messenger supplies additional data relevant to the descriptive logical process carried out by the council; unlike his predecessor, however, he ends his speech with an appeal that does not in fact address the intellect of his listeners:

> The Ottomites, reverend and gracious,
> Steering with due course towards the isle of Rhodes
> Have there injointed them with an after fleet.
>   ... Signior Montano,
> *Your trusty and most valiant servitor,*
> With his free duty recommends you thus,
> And *prays you to believe* him. (Ibid., ll. 33–42; my italics)

The effect of this appeal on the duke has not, to the best of my knowledge, been addressed by students of the play. Immediately after the messenger proclaims the worth of Montano as man and subject, and pleads for belief in the truthfulness of his report, the duke announces decisively:

> 'Tis *certain* then for Cyprus. (Ibid., l. 43; my italics)

Montano's messenger, however, has not supplied the council with data whose degree of certainty differs from that received up to this point. Thus, the information contained in this new message does not in fact enable the duke to alter the degree of certainty of his previous conclusion, certainly not from a status of high probability ('in all confidence') to one of absolute certainty (''Tis certain'). This significant transformation takes place in the mind of the duke only because a subject of his whom he has known for a long time – and of whom he apparently thinks highly – has protested his worth and pleaded for belief.

  Shakespeare, then, presents at this early stage of the play a highly rational character who chooses to pay heed to the non-intellectual faculties of the mind and, in keeping with their dictates, chooses the mental condition of believing (as opposed to 'knowing'). The circumstances in which the duke is placed during the Senate Scene are similar to those in which Othello will find himself later in the play; Othello, however, who can choose to *believe* Desdemona, insists instead on *knowing* with certainty whether or not she has committed adultery (and this is an impossibility, as we have seen). Unlike Othello, the duke is truly rational, and precisely for this reason he knows when he must abandon logical-descriptive thinking and turn to the emotional alternative.

Othello's situation, in which he seems to have the option of choosing to believe the woman he loves and be guided by this belief, is similar to that facing the speaker in Sonnet 138. As opposed to Othello, this speaker chooses belief; this choice, from our point of view, requires true mental strength, since (unlike Othello, who at first only *suspects* Desdemona), the speaker *knows* that his beloved is lying:

> When my love swears that she is made of truth,
> I do *believe* her, though I *know* she lies. (ll. 1–2; my italics)

The thematic similitude between this sonnet and *Othello* is reinforced by verbal similitude: the words 'believe', 'belief', 'think', and 'thought', which are used to indicate uncertainty, are the key words Shakespeare plants in both, in juxtaposition to 'know', 'knowing' and 'knowledge'.[91] The speaker in the sonnet chooses to live in a world based on the words *believe* and *think*; Othello – on the word *know*.

The arguments of this speaker can, of course, be presented in a negative light, as one critic has chosen to do, defining them as 'so cynical ... so self-conscious ... mutual deceit', 'schizophrenia' and 'a tissue of rationalisation he [the speaker] enriches himself with, perhaps as he approaches his mistress' chamber door';[92] however, it seems that broader and more useful implications can be unearthed when these fourteen lines are examined applying the terms discussed in this chapter. The speaker shares with us the considerations that have guided him to set aside his noetic rationality and choose 'the logic of

---

91   In numbers: the words 'think' and 'thought' occur in *Othello* 114 times; 'believe' and 'belief' – 12 times; 'know' in its various forms – 97 times.

92   Alice F. Moore, 'Self Deception in *Sonnet 138*'. *Shakespeare Quarterly* 40 (1989), pp. 15–17.

emotions', which has led him to the optimal response in the given situation: the emotional gain he derives from maintaining his relations with his unfaithful love, the flattery each enjoys from the false tongue of the other, and the illusion of youth regained, are all worthwhile for him and far more beneficial than busying himself with facts.

Othello, accordingly, acts with a complete lack of rationality for two reasons: he uses descriptive logic in a situation in which it has no validity (because the data available to him are incomplete and ambiguous); and he rejects the logic of the emotions, which in the given situation might have led to the optimal response, namely, belief. The absurdity of the illogical logic to which he adheres is best manifested in the following lines, which are in fact far more ironic than they first seem:

> OTHELLO: If she be false, O then heaven mocks itself;
> I'll not believe it! (III, iii, 280–281)

On the face of it, the veracity of this statement of Othello's is belied when he accepts Iago's 'proof' and rejects Desdemona's declarations of fidelity; yet Othello will in fact fulfil his declaration precisely: during the second half of the play he does not *believe* that Desdemona is unfaithful, but, having made obsessive and perverse use of his Reason, *knows* it.

5.4 'Addiction to Reason' in Shakespeare's Drama

As mentioned above, Shakespearean research often highlights the elements common to the tragedy *Othello* and medieval morality plays. Robert B. Heilman and Thomas McAlindon remark on the frequent appearance of the word 'General' in the play and its double meaning: in most instances it is used to indicate Othello's military title, General of the Venetian Army; sometimes it denotes the people in general; and at times the text suggests both these meanings (e.g.: III, i, 16). Thus the use of this word is one means of indicating that the most singular of Shakespeare's heroes can also be seen as a generic figure personi-fying the essence of human nature.[93]

Following this line of interpretation, the *psychomachia* within Othello's mind between the purportedly opposite entities, Reason and Passion, can be seen as representative of this same struggle within the human psyche. The problematic relationship between emotion and intellect has always preoccupied mankind and, in one way or another, troubled each and every human being. Since ancient times, the domi-nant voice in Western society has tended to prefer reason and to preach the suppression of immoderate passion. Jon Elster calls this tendency 'addiction to reason': he holds that the human being is a creature who desires, for the sake of his self-image, to believe that he acts according to the dictates of the intellect and, for this reason, he tends to implement his intellect obsessively, applying it even to mat-ters that have nothing to do with it. Just as all addictions are irrational, so too is the addiction to reason clearly irrational.[94] In light of Elster's observation, Othello can most assuredly be considered a generic figure representing mankind – a sort of Renaissance Everyman – because of the conspicuous way in which Shakespeare endows his character with the 'addiction to reason', that is, the obsessive and irrational desire to be rational.

Like mankind, Othello nourishes his self-image by imprisoning reality within the confines of reason, simplifying it,[95] or in less com-plimentary words, distorting it. Considering this human tendency from an anthropological perspective, F. G. Bailey sees it as the consequence of our need for a sense of security. Man, according to him, wants to feel that he is in control of himself and the world around him; to this end he formulates a clear set of rules, which he imposes on reality. Reality, of course, does not obey these rules (or in fact any other set of

93   Thomas McAlindon, *Shakespeare's Tragic Cosmos*, p. 135.
94   Jon Elster, *Solomonic Judgments* (Cambridge: Cambridge University Press, 1989), pp. 117–122; Jon Elster, *Alchemists of the Mind: Rationality and the Emotions*, pp. 290–291, 304.
95   Othello's tendency to simplify reality is clearly manifested in the Temptation Scene: 'IAGO: Men should be what they seem; / Or those that be not, would they might seem none! OTHELLO: Certain, men should be what they seem' (III, iii, 127–129).

258

rules one is capable of grasping) and is full of the unexpected, the irrational, and the strange. Man is aware of the constant contradiction between the rules he has formulated and reality, but cannot cease to formulate them and to delude himself that they are valid; to do so would be to doom himself to a constant sense of insecurity and inability to function properly.[96] Thought itself, argues Bailey, is merely the simplification of reality.[97]

Othello is perhaps the most highly developed Shakespearean embodiment of the rationalising Everyman, although he is by no means the only one. Brutus, in this respect, can be seen as Othello's prototype: as demonstrated in Chapter Two, Brutus' craving for Reason is manifested repeatedly in his use of conditional clauses and contrived, rigid textual structures that seek to limit reality to the confines of reason. As shown in Chapter Three, Shakespeare hints at Othello's 'addiction to reason' by employing the word 'satisfy' in contexts of logical proof; interestingly, he puts this very same word in Brutus' mouth as well, when the latter engages in seemingly logical rationales – and in association with the two favourite words of Shakespeare's rationalising characters, 'reason' and 'cause':

SERVANT: If Brutus will vouchsafe that Antony
              May safely come to him, and be resolved
              How Caesar hath deserved to lie in death,
              Mark Antony shall not love Caesar dead
              So well as Brutus living ...
BRUTUS: Tell him, so please him come unto this place,
              He shall be *satisfied* ... (III, i, 130–141; my italics)

BRUTUS: Our *reasons* are so full of good regard
              That were you, Antony, the son of Caesar
              You should be *satisfied*. (III, i, 224–226; my italics)

---

96   F. G. Bailey, *The Tactical Uses of Passion* (Ithaca, NY: Cornell University Press, 1983), pp. 11–21.
97   Ibid., p. 18.

<pre>
BRUTUS: Your master, Pindarus,
            In his own change, or by ill officers,
            Hath given me some *worthy cause* to wish
            Things done undone, but if he be at hand
            I shall be *satisfied*. (IV, ii, 6–10; my italics)
</pre>

It is no accident that this same word is also found in Caesar's vocabulary. As shown in Chapter Two, Caesar serves at times as a caricature of the rationalising Brutus; his use of the words 'satisfy' and 'satisfaction' in association with 'cause' is but one of the hints suggesting his affinity with Brutus, particularly their shared craving for reason:

<pre>
CAESAR: Decius, go tell them Caesar will not come.
DECIUS: Most mighty Caesar, let me know some *cause*,
          Lest I be laughed at when I tell them so.
CAESAR: The *cause* is in my will. I will not come:
          That is enough to *satisfy* the senate.
          But for your private *satisfaction*,
          Because I love you, I will let you know ...
          (II, ii, 68–74; my italics)

CAESAR: Know Caesar doth not wrong, nor without *cause*
          Will he be *satisfied*. (III, i, 47–48; my italics)
</pre>

Evidence that the addiction to reason is, from Shakespeare's point of view, a universally human tendency, can be found in the way he characterises the Roman crowd in *Julius Caesar*. As argued when examining the conduct of the citizens who resolve to put the poet Cinna to death (Chapter Two, 2.2.3), their reality-rationalising way of thinking is fundamentally identical to that of Brutus and Caesar. This tendency of the citizens also finds expression in their responses to Caesar's assassination and to the speeches of Brutus and Antony: Shakespeare puts the word 'satisfy' into their mouths as well, thus establishing their affinity with Brutus and Caesar, and hinting at one basic tendency common to all. The citizens' craving to 'be satisfied' is evident from the very first line of this scene,[98] and their reactions after

---

98   'ALL: We will be *satisfied*; let us be *satisfied*. / BRUTUS: Then follow me, and
     give me audience, friends. / ... And public *reasons* shall be rendered / Of Caesar's

hearing Brutus' 'cause' speech and the 'reasons' it contains, indicate their complete satisfaction. The style in which Antony opens his speech – an imitation in pentameter of Brutus' rationalising prose – is clear evidence that he is aware of the plebeian thirst for such pseudo-rationality. The pseudo-logical discourse the citizens conduct immediately following these Brutus-like lines, clearly shows that Antony knows how to provide them precisely what they yearn for.[99]

Characters who strive obsessively and irrationally for pure rationality are by no means exclusive to the plays upon which this study focuses. The following brief survey will seek to demonstrate this by pointing out the characterisation of several Shakespearean protagonists as being addicted to reason. King Lear serves as a good starting point: scholars justifiably tend to emphasise his irrational traits, manifested from the very outset of the play in his capricious decisions and his raging outbursts; however, it should be observed that Lear sees himself as rational, and compulsively applies his intellectual faculties even to matters that are totally irrelevant to the intellect. His fundamental error in banishing Cordelia is in fact an outcome of this tendency. On the basis of his assumption that passions can be measured and compared, he stages the love contest between his daughters; in this contest, he evaluates the measure of love that Goneril, Regan and Cordelia hold for him according to the words (*logos*) they speak. The result of Lear's erroneous premise and method is quite contrary to what he intended – Love is banished and the empty-hearted thrive. It is important to note that this way of thinking of Lear's is not a momentary whim, exclusive to the opening scene, but rather a consistent trait. Later in the play, he errs again in identifying and appraising Goneril's and Regan's true emotions; once again, his error stems from

---

death. 1 PLEBEIAN: I will hear Brutus speak. 2 PLEBEIAN: I will hear Cassius and *compare their reasons* ...' (III, ii, 1–9; my italics).

99   '1 PLEBEIAN: Methinks there is much *reason* in his sayings. 2 PLEBEIAN: If thou consider rightly of the matter, / Caesar has had great wrong. 3 PLEBEIAN: Has he, masters? / I fear there will a worse come in his place. 4 PLEBEIAN: Marked ye his words? He would not take the crown, / Therefore 'tis certain he was not ambitious' (III, ii, 100–105; my italics).

his inclination to examine the passions with intellectual tools, such as reasoning and calculations of amount and proportion:

> Regan, I think you are [glad]. I know what *reason*
> I have to think so. If thou shouldst not be glad,
> I would divorce me from thy mother's tomb,
> Sepulch'ring an adultress. (II, iv, 121–124; my italics)

> [*To Goneril*] I'll go with thee;
> Thy fifty yet doth double five and twenty,
> And thou art twice her love. (Ibid., 251–253)

The primary erroneous assumption which brings about this perverted way of thinking is hinted at twice during the opening scene: in his stormy outburst, disclaiming all his love, kinship and paternal care for Cordelia, Lear refers to himself and to his heart – the seat of passions – as two separate entities.[100]

This mental inclination of Lear's is not expressed by means of the many rhetorical schemes Shakespeare employs to characterise the comparable inclinations of Brutus and Othello; but precisely like them, the craving to impose reason on reality is perhaps Lear's most basic trait, the core around which the playwright has built his character – and from which stem his other traits and 'flaws', as it were.

For a representative example of characters 'addicted to reason' in Shakespearean comedy, let us take a glance at two of the main male characters in *Midsummer Night's Dream*: Theseus, in his famous speech at the beginning of the fifth act, reveals his obstinate preference for 'cool reason' and his absolute and reality-denying rejection of the irrational; Lysander, in attempting to explain the abrupt emotional metamorphosis he has undergone while asleep in the wood, due to which he abandoned Hermia and began to dote on Helena, prefers to see his faculty of reason as the cause behind it (II, ii, 121–128). His arbitrary attempt to justify his emotional change, do not agree at all with the events as seen by the audience on stage; even the shallow

---

100 'And as a stranger to *my heart* and *me* / Hold thee from this for ever' (I, i, 109–110); 'So be my grave my peace, as here *I* give / Her father's *heart* from her' (ibid., 119–120; my italics).

Bottom knows well that 'reason and love keep little company together now-a-days'.

In addition to these comic characters, Beatrice and Benedick from *Much Ado About Nothing* deserve special mention. Prior to their wedding, and independently of one another, the two carried on a love affair with the word 'wit' and its various meanings common at the time. This noun, appearing in the play no less than thirty-two times, is used to denote astuteness, verbal ingenuity, repartee, and at times even wisdom;[101] as previously noted, in Shakespeare's day this word was also commonly used to denote the intellect and the faculty of reason,[102] and *Much Ado* is no exception in this regard.[103] The sum total of meanings of the word 'wit' coincides with the sum total of the prominent characteristics of Beatrice and Benedick: both are considered by those around them to be witty and wise, and both operate intensively to establish and magnify this image by making obsessive use of their intellect and logic. Just like other reason-craving Shakespearean characters, Beatrice's and Benedick's addiction to reason is manifested in their untiring practice of imposing their rational ways of thinking on matters of passion: they deliberate on love with supposedly logical tools, and reject it by means of pseudo-rational arguments. These arguments are shaped and expressed using the same rhetorical schemes and style discussed in the context of Brutus and Othello: among these can be counted symmetry, inverted symmetry, contrived balance, 'if ... then ...' sentences, and sequences of short clauses that purportedly add up to complete logical arguments.[104]

Specifically, it is illuminating to note how similar some of the rhetorical devices and textual structures Shakespeare puts into Benedick's mouth are to those spoken by Brutus in his Forum Speech:

101 III, v, 56–57; V, i, 157–162 (see: *OED*, 'wit', n., 6a).
102 See Chapter Three, note 9.
103 III, i, 52, 89; V, i, 124, 128, 197.
104 I, i, 177–182, 195–196; II, i, 43–47, 209–213; II, iii, 6–10, 21–27, 188–199, 203–204, 208–212; V, i, 147–154.

BENEDICK: That a woman conceived me, I thank her; that she brought me up, I likewise give her most humble thanks: but that I will have a recheat winded in my forehead, or hang my bugle in an invisible baldrick, all women shall pardon me. (I, i, 177–180)

BRUTUS: As Caesar loved me, I weep for him; as he was fortunate, I rejoice at it; as he was valiant, I honour him; but, as he was ambitious, I slew him. (III, ii, 21–23)

BENEDICK: Because I will not do them the *wrong* to <u>mistrust any</u>, I will do myself the *right* to <u>trust none</u> ... (I, i, 180–181)

BRUTUS: Had you rather Caesar were *living*, and <u>die</u> all slaves, than that Caesar were <u>dead</u>, to *live* all freemen? (III, ii, 20–21; my italics)

BENEDICK: ... and the *fine* is, for the which I may go the *finer*, I will live a bachelor. (I, i, 181–182; my italics)

BRUTUS: *censure* me in your wisdom, and awake your *senses*, that you may the better judge ... (III, ii, 15–16; my italics)

Juxtaposing the rhetorical schemes and 'language of reason' employed by these two seemingly different protagonists, thus reveals their 'genetic' proximity and shared major characteristic.

Only the clever intrigue devised by the secondary characters, amplified by the catalysing emotional force of the events of the sub-plot, succeeds in breaking through the walls of intellect behind which Beatrice and Benedick have fortified themselves. When these walls begin to tremble, the two acknowledge their love; when the walls are close to collapse, they openly confess it. The central place of reason in their world, and its significant role in their denial of love, receive a symmetrical emphasis a moment before Love, in keeping with the tradition of comedy, emerges triumphant:

BENEDICK: Do not you love me?
BEATRICE: Why, no; *no more than Reason.*
BENEDICK: Why, then your uncle and the prince and Claudio
            Have been deceived; they swore you did.
BEATRICE: Do not you love me?
BENEDICK: Troth, no; *no more than Reason.* (V, iv, 74–77; my italics)

The word 'reason' appears capitalised in the above lines, in order to stress the secondary meaning concealed in these identical protestations by the two: the inner conflict that transpires in their minds during the play can be described as a struggle between their love for each other and their love of Reason; a moment before their wedding Beatrice and Benedick still find it difficult to devote themselves entirely to their new love and to forsake the old.

Concluding Remarks

Shakespeare's preoccupation with the passions, as presented throughout this study, cannot be considered unique in the time and place he composed his works. Many plays written and translated in early modern England display abundant awareness of the phenomenon of emotion, and considerable interest in its portrayal. This tendency appears to be directly linked to the interest frequently manifested by early modern English sources in the passions – not only in writings whose stated subject they were, but also in broader works dealing with philosophy, political thought and medicine. Playwrights, creating in a specific time and place, reflected in their works areas of interest common in the society to which they appealed; emotion was one such area of interest. The preoccupation of English writers with the passions stems in part from their interest in the classical sources: Elizabethan and Jacobean thinkers and essayists were deeply influenced by the numerous discussions of this subject in ancient works. Affected by this general trend, the playwrights of Shakespeare's time were captivated by the Roman dramatists' passion for the passions. In particular, English playwrights have adopted two salient tendencies of Roman drama: a constant focus on the emotional aspect of events, and directing the attention of the spectators to the outward manifestations of the characters' passions.

The clearest example of this is Seneca's *Tenne Tragedies*, which exerted a profound influence on the attributes of Elizabethan drama, inspiring both original dramatists and imitators. Seneca's great interest in the emotions was by no means dulled in the English translation. His characters comment frequently – in the Elizabethan vocabulary of the emotions – about the passions they and their fellow characters are experiencing. Particularly noteworthy in this regard is John Studley's translation of *Medea*, unequaled in the frequency of its references to the passions – describing their outward expressions and influence on mind and body – in Shakespeare's period or in any other. Of the nu-

merous original early-modern English plays showing a keen awareness of the emotions, the following are worthy of special note: *The
Spanish Tragedy* (1582–1592) by Kyd; the two parts of Marlowe's
Tamburlaine the Great (1587); *Every Man in his Humour* (1598),
Every Man out of his Humour (1599), and *Catiline* (1611), by Jonson;
and *The Revenger's Tragedy* (1607, possibly written by Thomas Middleton). The intense emotional consciousness of these plays is noticeable first and foremost at the verbal level: words from the semantic
field of emotion are frequently uttered by the characters, constantly
revealing the emotional aspect of the drama.

The uniqueness of Shakespeare, even within the context of plays
as full of emotional awareness as these, is the detailed presentation of
lengthy, ongoing and complex emotional processes, while portraying
the role of emotion in the human psyche and its reciprocal relationship
with sensory perception, imagination, thought, will, and, above all,
Reason. As briefly demonstrated below, the English playwrights
active during the reigns of Elizabeth and James tended to avoid portraying ongoing emotional processes: at most, they presented spectators with such processes in the most schematic manner. This is true
even of plays that grant emotion a position of importance, and consistently draw the audience's attention to it. The English playwrights focused primarily on supplying their audience with frequent 'emotional
snapshots', similar to those common in the Roman tragedies and their
translations. These 'snapshots' consist of brief reports uttered by the
characters, informing the spectators of their present emotional state
and its accompanying physiological and mental effects.

Shakespeare's treatment of the emotions was no less than revo-
lutionary. This becomes clear when the plays studied in this book are
compared to other plays of the period that seem to contain all the
'ingredients' necessary for the portrayal of complex and ongoing emotional processes. One such play is Jonson's *Catiline*: this tragedy
repeatedly draws the attention of the spectator to the emotional factor
in its fictional world,[1] and includes a number of well-constructed
speeches influenced by the classical rhetorical tradition, designed as

---

1   The word 'fear', for example, appears no less than fifty-eight times in the
     course of the play.

268

emotional appeals. An examination of the role of emotion in this play and the way in which it is represented, brings to mind *Julius Caesar*. After such an examination there seems to be no escaping speculation about the direct inspiration Jonson drew from Shakespeare's earlier drama of rage and fire: anger in *Catiline* is the primary fuel driving the plot; Catiline, who aspires to destroy Rome, is driven by this passion, as are most of his co-conspirators; anger has a very significant thematic role in *Catiline*[2] and is linked to an intricate array of fire imagery; this imagery analogises the anger of the conspirators to the fire with which they intend to burn Rome, as well as to an 'angry' storm that descends upon the city and is manifested on stage by means of various effects.

Unlike *Julius Caesar*, however, and despite the numerous attempts of its characters to exert emotional influence over their fellow characters, the plot of *Catiline* is not channelled through emotional appeals. As the play opens, the conspirators are already full of anger, desire for vengeance, and ambition; the emotional appeals Catiline addresses to them only attempt to intensify the existing passions and prevent them from fading. These emotional appeals cannot be categorised as channelling the plot, for two reasons: the text provides no indication as to the degree of their actual success; they do not generate emotion where none existed, nor do they act in opposition to an existing emotional inclination (as do the emotional appeals in *Julius Caesar*, and other appeals is the Shakespearean plays discussed in previous chapters).

In *Julius Caesar*, Cicero 'has had great wrong': in a play that focuses on public speeches and the ability to move audiences, the greatest of the moving orators was allotted by the greatest of playwrights only a tiny role, which includes not even a snippet of oration. Jonson amended this injustice in *Catiline*: he placed Cicero at the centre of the drama, and put into his mouth a profusion of long speeches that contain emotional appeals. These speeches are delivered

---

2   This is evident even from a cursory reading of *Catiline*, due to Jonson's frequent repetition of the following words (in parentheses: the number of appearances of each word): fury-furies-furious (21); anger (16); revenge-venge-vengeance (14); rage (5); fire (26); flame-enflame (11); burn (7).

on occasions of a juristic nature, in which Cicero attempts to persuade the senate of the guilt of Catiline and the conspirators. Yet his emotional appeals have no effect whatsoever on the main events of the play: Cicero's friends and countrymen are persuaded of Catiline's guilt only after they have realised that he is leading a hostile army towards Rome; in order to convince the senators of the guilt of Catiline's allies, Rome's arch-orator must produce material evidence, such as incriminating letters and a cache of weapons. In fact, Jonson channels the plot of this tragedy by the same means he uses in his comedies, namely, intrigues. The chief contriver of intrigues in *Catiline* is Cicero: failing to persuade the Romans of the guilt of the conspirators by means of emotional appeals, this great speaker turns to shady methods – he uses informers and has no qualms about paying a bribe to obtain the legal evidence he requires. That Jonson avoids depicting continuous emotional processes is particularly conspicuous in Cicero's long speech in scene IV, ii. This speech spans more than 300 lines and includes lengthy amplifications designed to arouse the senators' anger and fear towards the conspirators; this exceptionally massive oration, however, does not in fact draw from the addressees any response that might indicate the degree of its emotional influence, if any.

A similar tendency exists in other plays from Shakespeare's time that devote special attention to the passions. The emotional changes undergone by the characters in these plays – generated by emotional manipulations, intrigues, or the changing circumstances – are sudden and at times even appear arbitrary. Such is the case in Jonson's *Every Man out of his Humour*, a comedy in which the emotional and behavioural characteristics of the main characters go from one extreme to the other. Some of these changes do not occur on stage, but are instead reported succinctly and in retrospect: thus in scene V, vi, Fungoso reports that his obsessive aspiration to dress in fashionable garments has ceased, as has his envy of Fastidious Brisk, who always sports the latest fashion. The emotional changes Jonson does choose to present onstage are sudden, and do not afford a glimpse into the emotional mechanisms that brought them about. A typical example of this is the swift metamorphosis of Sordido, the egotistical miser, who turns into a man full of altruistic love seconds after his attempted suicide is thwarted by passers-by (III, ii). I do not of course mean to imply that this phenomenon constitutes a shortcoming in Jonson's writing, but rather to point out a general tendency it shares with that of other playwrights of the time, apart from Shakespeare. As to the particular play in question, one must of course consider that such sudden and arbitrary changes have ever characterised the comic tradition.

The two parts of Marlowe's *Tamburlaine the Great* may serve as yet another example from the tragic genre – which, compared to the comic genre, tends to make less use of arbitrary dramatic reversals. These two plays frequently demonstrate an awareness of the emotional factor, and draw the spectator's attention to the oratorical and persuasive powers of the hero.[3] On the face of it, emotional appeal might seem one of the central means enabling Tamburlaine to conquer such vast parts of the world: Marlowe repeatedly stresses the protagonist's intimidating appearance, the terror aroused by his fiery eyes and angry facial expression,[4] and his deliberate use of fear in his conquests. During sieges on enemy cities, for example, Tamburlaine establishes a routine of changing the colours of his tent, banners and weapons; his purpose in carrying out this practice is to indicate to the inhabitants of the besieged cities the mental transformation he supposedly undergoes as time passes: from mildness (white) to anger and bloodthirstiness (red), and on to an immutable resolution to destroy and massacre (black). However, a careful examination of these emotional appeals and their outcomes raises considerable doubt about their actual influence on subsequent events: several of Tamburlaine's enemies appear on stage expressing their great fear of the anticipated encounter with him;[5] others, by contrast, declare their self-confidence and absolute faith that they will defeat the Scythian shepherd;[6] not once does Marlowe portray any of Tamburlaine's enemies as being in a condition between these two extremes, that is, in the throes of an emotional process. In fact, in neither play is the audience witness to

3   See, e.g.: 1, I, ii, 210–211, 227–229; 1, II, i, 35–39; 1, II, iii, 25.
4   1, I, i, 55–56; 1, III, ii, 66–75; 1, IV, i, 12–16.
5   1, II, iv, 1–15; 1, IV, i, 12–16; 1, V, i, 1–23; 2, V, i, 2–9.
6   1, II, ii, 59–75; 1, III, i, 21–30, 45–49; 1, III, iii, 11–22, 75–81, 134–147; 1, IV, i, 31–36; 1, IV, iv, 61–68; 2, V, i, 10–23.

any success whatsoever of clear-cut emotional appeals:[7] the only speeches of persuasion that do succeed in changing the course of action pursued by certain characters are those involving considerations of personal benefit, rational argumentation, or a mysterious and unseen force. Such is the case when Tamburlaine first meets Theridamas and transforms him – as if by virtue of words – from enemy to ally (I, ii): this speech of persuasion opens with a touch of flattery (Tamburlaine notes that Theridamas has only 1000 horses, and claims that, judging by his imposing appearance, he is worthy to lead a much greater force); subsequently, Tamburlaine appeals to the reason of his addressee (arguing logically, as it were, that the heavens have destined him for continued military success and world rule, hence it would be wise on Theridamas' part to renounce fighting and join forces instead); this rational appeal harps especially upon the personal benefit of the addressee (should he renounce fighting and join forces, Theridamas is promised a partnership on the throne of world dominion). Marlowe does not enable the audience to determine which factor has persuaded Theridamas: the latter reports on having submitted to the outer appearance and words of the persuader (l. 228), but also describes a mysterious power at work during the speech, which has enticed his soul (l. 224).

Marlowe's refraining from portraying emotional processes in *Tamburlaine* is consistent, and is not limited to situations involving rhetorical persuasion. Thus, between scenes 1, I, ii and 1, III, ii, the captive princess Zenocrate undergoes a drastic change of heart, from hostility and contempt to lovesickness, with no possibility for the spectator to follow the emotional path that links these two conditions. The same is the case with Bajazeth's intensifying passions, which drive him to suicide: following his defeat by Tamburlaine, the emperor of the Turks is imprisoned in a cage and subjected to a series of humiliations, continuing from scene 1, IV, ii to 1, V, ii; during this

---

7   For example: the lengthiest emotional appeal of *Tamburlaine*'s two parts, that of the virgin of Damascus for Tamburlaine's mercy (1 V, ii, 11–42), is rejected out of hand. The moment the virgin ends her appeal, with no apparent signs of hesitation, Tamburlaine orders her execution together with that of her three companions, and their bodies are hoisted up on the city wall.

time Bajazeth openly expresses primarily anger and scorn for his captor, and there is nothing in his response to indicate his growing despair; this hidden passion emerges as if from nowhere near the end of the play, and drives him to smash his head against the bars of the cage.

Even against the background of plays full of emotional awareness, such as those surveyed above, Shakespeare's drama stands out from the point of view of this study: it portrays entire and complex emotional *processes*, and characterises the interaction between the mental faculties. Shakespeare's unique ability to represent emotional processes and to depict the place of emotions in the human psyche seems to have been the crucial factor that allowed him to write plots motivated by emotional manipulations. To the best of my knowledge, no playwright before or during Shakespeare's time composed plays whose plots are motivated through a similar technique, that is, plays whose course of action is changed radically, even reversed, before the spectators' very eyes, solely as a result of emotional appeals.

The fact that those of Shakespeare's plays motivated by emotional appeals were written in 1599 or thereafter appears to be related to his general development as a writer. A convincing portrayal of complex emotional processes – particularly those generated by emotional appeals – requires not only sharp insight, but also skill and sophistication in implementing traditional conventional rhetorical tools. This study has already pointed out that Shakespeare's use of rhetorical formulae became more diverse and sophisticated over time. Shakespearean drama written after 1599 contains more refined and original versions and combinations of the traditional rhetorical figures; in the earlier plays, by contrast, we encounter time and again conventional, bookish rhetorical displays: characters are often 'playing the orator', giving breath to standard figures from Roman and Elizabethan rhetorical treatises. In other words, Shakespeare's use of conventional rhetorical tools becomes unconventional over time.[8] As his rhetorical

8   Brian Vickers and Frank Kermode discuss the evolving subtlety and sophistication in Shakespeare's use of the rhetorical figures. Miriam Joseph points specifically to such evolving sophistication in Shakespeare's use of the figures of *pathos*. See: Frank Kermode, *Shakespeare's Language* (London: Penguin

tools become more refined and sophisticated, they clearly enable him to portray more refined and complex mental processes, including, of course, emotional processes. Excellence of technique, which is essential to excellent art, enables the dramatic poet to implement his theoretical insights in his plays, and makes it possible for the actors to realise them onstage. Among playwrights, Shakespeare is undoubtedly one of the greatest 'natural-born' psychologists of all time; the technical sophistication and subtlety he achieves in the course of his creative years enable him to bring his 'psychological' observations to the stage in an ever more credible and precise manner. Specifically, as it relates to this study, Shakespeare's growing skill in employing and hybridising diverse schemes, tropes, and lists of topics enables him to give shape to complete, complex and convincing processes of emotional persuasion.

The emotional processes in the four plays discussed here were examined in Chapter Five in the light of prevalent modern concepts of emotion. This comparative examination has indicated the existence of a significant correspondence between the emotional dynamics and the role of emotion in the human psyche in Shakespeare's dramatic world, and their parallels in the 'real' world – at least as they are conceptualised in current studies of the emotions. The point of utilising these theories has of course not been to 'force' them upon the plays, but rather to attempt to understand the Shakespearean emotional cosmos and microcosm by means of comparative tools. This comparison has revealed that, as held by contemporary research, emotions in the fictional Shakespearean world have a functional, beneficial value: they are by no means Man's archenemies (as in the stoic world view, often termed in a gross generalisation 'traditional') but rather his guiding angels; when used properly, they help to overcome obstacles, to realise goals, and to distinguish between friend and foe. The four

---

Books, 2000), pp. 25–82; Brian Vickers, 'Shakespeare's Use of Rhetoric', *A new Companion to Shakespeare Studies*, ed. K. Muir and S. Schoenbaum (Cambridge: Cambridge University Press, 1971); Miriam Joseph, *Shakespeare's Use of the Arts of Language* (New York: Columbia University Press, 1949), pp. 262–272.

plays – again, like contemporary research – expose the limitations of rational thinking, and point to emotion as a complementary mechanism compensating for the inadequacies of Reason. These plays also reflect human nature by representing the common aspiration to a self-image of a 'man of reason': several key characters display the irrational tendency to examine reality with rational tools alone, to perceive the passions as a negative factor, and to deny their legitimacy as a vital factor in thought processes. The figure of the 'Rationalising Man' is not limited to the plays that are the focus of this study, but, as has been demonstrated in brief, is clearly portrayed in a number of other Shakespearean plays.

Epilogue:
Shakespeare's Plays as Emotional Appeals
to 'Rationalising Man'

In the course of this study it has been my constant fault to narrow the reader's perspective. Discussion has consistently focused on a limited number of emotionally-charged events depicted in a few Shakespearean plays; broader perspectives, touching upon the reciprocal relations between these fictional events and audiences, have been firmly evaded. Hopefully this narrowing has helped to streamline the discussion, perhaps even to excite some passion in the readers; but now, in concluding the study, it is time to release the readers from the confines of fictional dramatic worlds: perspectives shall now be restored, and will regain their proper breadth.

The conclusions presented in Chapter Five have significant implications for the reciprocal dynamics between spectators of the plays discussed, and the emotional processes presented in them. I have chosen to end the study by demonstrating an awareness of this dynamics, thereby paving the way for further contemplation. Assuming that the 'addiction to reason' – displayed by the various characters surveyed above – reveals to some extent Shakespeare's own perception of mankind in general, it follows that his plays were written for 'Rationalising Man'. The spectator attending a Shakespearean play observes attempts by certain characters to apply reason to a fictional world that cannot be grasped by this faculty; at the same time, the spectator is himself in an identical situation, watching a play that renounces any attempt to subject itself to pure rationality. Shakespeare's plays are completely immune to the reductive effect of Man's rationalising mind: this can be demonstrated by briefly surveying three of their more general idiosyncratic characteristics.

First, the Shakespearean worlds are far too complex to be comprehended by intellectual tools alone. This is true not only of the typical theatregoer – who is subjected to a continual, fast-moving, one-way flow of information – but also of the expert who has pondered the play for many years. The amount of information Shakespeare compresses into every moment throughout his plays is unparalleled, in his period or in any other: the multiplicity of themes and of verbal and auditory devices, as well as the infinite ways in which they all interact, is too great to be grasped in its entirety. The extent of Shakespearean scholarship bears witness to this: thousands of men and women of reason continue to labour over the interpretation of the Bard's various works, which never cease to yield new findings.

Second, the plays are as full of textual gaps as a sieve, thus denying the spectator, the reader or the scholar a firm grip on the motives and actions of the characters. To the rational faculty of spectators and readers, these gaps constitute missing links in lines of argumentation that strive to make sense of the data provided by the play; in the absence of these links, one is forced to choose either to reconstruct them in an irrational manner, or to remain in the realm of doubt and uncertainty.

Third, Shakespeare's plays further evade the jurisdiction of rationality by being filled with what might be generally referred to as 'problems': the plays are replete with contradictions, and lack consistency in a most consistent manner. This does not refer to slight inconsistencies in units of measure, currency, or other numerical data, which may have been caused by inattention on the part of the playwright or copiers of his texts; the reference is to contradictions and inconsistencies whose nature and scope unmistakably attest to the

276

playwright's deceptive intent. A random, brief survey of such 'problems' in the plays under discussion would include the ambiguity built into the very foundations of *Henry V*, as elaborated in Chapter One and in Appendix B; the uncharacteristic error by the 'emotionally intelligent' Antony in recognising Cassius' true character, at the beginning of *Julius Caesar*;[9] the unanswerable questions arising from Iago's various explanations of his motives; and the shift of the dramatic action during scene V, vi of *Coriolanus* from the city of Antium to Corioles.[10]

These three characteristics of Shakespeare's fictional world coincide with three central characteristics of the 'real' world, as perceived by contemporary studies of the emotions:[11] the complexity of our world is too great to be encompassed by one's rational thinking, which would be drowned in a sea of data; the cosmos is infinite, and we humans, being constrained by time and place, are unable to resolve the numerous 'textual gaps' in our life stories; reality is paved with contradictions and inconsistencies, bringing us face to face with events and phenomena for which logical explanations are difficult to produce. Correspondingly, just as the individual simplifies this unsimplifiable world with the help of emotion, so is the spectator prone to simplify the fictional worlds of Shakespeare's plays, driven by the sway of his emotions – particularly those generated in him by the plays themselves. In a broad view, the plays can be regarded as emotional appeals in the form of highly developed amplification figures: they present in great detail the various circumstances that have brought about the extreme actions of their heroes, and thereby generate emotions in the audience.[12] These emotions – added to pre-existing factors such as basic beliefs, values, and mood – stimulate the

9   Oddly enough, it is Caesar, with his low 'emotional intelligence', who at the beginning of the play divines the hidden intentions of Cassius and the danger he presents. Even more oddly, the emotionally-gifted Antony disagrees with him (I, ii, 196–197). This moment is at odds with the otherwise consistent characterisations of Caesar and Antony throughout the play, and it is difficult to find a satisfactory explanation for it.

10   Compare lines 49 and 73 in this scene with lines 90–92.

11   See above, pp. 244–246, 251–252.

12   On the figure of amplification, see Chapter Three, pp. 142–144.

spectator to simplify the spectacle enacted before him: to patch over textual gaps, to ignore the broader, more complex picture presented by the play, and to overlook or resolve, as it were, the aforementioned 'problems'. This simplification, as stated, stems from the human need to counteract the threatening state of doubt and uncertainty. Shakespeare's plays appear to approach this need ambiguously: from a comprehensive view, in the cold light of reason, they defy it by presenting the audience with a fictional world that cannot be simplified; on the other hand, they are addressed to beings who are not endowed with pure rationality and whose thinking can by no means evade the simplifying effect of emotion; moreover, passion-inducing mechanisms built into these plays entice the human perceiver to ignore the unknown and the uncertain, and to impose his firm judgements and opinions. In other words, these unprecedentedly complex plays in fact seduce the spectator into divesting them of their complexity.

The idea of regarding Shakespeare's plays as emotional appeals addressed to 'Rationalising Man' is merely sketched here as a tentative, intuitive suggestion. Only further meticulous, systematic and consistent research can determine whether or not it has substance and can endure the assay of reason.

Appendix A
Shakespeare's Early Use of Emotional Appeal

The following survey aims to demonstrate the negligible effect of emotional appeals on the plots of Shakespeare's plays written before 1599. As briefly stated in the Introduction, although the early plays abound in attempts by various characters to emotionally manipulate their fellow characters, these attempts are for the most part unsuccessful. Even the rare appeals that do not fail to alter the opinion, will or course of action of certain characters, are not employed by the playwright for the purpose of channelling his plots.

Limitations of space do not permit a survey of Shakespeare's entire early drama; thus, seven representative plays, in which persuasive rhetoric and emotional appeals are employed by characters with particular intensity, have been chosen in order to illustrate this trend.

Titus Andronicus

Shakespeare's early revenge-tragedy, *Titus Andronicus* (1589–1594), is perhaps the most salient representative of the trend in question. As demonstrated below, not only does the plot of this play bypass several conspicuous emotional appeals scattered along its course: it is in fact based upon the characters' complete imperviousness to these appeals.[1]

---

1   One of the salient characteristics of the unique cosmos that Shakespeare has created in this play is the complete immunity to emotional appeals of its inhabitants, both human and divine. In fact, not only are the gods in this tragedy impervious to the appeals addressed to them by humans, but they delight in their tragedies (IV, i, 123–124; IV, i, 59–60). The goddess of justice is absent from *Titus'* world (IV, iii, 40–42); the goddess of revenge, by contrast, is ever present and can be easily summoned up from hell (ibid., 38–39).

From the perspective suggested in this study, the plot of *Titus Andronicus* can be described as a sequence of emotional appeals that fail to achieve their purpose: throughout this tragedy, characters plead for their own or their dear ones' lives, but the characters to whom these pleas are addressed are not moved in the slightest; undeterred, they carry out their bloody intentions, thereby infusing victims or their relatives with the desire for revenge and supplying the motivating force for the continuation of the circular plot.

The chain of revenge is initiated when Titus coldly rejects Tamora's plea for the life of her elder son Alarbus (I, i, 107–123). This plea is formulated as a typical emotional appeal, by means of which the captive queen seeks to awaken her addressee's sense of identification with her miserable state. As the Roman and Elizabethan rhetorical treatises repeatedly stress, one cannot stir up passion in others without expressing passion oneself: Tamora indeed tries to 'contaminate' Titus with her emotions, twice directing his attention to the tears she sheds while encouraging him to view the circumstances from her standpoint, stressing their similarity as parents who love their sons (ll. 108–111). This appeal fails to generate compassion in Titus: Alarbus is taken from his mother and two brothers, his 'limbs are lopped, / And entrails feed the sacrificing fire' (ll. 146–147). In this moment the driving force of the first half of the plot comes into existence: Tamora's thirst for revenge. The captive Goth queen, upon unexpectedly becoming empress of Rome, expresses her fierce resolution to massacre the family of the man who made her 'Kneel in the streets and beg for grace in vain' (I, i, 460).

The next significant emotional appeal to be so blocked is Lavinia's plea for the mercy of Tamora (II, ii). This plea is uttered after Tamora enthusiastically approves of her sons' suggestion to rape Titus' daughter. The extreme imperviousness to pity shown by the addressee is particularly jarring in this case because of her sex: women were considered in Shakespeare's time to be highly prone to pity,[2] and Lavinia indeed twice attempts to influence Tamora by referring to this convention (ll. 147, 136); the empress repels this effort by 'unsexing'

---

2   Thomas Wright, *The Passions of the Minde in Generall* (1604), p. 40.

herself, à la Lady Macbeth,[3] refusing even the maid's request to be 'merely' murdered, without first being raped (ll. 173–178). The cruelty of Chiron and Demetrius surpasses their mother's, and their atrocious abuse of Lavinia supplies the driving force for the second half of the revenge-plot.

Titus' plea to the tribunes for the life of his two sons, Martius and Quintus (III, i, 1–26), is the lengthiest emotional appeal in the play. It is also the most contrived, employing a variety of traditional rhetorical means of pleading for pity, such as personification and the figure of *apostrophe*.[4] Another conventional means employed by Titus is to direct the attention of the addressees to the tears shed by the pleader (the word 'tears' occurs no less than five times in this soliloquy). The sweeping tendency of the characters in *Titus Andronicus* to resist emotional appeals is ironically referred to in the second part of this speech, uttered after the tribunes have already left the scene. Titus, despite his extremely impassioned state, is well aware of the absence of his addressees; he stresses that pouring out his grief to the paving stones is far more sensible than expressing it before the tribunes: the stones cannot interrupt the speaker, and in receiving his tears they even seem to be weeping along with him (III, i, 36–41).

The general attitude of the characters toward appeals to mercy is epitomised in the *Tableaux* formed onstage in V, ii, when Titus prepares the execution of Chiron and Demetrius. Following his explicit orders, the mouths of the two are stopped; the text directs the attention of the audience to this visible fact no less than four times, stressing the inability of the gagged Goth boys to 'beg for grace'.[5]

---

3   The language employed by Tamora during this event attests to the manly perspective from which she observes her feminine victim; the suspension of her womanly qualities is indicated in the lines uttered by Lavinia, a moment before she is dragged off-stage by Chiron: 'TAMORA: What begg'st thou then, *Fond woman*? Let me go ... LAVINIA: No grace? *No womanhood*? ... TAMORA: Now will I hence to seek my lovely Moor, / And let my spleenful sons this trull deflower' (II, ii, 172–191; my italics).

4   See, e.g.: Cicero, *De Inventione*, I, LVI, 109, pp. 160–161; *Rhetorica ad Herennium*, IV, LIII, 66, pp. 400–401.

5   V, ii, 161, 164, 166–8, 178–179.

The plot of *Titus Andronicus* is based upon a series of appeals for mercy. This basic outline is particularly evident when the play is performed on stage, due to Shakespeare's repeated use of the act of kneeling. Characters resort to this gesture at least eight times during the play, reinforcing their pleas for mercy.[6] It should be noted that the act of kneeling, a conventional means of appealing for pity in the Roman rhetorical tradition, was bound to raise highly-charged connotations in the minds of Shakespeare's early modern spectators: key figures in Christian mythology, such as St. Paul and Mary Magdalene, employ this gesture when experiencing Christian grace for the first time. Significantly, Shakespeare generously scatters the word 'grace' throughout *Titus Andronicus*, often concomitantly with the act of kneeling.[7] At times, this word is used by characters who appeal for pity as a synonym for 'mercy'.[8]

From this survey's point of view, the closing scene of *Titus Andronicus* does not present the 'reformed' society typical of the tragic genre – a society whose redintegrative values ensure its immunity to further disasters. In fact, the new order established in this scene seems likely to reinforce the characters' existing imperviousness to emotional appeals, as elaborated above. As he will do in tragedies still to be written, Shakespeare crowns a seemingly moral and worthy young ruler at the end of *Titus Andronicus*. Lucius, son of Titus, is accepted by the surviving characters as Rome's new emperor. In his first public speech, this young ruler seems to be most fit to restore 'grace' to Roman society: addressing his 'gracious auditory', 'Rome's gracious governor' appears to be driven by sheer love – he even stresses the compassion aroused in the Goths when they beheld his fugitive tears (V, iii, 104–106). In contrast to his words, however, Lucius' very first actions as a ruler merely perpetuate the illness of Rome's self-destructive society – namely, the inability to overcome its thirst for re-

---

6   I, i, 106–107, 374–375, 464–465, 485; II, ii, 168, 288; III, i, 11–12, 206–210.
7   The word 'grace' occurs thirty-two times in *Titus Andronicus*; given the extreme cruelty shown by the characters, it does not seem coincidental that 'revenge' (and its derivatives) outnumbers it, appearing no less than forty-three times.
8   I, i, 444, 460, 485; II, ii, 182. See: *OED*, 'Grace', n., 15 a.

venge, and the complete immunity to compassion. The newly crowned emperor orders his men to bury Aaron the moor alive, and to 'let him stand and rave and cry for food' (ibid., 179). Wishing to prevent his subjects from being moved to pity by Aaron's raves and cries, Lucius utters an explicit threat: 'If anyone relieves or pities him / For the offence he dies' (ibid., 178–182). In addition, the new ruler decrees that Tamora's body be cast outside the city. This decree ends, as does the play itself, with a couplet in which 'pity' is rhymed with 'pity'; however, in this final couplet Lucius is in essence advocating the absence of pity.[9] His closing lines epitomise the fundamental narrative of revenge, in which the insusceptibility to compassion brings about insusceptibility to compassion in others:

> As for that ravenous tiger, Tamora ...
> ... throw her forth to beasts and birds to prey:
> Her life was beastly and devoid of pity,
> And being dead, let birds on her take pity. (V, iii, 194–199)

Henry VI and Richard III

The four plays that dramatise England's loss of the French throne and the War of the Roses, also known as the First Tetralogy (1592–1594), abound in emotional appeals. Characters in these plays frequently plead for mercy, steer fellow characters to action, incite to mutiny, generate hostility between key figures, and infuse anger, fear or shame – all for the sake of achieving their desired goals. The Tetralogy is particularly concerned with the undying human aspiration to honour and glory, and many of the emotional appeals in these plays are related to this ambition: characters seek to catalyse their rise in the social or political hierarchy, or to augment their influence, by emotionally manipulating others.[10] In this context, appeals by two femi-

9   See: Jonathan Bate, 'Introduction to *Titus Andronicus*', *Titus Andronicus*, ed. Jonathan Bate (London: Thomson, The Arden Shakespeare, 2002), p. 15.
10   See, e.g.: *1 Henry VI*, V, v, 1–21, 103–108; *3 Henry VI*, I, ii, 28–34.

nine characters are worthy of mention: Eleanor, the Douches of Gloucester, and Margaret, wife of Henry VI, seek to infuse their husbands with the desire for power and domination, in a manner similar to that employed by Lady Macbeth and her prototype, Eve (as portrayed in the medieval theatrical tradition).[11] As is to be expected in light of the general argument put forth in this survey, the considerable time and effort invested in their appeals are all in vain: the addressees of these ambitious women do not seem to be affected even slightly by their rhetoric, but rather continue to act in accordance with their original good intentions and humble personality.

Any changes in a character's course of action in the Tetralogy – such as joining forces with or deserting a leader, or granting patronage to certain subjects and holding them in favour over others – arise primarily from considerations of personal benefit.[12] In 2 Henry VI, there is a seeming exception to this rule, when the supporters of the rebel Jack Cade are overwhelmingly persuaded by the speech of Clifford, one of the king's men. In a comically abrupt turnabout, they desert their leader and instantly become the loyal subjects of Henry VI. This persuasive speech, however, cannot be strictly classified as an emotional appeal, because it is based for the most part on *ethos*: in it Clifford exploits the great reputation of Henry V, whose legendary reign is still far from being forgotten; he stresses before Cade's men a simple fact: their sovereign, Henry VI, is the son of France's renowned conqueror, whereas their present leader, Cade, is not. In order to vanquish France again, claims Clifford, the people must follow no other leader but the descendant of Henry V (IV, viii, 31–49). Cade's reaction to the sudden desertion of his men explicitly points to the principal rhetorical means exploited by Clifford:

---

11 *2 Henry VI*, I, ii, 1–16, 32–40; *3 Henry VI*, I, i, 217–258.

12 Clear-cut examples of this trend are the sharp political changeovers undergone by the house of York in the third part of the Tetralogy: on the sole basis of calculations of personal benefit, Clarence deserts his brothers Richard and Edward and turns to the side of Henry VI; similar calculations cause him, shortly after this desertion, to turn his back on the king and reunite with his brothers; it is in turn considerations of personal benefit that cause Richard and Edward to overlook their brother's defection, and receive him with open arms.

Was ever feather so lightly blown to and fro as this multitude? The *name* of Henry the Fifth hales them to an hundred mischiefs, and makes them leave me desolate. (Ibid., 51–53; my italics)

The emotional appeals of the First Tetralogy can be roughly classified into two main groups. The first contains brief and undeveloped appeals which seem, even as they are being uttered, to lack any substantial prospect of generating the desired influence upon their addressees.[13] The second group comprises elaborate, well-constructed appeals, employing the various figures and formulae of the rhetorical tradition.[14] This classification, however, pertains solely to the length and elaborateness of the appeals – as opposed to their actual power of influence. In fact, the potency of the emotional appeals in the Tetralogy cannot be evaluated at all, since they invariably fail to achieve their objectives – or, for the most part, to extract from their addressees even a dram of the desired emotion.

In addition to the emotional appeals whose failure is unequivocally clear (such as Lord Say's plea for his life, which served as an example in the Introduction) – a further class of appeals is typical of the Tetralogy. Such appeals, termed in Appendix B 'parasitic appeals', attempt to generate in their addressees the very passions that already sway them. In most cases, it is impossible to determine from the text to what extent, if any, such 'parasitic' appeals intensify these already-existing passions, and to what extent they contribute to the motivation of the addressees to act.[15] Notably salient in this category are the frequent manifestations of contempt between political and military rivals, which are particularly numerous and lengthy in *3 Henry VI*.[16] It seems that these appeals are directly connected to the exceptional ambition and desire for greatness typical of many characters in the

---

13   See. e.g.: *1 Henry VI*, III, i, 106–111; IV, ii, 3–14; V, iv, 59–64; *3 Henry VI*, I, iii, 12–20, 35–36, 39–45; V, iv, 39–49, 50–54, 55–57; V, v, 51–67.

14   See e.g.: *1 Henry VI*, IV, ii, 15–40; *2 Henry VI*, I, i, 72–100; II, iv, 19–25, 27–57; III, i, 4–41; III, ii, 73–121; *3 Henry VI*, I, i, 217–258; II, ii, 9–42; III, iii, 4–37; V, iv, 1–38, 73–82.

15   See, e.g.: *3 Henry VI*, I, ii, 22–34; II, iii, 14–22.

16   *1 Henry VI*, III, i, 27; IV, i, 89–107; *2 Henry VI*, V, i, 148–150, 151–156, 157–158; *3 Henry VI*, I, iv, 51–108, 118–149; II, ii, 81–177; II, iv, 5–11.

Tetralogy: one way these characters attempt to augment themselves is through the diminution of others, by means of curses, insults and demeaning expressions. These shows of contempt have no substantial effect on the development of the plot: they merely intensify existing anger and hostility on the part of the scorned characters, thus intensifying to some extent the sense of dramatic conflict in the plays.

In sharp contrast to the general trend described thus far, two persuasive speeches in the Tetralogy *do* achieve their objectives, and dramatically alter the emotional state of their addressees. I refer to Suffolk's description to Henry VI of Margaret's virtues and looks, which inflames the young king's love (referred to in *1 Henry VI*, V, v, 1–21); and to Gloucester's incitement of king Edward against their brother Clarence in *Richard III* (I, i, 32–40, 53–61). However, even these effectual emotional appeals cannot be regarded as exceptions to the trend in question, due to the simple fact that they are not uttered on stage: the audience only hears the characters report in retrospect about these appeals and their far-reaching influence. Moreover, Gloucester's incitement of Edward cannot be said to affect the course of the plot, because the passions it generates in the king dissolve shortly after they are aroused: the sedate Edward reverses his order to execute Clarence, inadvertently forcing Gloucester to act by himself in order to end his brother's life.

Against the background of the numerous ineffectual emotional appeals uttered throughout the Tetralogy, two speeches stand apart in their actual influence on the addressees' course of action: Joan la Pucelle's appeal to Burgundy to desert the English side and join the French (*1 Henry VI*, III, iii, 44–77); and Gloucester's aggressive courting of Ann in *Richard III* (I, ii, 49–228). In contrast to the off-stage appeals described in the preceding paragraph, these two speeches are uttered on stage, and their far-reaching effect on the addressees occurs before the spectators' very eyes. On the face of it, these two influential appeals would seem to be the exception that proves the rule: following Joan's speech, Burgundy does indeed desert the English camp and join the French; following Gloucester's rhetorical *tour de force*, Ann's rage and hatred are quenched and subsequently give way to love. However, as shown below, these speeches cannot be considered exceptions to the general tendency described in this Appendix, because they cannot be classified as clearcut emotional appeals: the plays provide substantial evidence that both Joan and Gloucester enjoy the aid of certain external forces, far more potent then the powers of emotional rhetoric. These forces, until the moment they forsake Joan and Gloucester, grant them success in all their doings, including, of course, rhetorical manipulations.

For a teen-aged shepherdess, Joan exhibits a most surprising mastery of rhetorical practice in the speech in question. Particularly salient is her use of two traditional tools of the rhetoric of emotional appeal: personification and *copia* (amplifying a given statement or idea by repeating it in varied forms). Joan appeals to Burgundy's compassion and shame by amplifying his unnatural conduct against his own country, against 'fertile France', and 'the most unnatural wounds' he has inflicted on 'her woeful breast' (III, iii, 44–57). The impact of this speech is immediate – too immediate, in fact, for a speech delivered by a human orator to a human addressee – and the emotional reversal experienced by Burgundy is abrupt beyond all plausibility: fourteen lines after Joan begins her appeal, he already states that he has relented (l. 59). Eighteen lines later, after Joan has appealed to his fear – by claiming that he is for the English but an 'instrument of ill' and will be 'thrust out like a fugitive' when Henry becomes the lord of France – the emotional transformation is complete, and Burgundy joins the French camp.

Toward the end of the play, the secret of Joan's rhetorical knowledge, skill and power is revealed: in the beginning of V, iii, in the midst of the fighting between the French and the English forces, she enters alone and invokes 'fiends' from 'the powerful regions under earth' (l. 7, SD; l. 11); she asks them to help her make France win this present battle; the fiends, who communicate with the French maid through bodily gestures, respond negatively to the request and depart; at this moment, Joan's triumphant time as a warrior,[17] prophetess and rhetorician[18] comes to an abrupt end. The tangible representa-

---

17 At the beginning of the play Joan displays miraculous combat skills, when she defeats the Dauphin in a duel.

18 Joan's loss of rhetorical prowess is evident in V, iv, when she fails to persuade her English captors to spare her life.

tion of the fiends, as well as the clear demonstration of Joan's dependency upon them, clearly reveal that all her previous accomplishments were achieved with the aid of 'the lordly monarch of the north' (l. 6),[19] who has chosen to confer his powers upon her for a limited time.

Richard Gloucester's emotional manipulation of Lady Ann seems at first to be the greatest rhetorical feat achieved by a character in the history of fiction. At the beginning of their encounter, Ann expresses intense hatred for the murderer of her husband and his father; at the end of this same encounter, however, she allows the murderer to put a ring on her finger, and consents to his request that they meet again. Immediately after Ann's exit, Richard expresses his impression that she is 'won' (I, ii, 233). Such subjective impressions should of course always be regarded with a degree of scepticism; however, this particular impression seems accurate enough, in light of Richard's and Ann's ensuing marriage. This rhetorical feat is particularly striking considering the special setting in which Shakespeare places it: Richard addresses Ann as she leads the coffin of his latest victim – none other than Henry VI, her late husband's father.

Indeed, Richard demonstrates in the scene in question lustrous rhetorical skills, appealing insistently to various, even contradictory, emotions in his addressee; however, it seems that so sharp and abrupt a change of heart as that undergone by Ann cannot be explained in terms of emotional rhetoric alone.[20] As in the case of *1 Henry VI* and

19   'The lordly monarch of the north' is either Lucifer or Zimimar, 'a devil frequently invoked by witches'. Michael Hattaway, 'Notes to *The First Part of King Henry VI*', *The First Part of King Henry VI*, ed. Michael Hattaway (Cambridge and New York: Cambridge University Press, 1990).

20   Ann's excessively abrupt change of heart in this scene poses significant pragmatic difficulties to contemporary directors and actors. It seems almost impossible to interpret this change as resulting from a continuous, 'realistic' process – that is, a process generated by forces which the modern spectator can comprehend, and whose effect on Ann's will can be seen as plausible. Laurence Olivier's cinematic adaptation of this scene reveals his concern with these difficulties: in order to present a convincing emotional process that will endure the modern spectator's test of realism, he has divided the scene into two parts, separated by another scene; the first part of Richard's wooing (I, ii, 49–114) takes place, as in Shakespeare's play, in the presence of Henry's coffin – when Ann's hatred for the murderer and grief for the victim are at their peak; the sec-

Joan la Pucelle discussed above, *Richard III*, too, hints at the existence of some hidden force that assists the protagonist in achieving his goals at the beginning of the play – among them the winning of Lady Ann. Thus, various utterances throughout the play may guide spectators to see Richard Gloucester as a 'black magician', a devil, or even *the* devil himself.[21] Phyllis Rackin convincingly shows how, in the course of the First Tetralogy, Shakespeare passes powers of witchcraft among several of his characters, including Richard and Joan (the powers of witchcraft that Joan enjoys in the first play of the Tetralogy, are in Richard's possession at the beginning of its last play).[22] In addition to this helpful observation, it should be noted that the playgoer of Shakespeare's time is likely to have ascribed Richard's powers and success to none other than God; such an assumption would have been based on the characterisation of the protagonist and the events in which he is involved, in accordance with the narrative of 'the scourge of God', common in medieval and Renaissance drama and literature. This narrative originated in the scriptures and certain classical sources, which on occasion describe wicked tyrannical rulers as the instruments of divine will – for example, *Isaiah* x refers to Assyria as the rod of God's anger, sent to punish the sinful people of Israel. Shakespeare's spectators, then, acquainted with this narrative and encouraged by the play's indirect allusions to it, were likely to have considered Richard's evil reign as God's punishment of England for the 'winter of discontent' it has brought upon itself.[23] According to

---

ond part of this scene (ll. 118–228) takes place beside Henry's tomb, which is already covered with a permanent tombstone; the significant time Olivier thus 'adds' to Ann's emotional process – several days or even weeks – allows her passions to subside; this intermission also allows Richard's seeds of love to sprout in Ann's mind. Interestingly, Olivier himself cannot point to any factor by which Ann's change of heart can be explained, other than 'pure magic'. See: Laurence Olivier, *On Acting* (London: Weidenfeld and Nicolson, 1986).

21 See, e.g.: I, ii, 34–35, 45, 50, 73, 91, 241; I, iii, 118, 298, 338; II, iv, 27–28; IV, iv, 418–419.

22 Phyllis Rackin, 'Engendering the Tragic Audience: The Case of *Richard III*', *Studies in the Literary Imagination* 26 (1), (1993), pp. 52–54.

23 See, e.g.: Antony Hammond, 'Introduction to *King Richard III*', pp. 102–104.

this interpretation, it is God who endows Richard with supreme powers and ensures his success during the first half of the play. The courting speech in question is one such divinely-assisted triumph. Richard's expression of astonishment at his unprecedented romantic success (ll. 232–259) can thus be interpreted not only as an ironic utterance of pride, but also as spontaneous and frank amazement at his all-too-easy conquest.

Richard's subsequent failure in a similar rhetorical task, undertaken in the second half of the play, reinforces the impression that his success in I, ii should not be ascribed solely to rhetorical prowess. In IV, iv, he seeks to neutralise the hatred of Elizabeth, the former queen, and to receive her consent to his marriage with her daughter. Following a long dialogue, during which Richard yet again reveals his rhetorical virtuosity and his mastery of emotional appeal (ll. 291–336, 397–417), Elizabeth grants her consent. Referring to her as 'Relenting fool, and shallow, changing woman' (l. 431) Richard reveals his complete confidence in his rhetorical success. However, as early as the next scene we are informed that Elizabeth has decided to marry her daughter to the invading Richmond. The text does not indicate whether or not Elizabeth was indeed persuaded by Richard's rhetoric and only later changed her mind, or was cunningly pretending to be persuaded. For our purposes, this question is irrelevant: for whatever reason, Richard fails in the final trial of rhetoric. He falls short of achieving his goal, which, it will be recalled, is markedly similar to the one he so impressively achieved at the beginning of the play. The divine or the devilish powers that sustained him during his pursuit of the crown have forsaken him, and, just as his military and political prowess fails, so does his rhetorical competence.

The Two Parts of *Henry IV*

The negligible effect of emotional appeals on the plots of *Henry IV*, parts one and two (1596–1598), will be demonstrated by examining two salient and passionate persuasion speeches. These speeches may seem at first to substantially affect the unfolding drama, because in their wake the addressees act precisely as intended by the speakers; however, a careful examination of the addressees in question – their character traits, objectives and ambitions – reveals that it is not the speeches, but their own motives and considerations that drive them to act as they do.

In scene III, ii of *1 Henry IV*, the king reproaches his son for the common way of life he is leading and for associating with such immoral figures as John Falstaff. The disgruntled father, who as monarch faces a rebellion, is deeply troubled that this wayward prince is destined to lead soldiers in the approaching confrontation. He thus addresses his son in a long speech, exhorting him to adopt a way of life more becoming to a prince and warrior. In order to infuse Hal with a potent blend of guilt, shame and envy, Henry chooses a rhetorical tactic based on a twofold comparison: he amplifies the similarities between his son and Richard II, who, claims Henry, lost his crown due to his common way of life (ll. 60–91); and he points out the dissimilarities between his son and Hotspur, whose reputation precedes him as the paragon of warrior-like virtues (ll. 93–117). The king's speech is well-constructed and flowing, and the comparisons upon which it is based are reinforced by means of exceptionally forceful imagery; when performed zealously enough by the actor, it can generate a powerful impression. Under the influence of this impression, as well as subsequent events in the play, it is tempting to see this emotional appeal as the crucial factor in the shaping of the plot: prince Hal not only proves himself a worthy warrior and commander in battle, but also defeats Hotspur in the decisive duel at Shrewsbury.

Putting the impression of this passionate speech aside, however, the bare text of the play does not enable us to determine to what extent, if any, it is the king's emotional appeal that drives Hal to his acts of valour. Moreover, the play shows from the outset that Hal assumes the disguise of commonness by choice, knowing full well that when the time comes he will unveil the exemplary prince hidden beneath. The playwright indicates this ability of Hal's to unmask himself at will by means of orchestrated transitions from prose to pentameter. Scene I, ii begins with the entrance of Hal and Falstaff, who is the very embodiment of commonness and loose behaviour, as the two are engaged in lively dialogue. Hal's first lines in the play are written in prose – a short monologue, yet long enough to be clearly recognised by the audience as prose (ll. 2–12). The playgoers of Shakespeare's time were familiar with the theatrical convention of alternating between prose and verse and of using the two modes to indicate the social class of characters. Thus, to the trained ears of the original audience of *Henry IV*, prince Hal's speaking in prose was a noticeable, even jarring, indication of his 'unprincely' behaviour. After his short exposition monologue, Hal continues to speak in prose – the fitting medium to discuss worldly matters with Falstaff and Poins. Toward the end of the scene, however, alone after the exit of his two friends, he delivers a soliloquy in exemplary pentameter. In this soliloquy he reveals his purpose in associating with such figures as Falstaff and Poins and in adopting their way of life (ll. 193–215). Hal analogises himself to the sun, who permits 'the base contagious clouds [namely, Falstaff and his gang] / To smother up his beauty from the world'; yet when the sun wishes 'again to be himself', he breaks through the clouds, now appearing – against the background of 'the foul and ugly mists' – far more glorious than before.

This soliloquy constitutes a sudden break in the prosodic norm established from the beginning of the scene, and Hal's fluent pentameter reveals his genuine princely qualities in the most straightforward manner. His sudden 'unsheathing' of the pentameter clearly demonstrates his ability to 'unsheathe' the inner prince at will. The brilliance of the blank verse against the background of the prose, analogous to the sun's breaking through the clouds, is thus the foretoken of Hal's reformation. Henry's passionate speech to his son should therefore be classified as a mere 'parasitic' emotional appeal: the motivation it seeks to infuse in its addressee already exists in him, hidden yet ready to be activated when circumstances demand it.

In *2 Henry IV* II, iii, Lady Percy and Lady Northumberland entreat the Earl of Northumberland to renounce his intention of joining the battles against the king; Lady Percy, in a long speech, seeks to instil in her late husband's father guilt and shame (ll. 9–45; 56–61). In *1 Henry IV*, Northumberland failed his son Hotspur and the rebels by not joining them in fighting against the king's army: led by his natural cowardice to remain in a safe, remote place, he played a passive yet crucial role in the rebels' defeat and his son's death. Seeking the most effectual tactic to influence Northumberland, Lady Percy tries to exploit his painful conscience; reaching the emotional climax of her appeal, she stresses that joining forces with the rebels now, when Hotspur is already dead, would be an insult to his spirit:

> Never, O never, do his ghost the wrong
> To hold your honour more precise and nice
> With others than with him! Let them alone. (II, iii, 39–41)

Northumberland's reaction to this speech attests, as it were, to its effectiveness in arousing his passions (ll. 45–47): shortly thereafter he utters his final decision not to join the battles (ll. 67–68). However, the actual impact of the emotional appeal in question is far from obvious, since Northumberland announces his decision only after Lady Percy and his wife fundamentally alter the nature of their plea: the two ladies substitute for their efforts of emotional persuasion, an appeal to the Earl's faculty of reason. They base their modified efforts on plain argumentation: Northumberland's best choice of action, at present, is to hide in Scotland until it becomes apparent how successful the rebels are; if they fare well, Northumberland can safely join them to tip the scales, with minimum risk to his own life (ll. 50–56). Throughout the two parts of *Henry IV*, Northumberland is consistently characterised as a selfish coward; this, combined with the fact that he abandons his original intent only after hearing a cold argument in support of his self-interest, diminishes the likelihood that Lady Percy's emotional appeal had any substantial role in his final decision, or in channelling the plot.

Appendix B
The Questionable Effect of Emotional Appeals in *Henry V*

Henry V can be seen as a link between the two stages of Shakespeare's dramatic writing as described in the Introduction, that is, between plays in which emotional appeals do not affect the plot and plays whose plots are clearly influenced by them. In this history play, apparently written in the spring or summer of 1599, we find a series of elaborate emotional appeals; the number, length and seeming potency of these appeals are without precedent in the plays Shakespeare wrote before this stage. Despite their centrality, however, it is not possible to determine to what degree, if any, each of them influences the course of the plot. In fact, there is no single emotional appeal in the play that can be said with certainty to bring about, by itself, a change in a character or characters that leads to a significant shift in the unfolding of events.

Henry V thus differs from, for example, the earlier *Titus Andronicus*, which contains numerous appeals that indubitably fail to achieve their ends and are thus uttered in vain. On the other hand, *Henry V* also differs from the later *Julius Caesar*, *Othello* and *Coriolanus*, in which it is clear that emotional appeals, directly and autonomously, alter the chain of events. In *Julius Caesar*, for the sake of illustration, Antony ascends to the pulpit and addresses the people, who but a brief moment earlier expressed their clear opinion supporting Caesar's assassination; by means of an emotional appeal Antony alters their opinion completely, and even arouses in them an intense passion that will incite them to a violent rebellion. The emotional appeal delivered by Antony alters the progression of the plot in an extreme manner, with no visible assistance from any other factor.

My decision to include *Henry V* in this study and to devote a chapter to it stems from a number of significant factors. First, the scope and seeming forcefulness of the emotional appeals in this play are, as stated, without precedent in Shakespeare's earlier drama; second, *Henry V* allots to emotional persuasion a central place in its thematic design; and third, the playwright does not indicate the failure of the play's emotional appeals: rather, he blurs the picture and prevents the spectator from determining to what extent, if any, they affect their addressees and the concatenation of the play's events. By comparison, *Troilus and Cressida*, which was also written after the 1599–1600 demarcation delineated in the Introduction, also abounds in emotional appeals; but in it, unlike in *Henry V*, Shakespeare supplies his audience with clear information indicating either that these appeals have failed, or that they have been addressed to a character already in the throes of powerful passions.[1] The ineffectiveness or outright failure of emotional appeals in *Troilus and Cressida* is the principal reason for my decision not to study it in this book.

The following survey will be devoted to reinforcing the general argument stated above: salient emotional appeals in *Henry V* will be reviewed, and their insignificant, ambiguous or questionable role in the shaping of the plot will be demonstrated. The reviewed emotional appeals, like the appeals in *Henry V* as a whole, can each be classified according to the following four categories:

1. Appeals that have a substantial emotional effect on characters, and bring about a significant change in their actions or behaviour, but have no substantial effect on the plot.

2. 'Parasitic' emotional appeals: appeals that do not influence the plot at all, although, immediately following them, events are seen to be channelled in the direction the appeals intend. Because the appeals are seemingly forceful and directed towards that very end to which events eventually lead, the audience is tempted to view them as the cause of these events. A closer examination of the text, however, proves that it is in fact other forces and factors, working parallel to

---

1   For example: the speech delivered by Ulysses, who tries to stir Achilles and renew his lost manliness and lust for warlike feats (III, iii, 146–191), fails to achieve its purpose, and Achilles continues to display behavioural characteristics considered 'effeminate' (III, iii, 239–243, 309–310); Pindarus' attempt to kindle in Cressida love for Troilus (I, ii, 54–271) is actually a case of 'bursting in through an open door' (ibid., 275–276).

these 'parasitic' appeals, that determine the ultimate reality. Even if we wish to examine to what extent, if any, these appeals serve as catalysts or enhance the forces that actually direct the plot, the lack of sufficient textual data prevents such an examination.

3. Appeals that do not deflect the course of the plot, although they do have a fairly forceful emotional effect on one or more characters. This effect does not overpower other forces, which are working in the opposite direction, and eventually fades away.

4. Emotional appeals that would seem to have a far-reaching effect on the plot, although the degree of their influence cannot be determined. The impact of such appeals cannot be determined because there are other forces influencing the plot in the same direction, and the play 'insists' on avoiding a hierarchical ranking of the various influential elements in its fictional world.

A typical example of an emotional appeal from the first category is the long speech Henry delivers at Southampton before his lords and soldiers, shortly before sailing to France (II, ii, 81–142). This speech is addressed to the Lords Grey, Cambridge and Scroop, whose conspiracy with France to murder Henry has been uncovered. Henry chooses to precede his speech with a theatrical prologue: he presents the three traitorous lords with three documents, decreeing them, as it were, regents appointed to rule in England during his absence; in fact, on each of the documents is written a proclamation advising the reader that the plot has been uncovered. Immediately after the three read the proclamations, Henry describes the physical change that has come over them; this physical change is an outward expression of an emotional change:

> Why, how now, gentlemen!
> What see you in those papers that you lose
> So much complexion? – Look ye how they change!
> Their cheeks are paper. – Why, what read you there,
> That hath so cowarded and chased your blood
> Out of appearance? (II, ii, 71–76)

Fear, according to Wright and Coeffeteau, is the passion that arises when one perceives a tangible danger to one's life: in times of such danger, the blood drains from the face to 'the fountain of life', the heart, in order to protect it; blood gives the face, in ordinary times, its reddish complexion, and when the blood deserts the face, it becomes white.[2] The pallor of Cambridge, Scroop and Grey, which Henry describes, is their natural response in light of what they know and what every playgoer of Shakespeare's day knew: that any crime considered to be treason – even seemingly minor ones such as 'shaving' the edges of coins – carries one and the same penalty, for which there is no reprieve.

The three conspirators appeal to Henry's mercy (II, ii, 76–78) and he, in response, expresses his astonishment that their natural shame does not prevent them from doing so (ibid., 81). In keeping with the way Shakespeare's contemporaries perceived the emotional mechanisms of the human body, it appears that shame and fear were understood as physiologically incompatible: someone whose life is in danger, whose blood has drained from his face, is incapable of feeling shame, since the latter passion involves the rushing of blood to the face (conversely: someone who is ashamed cannot feel fear).[3] Henry, for reasons he does not share with the soldiers and lords present on stage, intends the traitors to feel the full brunt of their shame, and for this to be witnessed by everyone in attendance. He apparently understands that the clear and present danger to the lives of the three traitors has generated in them fear so intense that it eliminates any potential for the arousal of shame; he therefore decides to assist Nature and circumstance by delivering a long, meticulously constructed appeal to the traitors' shame (II, ii, 81–142).

On the face of it, it would seem that this appeal accomplishes its purpose: the three lords express, not only joy that the plot has been discovered, but their complete preparedness to die (II, ii, 151–165). The willingness they express at the end of the speech is of course quite the opposite of what they showed at its opening, when they pleaded with Henry to show mercy and spare their lives. The radical

2   Thomas Wright, *The Passions of the Minde in Generall* (1604), pp. 33–34; F. N. Coeffeteau, *A Table of Humane Passions with their Causes and Effects* (1621), pp. 461–462, 497–498.

3   Ibid., p. 497; Thomas Wright, *The Passions of the Minde in Generall* (1604), p. 30.

change they exhibit at the end of the speech may seem to be the direct consequence of the emotional transformation effected by Henry's emotional appeal, and an indication that their fear has been replaced by shame: while fear impels a human being to protect himself, shame is liable, in extreme cases, to push him to end his life in order to stop the intolerable pain that accompanies it.[4] However, a healthy doubt should be cast as to the degree of real influence the speech has on the traitors, since the text provides no indication, such as an aside or a soliloquy, that their words reflect their thoughts – for example, Henry, having referred to their white complexion at the beginning of his speech, does not supply a complementary physiological-emotional reference at the end. But regardless of whether or not the appeal actually brings about a complete emotional transformation in its addressees, it has no effect on the progression of the plot: fearful or ashamed, pale or flushed, the three convicted Lords must march to their deaths.

An emotional appeal that undoubtedly has an effect on its addressees, but whose influence on the overall course of the plot is negligible, is that by which Henry urges his soldiers to renew their assault on the breach in the wall of Harfleur (III, i, 1–34). Insofar as it is possible to reconstruct what takes place on stage – from Henry's words and the original stage directions – Henry succeeds in altering his soldiers' emotional state and leading them to a renewed assault on the walls. The scene opens with the entrance of the king and of English soldiers bearing ladders, apparently in retreat, as Henry delivers his speech, 'Once more unto the breach, dear friends ...'. The text does not supply any responses by the addressees of the speech that might indicate an emotional change that has taken place in them; nevertheless, from the very fact that the soldiers follow their king off stage after the stirring closing lines, it can be determined that the king has realised his intention and induced in his soldiers the anger to counteract their fear[5] and motivate them to renew their attack. Yet

---

4   F. N. Coeffeteau, *A Table of Humane Passions with their Causes and Effects* (1621), p. 481.

5   On the role of anger as a motivator on the battlefield, particularly in this play and on this occasion, see Chapter One, pp. 40–51.

despite the emotional effectiveness of this appeal, it does not bring about any shift in the plot of the play: the assault by Henry and his soldiers, as we learn subsequently, does not achieve its objective. The English army apparently does not succeed in penetrating the city, which for the time being remains unconquered.

This goal is achieved only later, after a speech by which Henry attempts to arouse the fear of the ruler and people of Harfleur (III, iii, 1–43). This speech falls into the second of the four categories formulated above: that of the 'parasitic' emotional appeal. It is based primarily on a series of threats concerning the bitter fate that awaits the people of Harfleur should they refuse to surrender, and makes use of visual imagery of extreme cruelty. The content of the threats and imagery is amplified by alliterations, sound clusters, and other auditory devices occurring with exceptional intensity (e.g., 'The blind and bloody soldier with foul hand / Defile the locks of your shrill-shrieking daughters' [III, iii, 34–35]). An additional rhetorical device Henry employs to intensify the intimidation, is to plant a sense of guilt in his addressees, portraying them as the only factor in the onset of the future horrors he describes. According to him, the people of Harfleur will be solely responsible for the 'hot and forcing violation' of their own daughters, the dashing of their fathers' heads and the spitting of their infants upon pikes, because they themselves 'are cause' of these horrors, are 'proud of destruction' and 'guilty in defence' (ll. 4, 19, 43). But even this imposing speech, which spans 43 lines of increasing emotional intensity, is not the factor that brings about the downfall of Harfleur, and perhaps is not even a catalyst, as the words of the city's governor clearly attest:

> Our expectation hath this day an end.
> The Dauphin, whom of succors we entreated,
> Returns us that his powers are yet not ready
> To raise so great a siege. *Therefore*, great king,
> We yield our town and lives to thy soft mercy.
> Enter our gates, dispose of us and ours,
> For we no longer are defensible. (III, iii, 44–50; my italics)

This speech, then, does not serve the structural level of the play. T. W. Craik attempts to 'justify' its inclusion in the play, claiming that 'to stage the surrender without it would have been an anticlimax'.[6] It can be assumed that the inclusion of the speech was of great importance to the playwright, because it is an original (and lengthy) addition to the 'historical events' that served as the basic framework of the plot. In the two principal historical sources of which Shakespeare made use, there is no mention whatsoever of such a speech: the governors of Harfleur, according to Hall and Holinshed, realising that the city is about to be conquered and that no military reinforcement is expected to arrive, initiate the surrender in order to minimise loss of life.[7] In Shakespeare's adaptation, the threatening speech constitutes an important component of the thematic level, which allots considerable space to the emotional methods by which the prince can manipulate and control his subjects and enemies alike.

In the three cinematic versions of the play, this impressive speech has been shortened.[8] The significant abbreviation in Laurence Olivier's production (Henry-Olivier delivers only the first two lines of the speech), can be attributed to the director-actor's preference to portray an exemplary and moral ruler, and to completely suppress any textual hints that might lead spectators to doubt the purity of his intentions and his means of ruling. David Giles does not shorten the speech in so exaggerated a manner, but eliminates the lines in which Henry reveals, as it were, his excessive cruelty (33–40). By contrast, in Kenneth Branagh's realistic and mud-stained production the abridgement is not due to the harsh content of the speech, since Branagh includes those particular lines in his version and even delivers them with great fervour. It is widely recognised that the first victims in the process of abridging Shakespearean plays and adapting them for the modern audience are those elements classified as 'thematic' in nature, that is, which do not promote the plot. It would appear that this speech is a good case in point.

---

6   T. W. Craik, 'Introduction to *King Henry V*', p. 45.
7   Edward Hall, *The Union of the Two Noble and Illustre Families of Lancaster and York*, p. 61. Raphael Holinshed, 'Henrie the Fift, Prince of Wales', p. 73.
8   Laurence Olivier (dir.), *Henry V* (1945); David Giles (dir.), *Henry V* (1979); Kenneth Branagh (dir.), *Henry V* (1989).

The dispatch of tennis balls by the Dauphin to Henry can be defined, from our point of view, as an appeal to the addressee's emotion of anger. The various definitions relating to anger and the reasons for its arousal, from the writings of Aristotle onward, consistently emphasise the power of offence and the demonstration of scorn and contempt to ignite it.[9] Because the tennis balls are revealed in a public situation, in the presence of the king's men and the ambassadors of France, their potential for arousing anger is particularly great. Immediately after Exeter discloses to Henry the content of 'this tun of treasure' the French have brought with them, Henry launches on a long and seemingly furious speech (I, ii, 260–298). This speech describes the disasters of the impending war as the direct consequence of the lust for vengeance the tennis balls have aroused in Henry and, therefore, of 'the Dauphin's scorn' itself as the direct generator of the war (ll. 292–297).

The emotional tone of this eloquent speech, and the resolution it expresses, may create the impression that the Dauphin's scorn has indeed brought about Henry's final decision to initiate the war (or, in other words, that the course of the plot is altered by an emotional appeal). Even a scholar such as Goddard, in his intense desire to emphasise the negative aspects of the king's characterisation, overlooks the fact that the speech is delivered in public: whenever Henry is in the presence of his subjects, every word he utters must be examined first and foremost as a rhetorical means of influencing them. Goddard repeatedly refers to the speech as an uncontrolled outburst of anger that reveals the king's true nature, hidden until this moment behind the false image of an enlightened Christian ruler.[10] However, an examination of the thematic and structural constructions of the speech illustrates to what an extent the great emotional energy it expresses is governed and channelled by Reason: Henry receives the ball(s) sent to him by the Dauphin, and strikes back with a speech composed of imagery referring to the approaching war as a game of tennis; he builds and develops the flow of metaphors in a logical and conscious manner that would be impossible in the case of loss of emotional self-

9   See Chapter Three, p. 145.
10   Harold C. Goddard, *The Meaning of Shakespeare*, vol. I, pp. 225, 227, 231.

control. The eloquent flow of the speech – as well as the use of figures such as *climax* (ll. 284–289), guiding the actor to alternately increase and decrease pace and emotional intensity – also indicates that this is merely 'reasoned anger'. As shown in Chapter Five, Henry is characterised throughout the play by his outstanding emotional self-control and his abilities as an 'actor': being 'but a man' (IV, i, 102), he is quite likely to develop anger in response to scorn; being a highly skilled rhetorician he is able to control this emotion and channel it to suit his needs.[11]

This speech, both passionate and passion-inducing, is likely to captivate and ensnare the audience in the emotional manipulation Henry uses on the characters around him. However, it must be remembered that the king has announced beforehand that he is 'well resolved' to initiate war (I, ii, 223–234): it is therefore clear that declaring the diplomatic offence to be the cause of the war is factually incorrect. Henry's words are thus more of an opening shot in the psychological warfare that will accompany the 'actual' fighting in the fields of France. From this perspective, Henry's speech is an emotional appeal intended to arouse fear in the French, once their ambassadors have returned to their country and reported on its content. Indeed, the king's 'constant resolution', as expressed in this speech, reaches the ears of the French constable, and strongly impresses him (II, iv, 29–40). However, the effect of the fear-infusing speech in question, like that of the threatening ultimatum Exeter delivers to the French king (II, iv, 76–112), soon dissipates and does not influence the decisions and actions of the French. For this reason I classify these two speeches as belonging to the third category formulated above – that is, as emotional appeals that do not shift the course of the plot, but that *may* be perceived as having a forceful effect on one or more characters, an effect that does not influence their actions. The French fear of the English army – even if it existed at the beginning of the

---

11 When governed and exploited by the intellect, anger can serve as a tool: 'Pray be counselled. / I have a heart as little apt as yours, / But yet a brain that leads my use of anger / To better vantage' (Volumnia to Coriolanus, *Coriolanus*, III, ii, 29–32).

war,[12] and even if aroused in part by the reports of Henry's speech and Exeter's visit in the French court – subsequently gives way to pride and complacence.

Of course, the fear-inducing speech Henry delivers before the ambassadors of the Dauphin should also be considered as an emotional appeal intended to influence his own men, present on the occasion. The king's display of rage and resolution is likely to have a positive effect on the Englishmen who are listening to their sovereign: expressions of anger and desire for revenge on the part of a ruler would not have been perceived by early modern subjects (and playgoers) as they might be today – in a negative light.[13] However, one cannot measure the emotional influence of the speech on Henry's subjects, much less determine its part in the enthusiastic wave of enlistment that spreads through the realm (II, Chorus, 1–11), its effect on the fighting in France, or its role in the English victory.

A clear-cut example of the fourth category in the classification of emotional appeals suggested here is the famous St Crispin's Day speech (IV, iii, 18–67). This sweeping speech might seduce spectators into considering it the central factor in infusing the 'sick and famished' English soldiers with the strength of spirit that enables them to overcome their superior enemy. The scope of the speech, its location at the height of the plot, and its emotional impact, combine to encourage the spectator to regard the king's rhetorical skill as a key element in the English victory. Significantly, Shakespeare chooses not to provide his audience with any tactical details related to the battle itself, such as references by the characters to military manoeuvres or

---

12   On the dominant emotions in the French camp and the connection between them and the French performance in battle, see 1.2.3 and 1.3.3.

13   This can be concluded from Exeter's show of satisfaction at the end of Henry's speech (l. 299). The mild and civil Captain Gower is convinced that Henry, enraged at the murder of the English boys, has ordered the execution of the French prisoners (IV, vii, 35–38), and praises him for this: ''Tis certain there's not a boy left alive, and the cowardly rascals that ran from the battle ha' done this slaughter... carried away all that was in the king's tent, *wherefore* the king, most worthily, hath caused every soldier to cut his prisoner's throat. *O, 'tis a gallant king!'* (IV, vii, 5–10; my italics).

deployment of forces on the battlefield.[14] In addition, consideration must be given to the fact that, unlike other 'war' plays of Shakespeare's, in *Henry V* no characters are shown engaging in combat onstage. The complete omission of this dimension is intentional and manipulative: it inevitably leads the spectators to attach decisive weight to those factors the playwright does present, such as the speech in question. Holinshed and Hall, for example, report on an innovation made by the English army in this battle: wooden poles fitted at either end with sharp metal points, embedded diagonally in the earth with the exposed end pointing in the direction from which the enemy intended to attack.[15] A row of such rods made a kind of serrated fence that prevented enemy horsemen from reaching the soldiers standing behind it. In this way the 'historical' Henry deprived the French of their sting, as they had a large cavalry; England's military might was based on a formation of archers, whom the king chose to protect from the attacking horsemen by means of this barrier (Olivier's and Branagh's films 'correct' the historical wrong Shakespeare committed regarding this stratagem: both reconstruct the part of the poles in the battle and even devote a few seconds to the process of their being sharpened and embedded in the ground. In so doing, they provide spectators with an interesting historical reconstruction, but undermine the play's clear tendency to completely ignore actual fighting and tactics). Shakespeare, who used Holinshed as his main source and frequently even followed his wording closely, chose to omit from his work this historical-military datum, interesting and important in its own right; his consistent choice to withhold all such information en-

---

14   Although the theatrical medium does not allow for representations of entire battles or movements of troops on the battlefield, it does not prevent characters from describing to the audience military briefings and manoeuvres: 'I will lead forth my soldiers to the plain, / And thus my battle shall be ordered: / My foreward shall be drawn out all in length, / Consisting equally of horse and foot; / Our archers shall be placed in the midst. / John Duke of Norfolk, Thomas Earl of Surrey, / Shall have the leading of this foot and horse. / They thus directed, we will follow / In the main battle, whose puissance on either side / Shall be well winged with our chiefest horse' (*Richard III*, V, iii, 292–301).

15   Edward Hall, *The Union of the Two Noble and Illustre Families of Lancaster and York*, p. 66. Raphael Holinshed, 'Henrie the Fift, Prince of Wales', p. 79.

courages the audience to attach greater weight to Henry's speech and its effect, and to draw a direct connection between it and the English victory.

The text of the play clearly indicates that the St Crispin's Day speech has the desired effect on Westmoreland, its declared addressee. The latter provides his king with the 'cue' to begin the speech, when he expresses his wish that the English army be reinforced; at the end of the speech he expresses quite the opposite desire, embracing with excessive exaggeration the message directed to him:

> WESTMORLAND: O that we now had here
> But one ten thousand of those men in England
> That do no work today!
>
> ...
>
> KING: Thou dost not wish more help from England, coz?
> WESTMORLAND: God's will, my liege, would you and I alone,
> Without more help, could fight this royal battle! (IV, iii, 16–75)

Let us exaggeratedly assume that the king has exerted a similar influence on all the characters present in this scene (who constitute a theatrical representation of the army as a whole). Even in such case, it cannot be concluded that this speech, rather than some other factor, is the 'added value' that ultimately determines the outcome of the war. The play in fact supplies such an alternative factor, and at times even encourages the spectators (particularly fervent believers among them) to see it as the primary cause of the French defeat. Throughout the play Henry frequently expresses recognition of the power of God and its decisive influence on the outcome of the future war in France.[16] After the battle of Agincourt he by no means retreats from this practice, but repeatedly attributes the surprising victory to God.[17]

Shakespeare's choice of which numerical data to adopt from his historical sources and which to reject, also attests to his manipulative guidance of his audience to grasp the surprising English victory as divine intervention. The play emphasises again and again the disproportionate balance of power between the two armies – the French

16   I, ii, 290; III, vi, 168; IV, iii, 120; IV, iii, 131–132.
17   See: IV, vii, 86; IV, viii, 107–109, 112–113, 114–117.

camp outnumbers the sick and feeble English five-to-one; yet at the end of the battle the French are reported to have suffered 10,000 dead, as opposed to a mere twenty-nine on the English side. Holinshed, who also reports 10,000 French casualties, writes that some of his sources report twenty-nine English killed in the battle, but immediately adds that 'other writers of greater credit affirme, that there were slaine aboue fiue or six hundred persons'.[18] Shakespeare has chosen the lower and more unlikely number, thus increasing the spectator's temptation to ascribe the English victory to divine power.

An additional factor to which the audience might attribute the English success is the extreme complacence of the French. This emotional state, most inappropriate for men at war, results in inadequate physical preparedness,[19] as well as negligence and disorder in the ranks of the attacking forces. But just as it cannot be determined to what degree Henry's oratory and God influenced the outcome of the battle, neither is it possible to establish how fatal the French complacence was. Furthermore, the spectator may attribute the French complacence to a variety of factors such as their innate tendencies, Henry's rhetorical messages addressed through Montjoy the herald, or, of course, to God, cause of all causes.

The play, then, at different points in time, focuses the awareness of the audience on different factors that may have influenced the outcome of the battle. It is clear that at any given moment in which one of these factors is the focus of attention, that factor is likely to be perceived as more influential than the others; but at the end of the play, as has been said, not a single unequivocal piece of evidence has been presented that would make it possible to establish a hierarchy among the various factors that bring about the English victory.

The findings regarding emotional appeals so far presented should be linked to one of the play's most significant characteristics: the ambiguity which dominates almost all its aspects. *Henry V* provides its audience with different versions of the events it presents, of the reasons behind them, and of the characteristics and motives of its protagonist. These versions are not always in agreement with one

---

18   Raphael Holinshed, 'Henrie the Fift, Prince of Wales', p. 83.
19   See Chapter One, pp. 52–55.

another, and are sometimes even clearly contradictory. This ambiguity governs both the 'macro' level of the play, that is, the world it portrays and the events that take place in it, and the 'micro' level, or the inner world of its protagonist. In this regard, *Henry V* can be considered the harbinger of the great tragedies to come, in which the tragic dimension can be grasped as the consequence of the ambiguity that governs the worlds they portray (this is perhaps the most significant characteristic common to tragedies from classical times, which Shakespeare develops and elaborates upon). Nevertheless, the fact that *Henry V* precedes the great tragedies does not imply that it is 'less ambiguous': some scholars find it unusually ambiguous even by Shakespearean standards. Norman Rabkin, for example, stresses that while ambiguity is a significant characteristic in many Shakespearean plays, in *Henry V* it is a central theme.[20] Alexander Leggatt, following Rabkin, offers a similar insight:

> To a degree unusual even for him, Shakespeare is setting the material before us, leaving its contradictions intact, and inviting us to make of it what we can.[21]

The same is true of the emotional appeals in the play: Shakespeare presents them in all their splendour to his rhetoric-loving spectators, tempting them to let themselves be carried away by the forcefulness of these appeals and be impressed by their supposed shaping of events; at the same time he scatters facts and hints indicating quite a different dynamics, and does not resolve the contradiction he has created.

---

20   Norman Rabkin, 'Rabbits, Ducks and *Henry V*', *Shakespeare Quarterly* 28 (1977), p. 296.
21   Alexander Leggatt, *Shakespeare's Political Drama*, p. 125.

Appendix C
The Term *Ethos* as Used in this Study

'*Ethos*', in this study, refers to the way in which the speaker is perceived by his addressees – both in light of their previous knowledge of him and in light of their impression of him during his speech. Rhetoricians have always considered the image of the speaker in the eyes of his audience to be a critical factor in his success or failure to persuade; however, they do not agree on the manner in which the image of the speaker is shaped in the minds of his listeners.[1]

According to Aristotle, it is the 'personal character' of the speaker that makes us think him credible; he emphasises that the speaker must establish this 'personal character' *during the speech itself*, rather than relying upon people's previous opinion of him. Other rhetoricians, by contrast, attach greater weight to the addressees' acquaintance with the speaker prior to his speech, as well as to his public image. One such rhetorician is the influential Isocrates:

> ... for who does not know that words carry greater conviction when spoken by men of good repute than when spoken by men who live under a cloud, and that the argument which is made by a man's life is of more weight than that which is furnished by words? Therefore, the stronger a man's desire to persuade his hearers, the more zealously will he strive to be honourable and to have the esteem of his fellow citizens.[2]

An opinion similar to that of Isocrates is put forward by Cicero. In *De Oratore*, although he instructs his readers to present a pleasant and trustworthy personality while speaking, Cicero also acknowledges that the speaker's reputation is a highly influential preliminary factor:

---

1   See: James S. Baumlin, 'Ethos', *Encyclopedia of Rhetoric*, ed. Thomas Slone (Oxford: Oxford University Press, 2001), pp. 263–277.

2   Isocrates, *Antidosis*, 278, p. 339.

Now feelings are won over by a man's merit, achievement or reputable life, qualifications easier to embellish, if only they are real, than to fabricate where nonexistent.[3]

This approach is formulated with decisive simplicity in St Augustine's *On Christian Doctrine*:

> The life of the speaker has greater weight in determining whether he is obediently heard than any grandness of language.[4]

Thomas Wilson, too, is aware of the decisive influence of the speaker's reputation on the way in which his words are received. He advises orators to modestly summarise for the audience their contribution to the peace and security of the state, whether in military service or in public office.[5]

The term *ethos* as used in this study thus combines both approaches discussed above.[6] It is clear that prior knowledge about the speaker on the part of his listeners will, at the very least, affect the way in which they evaluate the beginning of his speech; it is no less clear that the impression they form of his character during the speech will also influence the way they judge his words – this impression may reinforce, cancel or alter their prior opinion, or may even create a conflict between their opinion of the speaker before his speech and their impression of him during it. In any case, it is clearly impossible to determine that either of these two factors is invariably more influential than the other: in any rhetorical analysis both must be taken into account, and examined specifically in the given situation.

---

3   Cicero, *De Oratore*, 2.182.
4   St Augustine, *On Christian Doctrine*, 4.59.
5   Thomas Wilson, *The Art of Rhetoric*, p. 135.
6   It should be noted that the *Oxford English Dictionary*, oddly, makes no reference to the meanings of the word '*ethos*' in rhetorical usage. The author of this entry provides only the general definition of the word, which derives from Aristotle's use of it in the rhetorical context: '[After Arist. *Rhet*. II, xii–xiv.] The characteristic spirit, prevalent tone of sentiment, of a people or community; the "genius" of an institution or system' (*OED*, 'ethos', n., 1).

Selected Bibliography

Rhetorica ad Herennium, trans. Harry Caplan (London: The Loeb Classical Library, Harvard University Press, 1999).

The Revenger's Tragedy, Thomas Middleton: Five Plays, ed. Bryan Loughrey and Neil Taylor (London and New York: Penguin Books, 1988).

Aristotle, *Nicomachean Ethics*, trans. and ed. Roger Crisp (New York and Cambridge: Cambridge University Press, 2000).

——, *On Rhetoric*, trans. George A. Kennedy (New York: Oxford University Press, 2007).

Aronson, Alex, 'Shakespeare and the Ocular Proof', *Shakespeare Quarterly* 21 (1970), pp. 411–429.

Babb, Laurence, *The Elizabethan Malady: A Study of Melancholia in English Literature from 1580 to 1642* (East Lansing: Michigan State College Press, 1951).

Bacon, Francis, *Essays* (1612), (London: Dent, 1972).

Bailey, F. G., *The Tactical Uses of Passion* (Ithaca, NY: Cornell University Press, 1983).

Bailey, John, 'Love and Identity: *Othello*', *Shakespeare Othello – A Casebook*, ed. John Wain (London: Macmillan, 1971), pp. 169–199.

Baldwin, T. W., *William Shakespeare's small latine & lesse Greeke* (Urbana: University of Illinois Press, 1944).

Barton, Anne, '*Julius Caesar* and *Coriolanus*: Shakespeare's Roman World of Words', *Shakespeare's Craft: Eight Lectures*, ed. Philip H. Highfill Jr (Carbondale: Southern Illinois University Press, 1982, pp. 24–47).

Barton, John, *Playing Shakespeare* (London: Methuen / Channel Four Television), 1984.

Baumlin, James S., 'Ethos', *Encyclopedia of Rhetoric*, ed. Thomas Slone (Oxford: Oxford University Press, 2001), pp. 263–277.

Beauregard, David N., '*Venus and Adonis*: Shakespeare's Representation of the Passions', *Shakespeare Studies* 8 (1976), pp. 83–98.

Ben-Ze'ev, Aaron, *The Subtlety of Emotions* (Cambridge, MA: MIT Press, 2000).

——, 'The Logic of Emotions', *Philosophy and the Emotions*, ed. Anthony Hatzimoysis (Cambridge: Cambridge University Press, 2003), pp. 147–162.

Bevington, David, 'Introduction to *Troilus and Cressida*', *Troilus and Cressida*, ed. David Bevington (London: The Arden Shakespeare, 1998), pp. 1–117.

Bliss, Lee, 'Introduction to *Coriolanus*', *Coriolanus*, ed. Lee Bliss (Cambridge, New York and Melbourne: Cambridge University Press, 2000), pp. 1–98.

Bosman, Jan and Hagendoorn, Louk, 'Effects of Literal and Metaphorical Persuasive Messages', *Metaphor and Symbolic Activity* 6 (4), (1991), pp. 271–292.

Bradley, Andrew Cecil, *Shakespearean Tragedy* (London and New York: Penguin Books), 1991.

Branagh, Kenneth, *Beginning* (London: St Martin's Press, 1991).

Brlek, Aleksandar, 'Ill Seen, Well Said: On the Uses of Rhetoric in *Julius Caesar* and *Coriolanus*', *Studia Romanica et Anglica Zagrabiensia* 43 (1998), pp. 161–71.

Brockbank, Philip, 'Introduction to *Coriolanus*', *Shakespeare's Coriolanus*, ed. Philip Brockbank (London and New York: Methuen, 1980), pp. 1–89.

Brothers, Leslie, 'A Biological Perspective on Empathy', *American Journal of Psychiatry* 146 (1989).

Brown, John Russell, *Shakespeare: The Tragedies* (New York: Palgrave, 2001).

Bruce, Yvonne, 'The Pathology of Rhetoric in *Coriolanus*', *Upstart Crow* 20 (2000), pp. 93–115.

Cacioppo, John T., Hatfield, Elaine and Rapson, Richard L., 'Emotional Contagion', *Current Directions in Psychological Science*, vol. 2 (3), (1993), pp. 96–99.

Calderwood, James L., '*Coriolanus*: Wordless Meaning and Meaningless Words', *Studies in English Literature* 6 (1966), pp. 211–224.

Campbell, Lily B., *Shakespeare's Tragic Heroes: Slaves of Passion* (New York: Barnes & Noble, 1960).

Campbell, Oscar James, *Shakespeare's Satire* (Hamden, CT and London: Archon Books, 1963).

Cantor, Paul, *Shakespeare's Rome: Republic and Empire* (Ithaca, NY: Cornell University Press, 1976).

Charney, Maurice, *Shakespeare's Roman Plays: The Function of Imagery in the Drama* (Cambridge: Harvard University Press, 1963).

——, *Shakespeare on Love and Lust* (New York: Columbia University Press, 2000).

Cialdini, Robert B., *The Psychological Influence of Persuasion* (New York: Quill / William Morrow, 1993).

Cicero, *De Divinatione*, ed. Arthur Stanley Pease (Darmstadt: Wissenschaftliche Buchgesellschaft, 1963).

——, *De Inventione*, ed. H. M. Hubbell (London: The Loeb Classical Library, Harvard University Press, 2000).

——, *De Oratore*, trans. James M. May and Jacob Wise (Oxford: Oxford University Press, 2001).

——, *Oratore*, ed. H. M. Hubbell (London: The Loeb Classical Library, Harvard University Press, 1962).

——, *Tusculan Disputations 3 and 4*, trans. Margaret Graver (Chicago: University of Chicago Press, 2002).

Cinthio, Giraldi, *Hecatommithi* (III, 7), *Othello*, ed. Alvin Kernan (New York: The New American Library, 1963), pp. 171–186.

Coeffeteau, F. N., *A Table of Humane Passions with their Causes and Effects*, trans. E. Grimeston (1621), (Ann Arbor, MI: University Microfilms, 1981).

Colman, E. A. M., 'The End of *Coriolanus*', *A Journal of English Literary History* 34 (1967), pp. 1–20.

312

Cooper, John M., 'Rhetoric, Dialectic, and the Passions', *Oxford Studies in Ancient Philosophy* 11 (1993), pp. 175–198.

Corbett, P. J., 'The Emotional Appeal', *Classical Rhetoric* (New York: Oxford University Press, 1965).

Cox, Leonard, *The Art or Craft of Rhethoryke* (1524), ed. F. E. Carpenter (New York: AMS Press, 1973).

Craik, T. W., 'Introduction to *King Henry V*', *King Henry V*, ed. T. W. Craik (London: The Arden Shakespeare, 2002), pp. 1–111.

Damasio, Antonio, *Descartes' Error* (New York: Grosset / Putnam, 1994).

D'Amico, Jack, 'Moral and Political Conscience: Machiavelli and Shakespeare's *Macbeth* and *Henry V*', *Italian Quarterly* 27 (105), 1986, pp. 31–41.

Davies, Sir John, *Nosce Teipsum (The Soul of Man)* (1599), *Silver poets of the sixteenth century* (London: J. M. Dent, 1947).

De Sousa, Ronald, 'Self-Deceptive Emotions', *Explaining Emotions*, ed. Amelie Rorty (London: University of California Press, 1980).

——, *The Rationality of Emotions* (Cambridge, MA: MIT Press, 1990).

Dixon, Peter, *Rhetoric* (London: Methuen, 1992).

Dorsch, T. S., 'Introduction to *Julius Caesar*', *Julius Caesar*, ed. T. S. Dorsch (London and New York: Methuen, The Arden Shakespeare, 1985), pp. vii–lxxii.

Ekman, P. and Davidson, Richard J. (eds), *The Nature of Emotion: Fundamental Questions* (New York: Oxford University Press, 1994).

——, 'Basic Emotions', *Handbook of Cognition and Emotions*, ed. T. Dalgleish and M. Power (Chichester: John Wiley and Sons, 1999), pp. 45–60.

Eliot, T. S., 'Shakespeare and the Stoicism of Seneca', *Shakespeare Othello – A Casebook*, ed. John Wain (London: Macmillan, 1971), pp. 69–72.

Elyot, Thomas, *The Book Named The Gouernour* (1531), ed. S. E. Lehmberg (London and New York: Everyman's Library, 1975).

——, *Dictionary* (1538), (Menston: Scolar Press, 1970).

——, *The Castel of Helthe* (1539), (New York: Scholars' Facsimiles & Reprints, 1979).

Elster, Jon, *Solomonic Judgments* (Cambridge: Cambridge University Press, 1989).

——, *Alchemists of the Mind: Rationality and the Emotions* (Cambridge: Cambridge University Press, 1999).

Enterline, Lynn, *The Rhetoric of the Body from Ovid to Shakespeare* (Cambridge: Cambridge University Press, 2000).

Erasmus, *De Copia*, *Collected Works of Erasmus: Literary and Educational Writings*, ed. Craig R. Thompson (Toronto: University of Toronto Press, 1989), vol. 2.

Evans, Dylan, *Emotion: A Very Short Introduction* (New York: Oxford University Press, 2003).

Evans, Phil, *Motivation and Emotion* (London: Routledge, 1989).

Fisher, Philip, 'Thinking about Killing: Hamlet and the Paths among the Passions', *Raritan* (1991), pp. 43–77.

Ford Martin, Paula, 'Emotional Intelligence', *Gale Encyclopedia of Psychology*, http://www.findarticles.com/g2699/0004/2699000455/p1/article.jhtml (2001).

Forset, Edward, *A Comparative Discourse of the Bodies Natural and Politique*, (London: printed for John Bull, 1606 and printed for Nathaniel Butter, 1624), (Farnborough, Hants: Gregg International Publishers, 1969).

Frijda, N. H., *The Emotions* (Cambridge: Cambridge University Press, 1986).

——, 'The Laws of Emotion', *American Psychologist* 43 (1988), pp. 349–358.

Frye, Northrop, *Northrop Frye on Shakespeare*, ed. Robert Sandler (New Haven and London: Yale University Press, 1986).

Gardner, Howard, *Frames of Mind: The Theory of Multiple Intelligences* (New York: Basic Books, 1983).

—— and Hatch, Thomas, 'Multiple Intelligences Go to School', *Educational Researcher* 18 (8), (1989).

——, *Multiple Intelligence: The Theory in Practice* (New York: Basic Books, 1993).

Gielgud, John, *Shakespeare: Hit or Miss?* (London: Sidgwick & Jackson, 1991).

Gilbert, Anthony, 'Techniques of Persuasion in *Julius Caesar* and *Othello*', *Neophilologus* 81 (1997), pp. 309–23.

Goddard, Harold C., *The Meaning of Shakespeare* (Chicago and London: The University of Chicago Press, 2003).

Goldman, Michael, 'Characterising in *Coriolanus*', *Shakespeare Survey* 34 (1981), pp. 73–84.

Goleman, Daniel, *Emotional Intelligence* (New York: Bantam Books, 1995).

Golomb, Harai, *Enjambment in Poetry: Language and Verse in Interaction, Meaning and Art* 3 (Tel Aviv: The Porter Institute, 1979).

Gomme, A. H., 'Notes to *Coriolanus*', *Coriolanus*, ed. A. H. Gomme (New York: Shakespeare Workshop, 1969).

Granville Barker, Harley, *Prefaces to Shakespeare* (London: Heinemann, 1995).

——, 'From *Henry V* to *Hamlet*', *Aspects of Shakespeare: Being British Academy Lectures* (Oxford: Clarendon Press, 1933).

Green, Lawrence D., 'Pathos', *Encyclopedia of Rhetoric*, ed. Thomas Slone (Oxford: Oxford University Press, 2001), pp. 554–569.

Greenblatt, Stephen, *Renaissance Self-Fashioning from More to Shakespeare* (Chicago: University of Chicago Press, 1980).

——, *Shakespearean Negotiations* (Berkeley and Oxford: Oxford University Press, 1988).

Griffith, Paul E., 'Basic Emotions, Complex Emotions, Machiavellian Emotions', *Philosophy and the Emotions*, ed. Anthony Hatzimoysis (Cambridge: Cambridge University Press, 2003).

Gurr, Andrew, 'Introduction to *King Henry V*', *King Henry V*, ed. Andrew Gurr (Cambridge: Cambridge University Press, 1992), pp. 1–55.

Hall, Edward, *The Union of the Two Noble and Illustre Families of Lancaster and York*, ed. H. Ellis (New York: AMS Press, 1965).

314

Hammond, Antony, 'Introduction to *King Richard III*', *King Richard III*, ed. Antony Hammond (Walton-on-Thames: Methuen, The Arden Shakespeare, 1981), pp. 1–119.

Harding, D. W., 'Women's Fantasy of Manhood: A Shakespeare Theme', *Shakespeare Quarterly* 20 (3), (1969), pp. 245–153.

Hattaway, Michael, 'Introduction to *King Henry VI*', *King Henry VI*, ed. Michael Hattaway (Cambridge and New York: Cambridge University Press, 1990), pp. 1–57.

Hawkes, Terence, *Shakespeare and the Reason* (London: Routledge & Kegan Paul, 1968).

——, 'Shakespeare and New Critical Approaches', *The Cambridge Companion to Shakespeare Studies*, ed. Stanley Wells (Cambridge: Cambridge University Press, 1986), pp. 287–302.

Heilman, Robert B., ''T'were Best not Know Myself: Othello, Lear, Macbeth', *Shakespeare Quarterly* 15 (1964), pp. 89–98.

——, *Magic in the Web: Action and Language in Othello* (Lexington: University of Kentucky Press, 1965).

Holinshed, Raphael, 'Henrie the Fift, Prince of Wales', *Chronicles* (1587), vol. 3 (New York: AMS Press, 1965).

Holllingshead, Stephen, *Shakespeare's Answer to Machiavelli* (North Carolina: Carolina Academic Press, 2005).

Honigmann, E. A. J., *Shakespeare: Seven Tragedies: The Dramatist's Manipulation of Response* (London: Macmillan), 1976.

——, 'Introduction to *King John*', *King John*, ed. E. A. J. Honigmann (London and New York: Methuen, 1983), pp. lxvi–lxvii.

Housman, John, 'Filming *Julius Caesar*', *Shakespeare Julius Caesar: A Casebook*, ed. Peter Ure (London: Macmillan, 1969), pp. 66–69.

Isocrates, *Antidosis*, trans. George Norlin (Cambridge, MA and London: Harvard University Press, 1982), 278, p. 339.

Jonson, Ben, *Catiline*, ed. W. F. Bolton and Jane F. Gardner (London: Edward Arnold, 1972).

——, *Every Man in his Humour*, ed. J. W. Lever (London: Edward Arnold, 1972).

——, *Every Man out of his Humour*, *Ben Jonson*, ed. C. H. Herford and Percy Simpson (Oxford: Clarendon Press, 1961).

Jorgensen, Paul A., 'Shakespeare's *Coriolanus*: Elizabethan Soldier', *PMLA* 64 (1949), pp. 221–235.

——, 'Perplex'd in the Extreme: The Role of Thought in *Othello*', *Shakespeare Quarterly* 15 (1964), pp. 265–275.

Joseph, Miriam, *Shakespeare's Use of the Art of Language* (New York: Columbia University Press, 1949).

——, *Rhetoric in Shakespeare's Time* (New York: Harcourt, Brace & World, Inc, 1962).

Kermode, Frank, *Shakespeare's Language* (London: Penguin Books, 2000).

Kern Paster, Gail, 'The Body and its Passions', *Shakespeare Studies* 29 (2001), pp. 44–50.

——, *Humoring the Body: Emotions and the Shakespearean Stage* (Chicago and London: University of Chicago Press, 2004).

——, Rowe, Katherine and Floyd-Wilson, Mary (eds.), *Reading the Early Modern Passions: Essays in the Cultural History of Emotion* (Philadelphia: University of Pennsylvania Press, 2004).

Kernan, Alvin, 'Introduction to *Othello*', *Othello*, ed. Alvin Kernan (New York: The New American Library, 1963), pp. xxiii–xxxv.

Kirschbaum, Leo, 'Shakespeare's Stage Blood', *Shakespeare Julius Caesar: A Casebook*, ed. Peter Ure (London: Macmillan, 1969), pp. 152–159.

Knights, L. C., 'Personality and Politics in *Julius Caesar*', *Shakespeare Julius Caesar: A Casebook*, ed. Peter Ure (London: Macmillan, 1969), pp. 121–139.

Knoepflmacher, U. C., 'The Humours as Symbolic Nucleus in Henry IV, Part I', *College English* 24 (1963), pp. 497–501.

Kokeritz, Helge, *Shakespeare's Pronunciation* (New Haven: Yale University Press, 1953).

Kyd, Thomas, *The Spanish Tragedy*, ed. J. R. Mulryne (London and Tonbridge: The New Mermaids, 1974).

La Primaudaye, Pierre de, *The French Academie* (London, 1618), (Ann Arbor, MI: University Microfilms).

Larsen, R. J., Kasimatis, M., and Frey, K., 'Facilitating the Furrowed Brow: An Unobtrusive Test of the Facial Hypothesis Applied to Unpleasant Affect', *Cognition and Emotion* 6 (1992), pp. 321–338.

Le Doux, J., *The Emotional Brain* (New York: Simon and Schuster, 1996).

Leggatt, Alexander, *Shakespeare's Political Drama: the History Plays and the Roman Plays* (London and New York: Routledge, 1988).

Levenson, Robert, 'Empathy: a Physiological Substrate', *Journal of Personality and Social Psychology* 63 (2), (1992).

Leavis, F. R., 'Diabolic Intellect and the Noble Moor', *Shakespeare Othello – A Casebook*, ed. John Wain (London: Macmillan, 1971).

Levy, Eric, 'The Problematic Relation between Reason and Emotion in *Hamlet*', *Renascence* (2001), pp. 83–95.

Luckyj, Christina, 'Volumnia's Silence', *Studies in English Literature* 31 (11), pp. 327–342.

Machiavelli, *Il Principe* (Milan: Signorelli, 1980).

——, *The Prince*, trans. Robert M. Adams (New York: W. W. Norton, 1977).

Marlowe, Christopher, *Tamburlaine the Great* (I, II), *The Complete Plays of Christopher Marlowe*, ed. J. B. Steane (New York: Penguin English Library, 1969), pp. 105–257.

Mayer, J.D and Salovey, P., 'What is Emotional Intelligence?' *Emotional Development, Emotional Literacy, and Emotional Intelligence: Implications for Educators*, ed. P. Salovey and D. Sluyter (New York: Basic Books, 1997).

McAlindon, Thomas, *Shakespeare's Tragic Cosmos* (Cambridge: Cambridge University Press, 1996).

McGuire, Philip C., '*Othello* as an "Assay of Reason"', *Shakespeare Quarterly* 24 (2), (1973), pp.198–209.

Miola, Robert, *Shakespeare's Rome* (Cambridge: Cambridge University Press, 1983).

Montaigne, *The Complete Essays*, trans. M. A. Screech (Harmondsworth: Penguin, 1993).

Moore, Alice F., 'Self Deception in *Sonnet 138*', *Shakespeare Quarterly* 40 (1989), pp. 15–17.

North, Thomas, 'The Life of Caius Martius Coriolanus', from Plutarch's *Lives of The Noble Greacians and Romans* (1579), *Shakespeare's Coriolanus*, ed. Philip Brockbank (London and New York: Methuen, 1980), pp. 313–368.

——, 'The Life of Julius Caesar', 'The Life of Marcus Brutus', from Plutarch's *Lives of The Noble Greacians and Romans* (1579), *Shakespeare's Julius Caesar*, ed. Marvin Spevack (Cambridge and New York: Cambridge University Press, 2000), pp. 154–183.

Nowottny, Winifred M. T., 'Justice and Love in *Othello*', *A Casebook on Othello*, ed. Leonard F. Dean (New York: Thomas Y. Cornwell Company, 1963).

Oatley, K., *Best Laid Schemes – The Psychology of Emotions* (Cambridge: Cambridge University Press 1992).

Oatley, K. and Jenkins, J. M., *Understanding Emotions* (Malden: Blackwell, 1996).

O'Keefe, Daniel J., 'Persuasion', *Encyclopedia of Rhetoric*, ed. Thomas Slone (Oxford: Oxford University Press, 2001), pp. 575–583.

Olivier, Laurence, *On Acting* (London: Weidenfeld and Nicolson), 1986.

Ortony, K., *The Cognitive Structure of Emotions* (Cambridge: Cambridge University Press, 1988).

Oz, Avraham, '*Julius Caesar* and the Prophetic Mind', *Assaph: Studies in the Theatre* 1 (1984), pp. 28–39.

——(ed.), *Marlow* (London and New York: Palgrave Macmillan, 2004).

Palmer, D. J., 'Tragic Error in *Julius Caesar*', *Shakespeare Quarterly* 21 (4), (1970), pp. 399–409.

Parker, Patricia, *Shakespeare from the Margins* (Chicago: University of Chicago Press, 1996).

Peacham, Henry, *The Garden of Eloquence* (1577), (Menston: The Scholar Press, 1971).

Plett, Heinrich F., 'Amplification', *Encyclopedia of Rhetoric*, ed. Thomas Slone (Oxford: Oxford University Press, 2001), pp. 25–26.

Pujante, Luis A., 'No Sense nor Feeling: A Note on *Coriolanus* IV, i', *Shakespeare Quarterly* 41 (1990), p. 489.

Putney, Rufus, 'Coriolanus and His Mother', *Twentieth Century Interpretations of Coriolanus* (Englewood Cliffs, NJ: Prentice-Hall, 1970), pp. 104–105.

Puttenham, George, *The Art of English Poesie* (1589), ed. Gladys D. Willcock and Alice Walker (Cambridge: Cambridge University Press, 1970).

317

Quintilian, *Institutio Oratoria*, trans. D. A. Russell (London: The Loeb Classical Library, Harvard University Press, 2001).

Rabkin, Norman, 'Rabbits, Ducks and *Henry V*', *Shakespeare Quarterly* 28 (1977), pp. 279–296.

Rackin, Phyllis, 'Engendering the Tragic Audience: The Case of *Richard III*', *Studies in the Literary Imagination* 26 (1), (1993), pp. 47–65.

Rainolde, Richard, *The Foundation of Rhetoric* (1563), ed. R. C. Alston (Menston: The Scholar Press, 1972).

Reid, Robert L., 'Humoral Psychology in Shakespeare's *Henriad*', *Comparative Drama* 30 (4), (1996), pp. 471–502.

Reynolds, Brian and Fitzpatrick, Joseph, 'Venetian Ideology or Transversal Power? Iago's Motives and the Means by which Othello Falls', *Othello: New Critical Essays*, ed. Philip C. Kolin (New York and London: Routledge, 2002), pp. 203–219.

Ridley, M. R., 'Introduction to *Othello*', *Othello*, ed. M. R. Ridley (London: The Arden Shakespeare, Methuen, 1984).

Roe, John, *Shakespeare and Machiavelli* (Cambridge: Brewer, 2002).

Rorty, Amelie Oksenberg, 'Explaining Emotions', *Explaining Emotions*, ed. Amelie Rorty (London: University of California Press, 1980).

Salovey, Peter and Mayer, John D., 'Emotional Intelligence', *Imagination, Cognition, and Personality* 9 (1990), pp. 185–211.

Sawday, Jonathan, *The Body Emblazoned: Dissection and the Human Body in Renaissance Culture* (London: Routledge, 1996).

Schanzer, Ernest, 'The Tragedy of Brutus', *Shakespeare Julius Caesar: A Casebook*, ed. Peter Ure (London: Macmillan, 1969), pp. 183–194.

Seneca, 'On Anger', *Seneca: Moral and political essays*, ed. and trans. John M. Cooper and J. R. Procope (Cambridge: Cambridge University Press, 1995).

——, *Seneca: His Tenne Tragedies* (1581), ed. Thomas Newton (Bloomington and London: Indiana University Press, 1964).

Simon, H. A., 'Motivational and Emotional Controls of Cognition', *Psychological Review* 74 (1), (1967), pp. 29–39.

Shakespeare, William, *All's Well that Ends Well*, ed. G. K. Hunter (London and New York: The Arden Shakespeare, 1997).

——, *Antony and Cleopatra*, ed. David Bevington (Cambridge and New York: Cambridge University Press, 1995).

——, *As You Like It*, ed. Alan Brissenden (Oxford and New York: Oxford University Press, 1994).

——, *Coriolanus*, ed. Lee Bliss (Cambridge and New York: Cambridge University Press, 2000).

——, *Hamlet*, ed. Harold Jenkins (Walton-on-Thames: The Arden Shakespeare, 1997).

——, *Julius Caesar*, ed. Marvin Spevack (Cambridge and New York: Cambridge University Press, 2000).

——, *The First Part of King Henry IV*, ed. P. H. Davison (London and New York: Penguin Books, 1994).

——, *The Second Part of King Henry IV*, ed. P. H. Davison (London and New York: Penguin Books, 1994).

——, *King Henry V*, ed. T. W. Craik (London: The Arden Shakespeare, 2002).

——, *The First Part of King Henry VI*, ed. Michael Hattaway (Cambridge and New York: Cambridge University Press, 1990).

——, *The Second Part of King Henry VI*, ed. Michael Hattaway (Cambridge and New York: Cambridge University Press, 1991).

——, *The Third Part of King Henry VI*, ed. Michael Hattaway (Cambridge and New York: Cambridge University Press, 1993).

——, *King John*, ed. E. A. J. Honigmann (London: Methuen, The Arden Shakespeare, 1962).

——, *King Lear*, ed. Jay L. Hallio (Cambridge and New York: Cambridge University Press, 2000).

——, *King Richard II*, ed. Andrew Gurr (Cambridge and New York: Cambridge University Press, 2000).

——, *King Richard III*, ed. Antony Hammond (Walton-on-Thames: Methuen, The Arden Shakespeare, 1981).

——, *Love's Labour's Lost*, ed. G. R. Hibbard (Oxford and New York: Oxford University Press, 1998).

——, *Macbeth*, ed. A. R. Braunmuller (Cambridge and New York: Cambridge University Press, 2001).

——, *The Merchant of Venice*, ed. M. M. Mahood (Cambridge and New York: Cambridge University Press, 2000).

——, *A Midsummer Night's Dream*, ed. Harold F. Brooks (London and New York: The Arden Shakespeare, 1996).

——, *Much Ado About Nothing*, ed. A. R. Humphreys (London: The Arden Shakespeare, 1991).

——, *Othello*, ed. Norman Sanders (Cambridge and New York: Cambridge University Press, 2000).

——, *Romeo and Juliet*, ed. Brian Gibbons (Walton-on-Thames: The Arden Shakespeare, 1998).

——, *The Sonnets*, ed. Katherine Duncan Jones (London: The Arden Shakespeare, 2002).

——, *Titus Andronicus*, ed. Jonathan Bate (London: Thomson, The Arden Shakespeare, 2002).

——, *Troilus and Cressida*, ed. David Bevington (London: Thomson, The Arden Shakespeare, 2001).

——, *Twelfth Night,* ed. Elizabeth Story Donno (Cambridge and New York: Cambridge University Press, 2000).

Sherry, Richard, *A Treatise on Schemes and Tropes* (1550), ed. Herbert W. Hildebrant (Gainesville, FL: Scholars' Facsimiles & Reprints, 1977).

Sicherman, Carol M., '*Coriolanus*: The Failure of Words', *A Journal of English Literary History* 39, (1977), pp. 189–207.

Slone, Thomas O., 'Introduction to *The Passions of the Minde in Generall*', *The Passions of the Minde in Generall* (1604), (Urbana, Chicago and London: University of Illinois Press, 1971, pp. xi–xlix).

Smith, Marion B., *Dualities in Shakespeare* (Toronto: University of Toronto Press, 1966).

Solmsen, Friedrich, 'Aristotle and Cicero on the Orator's Playing upon the Feelings', *Classical Philology* 33 (1938), pp. 390–404.

Sonnino, Lee. A, *A Handbook to Sixteenth Century Rhetoric* (London: Routledge & Kegan Paul, 1981).

Sternberg, Robert J., *Beyond I. Q.* (New York: Cambridge University Press, 1985).

Stewart, J. I. M., 'Character and Motive in *Julius Caesar*', *Shakespeare Julius Caesar: A Casebook*, ed. Peter Ure (London: Macmillan, 1969), pp. 110–120.

Strier, Richard, 'Against the Rule of Reason: Praise of Passion from Petrarch to Luther to Shakespeare to Herbert', *Reading the Early Modern Passions: Essays in the Cultural History of Emotion*, ed. Gail Kern Paster, Katherine Rowe and Mary Floyd-Wilson (Philadelphia: University of Pennsylvania Press, 2004), pp. 23–42.

Sullivan, Vickie, 'Princes to Act: Henry V as the Machiavellian Prince of Appearance', *Shakespeare's Political Pageant: Essays in Literature and Politics*, ed. Joseph Aulis and Vickie Sullivan (Lanham, MD: Rowman & Littlefield, 1996), pp. 125–152.

Traversy, Derek, '*Coriolanus*: Menenius', *Twentieth Century Interpretations of Coriolanus* (Englewood Cliffs, NJ: Prentice-Hall, 1970), pp. 108–109.

Trousdale, Marion, *Shakespeare and the Rhetoricians* (North Carolina: North Carolina University Press, 1982).

Vawter, Marvin L., 'Division 'tween Our Souls': Shakespeare's Stoic Brutus', *Shakespeare Studies* 7 (1974), pp. 173–196.

——, 'After Their Fashion: Cicero and Brutus in *Julius Caesar*', *Shakespeare Studies* 9 (1976), pp. 205–220.

Vickers, Brian, *The Artistry of Shakespeare's Prose* (London: Methuen, 1968).

——, *Classical Rhetoric in English Poetry* (London: Macmillan, 1970).

——, 'Shakespeare's Use of Rhetoric', *A New Companion to Shakespeare Studies*, ed. K. Muir and S. Schoenbaum (Cambridge: Cambridge University Press, 1971).

——, *Shakespeare: Coriolanus*, *Studies in English Literature* 58 (London: Edward Arnold, 1976).

——, 'The Power of Persuasion – Images of the Orator, Eliot to Shakespeare', *Renaissance Eloquence: Studies in the Theory and Practice of Renaissance Rhetoric*, ed. James Murphy (Berkeley: University of California Press, 1983), pp. 411–435.

———, 'A Test Case for Language Theory: *Othello*', *Appropriating Shakespeare: Contemporary Critical Quarrels* (New Haven: Yale University Press, 1993), pp. 74–91.

Walker, Alice and Willcock, Gladys D., 'Introduction to George's Puttenham's *The Arte of English Poesy*', *The Arte of English Poesy*, ed. Alice Walker and Gladys D. Willcock (Cambridge: Cambridge University Press, 1970), pp. lxxv–lxxx.

Walker, Jarrett, 'Voiceless Bodies and Bodyless Voices: The Drama of Human Perception in *Coriolanus*', *Shakespeare Quarterly* 43 (1992), pp. 170–185.

Wells, Robin Headlam, '*Julius Caesar*, Machiavelli, and the Uses of History', *Shakespeare Survey* 55 (2002), pp. 209–218.

Whitaker, Virgil K., 'Brutus and the Tragedy of Moral Choice', *Shakespeare Julius Caesar: A Casebook*, ed. Peter Ure (London: Macmillan, 1969), pp. 172–182.

Wilson, Thomas, *The Art of Rhetoric* (1560), ed. Peter E. Medine (Pennsylvania: Pennsylvania University Press, 1994).

Wisse, Jakob, *Ethos and Pathos from Aristotle to Cicero* (Amsterdam: Adolf M. Hekkert, 1989).

Wright, Thomas, *The Passions of the Minde in Generall* (1604), (Urbana, Chicago and London: University of Illinois Press, 1971).

Zajonc, R. B., Murphy, S. T., and Inglehart, M., 'Feeling and Facial Efference: Implications of the Vascular Theory of Emotion', *Psychological Review* 96 (1989), pp. 395–416.

Films Cited

Coriolanus, dir., Elijah Moshinsky (Alan Howard as Coriolanus, Joss Ackland as Menenius), BBC: The Complete Dramatic Works of William Shakespeare, 1984.

Henry V, dir., Laurence Olivier (Laurence Olivier as King Henry, Renee Asherson as Princess Katherine, Leslie Banks as the Chorus, Robert Newton as Pistol), Rank Film Distribution, 1945.

Henry V, dir., David Giles (David Gwillim as King Henry, Jocelyne Boisseau as Princess Katherine), BBC: The Complete Dramatic Works of William Shakespeare, 1979.

Henry V, dir., Kenneth Branagh (Kenneth Branagh as King Henry, Emma Thompson as Princess Katherine, Derek Jacobi as the Chorus, Brian Blessed as Exeter, Paul Scofield as France, Ian Holm as Fluellen), MGM / United Artists, 1989.

Julius Caesar, dir., Joseph L. Mankiewicz (Marlon Brando as Mark Antony, John Gielgud as Cassius, James Mason as Brutus), MGM, 1953.

Julius Caesar, dir. Stuart Burge (Jason Robards as Brutus, Charlton Heston as Mark Antony, Richard Johnson as Cassius, John Gielgud as Caesar), Commonwealth United Entertainment, 1970.

Julius Caesar, dir. Herbert Wise, (Richard Pasco as Brutus, Charles Gray as Caesar, Keith Michell as Mark Antony), BBC: The Complete Dramatic Works of William Shakespeare, 1979.

Looking for Richard, dir., Al Pacino (Al Pacino as himself/Richard III, Alec Baldwin as himself/Clarence), Fox Searchlight Pictures, 1996.

Much Ado About Nothing, dir. Stuart Burge (Robert Lindsay as Benedick, Cherie Lunghi as Beatrice), BBC: The Complete Dramatic Works of William Shakespeare, 1984.

Much Ado About Nothing, dir. Kenneth Branagh (Kenneth Branagh as Benedick, Emma Thompson as Beatrice, Denzel Washington as Don Pedro), Samuel Goldwyn Company, 1993.

Othello, dir., Orson Welles (Orson Welles as Othello, Micheál MacLiammóir as Iago), Marceau Films/United Artists , 1952.

Othello, dir., Stuart Burge (Laurence Olivier as Othello, Frank Finlay as Iago, Derek Jacobi as Cassio), 1965.

Othello, dir., Jonathan Miller (Anthony Hopkins as Othello, Bob Hoskins as Iago), BBC: The Complete Dramatic Works of William Shakespeare, 1981.

Othello, dir., Trevor Nunn (Willard White as Othello, Ian Mckellen as Iago), 1990.

Othello, dir., Oliver Parker (Laurence Fishburn as Othello, Kenneth Branagh as Iago), Columbia Pictures, 1995.

Playing Shakespeare, Created by John Barton, Channel Four Television Co., 1984.

Richard III, dir., Laurence Olivier (Laurence Olivier as Richard, Ralph Richardson as Buckingham, John Gielgud as Clarence), London Films, 1956.

Richard III, dir., Richard Loncraine (Ian McKellen as Richard, Nigel Hawthorne as Clarence), United Artists, 1995.

Richard III, dir., Jane Howell (Ron Cook as Richard), BBC: The Complete Dramatic Works of William Shakespeare, 1983.

A Shot in the Dark, dir. Blake Edwards (Peter Sellers as Inspector Clouseau), United Artists, 1964.

Index

his 'rational' emotional appeal to Brabantio's anger 123–128
Roe, John 26*n*
Rollins, Peter 22*n*
Romeo and Juliet 108*n*, 120*n*, 153
Rowe, Katherine 22*n*, 198*n*

sadness 47*n*, 72–73, 208
Salovey, Peter, and John D. Mayer 200–202, 205, 207, 217, 218, 219, 227
Schanzer, Ernest 72*n*, 88*n*, 95*n*, 103
Seneca: *Tenne Tragedies* 41*n*, 45*n*, 267
senses, the five 76, 83*n*, 107, 186, 206, 233, 236, 268
Shakespeare, William
    development as a writer 14–15, 273–274
    early and later use of emotional appeal 11–12, 14–16, 279–293
    plays as emotional appeals to 'Rationalising Man' 275–278
    preoccupation with the passions 19, 267–268, 273
    revolutionary treatment of the phenomenon of emotion 268
    unprecedented dramatic use of emotional appeal 273
shame 50–51, 155, 166–167, 176, 178, 178*n*, 188–196, 203–204, 226, 228–229, 232–233, 287, 291, 293, 298–299
    as a motivator on the battlefield 50–51, 166–167
    central place in Coriolanus' capitulation to his mother 155, 178, 188–196, 203–204, 226, 232–233
    physiological incompatibility with fear 51, 298
    physiological properties 51, 298
    shame and the desire for honour 178, 178*n*, 189, 189*n*, 191
Sherry, Richard 23, 124*n*, 126, 133

Shot in the Dark, A (film) *see* Clouseau, Jacques
Sicinius (*Coriolanus*) *see* Brutus and Sicinius
Simon, H. A. 245*n*
Smith, Allan 22*n*
Sonnets, The 45*n*, 86, 256–257
Sophists, the 161
Spanish Tragedy, The (Thomas Kyd) 268
spirits 27, 27*n*, 35*n*, 44*n*, 48, 56–57, 57*n*, 157*n*
Stewart, J. I. M. 95*n*
Strier, Richard 197–198
Studley, John 41*n*, 45*n*, 267
style (rhetoric) 89–90, 160–161, 213–214, 215–216, 234–235, 261, 263–264
Suetonius 186*n*
Sullivan, Vickie 26*n*
syntactical symmetry *see* figures of speech

Table of Humane Passions, A see Coefteteau, Nicolas
Talbot (*1 King Henry VI*) 40–41
Tamburlaine the Great (Marlowe) 106*n*, 268, 271–273
Taming of the Shrew, The 108*n*
Titus Andronicus 108*n*, 194*n*, 279–283, 295
Troilus and Cressida 41*n*, 296
    see also Hector
Twelfth Night 58*n*, 108*n*

Vawter, Marvin L. 102*n*
verse 292
    see also iambic pentameter; prose
Vickers, Brian 88*n*, 183*n*, 192, 234, 273*n*
Volumnia (*Coriolanus*) 154, 155, 177–196, 223–226, 232–233
    'emotional intelligence' 223–226